Prince

RONIN | RO

Prince

INSIDE THE MUSIC AND THE MASKS

ST. MARTIN'S PRESS ❦ NEW YORK

www.stmartins.com

Library of Congress Cataloging-in-Publication Data

Ro, Ronin.
    Prince : inside the music and the masks / Ronin Ro.—1st ed.
        p. cm.
    ISBN 978-0-312-38300-8
    1. Prince.   2. Rock musicians—United States—Biography.   I. Title.
    ML420.P974R67 2011
    781.66092—dc23
    [B]
                                                    2011026066

    P1

Contents

In this life? You're on your own.

—PRINCE, "LET'S GO CRAZY"

PART | ONE

The RISE

1

THIS THING CALLED LIFE

ON JUNE 7, 1958, AT MOUNT SINAI HOSPITAL IN MINNEAPOLIS, A baby was born. John Nelson faced his son in the crib and named him Prince Rogers Nelson—after his own musical stage name. "I named my son Prince because I wanted him to do everything I wanted to do," John later explained to Liz Jones.

They lived at 915 Logan Avenue, a humble home in North Minneapolis. John worked at Honeywell, an industrial supplier, and he and his wife Mattie—a former singer that John met while playing parties with his group, The Prince Rogers Trio—together cared for their first son. They were already trying to raise five kids on what John earned at Honeywell when Prince was born, but within a year Mattie was again pregnant. When their daughter, Tyka Evene, arrived in 1960, John saw his dream of a music career slip even further away.

Mattie also gave up her dream—since singing like Billie Holiday wouldn't pay the bills. She remained social, though, with a "wild side," Prince told *Rolling Stone*, while John was quiet, excited mostly by music.

Since John still played shows around town with The Prince Rogers Trio, and still sometimes answered to his stage name, Mattie took to calling their son "Skipper." Prince obviously knew about his father's history leading "his own big band, playing around the Midwest and stuff," and how his mother sang for the group. But he didn't truly understand what his father did until 1963. One day, his mother took him to a local theater. They took their seats, the lights dimmed, and John emerged from behind a curtain with a smile. People applauded as he sat at a piano. While he played, the curtain moved again, and scantily clad dancing girls came out. "People were screaming," Prince recalled, according to Per Nilsen. "From then on I think I wanted to be a musician."

The show took a hold of Prince, and for weeks after he tried to play any instrument within reach. He eventually settled, like his father, on the piano, and he would practice in the living room on John's. Then, in department stores, while Mattie shopped, Prince would rush to where the radios and instruments were kept to listen to music or play organs and pianos until his mother would get him. But piano wasn't enough. Prince would put two rocks in his hands, then smash them together to create a melody. He called this noise his first song. Soon, he'd use larger rocks to tap out a rhythm.

But while Prince was taking his first musical steps, John was finding the pursuit a rough life. He was, according to local reporter Neal Karlen, "a Jazz musician in the whitest metropolitan area in the country." With a wife and six kids to support, he continued to work at Honeywell, but he couldn't accept that he wouldn't someday be a music star. So he kept creating new melodies. Despite a limited income, John did things like install a TV in the living room wall. Or he'd parade around in new suits and shoes, as if about to take the stage. By 1966, John had bought himself a snazzy new white Thunderbird convertible. His dream seemed by turns impossible and just within reach. When he saw that Prince and his younger sister Tyka were interested in music, he encouraged them to play his piano, realizing he'd have to live his dream vicariously through them. While young Prince tapped out melodies, Tyka told *City Pages*, she sang, "because that's what my mom and dad did."

But just as quickly, moody John would see them bang away on the keys and tell them to get away from the piano. He needed it for his own dream, after all. Though the inner conflict persisted, inevitably he relented, and Prince showed him a melody he had written called "Funk Machine."

Monday through Friday, Prince attended elementary school, where other students sometimes insulted his diminutive size. By 1967, the fifth grader was being bussed to a school in an affluent, predominantly white suburb. He wasn't thrilled. One day in class, he turned to a page in a textbook that had a black-and-white photo of a young, dead black man hanging from a rope on a tree.

His sister Tyka recalled, according to Per Nilsen, that other students chased them back to the school bus many afternoons. "I didn't know it was because we were black," she said. Some days, other students by the bus protected them. But the next day would always bring another chase and more epithets. Inevitably, Prince tried to withdraw from the experience.

One morning he hid his socks, believing this would give his mother no choice but to let him stay home. No dice. She yelled, "You're going to get to that school and find some socks!" He sighed and kept dressing. "She couldn't have them calling me a nigger with no socks on," he told *PAPER Magazine*, in 1999.

Sundays, his mother took him to a wooden, two-story Seventh-day Adventist church where he was enrolled in a Bible study class. On these days, eight-year-old Prince bonded over music with his schoolmate, André Simon Anderson, the son of his dad's former bass player, Fred. "The most I got out of that was the experience of the choir," Prince said of church, according to Nilsen.

During this period, Prince's older half brother, Alfred—Mattie's son from her first marriage—was trying to dodge a few rules. In his room, Alfred sang along to his many James Brown records. He styled his hair in a Little Richard–type conk. He always seemed to have money. He also ignored John Nelson's curfews. Late at night, Alfred climbed out of a basement window and hit the street. With him gone, Prince and his cousin Charles tiptoed into his room to try on his clothes and play his James Brown records. Sometimes, Alfred caught them in the act. But he didn't mind.

In the end, things didn't end well for Alfred, Charles told author Per Nilsen years later. His recreational drug use led to confinement in a local mental institution.

Prince, himself, was born epileptic. As a child, he had seizures. While he trembled and shook, his parents stood nearby, wondering how to help. Still, "they did the best they could with what little they had," he explained.

There were other stressors. In 1981, Prince told New York *Newsday* that his father "felt hurt that he never got his break, because of having the wife and kids and stuff." With Mattie resenting this, "there were constant fights."

By 1968, Prince was watching things finally fall apart between his parents. They began having high-volume arguments that sometimes left Mattie in tears. Mattie and John had always been different. She was louder and more vivacious, while John was serious and strict. She had set aside music in the interest of her kids, while John did manage to play some shows in local clubs. "I think music is what broke her and my father up, and I don't think she wanted that for me," Prince later told *New York Rocker*. Serious musicians, like his father, could be moody. They needed space. Everything in their environment had to be just right. "My father was a great deal like that, and my mother didn't give him a lotta space. She wanted a husband per se."

Finally, John and Mattie called it quits. After thirteen years of marriage, they decided to separate and filed for divorce. John packed his stuff and moved into a small apartment near Minneapolis's downtown. Prince was shocked when John left. He didn't even take his piano. "Everything was cool I think, until my father left, and then it got kinda hairy," Prince said.

At home, it would now be only Prince, his mother, and Tyka. "He left when I was seven, so music left with him," Prince said. "But he did leave his piano." Prince faced the abandoned instrument. In the past, John had often kept the kids away from it. For good reason: they would just bang on it. With his father gone, Prince approached the piano; he was the only one that seemed to notice it was there. And he started to play it in earnest.

Meanwhile, Mattie took three jobs.

Prince spent much of his time nearby, on his cousin Charles's street. He told people not to call him "Prince." Referred to as "Skipper," he developed an acerbic sense of humor and coined numerous put-downs. But back at home, he'd return to being his father's son, playing melodies on the piano John left behind. At some point, Tyka stopped joining him. Though she never said who, someone, she said, had crushed her dream of singing, saying she was crazy to think she could be on stage. Prince taught her to draw and write stories. But he didn't abandon his own musical dream. Soon, he started practicing drums, playing on a box of old newspapers.

Mattie, however, didn't support Prince's musical aspirations. She wanted him in school, and later in college. She sent him to different schools, where he maintained high grades, but Prince viewed his studies as "pretty much my second interest. I didn't really care about that as much as I did about playing." Since music had destroyed his parents' marriage, he explained, "I don't think she wanted that for me."

Mattie eventually met Heyward Baker. With her divorce now official, Mattie married Baker and he moved into the house. Baker always brought the family presents. But, Prince told Barbara Graustark, "I disliked him immediately because he dealt with a lot of materialistic things."

Prince tried to build a relationship with Baker, as close as the one he had with John. But when Prince tried to engage Baker in conversation, Prince claimed, the man seemed to merely tolerate him. He mostly spoke up, Prince claimed, when Prince did something wrong. "I don't think they wanted me to be a musician," he said of Baker and his mother. They didn't want him to be like John. But the more they pushed, the more defiant

Prince became. Before long, he felt rejected, and bitter. He began to rattle off things he disliked about his new stepfather and "it kind of hurt our relationship."

Years later, Prince credited Baker for helping to improve the family's quality of life. The only time he had money during this period, Prince said later, "was when my step-dad lived there, and I know I was extremely bitter then."

By 1969, Mattie was pregnant with Baker's child, and Baker really started telling Prince what to do. In 1970, Mattie gave birth to Heyward's son, Prince's half brother, Omarr Julius Baker.

Over time, Prince became more and more impatient with his family's demands. One day, his mother told him to be home at nine. Prince told his cousin Charles that he was running away. Are you gonna come with me? he asked. Charles said he'd meet him at a certain time. But when he didn't show, Prince went downtown to his father John's small apartment. John heard him out and agreed to let his son move in. Prince transferred to Bryant Junior High.

During this period, Prince told *Musician* magazine, John was still working a day job but moonlighted in a downtown club "behind strippers." For weeks at a time, Prince barely saw John, except occasionally when John stood over the sink and shaved. "We didn't talk so much then."

Prince always liked sports. At Bryant, he made the junior varsity basketball team. His coach felt that even though Prince was short, he made for a good sixth or seventh man. Everyone on the team liked him, but he still had to work hard to prove himself. He had bigger kids taunting him, calling him Princess, or claiming he had the face of a German Shepherd.

The girls—on the other hand—loved him. But the bullies wouldn't let up. Soon, he was scared to walk up the steps and into the school.

In the seventh grade, Prince took up the saxophone, but that summer, he abandoned it, recommitting to keyboard. His musical skills continued to develop, though John still didn't take his son's music seriously, claiming he wasn't very good. "I didn't really think so either," Prince later admitted.

For a while, father and son got along. Prince followed John's rules. Inevitably, though, tempers flared. Published reports say that one day John found Prince and a girl in bed together. What exactly transpired is unknown, but after this incident, John's patience with the boy had run out. He kicked thirteen-year-old Prince out of the house—and onto the street.

———

Prince stood alone on Plymouth Avenue in north Minneapolis, near the McDonald's. He smelled cheeseburgers, and wished he could afford one. He crossed the street, entered the phone booth on the corner, and called his father. Could he come home?

John said no.

He called Tyka at the old house. Could she call John and change his mind?

It would take a few minutes. Call back.

When he did, he was relieved. Tyka said Prince could call their father and apologize, and John would let him come back home. Prince did, but to his surprise, John still said no.

Tears burst from his eyes, Prince later told *Rolling Stone,* and for two hours, he sat in the phone booth and cried.

With no other option, he retreated to Charles's house, where Prince's Aunt Olivia, his father's sister, invited him to stay. Olivia was old, and just as strict as John. Eventually, the tension between Prince and his father eased. Sometimes he would visit on the weekends. But with no room for a piano in his new home and without the money to afford one, Prince's piano playing days were over. To foster his musical interests, John got him an electric guitar. Prince tuned it to an unusual straight-A chord and taught himself to play.

At school one day, Prince was back on piano, playing with a band behind the school choir. His playing awed drummer Jimmy Harris, who was a year younger. Another day, he lifted a guitar and knocked out Chicago's intricate solo on "Make Me Smile." On another occasion, Jimmy Harris told the Minneapolis *Star Tribune,* "I made the mistake of getting up from the drums and he [Prince] sat there [at the drum set] and he killed 'em." He also had, Harris joked; with a hint of envy, "the biggest Afro in the world. That wasn't fair, either."

During this period, Prince reconnected with his old pal, André Simon Anderson, his friend from church. He and André had been in the same school for third grade, and saw each other when both of their mothers took them to the local Seventh-day Adventist church. But then the Andersons moved into a housing project. André's mother Bernadette and his father Fred, who was John Nelson's old bass player, then split.

Now, Bernadette was raising six kids on her own and had the family in a big, brick house on Twelfth and Russell in North Minneapolis. André felt they'd "moved up" into "kind of an upper class black neighborhood," and he was thrilled to see his friend Skipper again.

One day, Cousin Charles recalled, Charles told them both, "Let's start a band."

Fine.

So at the age of fourteen, Prince was in his first band. He played his guitar, tuned to that strange A-chord. André played bass. Charles was on drums. André's sister, Linda, got in on keyboards, while Terry Jackson and William Doughty, two friends, handled percussion. Initially, the band was named Phoenix, according to Charles, after Grand Funk Railroad's 1972 album *Phoenix*. But really, "we tried to imitate The Jackson 5. Prince was singing 'I Want You Back.'"

In September 1972, Prince started attending Central High School, near his father's apartment. According to a classmate interviewed for the Minneapolis *Star Tribune*, he still had a globular Afro and wispy mustache, and now wore dress shirts with huge collar points, baggy pants, platform shoes, and neckbands. When other students stared at him in the hall Prince would nod. In the lunchroom he sat with the biracial kids.

Despite his reported height of five foot four, he made the school basketball team. Assistant principal Don McMoore joked, "his hair made him look like he was six feet tall."

Prince reacted to taunts by putting up his dukes and hitting first. "I was a very good fighter," he claimed. "I never lost. . . . I don't know if I fight fair, but I go for it." Bernadette, André's mother, agreed. "He'd hit and run," she said, "but he'd get even."

This all changed once his father John remarried, and his teammate Duane Nelson suddenly became his half brother. People felt Duane (also on the school football team) had Prince's back. Prince also hung with school quarterback Paul Mitchell. Most afternoons after school, Prince's basketball coach, Mr. Nuness, would come in and discover the boys had sneaked into the school gym. They were usually in the middle of a game when Nuness chased them out, but they kept "bringing their bikes and their dogs in," Nuness recalled.

Other afternoons, Prince practiced with his band, which expanded its sound to include covers by jazzman Grover Washington and singer-songwriter Carole King. Sly Stone's deep tone began to inspire Prince's vocals. So did Stevie Wonder, who was producing melodies with over a dozen instruments. By August 1973, Prince's band had changed its name to Soul Explosion, after a local TV show André liked. They played high schools and the local YMCA. At a talent show, they battled an older group, Flyte Tyme. "We didn't have nothing," said André, referring to their equipment. But Soul Explosion—at the time just Prince, André, their drummer Charles, and a percussionist—asked their opponents, "Can we, like, play on your stuff, man?" In the end, Charles told a deejay for San Francisco radio station KPFA, the judges announced the winner: "Charles' Cousin and Friends." The group looked dejected until Charles said, "We won, we won!" Everyone laughed. Someone asked Charles, "Man, when did you change the band's name?"

By this time, Prince was making headway with the group, but his strict Aunt Olivia reportedly tired of the noise. And so, as *Rolling Stone* reported, once again the teenage Prince found himself kicked out of the house and onto the street.

Eventually, he wound up on André's doorstep. Once André's mother Bernadette spoke with Prince's father John, Prince moved his things into André's room and staged rehearsals in the basement. "The cutoff time for the music was ten each night," Bernadette recalled. But some nights Prince lowered the volume and quietly played guitar.

He also turned on the radio. With blacks representing less than 1 percent of the local population, station programmers felt there wasn't a demographic. So Prince listened to black station KUXL until eight thirty, then switched over to rock station KQRS. Soon, he counted Santana, Graham Central Station, Led Zeppelin, and Fleetwood Mac among his favorites. He also dug Jimi Hendrix's cover of Bob Dylan's "All Along the Watchtower" and considered Jimi "one of his heroes," local writer Neal Karlen recalled.

When he moved into the basement—a move inspired by André's untidiness—Prince used the weekly allowance John sent him to buy mirrors and a ten-dollar-swatch of rabbit fur. He hung them on his walls, along with the Hendrix posters his female friends brought over.

Sophomore year, Prince didn't make the school basketball lineup (for one of the city's finest teams). At the same time, Duane was moving in on girls that Prince liked. Prince would speak with one, watch Duane arrive, then see them leave as a couple. Prince poured his frustrations into a film class project. In the short movie, he reenacts such a scene, then depicts himself in the library reading a book on kung fu. He uses his newfound martial arts skills to get the girl and defeat his Duane-like competitor, a cast member told the Minneapolis *Star Tribune.* He also penned new lyrics about two-timing women who leave him for his best friend.

With basketball no longer an option, Prince threw himself into an extracurricular course, "The Business of Music," taught by a pianist that once played with Ray Charles. He also mapped out a trajectory toward rock stardom. "Not a musician, but a rock star," Prince's future employee Alan Leeds stressed. In Prince's mind, mass appeal would bring acceptance, power, and security, Leeds suggested.

At the time, other students were ostracizing him; he was an excellent ball player, but too short to make the team. His older brother's height made him more attractive to the ladies. Prince meanwhile felt he was in everyone's shadow. Leeds speculates that Prince told himself, *Okay, here's how I can get back at the world. Here's how I can get the girls and be the number one guy and get the attention that I never get.*

At sixteen, Prince kept writing songs. "I wrote like I was rich, had been everywhere, and been with every woman in the world," he said. "I always liked fantasy and fiction." Instead of tentative two-minute funk ditties, he brought his band seven-minute epics.

Before he knew it, André was planning his own changes. During one rehearsal, Prince saw André's shy, freckle-faced North High schoolmate Morris Day watching. Prince resented the intrusion but said nothing. Away from the group, André and Day had cut class and spent the day in Morris's home, where Morris mentioned he also played drums. After he rocked a few beats, André told him, "Man, you're good. We just happen to be having some scheduling problems with our current drummer," referring to Charles, who had been missing practices.

Within days, Prince saw André lead Day in to another rehearsal, this time to audition. Day got the gig. When Charles arrived another day, he saw Morris's drums in his usual spot, and asked, "Who sold me out?"

Everyone said, "Prince."

"It wasn't just me," Prince cried. "André, too!"

"Oh, so it's like that, huh?" Charles faced his replacement. "Morris, man, you're my friend, and you just took my band like that, man." Charles shook his head and left.

Now, Prince played lead guitar, André played bass, Linda handled keyboards, and Morris was on drums. They wore suede-cloth suits with zodiac signs on the back (Prince with Gemini, the twins). Morris's mother, Lavonne Daugherty, managed them: She shaped a professional image, named them "Grand Central Corporation," formed a company that technically owned every instrument, and booked as many shows as possible.

At age seventeen, though he had a local band with some success, Prince still loitered near the McDonald's on Plymouth and Penn. "I didn't have any money, so I'd just stand outside there and smell stuff." Being broke left him tired, bitter, and insecure, he continued. "I'd attack anybody." He couldn't keep a girlfriend for two weeks. "We'd argue about anything." Standing there, sniffing the air, he wished he had enough for a cheeseburger, he told reporter Neal Karlen.

Prince also wanted to leave school. "The only reason I stayed was because of André's mother," he later said. Bernadette was permissive about most activities but told him, "All I care about is you finishing school."

During their local shows, the band played the same old songs. "I hated top forty," Prince said. Everyone did. But white club owners and audiences expected it so they played "anything that was a hit; didn't matter who it was." It held the band back, but eventually earned them enough to finance demo tapes. It also let Prince include his family in his burgeoning career. Between sets, he'd let Tyka come out with her pals and perform the dance moves they picked up from Soul Train.

One time while performing, he saw his father John in the crowd, taking pictures.

Performing was great, but still, Prince had to do something more.

Minneapolis was behind the curve. New music and dances arrived three months later than they did in other cities. Prince had to ignore trends. "Otherwise, when we did split Minneapolis, we were gonna be way behind and dated." So down in the basement, he filled new lyrics with sexual fantasies and stories about "insane people" (perhaps inspired by half brother Alfred's institutionalization). "I liked the idea of being insane, of someone who grew up totally alone and ended up in a hospital," Prince explained in Musician magazine.

Prince used cassette tape recorders to overdub separate performances onto dual tapes. He kept playing tapes back and taping more sounds on the other deck, teaching himself to arrange and produce. He also mixed incongruent influences—Santana solos with James Brown yells, Sly Stone's elocution with his father John's unconventional piano playing (inspired, John claimed, by Duke Ellington and Thelonious Monk).

By December 1975, Prince met Linster Willie at a ski party. Married to Prince's cousin Shauntel, Linster was a Brooklyn transplant known locally as "Pepé," who was trying to get his disco group 94 East off the ground. "I remember thinking, 'Boy, he's got a big Afro,'" Pepé recalled. Pepé started attending the band's rehearsals in the attic of a South Minneapolis home. There, Prince played guitar while André handled bass, Morris Day played drums, Andre's sister Linda played keyboards, and William Doughty added percussion. One day, Pepé asked them to play an original song. "It was a disaster," Pepé recalled. The young band would play a song for three minutes, then improvise for ten. Then they leaped into Andre's work, "You Remind Me of Me." But Prince was singing "she" while André sang "he." "I couldn't believe they didn't take the time as a group to learn the words," Pepé continued. He asked them to stop, put their instruments down, and actually learn the lyric.

Even so, Pepé liked Grand Central's playing. Before Prince knew it, his manager was telling him Willie wanted to pay Prince and his band for session work. They agreed to play his disco stuff. "We were just trying to make some money," said André, who played bass, in a radio interview with KPFA.

Hopes were high in early 1976, when Morris's mother Lavonne got them into another studio to record six originals. The results so pleased Prince, he bragged about his group in the school newspaper that February. By early spring, Prince was done with school. Despite Day's mother's promise that Grand Central would have an album out that summer, that "wasn't fast enough for Prince," Bernadette recalled. "He wanted her to get them a contract right away."

Prince didn't give up, though. "I'm going to get out there and see if I can make it," he told Bernadette. But if he couldn't—if he failed at music like his father John—he still wouldn't waste his life in some local factory. He'd come back, enroll in college, and "major in music."

With no money, dependents, or girlfriends, and without a day job, Prince started writing more songs—up to four a day—about romantic relationships. "All fantasies," he shrugged, or about ex-girlfriends. He was "broke, and poor, and hungry," and dreaming of meeting people with money, success, and "a lot of food in their fridge." But he also faced reality. If one thing didn't work, Grand Central had to try another. He told the band they needed more instruments, assembling a twelve-piece outfit called "Shampagne." The rest went along, though only four people on stage actually played instruments. "Eight were faking," said Prince.

But things weren't working out. Conversations among the band members became arguments. The others resented Prince's changes. "It was always me against them," he said.

Still, Prince was joined by his bandmates for a session that spring at Moon-Sound, an eight-track studio that charged about thirty-five dollars an hour. He showed up early, sipping from a chocolate shake and ignoring Chris Moon, a young, bearded white man with an Afro. He set his beverage aside, bashed some drums, and played piano. Once everyone arrived, Shampagne worked on a few more songs.

Later, back at André's house, the phone rang for Prince. Moon, from the studio, said, "I've got an idea for you. I'm looking to put together some music that I have written." They were on acoustic guitar but needed some piano. He'd pay for Prince's work.

And so Prince returned to the South Minneapolis neighborhood to work with Moon. Twenty-four-year-old Moon had moved to town from Britain while in his teens, and tried his hand at everything from advertising, to professional photography, to real estate, to promoting local rock concerts. Now, instead of using his homemade studio to tape rock bands and advertising jingles, he wanted to give pop music a try.

Back at Moon-Sound, Prince finished the piano riffs. Did Moon need bass?

"Sure, but I don't want to pay for a bass player."

Prince added a bass line, drums, electric guitar, and cascading backup vocals. Awestruck, the studio owner proposed teaming up. He handed Prince a key to the place and handwritten instructions on how to run the equipment. "He'd stay the weekend, sleep on the studio floor," Moon recalled.

Prince had bigger aspirations now than his band could handle. "Do you want to stay here, or do you want to go to New York?" he finally asked.

His bandmates wanted to stay in town. "They liked their lifestyle, I guess," Prince said.

He was left with no choice: He left the group.

2

DON'T MAKE ME BLACK

THAT AUTUMN, PRINCE—NOW OUT OF SHAMPAGNE AND STILL nursing his dreams of stardom—spent an hour every day riding city buses to reach the studio. There, he played the new music he wrote for Moon's lyrics. Some afternoons, Moon rejected the music, urging him to try again. More sessions led to greater confidence. He told Moon he wanted to play everything himself, including drums. Moon said another drummer would play better. "You don't think I can do it, do you?" Prince asked, according to Steve Perry in *Musician* magazine.

Prince stopped acceding to requests for another take on a melody or vocal. "You can't even play anything," Prince said at one point. "Why should you be able to tell me what to do?" This was the mood when Moon taped Prince recording a song called "Aces." Moon asked for another take but Prince wouldn't do it.

Finally, Prince relented. "Okay this time. But only because you own the studio!"

What Moon couldn't know was Prince's discomfort at taking center stage. In Grand Central and Shampagne, friends surrounded him. "I never wanted to be a front man," Prince said. Now, it felt "spooky to be at the mike alone." He performed moves while singing but was never quite as comfortable as observers might have guessed.

Relations between the two became more tense, but through it all, Prince and Moon worked side by side at the board. Slowly but surely Prince learned the art of engineering. After six months, Prince was able to run an entire session himself. Prince also started to write more lyrics. Now, he was producing, writing, and playing every note. From the sidelines, Moon called for alternate bass lines or vocals, but Prince mostly ignored him.

Prince began to further sculpt his image. He practiced his autograph—inserting a heart over the "i" in his name. He also, Moon claimed, agreed to knock two years off his age and go simply by his first name. Most important, Moon continued, Prince listened to Moon stress the importance of attracting a white crossover audience.

But his image, as Moon told Steve Perry, still needed something. The final piece clicked. Moon began to write a lyric. "Angora fur, the Aegean Sea," he began. "It's a soft wet love that you have for me." Moon shared the lyric with Prince, which he called "Soft and Wet."

"I think we've got your marketing strategy worked out, and a song to go with it," Moon remembered telling him. "We'll have thousands of thirteen- and fourteen-year-old girls going crazy over you."

Prince offered what Moon called a rare smile.

After nine months, and with a few numbers on tape, Prince needed management. On the phone one day, he told his older half sister Sharon, then living in New Jersey, about his setbacks in trying to launch his career. Prince wanted to go to New York to get a deal. "Well come here and I'll help you," she answered. So, with four songs he and Moon chose from the album they recorded together, and with an invitation from his half sister, he left Minneapolis for New Jersey. He was sure his sister's winning personality could land him a deal. At the same time, Chris Moon said he'd call labels.

But after a week on the East Coast, he called Moon to ask why there weren't any meetings. According to Per Nilsen, Moon admitted he was having trouble—every time he called, receptionists took messages, but no one called back. Still, he kept at it. He told an Atlantic Records receptionist he represented Stevie Wonder. It worked. Within two minutes, a higher-up was on the phone. "This is Chris Moon, and I'm representing Prince. If you like Stevie Wonder, you're gonna love my artist. He's only eighteen, he plays all the instruments, and he's not blind!"

The executive laughed, Nilsen confirmed. "I don't know who this artist is but send him in tomorrow morning at nine." Ultimately, Atlantic rejected Prince's sound as "too Midwestern" and his songwriting as noncommercial. He would have kept at it, Prince said. But he told *Musician* magazine "that's when me and my sister kinda had a dispute." He was "running up sort of a bill there, at her place," he said evasively. She wanted him to sell his publishing "for like $380 or something like that, which I thought was kinda foolish." He said he could form his own publishing company.

Back home, Chris Moon wanted to get the songs out there. He thought of his associate Owen Husney.

Husney—only twenty-seven at the time—was a promoter, manager, studio owner, and ran a marketing company. He had played with the High Spirits in the mid to late sixties and achieved some success. That band lasted until late 1968, when their guitarist David Rivkin left. Though he'd abandoned a musical career, Husney excelled at advertising and still loved music.

There, in an office overlooking a small park with lakes, on the edge of downtown Minneapolis, Husney listened as Moon told him over the phone that "he had the next big thing in music," Husney remembered. Having heard this many times during his career, Husney didn't pay any attention to him.

After hearing the same claim every day for a week, Husney relented. "Finally on Friday I told him to come into my office, but for just a minute," Husney said. When the cassette began, Husney knew in one second ("being a musician myself") that Moon had something. The songs were pretty long—ten to twelve minutes apiece—but when Prince's tape ended, Husney said, "Not bad. Who are they?"

Moon replied, "It's one seventeen-year-old kid."

"Who?"

"Prince."

Husney wasn't as impressed by the songs as much as the fact that one guy had done everything.

"You gotta be kidding!" he told Moon. "I mean this is ridiculous. Where is he? Let's just get him on the phone now."

Moon said he was in New York with his older half sister Sharon. "I called him on the spot and told him to come back to Minneapolis." Husney added that he would protect his creativity, shop this new demo, and get him a record deal. "He said Okay, and came back to Minneapolis," Husney recalled.

Prince couldn't believe his luck. Husney's call came at the perfect moment—he was just leaving his half sister Sharon's house after their bickering over money. And while he liked Husney, Prince didn't yet commit to anything. Husney said he loved the self-produced tape; and no outsider should produce his records. "I don't know whether I really agreed with him at the time," Prince admitted. Husney's vehemence fascinated him but Prince still questioned whether he was "old enough or smart enough" to handle the job. "It sounded," Prince explained, "like a big term. You know, 'Producer' of an album."

He returned to André's basement, but this time with more confidence: There were people who wanted to manage him. Soon, he met Husney in person, and was impressed. Husney had experience promoting, and said Prince should produce his own records.

Word of Prince had begun to spread. A manager in LA now wanted to meet with him. Very suddenly, on the basis of that Moon tape, Prince was becoming a hot commodity. He reportedly made a quick trip to California, where this potential manager offered him a gold guitar. But there was something about the manager and his offer that said to Prince "back away."

In December 1976, Prince called Husney, who had left his job at the agency and raised fifty thousand dollars from investors toward a label.

Prince signed to Husney's American Artists, Inc., and the young musician saw life change for the better. Husney rented him an apartment downtown. And with Shampagne keeping his Stratocaster guitar (as the formation of that "company" had insisted), Husney bought Prince new instruments. He even provided a cash allowance.

"Owen believed in me," Prince later said. "He really did."

In early 1977, Husney tapped Bobby—a runner at his ad agency and the brother of his former bandmate David Rivkin—to watch over Prince. By now, Bobby had come by the studio and seen him in action at the piano. A drummer himself, Bobby recalled in the Minneapolis *Star Tribune*, "I was taken immediately."

Since Prince didn't drive, Bobby was charged with taking him to get his license. "We found an apartment," Bobby added. "We bought musical gear." They hung in his Pinto station wagon and caught Santana's show at Northrop Auditorium. Some nights, Bobby remembered, he helped move Husney's office furniture aside and, with André joining in, they played jam sessions that lasted until dawn.

Winter continued, and Husney installed Prince in Sound 80 Studios. It was time for him to record a *real* demo. At the mix board, Bobby's brother David, who had worked with Grand Central in the studio in 1975, engineered while Prince single-handedly performed 3 twelve-minute songs: a new version of Moon's "Soft and Wet," "Make It Through the Storm," and his schmaltzy new "Baby." "He did all the instruments," David told the *Star Tribune,* and Prince treated the studio itself as another.

Overdubs and multitracks banded together. Synthesizers created the illusion of a full orchestra, a horn section, or organ line. His songs drew from jazz, blues, pop, funk, and rock. "I got hip to Polymoogs," he said of these sessions. These polyphonic (two-handed) synthesizers let him avoid the piano and clavinet sounds heard on other albums.

Before a session, he hummed each part into a tiny cassette recorder. "The horn part, the guitar part, he had it all separated," David recalled. ("Prince: An Oral History," 2004) Before each take, Prince told himself this was his only shot. Whatever instrument he played had to sound perfect. The approach resulted in an entire band "playing with the same intensity." Come time to sing, Prince needed privacy. If someone stopped by, he had Rivkin turn off the lights. When Rivkin's wife saw him singing "Soft and Wet," Rivkin recalled in the *Star Tribune,* he glanced over at her with embarrassment.

No one could deny the young musician's immense talent. Husney was impressed with his young client. He had "the vision and astuteness of a forty-year-old man." He sat and listened, absorbing everything. He spent nights in the studio. He didn't "get high with the guys." Until now, Husney had dealt with hard-drinking, or drug-using musicians. "Not Prince," Husney continued. "That would destroy his chances of making it, and he wanted to make it."

During visits to Cliff Siegel's home, he sat for hours, watching tapes on Siegel's rare and expensive videocassette recorder. And despite—or perhaps because of—his height, he gave his all during their spirited games of basketball.

"He was always quiet and always a gentleman," Siegel recalled. He wasn't open about feelings but outlined goals—"to do films, be Number One, and produce other groups."

Husney thought it was a nice dream.

Husney remembered Prince's image taking shape during his late-night talks with Prince and André: there would be suggestive visuals, a cultivated mystique. They'd develop costly promotional kits, and retain control of ancillary rights. Husney also said "Prince Nelson" wouldn't do. He told him to drop the surname and simply refer to himself as "Prince."

It was time to put the image of Prince into place. They enlisted young photographer Robert Whitman. Prince fixed his Afro and chose an outfit—his managers helped decide which—and with Whitman carrying his Nikon 35mm camera, loaded with Tri-X black-and-white film, they hit the street. For one shot, Prince posed near a wall outside Schmidt Music Company, with the old building, aging cars, and a woman behind him. Other street shots showed him strolling in his extravagant getup. For one, he smiled as he raised his middle finger.

They traveled to Husney's well-appointed home, where Prince was photographed at a piano. Then he sat in a chair and held a guitar. Three or four sessions filled seventeen rolls of film. Some were standard head-shots. Others emphasized his Afro with dramatic lighting. After Whitman and his managers chose the most effective, they moved on to the press kit.

He didn't include press articles or "eight million pictures," Husney explained. Only one sentence per page. "The music would speak for it-self." Prince also reportedly shaved two years off his age, claiming he was only seventeen, to make him seem even more gifted. After creating fifteen kits, seven or eight went out to major labels. "And we sent the tape, itself, on a silver reel. It was reel-to-reel, not cassette," an older-fashioned, higher-quality medium for his music.

Despite all the attention that went into this extravagant packaging, Prince wasn't an easy sell. Many executives saw "a young black kid coming out of an island in the North" and didn't rush to buy in, Husney explained. But the package was undeniably compelling: a teen with a regal name playing, singing, and producing everything.

Husney called Warner, where Russ Thyret (who once co-wrote a hit with Stevie Wonder) could sign acts. He claimed CBS was flying Prince out to LA for a meeting. Did Warner want to meet? Thyret said yes. Then Husney called CBS and A&M to say Warner was flying Prince out. Do they want to meet? "I lied my way in everywhere to get him in," he told author Alex Hahn. "Jealousy is what makes this business go around."

Five major labels soon wanted meetings: Warner, CBS, A&M, RSO, and ABC-Dunhill.

———

That spring, Prince joined Husney and attorney Gary Levenson on a flight to Los Angeles. Many executives on the West Coast favored jeans, cowboy boots, and untucked shirts left open at the neck, so Husney and Levenson opted for three-piece suits. "We had one made for Prince, too," Husney told the *Star Tribune*.

At the meetings, he felt confident someone would want his 3 twelve-minute songs. He let his managers do the talking, and they played the demo. He would enter to mumble a few words, acting shy in spite of his open-collared shirts, tight jeans, pointy black boots, and long, feathered hair. CBS was intrigued, but they had reservations—and doubts—about his abilities. So they booked time at Village Recorders—they wanted to see if he could actually produce. Indignant, he nevertheless rerecorded "Just as Long as We're Together" for watchful executives.

After a flurry of meetings, they finally met with their first contact, Russ Thyret of Warner. Other executives wined and dined them, handled the check at fancy restaurants, and promised "homes in Beverly Hills." But Thyret met them at his home, sat on the floor, and talked music. "There was a real, genuine bonding there," said Husney. He hoped they'd wind up with the man. Prince meanwhile had concerns about marketing. Every major record company had a separate, black music department and felt it was easier to market whites as rock and blacks as funk, soul, R&B, or disco. To avoid people shoehorning him into disco, Prince emphasized a small-town upbringing among white and black friends.

"I'm an artist and I do a wide range of music," he told Thyret. "I'm not an R&B artist, I'm not a rock 'n' roller."

Thyret understood.

Back in Minneapolis, they were amazed. While RSO and ABC both passed, every other major company called Husney, even Herb Alpert, co-owner of A&M. Husney told A&M and CBS that Prince wanted to produce, and a three-album deal. A&M would agree to a two-record pact. Prince and his people weren't interested. CBS offered three but wanted Earth Wind & Fire's Verdine White producing. "That destroyed the possibility of Prince going with CBS," said Husney.

That left Warner. When Husney told them Prince needed to be his own producer, "they thought I needed valium."

Thyret passed his endorsement of Prince to Mo Ostin, the chair of Warner. Warner A&R man Lenny Waronker also urged Ostin to sign him. Waronker had worked with him since 1966, when thirty-nine-year-old

Ostin, vice president at Reprise, added the twenty-six-year-old to his artist development team. Ostin rose to become Warner chairperson in the early 1970s, but he promoted Waronker with him. Both were low-key, honest talent scouts used to dealing with capable eccentrics.

Ostin considered everything. "There was a fierce competition," Ostin told Roger Friedman. "Columbia wanted him. Lots of people. But we convinced him we had the mechanism to make him a star."

And so, Prince, just nineteen years old, signed with Warner on June 25, 1977. His contract reportedly called for three albums in twenty-seven months, the first to be recorded within six months. The three were to cost $180,000—the usual $60,000 per disc allocated to acts like The Ramones. If he submitted them by September 1979, Warner could renew the contract for two years (for another three albums) and an additional advance of $225,000. If Warner wanted a second option period after this—in September 1981, for a year and two more albums—the company would advance him yet another $250,000.

Husney called it perhaps the most lucrative contract ever offered to an unknown. "Well over a million dollars," he said. Another time, he said it set a precedent and was "the biggest record deal of 1977."

And with a record deal and steady income now secured, Prince breathed a big sigh of relief. He got an $80,000 advance up front. And if Warner exercised its options, he'd be paid for making music for five years, until September 1982, *and* have seven albums to his credit.

Suddenly, the anger that had driven him—the need to succeed not just to prove himself, but to but prove others wrong—dissipated. With his signature on "a piece of paper and a little money in my pocket, I was able to forgive," he told *Rolling Stone*. "Once I was eating every day, I became a much nicer person."

Warner was "taken with the simplicity of his music," an executive recalled. Still, some Warner executives were shocked by his ballad "Baby," Prince recalled, "'cause it was about a cat getting a girl pregnant." As summer continued, Ostin suggested a collaborator for Prince in the studio: Maurice White, leader (and drummer) of Earth Wind & Fire, a group whose slick sound made hits of "Serpentine Fire" and "Shining Star." Ostin figured White could mentor him. But Prince had already rejected CBS's attempt to include White's brother Verdine. He felt Earth Wind & Fire's horn-heavy sound was closer to disco, which he predicted would fade. When Husney ran Ostin's idea by him, Prince replied, "I gotta do my own album. Maurice White is not producing. You go tell the chairman of Warner Brothers that I'm producing." He then filled a lengthy memo with every reason it wouldn't work. Husney related it to Ostin, who continued to insist on a co-producer.

As CBS had when they were considering a deal with Prince, Warner executives were invited to a studio session to watch Prince do his thing. So after another flight from Minneapolis to Los Angeles, he reached Amigo Studios, set up his instruments, and again recorded his demo song, "Just as Long as We're Together." As Husney told it, whenever Waronker and other executives quietly entered and left the room Prince "thought these people were janitors." Waronker tells a different story. He says that Prince noticed him and producer Russ Titelman there when he arrived. To his amazement, Waronker said, he told Prince, "Play the drums" and Prince did, then added a bass line, and some guitar. After forty-five minutes, Waronker seemed convinced, according to Debby Miller in *Rolling Stone*. "We didn't want to insult him by making him go through the whole process, but he wanted to finish," Waronker recalled. By now, the Warner A&R man had decided, "This kid could do all of it, play all the instruments and know exactly what sound he wanted."

He told Prince, "Yeah, fine, that's good enough."

But, Husney later told author Alex Hahn that he still had doubts. "Okay, we're going to have to burn a record on the guy." Not the most glowing endorsement, but one that at least inspired sighs of relief at Prince's camp. They could record an album without a co-producer.

"We won," Husney said.

Before Waronker left, however, Prince had something he needed to say. He was lying on the floor, Waronker told the *Star Tribune*. As Waronker came his way, he faced him.

"Don't make me black," he insisted.

Waronker thought, *Whoa!*

"My idols are all over the place." He named a few from different genres.

"That, as much as anything, made me feel that we shouldn't mess around with this guy," Waronker later said.

Though he seemed to be given an assurance that he could produce, Prince said this session didn't resolve the issue entirely. "Warner's had a lot of problems with it at first, but Owen was fighting for control for me,"

Prince said. They made him do a demo. "So, I did it, and they said that's pretty good." They wanted *another* and he did that, too. "Then they said, 'Okay, you can produce your album.' And they waited a week to call me back and they said I couldn't."

The label's issue wasn't just concerning Prince's ear for his own music. Recording was difficult and costly. A producer needed more than a working knowledge of contraptions and sound levels. A one-man band and songwriter might also not have an intangible "record sense," the ability to recognize hit material. Warner wanted someone else involved, so everything stalled, frustrating Prince to no end. They went back and forth "a few more times," and in the end, both sides won. By late September, Ostin and Waronker enlisted veteran engineer Tommy Vicari, who worked with Santana, Billy Preston, and others, to executive produce—to protect the label's investment and ensure the debut had marketable moments. Vicari—and possibly Warner—chose to book time up north at the Record Plant in Sausalito, just across the Golden Gate Bridge from San Francisco—a peaceful setting far from Hollywood. The label also rented a home in Corte Madera with a great view of San Francisco Bay. Upon arrival, Prince, Vicari, Husney, and Husney's wife Britt all unpacked and chose beds.

Meanwhile, from the sidelines, Warner awaited the first album from their costly new prodigy. And as they would find in the weeks—and months—that followed, their fears of having a young, untested musician take the helm were well founded.

3

EVERYBODY OUT

PRINCE STARTED RECORDING HIS FIRST ALBUM, *FOR YOU*, ON
October 1, 1977. With Warner expecting results, he wasn't the same
blithe and playful Prince he had been while recording demos for Husney
back in Minnesota. He barely even spoke with Vicari or assistant engineer Steve Fontano, who told author Alex Hahn that "He was definitely
out to make a statement: 'I can do it all, and you can kiss my ass.'"
Prince viewed Vicari as a potential Warner-installed obstacle. If Vicari
suggested improvements, Prince replied with a few words, then ignored
his comments. When Vicari and Fontano tinkered with equipment,
Prince watched, asked questions, and then returned to ignoring them.
After a few weeks, Husney told Hahn, "Prince already wanted him
out . . . and Tommy was heartbroken, because he had just been treated
like shit."

Prince's repertoire was mostly rhythm and blues but he included a
few ballads and—despite his reported misgivings about the genre—more
than a few disco-worthy moments (open high hats whisking along during
breaks, synthesizers playing upbeat riffs, artificial drumrolls, winding
guitar riffs).

One session, he knocked out a mellow drumbeat. Minutes later, with
bass guitar in hand, he played a taut funklike bass line. On the guitar, he
added sinuous melodies. Next, behind the synthesizer, he played sharp
notes, and droning, dreamlike riffs that would have been at home on a
disco single. Then, behind the mic, he sang his mellow lyric, "Soft and
Wet." It was a come-on to a young woman, with cheesy singles-bar lines
("Hey lover," he utters). But Prince thought it worked, and kept adding
backup vocals, cooing its chorus, and offering feminine cries.

"He seemed to be one of these guys who could hear the entire song in
his head, before he even played it," assistant engineer Fontano explained
to Hahn.

He wanted to handle everything himself. When he finished basic tracks, Prince insisted on having his friend and previous studio engineer David Rivkin come west from Minneapolis to the Bay Area to tape vocals. Once Rivkin arrived, Prince relaxed, and they hung out together after work. André also came out west, to show support for his friend and contribute. In the wings, he hoped to play bass, but the opportunity never materialized. Prince felt he had to gain Warner's confidence, make his name, and deliver parts that met his own increasingly high standard for excellence. So André was left to kill time by telling people he'd create his own album. "He kept saying, 'I'm going to do my thing,'" Rivkin recalled.

Only when Prince finished recording for the day would they hang and explore the area.

In the studio, Prince continued to insist on flawlessness, especially when it came to his vocals. He kept Rivkin at the board for hours. But with his many takes, Rivkin felt everything sounded canned. In other hands, the title track "For You" would be a pleasant little vocal showcase. But he filled the track with forty-six time-consuming overdubs. Rivkin understood Prince was under pressure and wanted to silence doubts about his production abilities. But Rivkin felt he was cluttering the song, as well as "Soft and Wet," whose catchy melody was buried under too many keyboard flourishes.

Worst of all from the label's perspective, the album went over budget—*way* over budget. "It was really big," he told *Musician*, "over $100,000." The Warner contract meanwhile called for $60,000. Either way, Prince kept creating new ideas. "I went in and kept going and kept going and kept going. I got in a lot of trouble for it."

They were recording at the Record Plant with Vicari one afternoon when Lenny Waronker and Warner Bros. head Mo Ostin flew in to observe. Prince didn't want them there, but Husney, in the interest of brokering a peace between his artist and the label, worked to make them feel welcome. During the playback of Prince's ballad "So Blue," Husney told the *Star Tribune*, Waronker said, "Great song, but there's no bass."

Prince's turn was sudden. "That's it. Everybody out. Get out."

Husney turned pale. *It's all over,* he thought, as the label execs shuffled out. "Don't worry about it," Waronker said, reassuringly. "The song is great. I get where he's coming from. I'm with him."

———

In late December 1977, after three grueling months of long sessions, everyone was weary. Prince's flawlessly produced songs sounded like professional products, but the actual songwriting was a jarring mix of funk, rock, and soul. His maudlin ballad "Crazy You" sat next to his over-wrought hard rock number, "I'm Yours." Prince hoped the variety—a rock number with wailing riffs, a ballad, and two folksy numbers with acoustic instruments—would prevent anyone from shoehorning him into disco, funk, or R&B. But four songs were the usual fast-paced dance stuff. And for all his talk of rock influences and not being pigeonholed, most of *For You* was R&B and disco.

Still, he left Sound Labs after final touches and turned it in. Warner executives didn't know what to say about its cost. He had just spent $170,000 on *one* album when Warner wanted *three* for $180,000.

Either way, Prince was done with the Record Plant. He booked time at Sound Labs Studios in Hollywood, where he spent January and February mixing it all down.

Externally, Prince exuded pride. But was *For You* too perfect? It didn't truly reflect him as a person, he later decided. It was, he said, "like a machine." He had entered too many sessions after too little sleep. "I didn't really feel like recording for eighty percent of the record." But with costs exceeding almost a hundred thousand dollars, he had to do "something great. So, by that time, I didn't want to make any mistakes." He resented that Warner installed Vicari as an executive producer; he implied the man tried to control sessions.

Still, Warner deemed the songs good enough to release, and planned an early spring date. They hired an art director for the cover, but Prince's creative control extended beyond the studio. He posed instead for photographer Joe Giannetti, a shot of his head in a dark room, his Afro illuminated with dramatic candlelight. Try as he might, the shot only made him look more like a disco artist.

Back in Minneapolis, Prince was "a physical wreck," he said, but proud all the same. With his almost unprecedented record deal and an upcoming album he felt good. He also found that the same people who had once predicted he'd fail were suddenly deferential, eager to befriend the rising star.

"And it made me a much better person," he said of his newfound acceptance. "It took a lot of bitterness out of me."

———

Before releasing *For You* on April 7, 1978, Warner sent the media publicity materials. At black teen magazines, editors asked writers to create features that mentioned Prince's use of synthesizers, his one-man band approach, his extraordinary deal, and his status as producer.

When *For You* was released, it charted at No. 21 on music trade journal *Billboard*'s Soul Chart; but only made it to No. 163 on the Pop Chart, meaning few white stations paid attention. There also weren't many reviews. Those that did run offered kind words but focused on his age or his one-man-band approach. Prince kept watching the charts, hoping for a leap in sales. When the album failed to rise higher, he stopped watching. With sales at only 150,000 copies in America, for the moment (though this would change dramatically over the years), he watched as the mainstream media and music press continued to glorify soundtrack albums for musicals *Saturday Night Fever* and *Grease*, and the white disco act The Bee Gees, while his album languished.

His manager Owen Husney, however, took a different view of Prince's success. If black markets were his audience, then they should be cultivated with a quickly arranged publicity tour. Warner helped, releasing the track "Soft and Wet" as a single in June. By the time Prince arrived at a North Carolina record store for a routine signing, his single was No. 12 on the Soul Singles Chart.

Prince was astounded to find a crowd of three thousand teens screaming they loved him. After taking his seat at a tiny table near a member of the black funk act Cameo, he reached for a pen, signed posters, and autographs—and noticed the line in front of *his* table was longer. Kids from eleven to twenty were awed by his age. They asked if Prince was really his name, the meaning behind "Soft and Wet," and whether he really played every note. The crowd got rowdy, so Pepé—who had traveled with Prince to North Carolina and was a de facto bodyguard—suggested they leave. "Just let me sign a few more albums," he answered, basking in the attention.

"Okay, but the next time I whisper into your ear, just grab on to me and we are getting out of here."

Within twenty minutes, Pepé gave the sign. Leaping to his feet, Prince raced for the back door, to a car outside. Behind him, Warner reps doled out posters to fans. Author Per Nilsen reported that, at his hotel, he asked Pepé, "How can they love me? They don't even know me." He added that he felt like "a piece of meat" on display.

Husney accompanied him as he visited radio stations in other key markets. Though their reception was strong, they still didn't have any money, Husney recalled. They were sharing hotel rooms. Even worse, Prince kept falling asleep with a loud radio playing. One night in San Francisco, Husney had had enough. It was 4:00 A.M., Husney told the *Star Tribune,* and he reached over and turned off the radio. Prince quickly sat up. "Never, ever turn off the radio," he said. "Music soothes the savage beast." After flipping it back on, his back hit the mattress, and he instantly dozed off.

In Minneapolis, Prince finally had a place of his own, a yellow number at 5215 France Avenue, in Edina, a quiet suburb of the city. He stored his drums, instruments, and a TEAC four-track reel-to-reel in the basement. He didn't have furniture or carpet, his cousin Charles told Per Nilsen, but eventually set a rocking chair, and some early video games like Light Tennis, or Pong (released in 1977) near a tiny TV.

In the months after *For You,* inactivity got to him. He hoped Warner would provide tour support money (another loan he'd repay from royalties). Predicting they would, he told a writer he was forming a band for a national tour. "So far I only have a bass player, André Anderson, from Shampagne," he said. He vowed to hold auditions in New York for two keyboardists. He still had to "figure out who's going to fit" but he wanted a personality group. And while no horn players would be on stage, "I'm going to pick up a flute pretty soon."

And Warner didn't disappoint, providing for a small tour. Around late summer, they held auditions in LA. As usual, Prince didn't speak much. While many worthy candidates auditioned, he didn't pick anyone.

As autumn 1978 began, he took a new approach to recruiting. He placed an ad in a local paper that read: "Warner Bros. recording artist seeks guitarist and keyboardist." Prince's cousin Charles soon steered Gayle Chapman over to Prince's house on France Avenue. The white, blond keyboardist had bought a copy of *For You* ("the first one, with him in the fluffy hairdo," she said) and played it at full volume in her living room while thinking, *in order for Prince to tour, he will need a band.*

After auditioning her, Prince added Gayle to the group, which at the time included only bassist André. Then he recruited Bobby Rivkin to play drums. Jimmy Jam, of his old rival band Flyte Tyme, tried out but Prince rejected him. He wanted a young musician named Sue Ann Carwell on the stage with him. He had hopes for a project she was at work on, under the name of Suzy Stone, and he mentored her, telling her during one talk, "Whatever you do, go the other way. Be different."

He ultimately invited her to sing backup near André, Bobby Z (Rivkin), and Gayle Chapman, and to help William Doughty play the congas on "Just as Long as We're Together." But she tired of the group and backed out.

"I didn't really believe in Prince," she admitted.

The band was starting to take shape. For weeks, he invited local keyboardist Ricky Peterson to jam sessions. He wanted him in the group and laid out the rules, Peterson recalled in the Minneapolis *Star Tribune*. "This is what you can't do: You can't drink; you have to show up on time. . . ." Peterson listened, but thought, *This sounds like horrible boot camp*, and coming from someone that didn't even have a career yet. "I said 'no' to Prince," he explained.

Bobby Z invited his friend Matt Fink to try out. Fink loved the British Invasion (The Stones, The Beatles, and The Who) as much as he did James Brown, Stevie Wonder, Ray Charles, and contemporary acts Earth Wind & Fire, Steely Dan, Elton John, Yes, and David Bowie. He sounded like a good match for Prince.

Fink would eventually make the cut. And while Prince already owned some keyboards, Fink brought a few of his own. Even more impressive was how he handled the ARP pro-soloist, a chunky wood-paneled analogue synthesizer with thirty preset sounds that most players set on top of a large organ. Finally, after about four months, Husney began to schedule auditions for local guitarists.

On a cold winter day, Prince held auditions at Del's Tire Mart, a shop near the river and the University of Minneapolis campus, with enough space in a back room to hold his equipment and rehearsals. He was running two hours late. He strolled toward the entrance, surrounded by André, drummer Bobby Rivkin, and manager Owen Husney. Warner had released his single "Just as Long as We're Together" (backed with "In Love") on November 21, 1978, but it reached only 91 on the Soul Chart. More than just a new band member, Prince was likely thinking that day about how he could elevate himself to the next level of success.

Inside, he crossed the huge space, entering the rear room, where he found his equipment and headed for the keyboard. As he turned it on, he could hear, behind him, others opening the door, and a stream of musicians pouring in. After he was introduced to the group, Prince sat behind an Oberheim polyphonic synthesizer and Hohner Clavinette keyboard. He saw a black guitarist tell Husney he had only fifteen minutes to spare. Could he go first?

The man was Desmond ("Dez") D'Andréa Dickerson, born 1955, a guitarist with straightened frizzy hair. Dez could play faithful covers of Hendrix, Grand Funk Railroad, Cream, and Led Zeppelin. At home, he had heard his little sister's copy of *For You* and decided *it's okay, but they should have signed me: I could have done a much better record.* Clearly, Dez had put his reservations behind him, because now, Husney agreed to give him the first go at auditioning.

"I was headed out of town to do a gig with my band Romeo," Dez explained. With Prince arriving two hours late, he added, "I needed to get down the road."

Prince didn't speak to him. The frizzy-haired guitarist strapped on his guitar, and Prince started playing a riff. Once André and Bobby determined the tempo and key they joined in.

Dez watched for a minute, taking it in. He then played rhythm.

Prince was pleased with what he was hearing: Dez was capable, but he didn't try to showboat. With a nod he signaled to Dez, who began to play a restrained solo, then quickly returned to the rhythm. A team player.

Fifteen minutes later, Dez apologized and said he had to go.

In a suprising turn, Prince said he'd walk Dez out. It was cold out, others were waiting, but he had liked what he heard. "It was obvious from the kinds of questions he asked that I had passed muster," Dez recalled. The guitarist meanwhile thought Prince was "very thoughtful, not overly verbose." Prince asked Dez his career goals. "I told him it was to front my own thing," Dez explained, "which I had always done until that time." He asked about Dez's musical tastes, influences, and his work ethic. After ten minutes, he shook Dez's hand, asked him to learn a few songs from his album, then went back in. Dez meanwhile pointed his ride toward I-94 and the Wisconsin border and stomped on the gas pedal.

While dealing with Warner and the media in the months that followed, Prince avoided eye contact. He paused midsentence. He remained quiet. He spoke slowly and in a hushed tone. He backed out of interviews and public appearances. Either he was trying to cultivate an air of mystery or he was just being cautious. Either way, to his dismay, it backfired.

"Everybody at Warner Brothers has a big impression I'm really quiet," he explained. "'If he doesn't talk, he probably won't dance or sing too much.' I have to put to rest all those accusations." He needed them to invest in a tour, after all, and a reputation as a shy, retiring artist wouldn't do. The only solution was to prove his talents as a performer.

It was time to arrange his debut.

Starting in December 1978, Prince invited the new band—five local unknowns, only one older than twenty-three—to his west Minneapolis home for a series of rehearsals, where he struggled to get used to again involving others in his music. For weeks, he worked out arrangements with them. It was hard performing for others, even just for the band at first—he hadn't done it since leaving Shampagne, after all.

Prince was still nervous before the first show. He told himself he'd hide his fear of a large audience, "block out the fact that there are people out there." He'd focus on the music, playing different instruments on specific songs. He threw himself into promoting the event, having a band-mate invite Jon Bream of the Minneapolis *Star Tribune* over to talk. Bream had been one of the first reporters to notice Prince, and he had visited him as he recorded the album in California.

For forty-five minutes, Prince hid his face with a cap and let Bream do most of the talking. Then, at last, Prince relaxed, and he spoke for another forty-five minutes. He missed out on a lot by focusing on his career, he said, but didn't regret it. He *liked* playing music. He liked sports, too, but he abandoned them in the interest of furthering his musical development. Same with college. "I certainly don't have time for that." He told himself someday he'd realize another dream: having a kid. But for now, he was too busy.

A booking agency was arranging a short tour, he told Bream. After he toured, there was the obligation of a second album.

With Bream preparing to leave, Prince laughed. "I've never talked this much in my life. I swear."

In early January 1979, Prince and his new band arrived at 2027 West Broadway, the North Minneapolis movie theater called the Capri, described by Dez as "an old classic" venue. Bream claimed Prince could have debuted at New York's Madison Square Garden if he wanted; he chose to do two consecutive nights in his hometown.

In the three years since Prince arrived on the Minneapolis music scene, he had performed for only very small audiences. There were just three hundred people at his debut performance, but it was still the largest show he had played in ages. He and his band waited backstage at the aging movie theater, hearing local music fans—most of them teenage girls— pile into the auditorium, slide into red seats, and buzz with anticipation. Family members and friends were present.

KUXL's jive-talking emcee Carl Ray took the stage, introducing Prince as the next Stevie Wonder. Without further ado, Prince and his band took the tiny stage. For this show, he wore jeans, leg warmers, a slack blouse, a vest, and a raincoat that he hoped—along with his deeper voice during this performance—would position him closer to Mick Jagger, Sly Stone, and Jimi Hendrix than the blow-dried, flashy, polyester-clad Bee Gees set.

Bassist André and guitarist Dez played amid flashy pyrotechnics. Both knew—like every other band member—that Warner executives might attend the show to see if Prince was ready to tour. But Dez's new wireless guitar setup made the sound system act up. "There were radio frequency problems in the building," Dez recalled, and the music store that sold them the system hadn't properly addressed them. Prince was focused on his own falsetto when a blast of feedback burst from the system. He kept singing but more noise erupted. He soldiered on, playing his gentle acoustic ballad, "So Blue," even as the system emitted an annoying buzz. They stopped a few times to handle technical problems. Still, Prince remained unfazed. He didn't address the band or audience during these moments. Instead, he resumed playing and showed his command of different instruments. He played his album's delicate title track. He did a jazz-rock-funk groove and his dance-oriented lead single, "Soft and Wet." He threw in a few new funk tunes, too, then closed with his new single, the much-recorded "Just as Long as We're Together," which Bream dubbed contagious enough for soul, pop, and disco audiences alike.

"As a whole, Prince's performance clearly indicated he has extraordinary talent," Bream wrote of the night. More experience and refinement would, he added, guarantee "a royal future for Prince."

The first night went off well, all things considered, but with Warner executives flying in for his second night, January 7, 1979, there was much more pressure. It was also an audition of sorts, to determine if Prince was ready to earn money on the road, with Warner providing tour support. Before the show, Pepé led the Warner people to choice spots on the balcony.

Prince meanwhile was somewhat nervous, Dez recalled. In light of the technical problems the night before, Prince had been extremely cautious this time. He made sure the equipment worked and that there would be no feedback. Another glitch like that was the last thing he needed.

The executives, meanwhile, watched tentatively; their limo sat outside with the engine running as Prince performed. It was a relatively small audience, but they were responsive. Women screamed whenever he performed a dance move.

Pepé, meanwhile, watched the Warner executives. He wanted to determine their reaction, but he couldn't tell. Warner executive Carl Scott, however, liked what he saw. "It was unbelievable," he said later. "I just couldn't believe I was watching it." There was genius and magic taking place "but I didn't know what it was."

It was heartbreaking, then, when they decided he wasn't ready yet.

Prince told the band Warner wanted him to record another album before touring. He didn't say much, but his band members sensed he was down on himself. Dez understood. As he told the *Star Tribune*, "We were still individuals and not a band yet." Still, they tried to cheer him up, Dez saying, "Put it behind you. We did fine."

Though Warner let him do as he pleased with his debut—even going way over budget on the recording—Prince began to question what he heard from Husney and Warner. He had tried not to make waves, he claimed, "because I was brand new, and stuff like that." But clearly that wasn't working. He had to do it his way. If he didn't, "sooner or later down the road I'm going to be in a corner sucking my thumb or something," he later said to *Musician*. He only had one career. He wouldn't ruin it. "I just want to do what I'm really about."

The lack of a tour really gnawed at him. He kept rehearsing his band nonstop, working out what he wanted to do on stage. But nothing was set.

This more than any other moment was when Prince's relationship with Husney, one of Prince's first, biggest supporters, began to sour. He later cited the label as a factor in the dissolution of their professional relationship. "I was being real stubborn and bullheaded, and Owen didn't realize how to get it out of me, and make me stop," he said. "And, I don't know, our friendship died slowly after that. It just got strange." It may have been the label's decision not to tour, but it was his manager who endured the fallout.

Pepé felt it was simpler than this. At the time, Prince kept his drums in the basement of Pepé's apartment. It was freezing down there, so Prince called Owen for a space heater. Busy waiting for a return call from William Morris, Owen couldn't drop everything and bring it over.

Warner did what it could for the debut. But not even the singles "Soft and Wet" and "Just as Long as We're Together" could help the album rise above No. 163 during its five-week stay on the Pop Chart. During this period, Prince formed Ecnirp Music, his name in reverse, and registered "Do Me Baby" and other new works as his own creation.

When Warner called for another album and advanced him thirty thousand dollars, he needed representation more than ever. He was introduced to Don Taylor, a manager that handled reggae talents Jimmy Cliff and Bob Marley. Taylor assigned employee Karen Baxter to handle Prince's project. Baxter soon regretted it. "This guy was just too weird for me," Taylor told author Per Nilsen. "I never knew where he was coming from."

At Warner, executive Carl Scott remained a supporter. He let Bob Cavallo and Joe Ruffalo know Prince needed a manager. The duo, childhood friends from New York, handled funk and R&B stars Earth Wind & Fire, and Ray Parker, Jr. They also worked with one of Prince's idols, Sly Stone. Scott told them to pay attention to this guy. Maybe talk with him. They wouldn't regret it. Prince heard from them, they hit it off, and Cavallo and Ruffalo became his new managers after buying the unexpired part of his contract with Husney and American Artists, valued, Per Nilsen explained, "at some $50,000."

And as two of their employees arrived in Minneapolis to help with day-to-day chores Prince began to focus on the next step in his career: a second album.

4

PRIVATE JOY

WITH MANAGEMENT FIRMLY SQUARED AWAY, PRINCE COULD write his next album in peace. "After the first record, I put myself in a hole, because I'd spent a lot of money to make it," Prince said. With *Prince*, he wanted to "remedy all that" by consciously creating a "'hit album.'" He began to craft danceable works.

But he still didn't want a producer. New co-manager Cavallo invited engineer Gary Brandt to get involved since Prince had refused to work with Maurice White from Earth Wind & Fire. Cavallo felt Brandt, even as engineer, could help get the best sound.

In late April 1979, Prince packed his bags and caught a flight to Los Angeles, where he moved into another rented house on the edge of town, sharing it with Perry Jones and Jones's cousin Tony Winfrey, both affiliated with Prince's new managers Cavallo and Ruffalo.

Alpha Studio was located in Brandt's home just outside of Los Angeles. Where Prince spent five months recording and mixing *For You*, his managers booked just a month for his second album. With a lower budget, he planned to knock this out quickly. He'd work without an "executive producer," record only the songs he'd written, and limit himself to sixteen tracks (though the studio's two 24-track recorders could provide 48).

Some days his limo—arranged by new managers—dropped him off in the early afternoon. Most times, it arrived at night. He asked Brandt to keep women out of the studio. Instead of creating music on the spot, he wanted to re-create only his nine home demos, and improve them, if possible. At the board, Brandt watched him work. "He already had everything in his head," he told Per Nilsen. "He knew where the parts were going so it was just basically getting it onto tape." But he soon began to add new melodies and arrangements.

He usually made each session last about twelve hours. And since "he knew little about quality rerecording," Brandt told Housequake.com, he let Brandt determine how sounds were processed and recorded. When Brandt proposed where to place microphones, he was "reasonably open-minded"—a big step from when he was recording *For You*. Brandt felt comfortable enough to slide levers or twist various knobs on the mix board while playing songs back, auditioning various echoes, delays, and effects that, he felt, Prince never considered.

"I Wanna Be Your Lover," now one of Prince's most revered tracks, was about a jilted, penniless suitor vowing he could make a woman happy. He sat behind the drum kit, ready to bang it out. Brandt used a customized AKG 452 microphone to record his snare. With the basic track down, he added funk riffs on guitar and bouncy synthesizer melodies.

They kept recording. Now instead of the AKG 452 mic, he wanted a Shure SM57, an old horse when it comes to studio recording. Brandt felt it was a mistake. Prince insisted and got his way, Brandt recalled, but "the rest of the tracks sounded less snappy."

He sang in his falsetto again and kept trying to cover all bases by setting pop-rock and almost folk numbers alongside funk and R&B. Only this time it worked: The music wasn't as cluttered. The synth wasn't in everyone's face like on *For You*. Some songs, he actually used a piano. He also threw in two rock-flavored cuts.

By June 13, 1979, he had his nine songs down, and he sat with Brandt to create rough mixes. He figured he'd tape them, study them at home, form ideas, then return, and perform the real mix.

But Brandt had two other projects booked. "He expected me to do anything he wanted but he wasn't even known at the time." His managers told him Brandt was busy. He told them to change Brandt's mind. Brandt couldn't do it; two complete album projects were bringing four months of income. "Warners [sic] would never have done that at the time so that was that." His managers got him into Hollywood Sound Recorders, in Los Angeles, where he recorded final touches and overdubs, mixed everything, and, after having some second thoughts, yanked two songs, "Oh Baby" and "Darling Marie," from the album.

After publishing every song through Ecnirp Music Inc. and BMI, he moved on to the cover. Again, he created the concept. Photographer Jurgen Reisch snapped a shot of him against a light blue backdrop, without a shirt, expressionless, his hair blown out. The rear sleeve photo found him in underwear, with long hair and an earring, riding a winged horse (created by superimposing dove wings on an image of a rented horse). He wanted calligraphy; Terry Taylor provided it. Finally, he sat to write the credits. He included a list of thank-yous. God was first. Then band members, friends, Warner, Pepé, various attorneys and managers, Cynthia Horner (editor of black teen fanzine *Right On*), "and all the beautiful people who got into my first album, I love you all."

And just as quickly as he had begun the album, he moved on to the next.

Within weeks, Prince had his band joining him to record a rock album under the group name The Rebels. It was a good time to shift gears. Labels were glutting the market with so many disco singles and albums, even ardent fans were bored with the sound. And many rock radio stations were staunchly opposing music with any disco or dance influence. This album, he revealed, would feature "everything from New Wave to R&B," Dez recalled. Dez was delighted. Recently, he had introduced Prince to the music of The Cars, a Boston-based New Wave group whose works fused Doors-like keyboards to roaring guitars and Ric Ocasek's icy vocals.

Prince's band arrived in Boulder, Colorado. In the studio July 10, they started a collaborative album. After hearing they'd write and receive credit, guitarist Dez, bassist André, keyboard players Gayle and Matt, and drummer Bobby brought their best ideas. "I wasn't sure what he'd want," Dez said of the rock material. "I just presented what I liked." For eleven days, until July 21, Prince and the band recorded Dez's "Too Long," "Disco Away," and an instrumental. Dez was thrilled. "We had a blast," he recalled. "We worked, we played, we ate lots of shrimp." Even better, "I was allowed to do what I wanted to do." They moved on to André's song, "Thrill You or Kill You" and another of Andre's melodies. Prince meanwhile wrote four: "You," "If I Love You Tonight," "Turn Me On," and "Hard to Get." "You" mixed forceful guitars with lighthearted synth effects and Gayle singing in a high voice that evoked Prince's falsetto. There were few lyrics and the ones there were sounded "quite odd," the magazine *Uptown* noted. "You, you drive a girl to rape," she sang. At another point: "It's true; I'd kill myself if I didn't make love to you." Still, Gayle had no problem with the material. If anything, she thought the songs were "Different, fun, great to play with the musicians in the group."

"If I Love You Tonight," meanwhile, was as gloomy as his *Prince* number "It's Gonna Be Lonely," with a downbeat chorus ("All I need is some company to help me through the night"). Still, everyone was excited about the album's imminent release. "They were mostly our songs, not all his," Gayle explained. It was "rock that was consistent with his sound," Dez said, "as opposed to what a purely rock-oriented band might play."

Then, without a warning, Prince pulled the plug on the project. "It just kind of went away," Dez said.

Prince never explained why.

"Prince had the open doors," Gayle Chapman said. "He gleaned what he could, made use of what worked, and ran with it."

On October 19, 1979, Warner released Prince's second album, called simply *Prince*. Some reviews called it glossy, unoriginal, even sophomoric. Others focused on his inventiveness, his odd fusion sound, and vastly improved songwriting. Prince said years later it all sounded "pretty contrived." Emerging just a year after *For You*, *Prince* certainly found him showing improvement on a number of fronts. "I Wanna Be Your Lover" crystallized what Prince was about as a performer, the lonely underdog that craved—but also sometimes rejected—acceptance and love. "Sexy Dancer" fitted his tight new sound to a post-disco anthem. "Do Me Baby" was a stately slow jam. Everything sounded more confident; he was writing better songs and hinting at the darker places his ballads would head in years to come. *Prince* was a big step up from *For You* and announced the arrival of a talented, determined R&B act with a new sound and, more importantly, a distinct worldview. But his sound was still in transition; the album wasn't enough to make him as big a name as Michael Jackson and Kool & The Gang, the acts Prince reportedly viewed as his biggest competition.

Within weeks, *Prince* debuted on the charts. One single had become a runaway hit. The poignant disco number, "I Wanna Be Your Lover," topped *Billboard*'s Soul Chart, Prince's first Soul No. 1, and it reached No. 11 on the Pop Chart. Radio stations nationwide kept playing every note of it. Sales passed 500,000 (his first Gold-certified single).

"It surprised me that it became a hit," he said. He wasn't trying to create one. "I basically make songs I like." Regardless, life for Prince changed immediately. Warner executives couldn't be happier now. Some felt confident he could go on to deliver variations of this hit.

On the strength of the single, *Prince* made the *Billboard* 200. The album was quickly racing toward the 500,000 sales mark. His record deal in 1977 may have hinted at Prince's potential for commercial success, but the brisk sales of *Prince* cemented it.

Success with the rock market, however, eluded him. Warner released his guitar-heavy "Why You Wanna Treat Me So Bad?" as a single but it landed on the R&B Chart.

Still, with his sophomore work selling more copies, and its single popular on black and pop radio, Warner felt there was no more need to wait: He was ready to tour.

The two Prince albums may have created a cult following in Detroit and northern cities, but it was the success of his single that got him invited onto the high-rated Saturday morning dance show *American Bandstand*.

January 25, 1980, in the green room, host Dick Clark entered and greeted Prince and his band. Once he left, Prince faced the band members. His expression made Dez think, *Uh oh, something's coming.*

"This is what we're going to do," Prince began. "When Dick Clark talks to you, don't say anything." When cameras rolled, he continued, they'd play two songs then join Clark for the usual banter. But when Clark posed questions, they should stay shut. It was rude, weird, and nothing a relative newcomer should pull, but Prince was out to make a statement.

They performed his pop hit "I Wanna Be Your Lover," along with "Why You Wanna Treat Me So Bad." Then the band surrounded him and Clark. Cameras rolled. Clark expressed amazement that he hailed from Minneapolis of all places.

"That tripped me out," Prince recalled in the *Star Tribune*. Clark kept talking but the comment ate at him. "That really gave me an attitude for the rest of the talk."

Clark asked how long he'd been playing.

Prince stared at him and held up four fingers. He adopted a lewd facial expression.

The appearance might have put off some viewers, but it made its mark. Dez felt it was pure genius. "Dick Clark talks about it to this day."

The *Bandstand* appearance and another on the NBC musical variety show *The Midnight Special* left people wanting more. His hit remained on radio. *Prince* sales—and those of his single "I Wanna Be Your Lover"—now soared past the 500,000 mark. As February 1980 approached, the Recording Industry Association of America began the process by which to certify the album Gold.

To maintain career momentum, his handlers asked New York–based publicity legend Howard Bloom for ideas on how to expand Prince's white audience. As author Roy Shuker reported, Bloom felt Prince's next tour "could be critical." They should book two dates in each regional market, Bloom wrote. Have Prince open for a major black headliner like Cameo or Parliament, and play each town's New Wave dance club. "The idea is to go after the black and white audience simultaneously," Bloom explained. "Neither date will conflict with the other. The white kids who would go see Prince at the Ritz would never go to the Felt Forum (a New York funk auditorium) to see Cameo," he wrote. "The black kids who flock to see Cameo wouldn't think of going to the Ritz."

Before they knew it, they had their chance to put the plan into effect.

Rick James (born James Ambrose Johnson, Jr. in Buffalo, New York) needed an opening act. James was a decade older and known for sporting braids, leather outfits, and boots in the P-Funk mold. By autumn 1979, his *Fire It Up* was in stores. His third release in eighteen months, it included the usual rock and R&B, disco, and a hit single called "Love Gun." When none of its songs crossed over, James filled his fourth album *Garden of Love* with ballads. Motown released *Garden* on New Year's Day, 1980. "Big Time" became a hit, but James now heard segments of his black audience claiming he recorded soft-lit ballads for white approval.

He needed to get back out there to command crowds, to yell, to serenade marijuana and sex, and to make lewd gestures to his female backup singers—to reestablish himself, in short. But for this latest tour—called Fire It Up—James needed a strong opening act. "There was a record burning up the airwaves called 'I Wanna Be Your Lover' by some cat named Prince," James remembered in his memoir. He liked that Prince played guitar. James's handlers all agreed Prince would be great. James bought his album "and really enjoyed it, especially 'Sexy Dancer.' I thought the kid was pretty funky." He asked Warner for a video, watched it, and felt Prince reminded him of himself, "except that he didn't move as much."

He invited Prince to open during the Fire It Up Tour. Prince accepted, and suddenly he found himself with a chance to perform before thousands. The two musicians finally met in late January. James entered through a venue's backstage entrance and saw Prince behind Bobby Z's drums "playing some bullshit beat." They'd be sharing stages for thirty-eight shows during the next nine weeks, but James sat behind his group's drum set "where he [Prince] could see me," James recalled, and started "playing some serious shit." Prince watched him, James claimed, "and just got his little ass up and walked away."

When Prince finally performed, Rick James said, "I felt sorry for him." He was a "little dude" in high heels and a trench coat, standing in one spot on stage while playing New Wave. "Then at the end of his set he'd take off his trench coat and he'd be wearing little girl's bloomers." James laughed. Men in the audience "just booed this poor thing to death." He let Prince keep opening—but he came to regret it.

Every time James played, the headliner recalled, he saw Prince on the side of the stage "just staring and watching everything I did, like a kid in school." James approached during a song and pointed his bass "right in his face," grabbed his own crotch, gave Prince the finger, then kept playing. "He was remembering everything I did, like a computer," James alleged. He kept doing what he called trademark moves: flipping the microphone stand, catching it "backwards, you name it," doing call and response chants, with a hand on an ear while the crowd yelled back.

One night, James entered an arena and heard the crowd chanting. He rushed to see what was happening. "Here's Prince doing my chants," James claimed in his 2007 memoir, *Memoirs of a Super Freak*. Prince was also "stalking the stage" like him, James insisted in print, doing his "funk sign"—holding up his thumb, forefinger, and pinky (a move today's metal fans call "devil horns")—"flipping the microphone and everything. The boy had stolen my whole show." James was furious and so were his band members. But it kept happening night after night, he maintained. He saw more of his routine. It reached a point where James couldn't do his own show, he said, because after the crowd saw Prince doing it, it "started to look like I was copying him."

Despite James's claims, Prince was actually wary of similarities. At the time, Prince's keyboardist Matt Fink had an image that consisted of a black-striped jail suit. But after a few shows—in which James donned one before his tune "Bustin' Out of L Seven"—he asked Fink for other costume ideas. "How about a guy in a doctor suit?" Fink replied. Prince liked it. That day, wardrobe people found scrubs at a uniform shop, Fink recalled, "and I have been Dr. Fink ever since."

Though James spoke frequently of a competition, his onetime protégé Teena Marie explained, "It wasn't really Prince. It was more Rick than anything." While Prince ignored him, James privately loved Prince's music, she said, "although he would never admit to it." (James, in fact, did later publicly credit Prince with being "a great player and a very innovative person." But that came later).

The tour continued. Furious songwriting sessions in various hotel rooms found him incorporating new influences. Sitting with a guitar after a Birmingham date led to "When You Were Mine," an upbeat number with a melancholy message and a John Lennon–like vocal arrangement.

He soon showed the band the up-tempo pop song. Its high-pitched organ, snare-heavy beat, and vocals (including backup) all screamed early Beatles. "It was probably inspired by an old girlfriend," said Fink.

Between concerts, Prince taught them another new song, "Head." It described his meeting with a bride minutes before her wedding. She was in her gown, he sang, but still wanted to perform fellatio. He felt the shock value would draw more fans and reporters—but it had an immediate effect on the band. He wanted to perform "Head" on stage, with the blond—and religious—Gayle leaving her keyboard. As everyone played its cyclic groove, chanting its one-word title, she would perform a back bend. "The idea was in part inspired by Bob Fosse's dance theater," Gayle recalled. Once she bent, she added, "He would finger keyboard parts on my stomach in rhythm with what Matt was playing." Other times, he'd play guitar. She'd kneel before him and bend backward "and he walked right over me. No hand gestures or funny mouth position." Then, on two occasions, when the song ended, they French-kissed for about thirty seconds.

Within a few shows Gayle left the band. She did so, she said, for "a number of reasons, the biggest of which was I needed more out of life than working as an employee in his band could offer at the time." She stopped by his house on Orofino Bay on Lake Minnetonka. When they finished talking, they were still friends, she added. He told her if she ever needed his help, she should reach out. "And we left it at that," she said.

It was back home in Minnesota, between dates, that Prince steered his tiny Fiat through the Minneapolis-St. Paul airport to pick up a recent high school graduate. She asked if she could smoke. He said sure. "I don't think his ashtray had ever been used," she recalled in the *Star Tribune*. "He was really romancing me."

The young woman's name was Lisa Coleman, and her father was a veteran session musician. By age nine, Lisa was studying classical piano. In 1971, her father had her join six other kids in a group that released a bubblegum pop album. After it flopped, Lisa attended Hollywood High and earned independent-study credits with original melodies and Joni Mitchell–style lyrics. "I basically just stayed home from school and wrote songs."

As an English major at Los Angeles Community College, Coleman maintained a 4.0 average and read voraciously—before dropping out. She was working for a documentary-film company's shipping department (on the dock), and teaching piano when a friend at Cavallo-Ruffalo said Prince needed a replacement for Gayle Chapman. Coleman recorded a demo, and mailed it in.

Prince was struck by it. He asked his managers to invite her to Minneapolis for a private audition. With Lisa now in Minnesota, Prince's Fiat reached his house. He led her into his downstairs workspace and pointed at the piano. "You can go play, and I'll be right back." He was heading upstairs to change clothes. Suspecting he heard every note, she sped through a Mozart concerto she had been working on. "He came bounding down the stairs," she said. He lifted a guitar and they jammed. "From the first chord, we hit it off."

She stayed the weekend in his spare bedroom. She walked through the house and peeked into his bedroom, where she saw the poster for the Kristofferson and Streisand remake *A Star Is Born* on a wall. "I thought that was so cute," she recalled.

Prince meanwhile liked her look, and started thinking of penning a song that urged her to leave her boyfriend and join him for a movie—and more. Whether anything romantic transpired between them is unknown. What is known, however, is that in later years, Lisa would form a romantic involvement that would last for about two decades, with another woman.

Now, with an invitation to play in Prince's band, Coleman had about a week to relocate. But she was elated. He played well and had an integrated band. "When I first joined the band," she told *Rolling Stone*, "I got solace from the fact that here were some other people so different that they only fit in there."

With Coleman replacing Gayle in the band, he was able to return his focus to his next album, which he had taken to calling *Dirty Mind,* songs which he had begun writing during his tour with James. He knocked out new songs called "American Jam," "Big Brass Bed," "Plastic Love Affair," "Eros," "Bulgaria," "Rough," "When the Shit Comes Down," and his maudlin "Lisa." New ideas kept coming, so he left enough songs off to fill another full-length work.

His mood became as dark as some of his song themes. As Prince told *Rolling Stone*'s Neal Karlen, "fits of depression" at this stage had left him "physically ill." He frequently reached for the phone to "call people to help get me out of it."

His song "Sister" was another fast, shocking song. After singing about sleeping with his sister—and enjoying it—he'd croon, "Oh sister, don't put me on the street again." The song's narrator is confused, scared, willing to do anything to avoid homelessness.

The tour with Rick James continued, and so did his bedevilment. Eventually, James's frustrations boiled over. He told Prince's manager if he stole any more of James's moves he was off the tour. Another day, both managers and bands had a meeting. In Prince's room, James's band—tall men in braids and leather—sat at one side, James explained, while Prince's band—"in their eyelashes and makeup"—sat at the other looking "very afraid." James's band seemed ready to physically attack.

According to James's memoir, Prince sat on a bed during the meeting and mostly stayed quiet. "He acted like a little bitch while his band and mine patched up their differences," James claimed. After this talk, James said, "things went back to normal," namely, James upstaging Prince every night.

Yet, despite alleged tensions—apparently caused by James himself—James invited them all to his birthday party. Prince attended that night and sat at a table but didn't drink. James, who loved partying almost as much as funk, claimed he then walked up, grabbed the back of Prince's hair, and forced cognac into his mouth. "He spit it out like a little bitch and I laughed and walked away," James claimed in print. He loved, James admitted, "fucking with him like that."

By spring 1980, the shows, and Rick James, were behind him. Thanks to his long and winding dance hit "I Wanna Be Your Lover," *Prince* reached No. 3 on *Billboard*'s Soul Album Chart—staying there twenty-three weeks—and No. 22 on the Pop Chart. But after the lead single, Warner shipped "Why You Wanna Treat Me So Bad?" to stores and sold few copies of the funk-rock single. Warner decided to shift gears, putting out his schmaltzy ballad "Still Waiting." Same thing. Little interest. By May, after a twenty-eight-week stay on the Pop Chart, *Prince* vanished.

Prince himself left his first house in Edina, and carted his possessions and makeshift sixteen-track studio into a rental in a secluded, costly western suburb near Lake Minnetonka. There he worked mostly alone in his densely packed basement on *Dirty Mind*. At the end of the Rick James tour, Prince had searched in vain for his synthesizers, only to find they were gone. Rick James, Teena Marie explained, had taken them and was using them in Sausalito, California, to record his next album, *Street Songs*. Only when James finished recording would he write thank you on a postcard and send it and the equipment back to Prince. The theft only added to Prince's agitation. But he kept working.

He recorded most songs quickly, during all-night sessions. As usual, he used his falsetto on a few numbers. He hoped lyrics would shock people and draw attention. He wrote about oral sex ("Head"), incest ("Sister"), orgies ("Uptown"), bedding a woman in her "daddy's car" (the title track); satisfying another ("Jack U Off"), and an ill-fated threesome ("When You Were Mine").

Musically, he abandoned horns, cluttered keyboards, and excessive overdubs and turned to electronic instruments he hoped would differentiate him from other acts on the market. His drum machine created pounding dance beats, synthesizers delivered icy melodies, and he strummed a few minimal riffs on guitar. "He really found himself with that album," drummer Bobby Z felt. He wrote better songs, and "the roughness of it gave it an edge. It was a little more garage sounding."

With more songs in the can, he played his albums back to back, and heard the difference. His first two had more falsetto, serenading women or else begging them to stay. "I was in love a lot back then when I used to make those records. The emotion meant more."

Now, he felt that he had been gullible, he told *Musician* magazine. "I believed in everybody around me. I believed in Owen, I believed in Warner Brothers, I believed in everybody. If someone said something good to me, I believed it." He hinted that he had been pressured to write ballads. And he once liked romantic themes, felt good singing those words. But much had happened the past three years. His new stuff reflected his anger. His lyrics avoided talk of deep feelings or romance. Song after song said he wanted a good time. "I'm screaming more now than I used to."

He also remained open to including his band members. During one performance rehearsal, he heard Fink play an intriguing synthesizer groove. At day's end, he invited Fink to his home, played Fink the basic track of "Dirty Mind," then had him re-create the riff. He wrote a bridge and altered a few things "and that was it," Fink recalled. "I got home about one in the morning." After another hour of work, Prince put it on tape.

Ten hours later, at rehearsal, he showed the band a rough mix complete with vocals. "He had stayed up, written lyrics, and finished the whole thing after I left," Fink said. "We were amazed." He and Fink worked the same way for "Head." As the song blared from speakers, Fink improvised five or six solos. "Prince had final approval of course," he said, but Fink's ideas made the cut.

He created another song after letting Morris Day use his studio. Once the freckly faced black drummer left, Prince listened to one of his grooves and wrote a lyric called "Partyup." He rerecorded Morris's track and then offered him a choice of ten thousand dollars or help landing a record deal. Morris, who washed cars for a living, wanted the deal.

Keyboards dominated *Dirty Mind*, but Prince also used the tougher sounding Oberheim synthesizer and an electric piano. "When You Were Mine" had a sixties Farfisa-style organ sound that evoked sixties garage rock. Minimal guitar—letting falsetto, large drums, and throbbing bass carry tunes—added to his gripping new sound. The songs were far more aggressive than anything on *For You* or *Prince*. Within twelve days, he had finished the album. "I became totally engulfed in it," he said. And no one was able to tell him to include ballads. "It really felt like me for once."

With another album recorded, he had to make sure the cover reflected his bold new direction. In a studio one hot summer day, with the band rehearsing in the background, he slipped a scarf around his neck, like an outlaw, then slid into his long duster coat. The raincoat had a studded right shoulder and a round button, pinned to his left lapel, which read, "Rude Boy." Then he stared down photographer Allen Beaulieu's camera while standing in front of what resembled a bedspring hanging on a wall. To Beaulieu's surprise, Prince opened the coat to reveal nothing but black briefs and matching thigh-high boots. His straightened, spiky hair, his "rude boy" button, and the rumpled raincoat made him fit in with this emerging "New Wave" market. The band photo meanwhile, also black and white, with male and female members, would soon strike one rock writer as furthering the new wave, two-tone checkerboard motif. Come time to list credits, he also included pseudonymous Jamie Starr as engineer—Matt Fink said that was Prince not wanting "it to seem like he did *everything*."

Prince took his heartfelt home-recorded demos to California to redo them. After playing them for one of his managers, he heard the man say,

"This is the best stuff I've heard in a long time. This should be your album." Prince felt the same way. This album held the sort of music he really wanted to hear.

His managers submitted the tapes to Warner as is. But Warner didn't know what to think. The label expected more hits like "I Wanna Be Your Lover." But during his visits to the label, Prince was a changed man. With *Dirty Mind* possibly the final album on the contract, he marched down office corridors in bikini briefs, high heels, makeup, and an open, flapping trench coat. Gone was the shy, retiring musician who let his managers do the talking. He told the label to release these home demos—which included a few lyrics no radio deejay would play. Warner for their part "flinched at just about everything," he recalled. One person, he remembered, said, "The sound of it is fine. The songs we ain't so sure about. We can't get this on the radio. It's not like your last album at all."

He answered, "But it's like me; more so than the last album; much more so than the first one."

Other employees kept complaining about its low-fidelity and lyrics. But after more discussion, Warner finally agreed to release *Dirty Mind* as is.

In Los Angeles that June, Prince booked time at Hollywood Sound Recorders and mixed the album. For a week and a half, he made a number of important creative decisions. On some numbers, harmonies were a bit messy. But he left them on. He also resisted the urge to add new elements, or improve what grooves he did set over drums. "The rhythm tracks I kept pretty basic," he said later. "I didn't try a lotta fancy stuff so I didn't have to go back and do things over." People in Warner's promotion department predicted these lyrics, not to mention releasing *demos*, simply wouldn't work, but his managers supported him. "Sure it was a risky record," Bob Cavallo conceded. "Some thought we were losing our minds." But it was brilliant and sure to impress reporters. In the end, Warner rolled with it.

With Warner's decision to renew on the line, there was more than just the provocative new album's success at stake for Prince.

5

I MAY NOT BE A STAR

ON OCTOBER 8, 1980, WARNER RELEASED *DIRTY MIND*. CRITICS
called it a winning fusion of rock, pop, and soul, with risqué themes, flam-
boyance, and falsettos. *Rolling Stone* gave it four and a half stars. *The Village
Voice* placed it in that year's Top Ten. The *Los Angeles Times* and *Newsweek*
sang its praise. Critically, it was his most successful album to date (and
perhaps ever). But not everyone liked its frankness. After Prince played
him the album, his own father John Nelson complained, "You're swearing
on the record. Why do you have to do that?"

"Because I swear."

Instead of sticking with his chart-topping sound ("I Wanna Be Your
Lover"), and treading the Michael Jackson and Kool & The Gang territory
of his previous albums, this album found Prince exploring the darker
themes hinted at on his first two LPs. Musically, he had unveiled a funk-
filled twist on electronic dance music. *Prince* was a great album but *Dirty
Mind* showed he could do more than master existing forms; he could mix
them and create new ones. Critics today often focus on its vulgarity and
hedonism when in fact *Dirty Mind* also found him expanding his thematic
repertoire to include social commentary, an area he would approach in
earnest later in his career. Writers may go on about *Dirty Mind*'s cold,
electronic sound, but Prince also filled tracks with warm beats, intimate
lyrics, poignant synthesizers, and impassioned choruses. Though it would
sell fewer copies, creatively, *Dirty Mind* undeniably marks a step up from
For You and *Prince*—a radical departure from disco, slow jams, and acoustic folk. It would also serve to introduce him to the mostly white rock
press and inspire countless other dance acts in the decade to come.

But *Dirty Mind* alienated important segments of the industry. Warner
included an atypical sticker asking deejays to "audition prior to airing."
They ended up not being able to play some lyrics. His cover shot meanwhile frightened record-store owners. Many saw him in those briefs and

refused to set the cover on their shelves. But satisfied customers recommended it to friends. Left-leaning news outlets championed his work. *Dirty Mind* reached No. 45 on *Billboard*'s Pop Chart and No. 7 on the Soul Chart. Sales were low but reporters and Warner understood he wouldn't let them pigeonhole him in one genre or market.

At the same time, Prince resisted Warner's plan to have him meet radio disc jockeys and promotion people. "Originally I didn't want to do any of that, because it was basically a stroking game and I didn't want to get involved in it at all," Prince told *New York Rocker*'s Andy Schwartz. Ultimately, he agreed to meet a few and saw they weren't saying, "Well, this cat gave me a television set so I'm gonna play his jam, and it's been nice meeting you." They had genuine interest in his music.

But his interviews were just as off-putting as some of his newest lyrics. By now, his mother Mattie had earned her master's in social work from the University of Minnesota and started working as a social worker in local schools. Even so, Prince told one reporter that she reared him on her soft porn novels. Prince also maintained he was half white, a claim that, while patently false, still attracted white pop critics that had ignored his first two albums. He went on to suggest to Barbara Graustark, of *Musician,* that the stories on *Dirty Mind* (including the incest story "Sister") were serious.

With his new, bolder attitude and look, Prince was aiming for nothing short of a complete reinvention.

And he thought the response he was receiving was just fine. But at Warner, publicist Bob Merlis believed he had a "problematic" relationship with reporters. "He just didn't talk," said Merlis. "When he did do a few interviews, they were strange. They had non sequiturs." Warner tried to spur sales by releasing "Uptown" as the first single. It didn't chart in the R&B Top 5. *Dirty Mind* was selling less than *Prince* and stalling any momentum his low-level hits may have had on the radio. "Like many relatively new artists, he was only as good as his last single," future employee Alan Leeds explained.

On December 4, 1980, Prince and the band traveled to Buffalo, New York, to prepare for his second national tour. The public had his second single, "Dirty Mind." "The record's not doing phenomenally well sales-wise, and airplay is pretty minimal," Prince admitted. It sold half what

Prince did. But he planned to fill ninety-minute sets with everything on the album.

In late December, he either—depending on which report you believed—took a two-week break or ended the short tour due to someone's illness. Regardless of why, he was frustrated with how critics had reacted to his performances. "They didn't understand that we are trying to bridge the worlds of rock, funk, jazz, and whatever," he said. They expected songs as mellow as his albums. Older people and rock fans were just as hostile. "They thought we were gay or freaks."

The February issue of *Rolling Stone* included the article "Will the Little Girls Understand?" and championed Prince to the rock journal's largely white audience. Writer Bill Adler praised his interracial band, while calling him a star and mentioning he had "the potential of being a crossover artist." Just as quickly producers invited Prince to perform on NBC's high-rated *Saturday Night Live*.

And so on February 21, 1981, he was in Manhattan, on the set of what has become a rite of passage for any rising talent. Charlene Tilton, a curvy young blond from the CBS weekly nighttime soap *Dallas*, was hosting. He and Todd Rundgren were the musical guests. Rundgren did two meditative works off his newest album. For his part, Prince delivered a rousing "Partyup."

Back home, Prince was still looking to perform. One night he took the stage at Sam's, a former bus terminal turned nightclub, to a house so packed some customers sat on bars or hung from balcony railings. National audiences might have had their doubts about Prince, but he was a star in Minneapolis. "There's no place like home," he said three times. His ninety-five-minute set found him stripping down to briefs and strutting across stage like Mick Jagger to dance near André and second guitarist Dez. He also shocked people with between-song banter in his natural voice. Then, during his encore, "Bambi," he humped a mic stand and rubbed his guitar neck suggestively. *Star Tribune* critic Jon Bream wrote, "Minneapolis finally has its own bona fide rock star."

The Rebels were short-lived, but Prince still wanted to create a side project to express different sides of his personality—more than ever after seeing November 1980's *The Idolmaker* (about a songwriter making stars of a bar-band saxophonist and a waiter). But instead of The Rebels, he chose a band he called The Time. In California, management employee Steve Fargnoli thought it was a great idea; if Prince planned to hole up and record anyway, he may as well profit from it.

The Time didn't officially exist, but in the home studio in the basement of his new two-story house near Lake Riley in Chanhassen, he spent part of April creating songs and combing through outtakes to come up with music for them.

In the studio, he made his own bandmates laugh. Some days, he'd leave a microphone on while cooking a grilled cheese sandwich. Or he'd press the Record button and race toward the drum set with the recorder capturing the noise he made leaping over objects, tripping on wires, and sliding into his seat. Usually, he taped the lyric sheet, torn from a notebook, to the kit. But some songs, "You'd hear him like kind'a grunting and singing a little bit of the song on the drum track," bandmate Lisa remembered.

Soon, he involved a few of his band members in the new project. "He called me up with the title and asked me to write lyrics," Dez said of a new song called "Cool." Within twenty minutes, Dez called back to say it was done. "He asked me if I had any songs I wanted to submit." Dez sent a complete demo of "After Hi School." Lisa Coleman wrote "The Stick." Prince threw in "Oh, Baby," originally recorded with Gary Brandt two years ago. But André was reluctant to contribute. Their relationship, Dez explained, "was already changing." Now, André reserved his songs for his own side project The Girls. Prince kept asking for material, he recalled, until he finally thought, *You know what, I don't wanna hassle about this song. Take the song. Take the credit. I don't care. I'll write some other songs.*

With material ready, Prince now needed people to re-create the new songs on stage. He looked first to Flyte Tyme. Since 1973, this local unsigned band had played the sort of funk that made a million-selling hit of "I Wanna Be Your Lover." And they could use the break. They were still trying to earn money with shows in bars and clubs. One club owner had told band member Terry Lewis, "You've got too many black guys in the band." They tried to unveil originals to apathetic audiences. They hadn't made any progress with an album. They were also tired of Top 40 covers. "Prince, though, he had the ambition and the contracts," said group member Monte Moir.

He met the band and their singer Alexander O'Neal in a diner. According to Jellybean Johnson in *Tones* magazine, "This is what's going to happen," he began. He'd do the music, they'd play it on stage, and they'd tell reporters they did the music. They were into it. But after the meeting, singer O'Neal had second thoughts and backed out.

With a vacancy for a band front man, Prince remembered Morris Day. Day had let him include his song "Partyup" on *Dirty Mind*. He had also played with Prince back in the days of Grand Central. Morris was offered the opportunity, and he happily joined the group. He reportedly suggested adding guitarist Jesse Johnson. Johnson hailed from Illinois. He had become a huge Hendrix fan when he was fourteen and could now play every one of Jimi's songs. Prince agreed to the addition.

Once he recruited every member, Prince played the new band the completed music. Each number had his voice singing the lyric.

When Morris came over, Prince coached Morris on how to match every phrase and intonation. One time, Lisa Coleman watched. "Morris had some hard times," she told the Minneapolis *Star Tribune*. He kept blowing takes on a vocal. Stress—and Prince—made him cry. Lisa understood. He pushed hard but rarely included positive reinforcement. It was always a Machiavellian "you *will* do it." Eventually, Morris got everything right.

Within two weeks, Prince finished the six songs. By April 28, he was in sunny Los Angeles, mixing them at Hollywood Sunset Sound. Forty-eight hours later, he was done and The Time's first album was complete. Coyly, instead of removing his voice entirely, Prince left it on, so people could occasionally hear it right alongside Day. At Warner, executives viewed *The Time* as a welcome return for Prince to the warmer sound of "I Wanna Be Your Lover," which sold a million copies. The label quickly signed the band.

On August 14, Prince again entered Sunset Sound Studio, this time to spend nine days completing a new album, *Controversy*. At this point, he could have gone to another record label. But after seeing Warner release and support his controversial change of pace *Dirty Mind*, he wanted to stay on their roster and get them another LP. By this point, he had already taped a few songs in his new, professional-quality home studio. Until then, he hadn't let band members record on songs because he didn't know "exactly which direction I wanted to go in." This time he decided to involve them. He even decided to give them credit for composing, arranging, and performing.

"I usually change directions with each record," he told Robert Hilburn. But he also had another batch of strong ideas. Tinkering with a guitar, for instance, had led to "Ronnie, Talk to Russia." Playing drums resulted in his title track, "Controversy." And instead of sexual themes, he included more politics and religion in his music. He knew they would shock and make headlines. His title track was a reaction to interview questions about race and sexual proclivities. "Ronnie, Talk to Russia" was upbeat but urged the current U.S. President, Ronald Reagan, to enter peace talks with the Soviet Union "before it's too late." For "Annie Christian," he set bits of roaring guitar to a bald-drum-machine beat. With a booming messianic voice, he rails against a flurry of current events (child murders in the South, Lennon's killing, federal agents videotaping an illegal deal in the Abscam scandal), and hinted that the devil made them all do it. In "Sexuality," he discussed education and a new generation that would escape old prejudices. He also made sure "Do Me, Baby" was ready.

He had just a couple more pieces to contribute to the recording. Back in his home studio, he filled the dim control room with perfumed candles and chiffon drapes. When an engineer arrived, he told him to turn the recorder on, then get going. Locking the door behind him, Prince taped a series of falsettos and come-on vocals.

By August 23, *Controversy* was finished. His bass-and-drum funk sounded tighter. His slow jam was more confident. His fifties-styled rock sounded more authentic. His keyboards incorporated more New Wave influences. As with *Dirty Mind*, he applied a bit of studio gimmickry to create one consistent sound for the album. Though not as groundbreaking as that previous album, *Controversy* has to be considered another strong, compelling, and experimental Prince album, from what many consider his golden era. Even today, *Controversy* remains as engaging, enjoyable, and—in most cases—as innovative as it was upon its release.

Prince felt the album was a bit erratic but he submitted it to Warner. And with another provocative new album in the can, he looked forward to getting out there, promoting it, and regaining ground.

Warner released "Controversy," and his *Dirty Mind* number "When You Were Mine" as a single on September 2, 1981. Once again, Al Beaulieu took the cover photo of him staring at the camera. Only this time he wore a purple coat and white Jimi-like shirt. For Jill Jones, who would sing backup for Prince, nothing had changed. "*Dirty Mind* is when it started," Jill said of his look. "The fabrics just became better as money came in."

Black radio loved the new song. But Prince had no time to celebrate. His managers had some tour dates booked.

With André gone from the band—he had left in June to work with Prince's former manager Owen Husney on his solo career—Prince needed a replacement fast. He remembered Mark Brown (sometimes "Brown Mark").

Brown was a young black bassist who had played with the local band Fantasy while in tenth grade, and battled Flyte Time and Cohesion. Prince also enjoyed Brown's playing during a 1980 gig at Sam's, the bus terminal turned nightclub. He called to offer the recent high school graduate a spot in the group. Brown accepted and immediately saw "how serious [Prince] was about his music." He kept everyone on his or her toes. If they wanted to "play around" or act unprofessional they could "go someplace else," Brown recalled. And with the tour starting soon, Prince had no time to stop and teach anyone. "He'll give you a couple of weeks, and if you're not on his level, he'll get rid of you just that quick."

While the band rehearsed for the Controversy Tour, The Time continued to play. He let Jerome Benton act as Day's onstage valet. Jerome was a skilled dancer, a great comedian, and was willing to take artistic direction. By October 7, Prince felt they were ready for a low-key local gig. He joined them at the downtown club Sam's and stood near the soundboard again, enjoying every practiced move and deciding they were ready for the tour.

He received even better news. The legendary Rolling Stones wanted him to open a few shows at the Los Angeles Coliseum. At this point, *Dirty Mind* had finally drawn the interest of rock critics. At the same time, his look was evolving. "Prince was in his full *Dirty Mind* regalia with the bikini and the trench coat," Dez explained. Mick Jagger hadn't forgotten seeing the long hair, regalia, and stage mannerisms during Prince's November 1980 show for *Dirty Mind*.

He was offered the opening slot on their tour, including him at the bottom of a bill that also included the upbeat J. Geils Band, and the blues-based George Thorogood and the Destroyers.

When Prince learned The Stones wanted him at their shows, he was stunned. He had repeatedly told Dez he wanted his own band to be like a black version of the Rolling Stones, "with him being Mick and me being Keith," Dez explained.

Prince couldn't have been happier.

Warner meanwhile saw it as a wonderful way to introduce his latest work *Controversy*, which would arrive in stores in under two weeks.

Dez tried to hold his tongue. For weeks, he had warned Prince that the Stones audience might reject them. The rest of the band was too delighted to be very much concerned.

They flew West and eventually pulled up to the Coliseum in LA and entered an area filled with as many tents and trailers as a circus or fair. Everywhere they looked, they saw cables, generators, and technicians. Finally, Security led them into a tent filled with flowers, mirrors, lights, and a banquet of fruits, cold cuts, and assorted breads. Behind them, they heard the crowd roar.

Dez was just as excited. A burgeoning Christian, he still felt uncomfortable performing some of Prince's material. But he felt they were set to reach the big time. Recently, fans at Denver's Rainbow Theater had caused Prince's "first all-out fan riot," and now, he was at the enormous Coliseum, opening for the band he said served as their template for success. Decades later, he still remembered it "as an incredible moment."

Prince was ecstatic as Security lined their motley crew up at 2:00. The walk toward the stage felt, Brown said, "like a scene from the movie *Gladiator*." They walked toward a stairway leading down to enormous white curtains. After passing through the drapes, they saw musical equipment all over the place; and technicians rushing in every direction. They circled stacks of amps and speakers and were finally onstage. But they couldn't see the crowd yet because of more huge curtains up ahead. Prince faced the band then gave them the ready signal. With the curtains splitting, Bobby started hitting the drums.

Prince faced a sea of people, all standing. It was sweltering, and fans were sweating, screaming, dancing to the beat, and holding beer cans and bottles aloft. On each side, arena employees aimed giant water hoses at the crowd, to prevent dehydration.

The crowd, Bobby noted, had waited since six in the morning for the Stones, and was now "peaking on all their drugs." On stage, Prince rushed out in his trench coat and black underwear. He led the band through "Uptown," the crowd noise drowning out the music. When the song ended, Brown recalled, "I noticed people not liking what they were hearing." These Stones fans—many of them bikers—wanted rock music. To his credit, Prince immediately changed the set list. They immediately played "Bambi" from his second album. But he changed it, singing not in his falsetto but in a deeper, more masculine voice. Then he filled its closing moments with him soloing on lead guitar. "Put your hands together," he shouted. "Right here. Come on!" Then he yelled, "Rock and Roll California!"

Dez meanwhile told the crowd, "Get ready for the Stones!"

They went into "When You Were Mine" from *Dirty Mind*, with Dez assisting on vocals and Prince using his deeper, natural voice. When this ended, the crowd applauded. But then, Prince started "Jack U Off," an unreleased number from *Controversy*. With its cluttered arrangements, tempo, and the arena's speakers, it was hard to hear. The falsetto and the audiences—yelling, booing, high on drugs—created a recipe for disaster. Still, the band played their speedy keyboard music over drum machine beats and handclaps, while Prince did some of his signature moves. For the crowd, this sounded like disco during an extremely divisive period in pop music. Even worse, Bobby recalled, the crowd "thought we were saying 'fuck you' or something. Then stuff came flying like you wouldn't believe." Prince sang its final lyric: "And as a matter of fact . . . you can jack me off!" The band stopped playing, but now the crowd was booing. Eventually, the jeers died down and Prince felt confident enough to start "Uptown."

Mark Brown, playing his first show to one of the group's largest crowds, struck the first note. An orange from the throng hit his bass. "Knocked him out of tune," said Bobby. Prince saw the flying objects and heard the jeers. Initially, he told Robert Hilburn, he thought they were just having fun. *Well, we just better play*, he thought. Dez echoed the sentiment. Dez came within earshot, and told him. "Show 'em we can play, and then it'll simmer down." Prince kept performing. But then his eyes landed on "one dude right in the front," and he saw "the hatred all over his face." The guy wouldn't stop throwing things. After fourteen minutes, he had had enough. He didn't want to perform anymore. "I just wanted to fight him. I got really angry." He felt like inviting the guy outside to work this out. "You know? How dare you throw something at me?" Prince left the stage.

"I'm sure wearing underwear and a trench coat didn't help matters but if you throw trash at anybody, it's because you weren't trained right at home," he said.

Dez recalled, "I look around and Prince is gone." He returned to the stage and leaped into a fiery guitar solo that seemed to subdue the angry crowd.

Prince launched his final song, "Why You Wanna Treat Me So Bad?," another guitar-heavy older work. Dez joined in playing its riffs, but Prince's vocal sounded deflated. After ending the set to polite applause, Prince marched offstage, through the curtains, and out of the arena. Then, Dez recalled, the crowd really started to boo.

Prince was gone, leaving Matt Fink and Bobby Z backstage. The Stones Bill Wyman, Charlie Watts, and Mick Jagger offered their advice, suggesting they hang in there. But by then Prince, furious, was already on his way to a flight back to Minneapolis. Manager Steve Fargnoli said that Prince wouldn't return for any more shows on the tour.

The band faced each other in defeat. Mainstream rock audiences didn't want them, drummer Bobby thought. "I was almost in tears. It was catastrophic."

They returned to their hotel rooms to wait. Promoter Bill Graham and Mick Jagger worried about how to convince Prince to return for the second show. Understandably, Prince wasn't interested. "He was really, really unhappy," said Bobby. Eventually, Jagger reached him on the telephone. "He said he didn't want to do any more shows," Jagger recalled. Jagger kept asking him to return. He wouldn't. Drummer Bobby noted, "We had to do it." He refused until Dez—at Fargnoli's urging—called. He heard the guitarist describe gigs in biker bars that, until then, had never entertained blacks. "You can't let them run you out of town," he added.

Dez was right. Prince returned to LA.

They couldn't even change the set list to emphasize more rock. There was no time. Right after Friday night's first concert, the venue covered the stage and prepared for Saturday's football game with the Rams.

At their next show, new bassist Mark Brown walked onstage for the second time. The eighteen-year-old faced about 110,000 people in the Coliseum and this time froze like a deer in the headlights. Prince came out in his bikini and trench coat. From his vantage point at the drum kit, Bobby felt Prince had an angel watching over him. Just as he started the first song and did a stage move—ducking his head—"a bottle crashed against the drum riser." Someone threw a fifth of Jack Daniel's. Then a gallon container slammed into Mark's bass guitar and exploded. Indignant, Prince walked off stage in the middle of the lengthy "Uptown," leaving them without an ending. People hurled Coke cups. Unaware of Prince's departure, Dez kept playing, pointing at crowd members, smiling and waving. But then he looked around and saw their front man had left the stage. That didn't stop the crowd, though; they kept throwing things. "So I signaled to the rest of the guys: Let's do likewise."

But then, Bobby recalled, Prince came right back, and ended the song "and then that was it." It was tough, but they got through their set.

Prince, however, wanted nothing to do with the tour.

"The other shows we were scheduled to do with them were cancelled," Dez explained. "We never opened for anyone again."

6

ALL THE THINGS PEOPLE SAY

ON OCTOBER 14, 1981, WARNER RELEASED *CONTROVERSY*,
Prince's fourth album. With relief, he saw his return to lighter dance fare
sell almost twice as well as *Dirty Mind*. It went Gold within months and
reached No. 21 on the U.S. Album Chart, his highest album placement yet.
But critics offered mixed reviews. One thought it was "refreshingly relevant" while another grumbled about "a repetitive jerky Bee Gees pastiche."
And as usual, a few stretched, claiming the music—mostly dance music,
drum machines like those on early rap singles—transcended "black" dance
music for "white" rock and pop. They also remained divided between
whether he was doing smut or had toned down things since *Dirty Mind*. It
was all "senseless noise," Prince's future employee Alan Leeds felt, "and
particularly aggravating" since his first single had "a witty lyric and catchy
funk groove." The single "Controversy" also got him back onto black radio.

November 20, 1981, the Controversy Tour started in Pittsburgh. The
Time opened for him. Instead of the bikini briefs and leg warmers that
inspired derision during the Stones gig, Prince wore a purple trench coat,
conservative black trousers, a vest, a white shirt, and even a bow tie. He
also improved his stage presentation. Huge red-lit Venetian blinds were
everywhere. On an upper level—almost a balcony over the band and
crowd—he stepped into view behind a blind, his silhouette fused with
purple smoke. Bobby Z hit the drums and suddenly Prince appeared, leaping
into "Uptown." When it ended, he slid down the fireman's pole at center
stage and landed in time to start "Why You Wanna Treat Me So Bad?"

Normally, he felt uneasy taking the stage, especially as front man, he
told *Musician*. This changed. "There was something about coming down
the pole and going out in front," Prince explained. "I felt real comfortable." Each show ended with him spreading his arms in front of a backlit
silhouette of a cross.

The tour moved from city to city, attracting more rock writers. After playing St. Louis, he flew to Los Angeles, to duck into Sunset Sound and expand his dance track, "Let's Work" for a single. He got Warner this new remix, but also worked on the dance-driven "Baby I'm a Star," and "Rearrange," a new work that consisted mostly of him saying, "Rearrange your mind." But these he set aside, for now.

Warner released his funk song "Let's Work," backed with "Ronnie, Talk to Russia," on January 6, 1982. Its cover showed him in a gray suit without a shirt, with spiky hair and a brown guitar in hand. He looked like a new wave act from MTV.

His managers felt he needed more security. And they had the perfect candidate, too. In Tampa, before his January 1982 show, he held a band meeting in his hotel room and introduced his new guard "Big Chick." Born Charles Huntsberry, Chick stood six foot eight inches tall, weighed almost four hundred pounds, and had a long white beard some compared to Santa Claus. His resume included some law enforcement in Tennessee and protecting the metal band AC/DC. But later that same day, Prince told Dez he was letting Chick go.

"Why?"

"He's just too big. He scares me."

Dez, who chatted with Chick on the tour bus, said, "I think he's a good guy. You should give him a chance." Chick stayed with the entourage, which grew to include another member in January.

By this point, Prince had chosen his pal Susan Moonsie, wardrobe assistant Brenda Bennett, and Cavallo, Ruffalo & Fargnoli employee Jamie Shoop to be in his next side project, The Hookers. Then, at a club one night, he met twenty-two-year-old former model Denise Matthews.

Born in Ontario to Scottish and Eurasian parents, Matthews had modeled and—as "D.D. Winters"—appeared in the low budget Canadian slasher *Terror Train*, and *Tanya's Island*. "I really did think Prince was gay when I first met him," Matthews told author Liz Jones. But after they went out to dinner, she added, "I realized he was definitely *not* gay."

For weeks after the meeting, he thought of her. He changed his plan for The Hookers: He'd create the group around her, he said. His plan for risqué themes and lingerie excited her. He said he wanted to call her "Vagina" (pronounced: "Va-GEE-na").

Prince was excited at the prospect, but before he could get any further, he had to handle other business.

———

The second leg of the tour, in February, found Prince sometimes demoting The Time from the bill. With their debut finding an audience (selling 500,000 copies in only seven months), he was allegedly threatened—even terrified—by the band's success. It didn't help that one reviewer wrote, "Morris led the band to the point where it now often steals the show . . . even from Prince." Prince kept removing them from bills, even though editors at *Rolling Stone* had decided that he—not The Time—would be on their cover.

Prince let Time members sit in on sessions for his girl group idea. Denise Matthews was to call herself Vanity, now, and lead a group that Prince decided to call Vanity 6. While he averaged a song a day of new material, The Time stood on the sidelines, watching and learning. "He would record everything way too loud," Jimmy Jam felt. But it made for more excitement and gave each song an edge. He set most songs to catchy synthesizers and mechanical beats from his Linn LM-1. In some ways, *Uptown* magazine felt, this lighter, playful music was his version of the day's popular electro-pop sound.

With an album for Vanity 6 recorded, Prince turned his focus to their image. Cover photos were shot in different rooms of his house. Each member added a suggestive quality to her basic lingerie and heels. Vanity, in revealing black teddy, knee-high black leather boots, and tuxedo coat, looked sultry, glamorous, and mysterious. Brenda wore leather belts and straps studded with silver conch shells, a chain-link belt, and a cigarette to give her a "bad girl" persona. Susan's lace-trimmed white camisole and demure pose offered a spin on the good girl archetype. On the sidelines, Matthews felt, "it was all about being sexy, getting slimmer, and getting cuter."

Downstairs from the living room of his Chanhassen home, en route to the master bedroom, Prince kept a narrow little workroom filled with recording equipment. He called this setup "Uptown" and he elected to record his entire new album here. Some tracks dated from the *Dirty Mind* sessions or earlier. But unlike that album, this time around he was using a twenty-four-track recorder. Many nights at three, he would invite Bobby Z to the studio. Sometimes the drummer came, sometimes he didn't. So he found himself relying more on technology. Appropriately, he named the album-to-be *1999*.

Prince turned to the Roger Linn drum machine he got in 1981. One of the first ever created, it let him create an original beat in five seconds. With technology providing instant results, 1999 morphed into becoming all about Prince running computers. But there were drawbacks. When he heard sounds in his head, he worked with the tools in front of him. He didn't think in terms of instruments. The sounds now dictated how he developed ideas. Another change was that Prince no longer limited himself to re-creating demos or a set number of songs in the studio. He recorded new ideas as they arrived. Thus, March 30, 1982, found him knocking out another quick groove and singing a new song, "Let's Pretend We're Married." Then he tried "Turn It Up," another shuffling work with drum machine and throbbing bass. He threw in drumrolls, synth overdubs, and his voice wailing "Turn it up. Turn it up, baby. Work me like a radio." He kept revisiting it, trying other ideas, then set it aside when he created the similarly paced "Delirious."

Another morning, after recording all night, Prince sat in Lisa Coleman's pink Edsel. At this point, Lisa—a platonic bandmate—was sometimes staying in his home, or with one of his ex-girlfriends, and continued to appear on some of his songs. He was dozing off, but an idea arrived. "I guess I should have known by the way you parked your car sideways that it wouldn't last," he thought. As more lyrics came, he jotted them down between short naps. He started creating a track filled with pensive synthesizer, and a lyric called "Little Red Corvette."

By April, he was at Sunset Sound again. There, husband and wife team David Leonard and Peggy McCreary helped him record and mix the new songs. Usually, he recorded drums or piano. "Then he puts on bass, and builds from there: keyboards, guitars, vocals," remembered McCreary. He started in the morning and was usually finished that night. He left with a basic mix but returned the next day to improve it. "We do it all in one or two days, very rarely three days," she said. "That's different to me!"

Talented musicians surrounded him, but he found it easier to work alone. "I have a communication problem sometimes when I'm trying to describe music," he explained. Then there was the fact that some sessions lasted so long he wore two or three engineers out. "He'd work three days straight without sleeping," Dez recalled. Dez usually stopped by once a song was almost finished.

He also wanted engineers to move quickly. If Peggy took too long preparing to record a fleeting idea, he'd say forget it; it was an omen, it wasn't happening. If he suddenly wanted a different drum sound, she had it ready in less than five minutes. In the control booth, hearing a song, he might create a vocal hook immediately. He'd reach for the mic she now kept nearby to punch in the new part without returning to the other room.

On April 3, he was trying new ideas. He filled "Extra Loveable" with rock guitar, Linn drumbeats, and a lyric inviting his girl to join him for a bath. He could be "very cruel" and rape her, he sang. Three days later, he recorded "If It'll Make U Happy," a sensitive three-chord number in which he left his girl then changed his mind. "I really love you baby, no matter what your friends may say."

He shifted gears again, filling his funky "Lady Cab Driver" with street sounds "and almost a kind of rap," said Bobby.

His attitude in the studio was "anything goes," Bobby explained. Prince tried experimental sounds and backwards-recorded tracks. He avoided the disco hi-hats and grooves this time. He was just having fun, finally. He was keeping things loose, seeing what came out. April 20, for instance, during "D.M.S.R.," he ad-libbed, "All the white people clap your hands on the four now: one, two, three [clap]." By April 25, he had recorded a windy rock ballad called "Free" and let Lisa Coleman's brunette friend Wendy Melvoin sing backup.

Wendy lived near Lisa in California until her divorced mother moved her to North Conway, New Hampshire. After graduating from high school, she returned to Los Angeles, waited tables, worked as a secretary, and planned to attend a music college. She kept showing up at the studio to visit Lisa. Prince decided she'd also sound good on "Irresistible Bitch."

A day after "Free," April 26, he asked engineer Peggy McCreary to bring a bottle of wine to the studio. This way, he'd sound pretty bummed out while crooning the downbeat lyric on his ballad "How Come You Don't Call Me Anymore." Two days later, he shifted gears again, creating the upbeat but equally mordant "Something in the Water (Does Not Compute)," with synthesizers, Linn drum, and lyrics as ominous as his keyboard textures. Drummer Bobby Z said, "The groove got settled. He knew it was back to dance. There wasn't anymore of the 'Ronnie, Talk to Russia' kind of songs." This new feel was Bohemian yet "still very funky," Bobby added. "I think he found his groove and the groove never left."

Back home in Minneapolis, on May 9, he refined "Little Red Corvette." Dez visited his home studio. They were alone, and he played Dez what he had. He wailed the lyric and when it ended, Dez lifted his guitar. Prince started recording. "He would always let me play what I wanted to." Dez offered three different solos. Prince then "comped" them into one, connecting different sections. "I was finished within half an hour!"

He kept working on his fifth album, and found that the songs kept mentioning the color purple. His fascination with the color—also favored by his hometown's pro football team the Minnesota Vikings—stretched back to an early demo on which he mentioned a "purple lawn." He must surely have been thinking, too, of one of his idols, Jimi Hendrix and his rock classic called "Purple Haze." Either way, Prince used the word now to describe a bloody conflict waged in blue skies, between angels and demons, which would cause red and blue to mix. He tried the word in a title for a droning dance number called "Purple Music."

July 6, he was again at Sunset Sound, recording another rock ballad. Titled "Moonbeam Levels," its description of future events evoked Jimi Hendrix's "1983." He was still working on July 16, when Warner released his hysterical ballad "Do Me Baby" backed with "Private Joy," both off last year's *Controversy*, on a promotional single not sold in stores.

Music fans however ignored the numbers.

By month's end, he played his managers a number of his new bass-and-drum-machine anthems, including some thrown together in his home studio. The songs lasted six minutes each, but the grooves were compelling enough to carry them. He wanted every note of it released—on two discs. The first album would have tight, well-written works that invariably led to passionate Sly-like exhortations, synth riffs, and hand claps. The second album held slower, mood pieces.

They listened intently to "Let's Pretend We're Married," "Delirious," "D.M.S.R.," and "Little Red Corvette." His managers liked them but urged him to include something like *Controversy*, a title track with a main theme. "He yelled at us and then he went back to Minneapolis and kept recording," Bob Cavallo told author Alex Hahn.

Back home, he returned to his new trademark, purple skies, and fear of nuclear war. He programmed another dance beat and recorded a Sly-like multiplayer vocal about a dream, a nuclear "judgment day" in which the sky was "all purple" with "people runnin' everywhere." Then, on the keyboard, he played a synth line that some felt unconsciously mimicked one on The Mamas & the Papas sixties classic "Monday, Monday." "I think he was trying to become as mainstream as possible," his keyboardist Matt Fink explained. "To some extent, he was trying to make the music sound nice, something that would be pleasing to the ear of the average person who listens to the radio, yet send a message. I mean, '1999' was pretty different for a message," Fink continued. "Not your average bubblegum hit." Its lyrics discussed dancing in the face of Armageddon.

Prince's eleven songs lasted nearly seventy minutes. Three songs ran over eight minutes each. Warner wasn't thrilled with a double album from someone that wasn't a superstar yet, but they considered the newest Time album *What Time Is It?* Warner had tested the water with lead single "777-9311" and saw it reach No. 2 on the Black Chart and No. 88 on the Pop Chart. And since August 25, the entire album was selling faster than their debut. Warner agreed to a double album.

They started planning a cover. Prince wanted purple on it. His name would be in huge letters, but over part of the letter "i" in his name, he added, in small, backward lettering, "and the Revolution." "I wanted community more than anything else," he said. "He was setting the public up for something that was yet to come," Bobby Z added. It was the name he would assign this band.

Prince told them it was time to create a video. MTV had rejected the cheap-looking clips for "Dirty Mind," "Uptown," and "Controversy." Lisa Coleman said, "We weren't even allowed on MTV at first. It was all like, you know, white hair bands." And she didn't think MTV would want this one, either, but still the band—and sexy blond Jill Jones—performed "1999" for cameras, on a set with red-lit Venetian blinds.

This time, things were different. "It looked as though he had more money to spend and his interest in film and marketing started to increase," Jill Jones recalled. "He started to single out professionals instead of amateurs. Peers." He was, she added, "Professional. Focused. Well rehearsed."

September 24, Warner released "1999" as a single. It made No. 4 on the Black Chart, but got no higher than No. 44 on the Pop chart. Still, it improved upon his last commercial single, "Let's Work."

With Warner about to release his double-album and three works— The Time's second album, his "1999" single, and *Vanity 6*—doing well in the three months spanning August to October, Prince planned his most ambitious tour yet. Vanity 6 was on the bill, so he invited Jill Jones, fresh from her appearance in the "1999" video—and his girlfriend at the time—to sing backup. "I was hired as an employee," she said. "Work for Hire."

He next decided The Time needed some work. He sat with them, and showed videos of Muhammad Ali taunting old champion Sonny Liston.

Next, while they rehearsed, he saw they had trouble with their Prince-written "777- 9311." One session, he faced keyboardist Jimmy Jam. "Jimmy, you're just doing the bass with your left hand. You're not using your right hand."

Jam said there was no part there.

"Well, you make a part there! You add something. You got to make it better than the record. No hands can be lazy. You got to play!"

The band sometimes felt Prince was too hard on them. But he respected their talent, to the point where he later publicly admitted, "To this day, they're the only band I've ever been afraid of." After they devoted a few more rehearsals to the routine, Prince returned to find the group proud of their progress. Some members even said, "Teach! Prince, check this out! We're jammin'!"

But Prince frowned. "Okay, who's not singing? Everybody's gotta sing a harmony part."

Someone noted it had few harmony parts.

"Doesn't matter. Gonna be better now than it is on the record."

The band sighed. But they sang during three more rehearsals.

Prince showed up again. "Okay, where's the choreography? You guys got to be steppin'!"

Terry Lewis, Morris Day, and Jesse Johnson were stepping and "having a great time," Jam recalled. But it wasn't enough.

"Jimmy Jam, what about you?"

"What about me? I'm the keyboard player."

"No, you got to step with them, too."

"What! I gotta play with both hands, sing a note, and be steppin' at the same time? Forget it. I can't do that shit."

Prince left. He had other details, and bands, to deal with. Jam considered his request. The next few rehearsals—"about four solid hours of playing at each one"—were difficult, but Jam could soon "do the shit in my sleep." Jam could play his keyboard part, pull a handkerchief to wipe his face, stow it away, and perform a dance step.

"That's what Prince did, time and again," Jam said. "He taught us we could do things we'd never believed we could."

Jesse Johnson however believed "his real knack is trying to discourage people, and keep them from being confident." He claimed Prince once said no one would recognize them on the street; they laughed because fans usually mobbed them during shopping trips. "He likes to tell you stuff like that, because of course if you got people believing that, they're always gonna be there, accepting that small paycheck and feeling happy."

7

PARTIES WEREN'T MEANT TO LAST

WARNER RELEASED *1999* ON OCTOBER 27. THE REVIEWS WERE
generally supportive. But *Rolling Stone* called "All the Critics" and "D.M.S.R."
obvious filler, where Prince saw them as two of his best new songs. He
granted an interview to the *Los Angeles Times* to promote *1999*, but then,
he announced he'd never speak to reporters again and walked out. "He's
afraid he might say something wrong or say too much," said a former aide-
de-camp. Numerous tabloids and magazines offered cover stories, but his
managers referred them to a public relations firm, which repeated Prince
wouldn't talk. With his retreat, rumors continued.

Prince meanwhile continued to plan his most ambitious tour yet.
While conferring with Roy Bennett, his production designer since 1981's
Dirty Mind Tour, he heard Bennett pitch an odd concept: Prince could perform a few lewd stage moves near a woman reclining in a first-class airplane seat. He rejected this. "Prince felt we had to be careful not to be so
suggestive that it would upset people," Bennett recalled. "He'd be the
one to say we had to be careful about going too far." Instead, he asked
Bennett to create a brass bed he could use during the finale of his ballad
"International Lover."

The Time got just as much mileage out of bawdy lyrics, synths playing horn lines, and their look as Prince did. Until now, they and Vanity 6
accepted that Prince would hand them completed albums and expect their
singers to match his guide vocals. It wasn't the best arrangement but
Prince at least let them claim they wrote and created their works. He had
credited their album to "Jamie Starr," the pen name he also used on *Dirty
Mind*. Reporters, however, kept bringing Prince up, asking why The Time
used the same sexual themes he did. Questions about Starr led to icy tension between him and the band, a writer felt.

Reporters began wondering if Jaime Starr existed. In response, Morris said Jamie was an engineer and co-producer. "Of course he's real."

Manager Steve Fargnoli claimed Starr didn't grant telephone interviews since he was "in and out of Minneapolis," "a reclusive maniac" and might not be around for months. But Prince's old pal Sue Ann Carwell (once known as Suzy Stone) said it plainly: "Prince is Jamie Starr."

People tied to the band wondered if Prince encouraged the disclosure to attract more attention. Alan Leeds meanwhile said, "To my knowledge, he discouraged anyone 'leaking' that he was Jamie Starr. He preferred the mystique of it all."

Either way, The Time coped with the revelation. "When people came to realize how big a role he played in some of these projects, they started to lose a little respect," said Alan Leeds.

Once people learned Vanity 6 was really his concept (from lingerie to lyrics and the music) "it wasn't the same." But live shows didn't suffer. One reporter spoke for many when he noted, during the tour, The (actual) Time now outplayed "whoever it was on the first Time record."

By December 16, when Prince arrived at The Time's sound check in Nashville's Municipal Auditorium, morale was low. Various band members sensed he feared they'd upstage him. Tensions mounted.

Prince kept playing his dates, videotaping every show. On his tour bus, he scanned the footage for missteps. And some nights, he had the band nearby, offering commentary and suggestions while the videos played.

During a tour break in New York City, Prince strolled down a hotel corridor, bound for his room. He heard guitar playing from behind Lisa's door. He approached and knocked. "Who's playing," he asked, "'cause I know it ain't you."

Lisa answered. He saw her good friend Wendy there. Both their families were in town for Christmas and Wendy was spending a few days in the room. She was also holding a guitar. "I played some hotshot progression," she recalled. His eyes twinkled. "I didn't know you played."

He asked to hear more. "He was impressed," Wendy said. "I was shocked. I was this kid, just out of high school. I had no real performing experience."

In late January 1983, Prince ended his month-long break and continued the 1999 Tour. As February began, program directors at rock radio stations heard his plaintive new single, "Little Red Corvette," and enjoyed its conservative, moralistic lyric—a wounded man urging a fast woman to "slow down"—and its fiery guitar work. They added it to play lists and a new audience helped it quickly reach No. 6 on the *Billboard* Hot 100 singles chart. And where his songs usually did better with R&B listeners, this one kept climbing higher on the Pop Chart. Then MTV started playing the clip, Prince in a shiny purple jacket and frilly white shirt. Fans ate it up.

As the second leg of the tour continued, he found himself booked into stadiums and ice-hockey rinks for crowds of twenty thousand. And during shows, he faced audiences that were now 50 to 75 percent white. With "Corvette," and then "1999" crossing over, demand for tickets had him leaving small theaters behind. Rock fans considered him "a dynamo [that] could write brilliant songs, outperform just about every rival, and sell out arenas," said associate Alan Leeds.

Now when the band left the dressing room and marched toward another stage, they could already hear crowds screaming for them. Screaming fans were nothing new, Dickerson noted, but the cries carried a new intensity. "We could see we were at a turning point," he explained.

By month's end, the *Village Voice* Pazz & Jop critics' poll had 1999 at No. 6 in their albums of the year, over Michael Jackson's new *Thriller* (No. 15), The Clash, Paul McCartney, Aretha Franklin, Fleetwood Mac, even his idol Joni Mitchell.

MTV started airing Michael Jackson's video for "Billie Jean" on March 2, a week after the song reached No. 1 on *Billboard's* Hot 100. While *Thriller* had already sold 2 million copies since its late 1982 release, "Beat It" now inspired sales of 800,000 every seven days.

But Prince was on the rise, too. March 21, rock fans paid top dollar to see him play Radio City Music Hall. That night, a riot flare burst from the drum kit on the dark stage. "Controversy" pulsed. Prince rode a backstage platform—an elevator—until his silhouette appeared on the *Controversy* blinds. His set list included his usual electronic funk—"Sexuality," "Let's Work," "Dirty Mind"—but sped up and rearranged. It also included "Little Red Corvette" and live instruments. Everything came together. Roy Bennett's light show included purple and pink police lights. The integrated band re-created moves from videos. Midway through "Let's Work," he and Dez did "a classic Rolling Stones move," a critic reported, standing back to back like Ron Wood and Keith Richards.

Between shows, Prince relaxed by playing basketball or video games. "We thought *Space Invaders* was incredible," Dez said. But once Prince started traveling on his own rented tour bus with Fargnoli and Chick, his band felt demoted to backing musicians. Others joined in blaming Fargnoli for Prince's increasing isolation. "He only cared about Prince and his money," Mark Brown said.

"Steve seemed very possessive and protective," Dez explained. With the album gaining momentum, Dez added that people in the entourage were exhibiting many "unhealthy attitudes."

For his part, Prince was plotting his next move—something big.

There was tension among Prince's team of musicians. Morris continued to tell Prince he was The Time's main draw and deserved a raise. Dez was more crestfallen than other band members. "Originally, Prince wanted to be a black version of the Rolling Stones," Dez said. "His Mick to my Keith," he added. But Prince's calculations and endless rehearsals had Dez feeling constrained.

"It began to feel more programmed than I would have liked," Dez said.

At the same time, Dez still had trouble with some of the more outrageous songs. He and a few other band members watched Christian television on days off and Dez sometimes uttered "the salvation prayer" under his breath while performing onstage.

By spring, Dez recalled, "I arranged with Prince to opt out of soundchecks entirely." Usually, Prince started these long rehearsals at two—"as soon as the gear was up and running," Dez recalled—and kept the band on stage until six. "It was always intense," Dez explained, particularly when Prince controlled every move. Then, after about four hours, he'd always end with about sixteen bars from "Controversy."

With Dez absent, he turned to Lisa Coleman's brunette pal Wendy, who sometimes rode on the tour bus. Would she mind stepping in? Wendy strapped her guitar on and played "Controversy." Prince liked how she handled the song's scratchy rhythm guitar, and had her sit in a few more times. The others sensed he wanted her in for good. They were right. He invited her to join. "I was just in the right place in the right time," she said. Dez felt she was being "opportunistic." This wasn't Dez's style—undermining a band member—but Dez reluctantly conceded that positioning herself as a possible replacement was a good move.

Relationships with others were being challenged, too. Vanity was barely speaking to Prince, riding on a separate bus, unhappy because he was seeing both her and Vanity 6 member Susan Moonsie, Per Nilsen reported. "All of us girls were on one bus!" Jill Jones recalled. "He had his own."

In March, England's *New Music Express* flew in writer Barney Hoskyns from Los Angeles to accompany the tour. "He came to the door of his dressing room and shook my hand," Hoskyns recalled. For two days, Prince avoided conversation. "He occasionally glanced at me but otherwise seemed indifferent. . . . Remember he had just made a huge deal about never talking to the press again," Hoskyns explained. But this seemed to extend to more than reporters. Hoskyns observed "a more or less total separation between Prince and everybody else." Lisa took the writer to a party after their Minneapolis show. Then Vanity "sort of took me under her wing," Hoskyns recalled.

After their exhausting March 13, 1983, show at Kalamazoo, Michigan's Wings Stadium, the line of tour buses left I-94 in northern Indiana. Between shows, Prince would ride in his own bus, filling pages in a purple notebook. He carried it wherever he went. The secrecy was confounding.

That cold night, the flamboyant entourage stood outside a huge truck-stop diner. The Time, Vanity 6, and The Revolution mingled with roadies, technicians, and tour personnel. They were dressed strangely, compared to local residents, but Hoskyns noted "Prince was already enough of a star for this not to be an issue." Only when everyone settled in at booths did Prince enter with giant, bearded Chick. "No one said anything overt but there was an implicit feeling of 'His Majesty has just entered the building . . .'" Hoskyns recalled.

They silently passed tables, and crossed the room. At a far-off table, Prince and Chick sat in relative silence. The band didn't comment on this. "It just seemed to be accepted that he was so brilliant and important that he couldn't consort with mere mortals," Hoskyns quipped.

March 24, Jimmy Jam and Terry Lewis missed a Time concert at San Antonio's HemisFair Arena. Prince had valet Jerome Benton strap on a bass guitar and pretend to pluck the instrument. Backstage, Prince held his own bass and played every note. Lisa Coleman played Jam's parts. The duo returned for the next show, with an explanation. After recording with the S.O.S. Band in Atlanta, a snowstorm trapped them in an airport. Prince wasn't satisfied, though. He fined each $3,000, *Uptown* magazine reported. "He thought we were off seeing some girls," Jam told *Uptown's*

Sam Sandberg. But then Prince saw them near the S.O.S. Band in a photo in "*Billboard* magazine or something," Jam added. "Seems like it was okay to be off meeting girls, but not okay to be furthering our own independent careers."

In Los Angeles on March 28, Prince yanked the group from the bill. People whispered that he didn't want The Time upstaging him in front of big city audiences that might include Warner executives. Prince thought it was more important for them to focus on their own career, especially now that he was going to let them have a hand in their third album.

8

BE GLAD THAT YOU ARE FREE

JACKSON'S *THRILLER* CONTINUED TO SELL. BUT WARNER HAD their own slick-haired black musician in shiny clothes. Though they had already promoted the "1999" single, executives chose to send it out again that spring, this time to Pop Radio. Since "Little Red Corvette," these stations had eagerly embraced Prince as an exciting new pop act. It reached No. 12. With "Little Red Corvette" and the reissued "1999" on the charts, the double album soon reached No. 9 on *Billboard's* Pop Chart and No. 4 on what *Billboard* now called the Black Chart.

But the neck and neck race continued. Epic and Michael Jackson had another video ready. This one, "Beat It," cost over $150,000 and involved a Broadway choreographer. In it, Jackson wore a red leather jacket with his black high waters and glove. He snapped his fingers, danced and yelled, and led dozens of extras in choreographed dance routines. MTV quickly put it in heavy rotation, raising *Thriller's* sales even more.

Prince, meanwhile, continued to tour.

April 8, he pulled The Time from the bill in Detroit, one of his major, most reliable markets—billing the show as simply Prince with Vanity 6. One musician was impressed by the music. Before twenty thousand of his own fans in Tulsa, John Cougar ran backstage for his cassette deck, then played a tape of "Little Red Corvette" into his microphone. Cougar kept trying, unsuccessfully, to invite Prince onto his new album.

In April, Prince was back in *Rolling Stone*. "There just don't seem to be any bounds to Prince's nerve or talent," the magazine opined. "Each album is better than the last (he's made five), each stage show more outrageous." The feature noted his tour grossed almost $7 million from November 1982 to March 1983, his double album *1999* sold almost 750,000 copies, and "Little Red Corvette" was "closing in on the Top 20 on *Billboard's* Hot 100 chart." Further, two side projects landed in the Black Chart's Top 10 that winter: Vanity 6 "whose 'Nasty Girls' was a disco smash, and

The Time, the tightest, funkiest live band in America." At only twenty-two Prince was "the father of it all," but equally mysterious. He wouldn't discuss his past. He didn't dress like the Commodores or like Bruce Springsteen. His eye makeup and hairstyle evoked Little Richard.

Prince tried to move past his provocative *Dirty Mind* image. "My songs are more about love than they are about sex," he said. Co-manager Fargnoli said he wasn't playing a role. "His persona is Prince, onstage and offstage." Prince was also just as outspoken and outrageous "in his business dealings." Prince was shy, Fargnoli added, but demanding of himself and everyone around him. "You always have to be on your toes. He doesn't play by the rules."

His androgynous look, name, and lyrics, *Rolling Stone* noted, continued to scare some whites, and rock radio wasn't playing much of his music. They were claiming heavy-metal listeners didn't want funk even as his popularity on MTV made his audience as "integrated as that of the old soul stars," 40 percent white during concerts.

At Warner, executive Russ Thyret superintended the effort to push the song "Delirious" to pop radio. Thyret had wanted to do this for a while but every time he had the pop department start promoting one single, Prince's managers submitted another new album. With Prince touring this year, not releasing something new, Thyret hoped to get the innocuous dance track into record shops on August 18.

On the tour bus, Prince kept filling pages in his notebook, concealing what he wrote. With *1999* sales rising even higher, his contract with Cavallo, Ruffalo & Fargnoli about to end, and Steve Fargnoli, traveling with the tour, urging him to stick with the agency, Prince figured the time was right. He pulled Fargnoli aside and said his newfound fame was great but he wanted more. He kept talking. Later, Fargnoli grabbed a phone and called Bob Cavallo. "It's very simple," Fargnoli reported. "He wants a movie. If we don't get him a film deal with a major studio, he won't stay with us." None of them knew the film business. They managed Weather Report, Earth Wind & Fire, and Raydio's Ray Parker, Jr—musicians, in short.

The next day, Cavallo had put piles of press clippings together. *For You* had yet to sell 400,000 copies in six years. But his next three (*Prince, Dirty Mind*, and *Controversy*) all went Gold (sales of 500,000 copies). And since late 1982, *1999* had sold nearly 3 million copies. It was on the Pop Charts ninety weeks after its release, thanks to its title track, "Delirious," and "Little Red Corvette." Still, a movie was a difficult sell. Most of the audience had never heard of Prince.

It was shopped around, and many studio executives and filmmakers declined. During his own meetings at major studios, Fargnoli saw many laugh at his pitch. Few believed Prince would carry a bankable film. Richard Pryor's production company was mildly interested but nothing happened. In the end, Cavallo turned to Warner Bros. Records Chairman Mo Ostin for a loan. The double-album idea had worked. And that year MTV kept his videos in constant rotation. Prince was now an unlikely superstar in the making. And his next album could potentially create a cultural explosion. If he insisted on releasing this movie with it, then fine. Mo Ostin acquiesced. Mo didn't need to see the script, either. He signed Prince and believed in him. He would personally loan them the money.

Back on the road, with the tour winding down, Prince sat with Matt Fink and told him the next step was a movie. Fink faced him with amazement. "It's already in the works," Prince added.

Fink wondered if he could pull it off.

Eventually, the tour reached Los Angeles, and Prince booked two days at Sunset Sound. There, he started the third Time album, called *Ice Cream Castles.*

During a break from recording, he made time to see Stevie Nicks, lead singer of Fleetwood Mac. Though still with her group, Nicks had seen her 1981 solo debut *Bella Donna* become a major hit. She joined her band for 1982's group effort *Mirage* then started her second solo album *The Wild Heart.* She was looking for a sound like the one on "Little Red Corvette," which she loved. After writing "Stand Back," she called to ask if Prince would help. He agreed.

Prince arrived at her session at the S.I.R. studio and heard Nicks play him her song. He liked it. He approached the piano, quickly tapped out an improvised keyboard track with two fingers, then left. She felt his contribution merited half of the songwriting credit. Since she recorded for rival label, Modern Records, however, they left his name off the album, *Uptown* magazine noted, "to avoid criticism from Warner Brothers."

Prince returned to Sunset Sound and his work with The Time. The situation with Jam and Lewis weighed heavily on his mind. Allegedly, Per Nilsen reported, he suspected they helped The Whispers create "Keep On

Loving Me," a song that sounded like The Time. "Prince swore we did that record," said Jam. If anything, the song's producer Leon Sylvers just wanted to try the Minneapolis sound. Either way, on April 18, Prince summoned both to Sunset. When they arrived, Prince called them into a lounge. With Morris and Jesse watching, Prince faced Jam and Lewis, and said, according to Jam's quote in Nilsen's book, "I told you guys how I felt about you doing the outside production and I realize that's what you want to do, so I feel at this time it's best to part ways."

And just like that they were fired. Some band members believed it was a ploy to dissuade them from outside production work. But the duo really was gone. Disbelief turned to anger. Keyboardist Monte Moir and drummer Jellybean Johnson quit and Prince invited them back. Jellybean Johnson hadn't held a job in years, and had to support a family. "I needed the money so I went back." Prince soon had Jellybean call Terry Lewis, Jam claimed. "Prince wanted Terry back, but not me." Terry, however, told Jellybean, No way. They were a team: "It's me and Jimmy and we're doing our own thing."

During the same trip, Prince and Fargnoli went to an Italian restaurant in Hollywood where they waited to meet William Blinn, whose credits included the Emmy-winning TV movie *Brian's Song*, a few episodes of *Starsky and Hutch*, and an installment of *Roots*. Most recently, Blinn had executive-produced the second season of NBC's *Fame*. He was waiting to hear if the network would commit to more episodes. Prince's managers wanted him to turn a vaguely conceived idea into a script—and he was interested. Manager Joe Ruffalo felt he had a "sense of music." Blinn didn't know much about Prince. "I seem to be strange casting for this kind of project," he later said.

When Blinn arrived, Prince ordered spaghetti with tomato sauce and some orange juice. Blinn thought Prince was "not conversationally accessible," but agreed to work on the script in Minneapolis. They would let Blinn write *and* direct.

Prince took a moment to reflect back with pride. He had played thirty-nine dates last year, and already fifty-one since January. It was only April but reporters already called his tour one of 1983's biggest earners. He was achieving the kind of stardom he had dreamed of.

After London shows on April 18 and 19, Prince finally left the road and leaped into creating the *Vanity 6* follow-up. But writer-director William Blinn wanted to meet. In Minneapolis, Blinn arranged a few appointments, but Prince had to cancel. He had a lot going on.

One day in April, Dez arrived at his house. In his basement studio, where they had created "Corvette" and other hits, he told Dez, "We're at a crossroads with this film. We're making a big investment. I need you to either bail now or make a three-year commitment to stay with the program." He'd understand if Dez did the "solo thing," Prince added. "I'll help you do it, my people will manage you, and the whole bit." Dez needed time to consider. At home, he prayed for guidance. He decided he was too unhappy. Three more years wasn't an option. He told Prince, who understood. He could have been angry; instead he sent Dez a salary "for a long time," Dez recalled.

Suddenly, Prince learned Blinn wanted to leave town *and* the project. "Look," Blinn apparently said, "I want out of this. You've got a rock 'n' roll crazy on your hands. I know he's very gifted, but frankly life's too short."

Blinn left Minneapolis. But within days, Prince called him to say he'd been under stress and that he wanted to talk. So Blinn returned, and in his purple home, Prince approached his piano. He played some of the songs he wanted in the film. Prince included one by his father, and mentioned the broad strokes of John's life: performing, marrying a singer, leaving home. He discussed how he came to live with André's family. To Blinn, music was "obviously a cloak and a shield and a whole bunch of things for [Prince]. It's a womb." Blinn got the sense this time that Prince was serious, and so he agreed to write the project, which they had taken to calling *Dreams*. Prince wanted his character's music to be "a kind of life force," Blinn recalled, "and his home life representing the opposite of that."

Blinn thought, "this picture was either going to be really big or fall right on its ass."

In May 1983, Prince's double set *1999* finally passed the 1 million sales mark and was certified Platinum. It should have been a major moment. But all anyone wanted to talk about was Michael Jackson, again. This time, in early May, Jackson stole the show during the NBC-TV special *Motown 25*. That night, forty-five million viewers saw him perform "Billie Jean" and his new dance step the "Moonwalk" (borrowed from break-dancing).

Prince was still writing new songs, and listening to his usual favorites

(Sly & The Family Stone, James Brown, Joni Mitchell, even some Miles Davis) but Alan Leeds recalled, "Of course he knew what Michael Jackson was accomplishing." At one point, he even discussed the *Thriller* star with Jill Jones. Ever competitive, Prince put aside his feelings to focus on creating the film that would break him out.

Blinn completed his draft of *Dreams* on May 23. In it, Blinn depicted a character called only "the Kid," who was haunted by memories of his father killing his mother, then himself. Blinn included the local music scene, and Vanity would play the role of one of the Kid's girlfriends, a soothing presence. Blinn told Prince's managers, "You're clearly heading for an R-rated picture." They didn't mind. "They felt they wanted to broaden Prince's audience."

The warehouse on Highway 7 in St. Louis Park was a huge depot with cement walls. It was an unlikely spot for a new studio.

A difficult tour had only ended a few weeks ago, but Prince had workers carry his recording equipment into the structure he had recently purchased. They put the mixing board at the center of the enormous loft. Once workers erected a soundstage, Prince and the band started creating songs for *Dreams*. Some days, a business a hundred yards away complained about the noise. Other days, truck drivers sat outside the loading dock and ate their lunches while listening to them play.

During this period, Alan Leeds says Prince wanted more "creative control and authority over every aspect of his career." And this included his image. Prince had sewing tables placed inside, and Marie France, a talented costume designer, joined two other designers in creating new outfits. Before he knew it, the trio had come up with a new look—his purple raincoat, ruffled shirts, and skintight pants that were equal parts new wave, late-period Beatles, and Jimi Hendrix.

Prince prepared everyone for the movie, and a world tour. Blinn hired Don Amendolia to help. "We started taking acting lessons every day," said The Time's Jellybean Johnson. "We were taking ballet, pirouetting and shit across the floor."

Lisa Coleman came in from Los Angeles for the sessions, which Matt Fink felt were "like boot camp." Prince stayed on The Revolution, The Time, and Vanity 6, telling all to stay disciplined and dedicated. "He just worked nonstop," said Fink. "He never slept."

In one room, The Time might be practicing. In another, he put The Revolution through paces. Everyone was nervous around him. But not Wendy. One summer day, he was at a keyboard, playing with no shirt on. She reached over and yanked his underarm hair. He pressed his elbow against his side. "Don't!" He kept playing.

She did it again.

"Cut it out!"

They started play fighting, slapping each other. No one else dared be as informal with him. He dug that about her. Despite the flirtatious rapport, Prince's attraction to Wendy wasn't a romantic one. If anything he liked that she was new to the business and still enthusiastic; honest enough to speak out if she disliked something; friendly enough to crack jokes; and humble enough to accept his mentoring and advice. He was smitten, however, with her twin sister, Susannah, who came to town to visit Wendy, met him at a party in Dez's home, mentioned she already had a boyfriend, but accepted the flowers Prince now sent to her California home every day.

Prince monitored the script. With Blinn halfway through a second draft, Prince decided he wanted "purple" in the title. Blinn thought it strange but understood he identified with the color. It was dark, passionate, foreboding, and had "a certain royalty to it, too." Prince wanted to call the film and the album that would accompany it *Purple Rain*.

Then he was thrown a curve ball. He learned Blinn had left the project—NBC wanted him on another season of *Fame*.

With Blinn gone, they had a partially finished script but no director. His manager Bob Cavallo scouted directors. First choice, *Reckless*'s James Foley, couldn't do it; he suggested *Reckless*'s editor Albert Magnoli. Magnoli had recently graduated from U.S.C. grad school, where he studied film. And while the thirty-year-old had yet to direct a feature, his student short *Jazz*—detailing the lives of a few black musicians in LA—won over a dozen awards.

Prince's managers called to say they liked it. Magnoli thanked them. He knew Prince only from "1999," "Little Red Corvette," and a *Rolling Stone* profile, but he agreed to read Blinn's script. When they next spoke, he told Cavallo a new deal with Paramount prevented him from doing their film. Cavallo was stunned. "Listen, I'm offering you the possibility of getting behind this and you're telling me you're too busy!"

Magnoli felt Blinn's script needed work, and he wasn't interested in pursuing it. But Cavallo was persistent; he wanted to meet for breakfast.

At the table, Cavallo asked what they should do.

"This is what I would do," Magnoli answered. He described a story. "It just came out." The script already had the Kid, Morris, and a girl in the middle. But he thought *Where do you go with this?* He outlined Prince's story arc, described Morris's, and explained Vanity's character. Then he suggested having the Kid's mother and father—an interracial couple—alive and fighting whenever the Kid came home. Within minutes, improvising, he shaped the film's world. And simultaneously, he said, "I had convinced myself that this would be an extremely exciting film to make."

Cavallo was pleased. Now all he needed was Prince's approval. Prince met with Magnoli in Minneapolis. Over dinner, Magnoli spoke for twenty-five minutes, outlining his story then "working off what was emanating from him." Magnoli devoted much of his pitch to the parents: the musician father and the mother as "sort of a woman wandering the streets." If Prince visibly reacted to anything, Magnoli lingered on that point. Finally, Prince said, "Okay, let's take a ride." After driving through town for a bit, he faced Magnoli. "I don't get it. This is the first time I met you, but you've told me more about what I've experienced than anybody in my life."

With that, he agreed to hire Magnoli.

"Al and Prince were writing it as they were going," Wendy remembered. That entire summer, Magnoli kept calling band members into meetings. When Wendy sat with him, he asked, "What is your relationship with Prince?" Then, "How would you see a situation arise?" She thought *Blah, blah, blah.* But within ten days, she saw new script pages materialize from their meetings.

After three weeks, Magnoli started reworking Blinn's draft. Magnoli rewrote 90 percent but "the story changed hardly at all." He based characters on Morris, Prince, and others, then exaggerated or downplayed attributes and had them act out a fictional story. "There's music," Magnoli explained. "That means there's night, there's bars, there are alleys." From here, the plot unfolded. "A girl comes into town to a club. She sweeps out of a cab in black. There's Prince—he's a dark figure. There's Morris—he's a light figure. There's the girl—she's a mystery." The Kid was popular in the local music scene but at home, his parents' fights left him "humiliated, frightened, and damaged," Magnoli added. He was too introverted to co-operate with his band or love the new girl. When she fled to Morris, he socked her, realized he was just like his father, then let everyone know he had changed by singing a power ballad. By the finale, Magnoli added, "he has learned to let others into his world . . . he has learned to love."

Magnoli's biggest change to the script was with the parents. He cut what Blinn planned as an offscreen murder-suicide, and included the Kid's parents as characters. While Prince's own mother never considered themselves other than black, the script showed Prince's character the Kid as the product of a mixed marriage. They also "jacked up" the father character, Neal Karlen explained. In a few scenes, he berated or beat his wife; he fought with his son; he pulled a gun. They included elements of his biography "to make the story pop more," Prince said, "but it was a story." The real John never touched guns or cursed at his mother, Prince claimed. "He never swore, still doesn't, and never drinks."

It was at this same time that Prince asked Magnoli, "What should I have as a vehicle? I was thinking of a motorcycle."

9

YOU SAY YOU WANT A LEADER

WHILE WORKING ON *PURPLE RAIN*, PRINCE INCLUDED THE REVO-
lution more than ever. "We were recording and writing and doing it,"
drummer Bobby Z remembered. "We all worked hard and did this music
together." Bobby credited Wendy with changing things for the better.
Wendy meanwhile felt Prince "definitely" enjoyed group sessions more
than he had.

Instead of recording everything then teaching them how to play it
live, he doled out parts of a song or cassettes and solicited input. They
jammed until they found a groove they liked, Wendy explained, then individual players took over when a section played to a particular strength.
Ultimately, he included The Revolution on six of nine songs. He also
shared credit for composing, arranging, and producing.

At some point, Prince brought out his idea for "Let's Go Crazy." He
started this with a mood-setting church organ and his filtered voice saying
there was something else—"the afterworld." In this world of never-ending
happiness, you could always see the sun, day or night, he added. Instead of
relying on a shrink in Beverly Hills, people should simply accept that this
life was harder than the afterworld. "In this life, you're on your own!" His
chunky guitar chords and pop keyboards followed to a quick beat. His vocal
was drenched in reverb. His guitar roared through the entire song. He
threw in a few high-pitched squeals.

People around him loved the track, but they frowned on its overt religious message. They knew he had dedicated five albums to God—even
Dirty Mind—but they also knew the religious theme weighed down what
was otherwise a great party track. Prince ignored them. His song was
about God and "the de-elevation of sin."

One August day, he started working on something called "Computer
Blue." He had considered this rock suite since the second part of the 1999
Tour in early 1983. That day, Matt Fink improvised a slinky synth groove

during a rehearsal. Prince loved it and said, "Let's turn that into a song!" Now, Prince wanted to inflate it to include a riff his father John used to play. He had Wendy and Lisa greet each other by name over a pounding bass drum and whiny noises. He screeched, and a thrashing rock beat started. He played more roaring guitar, and sang about loneliness. The results were strange and catchy—but it still needed something. He'd finish it at some point. Maybe in California.

August 3, he again brought out "Baby I'm a Star," a song he had recorded once during the Controversy Tour. Fink remembered improvising riffs "over the track for several takes until I got one Prince and I liked." Prince also worked on a smooth instrumental called "Electric Intercourse," then filled his dance number "I Would Die 4 U" with more religious subtext. He also started "Purple Rain," a guitar-heavy power ballad in the "Free" tradition, and one as expansive as any on Jimi's *Electric Ladyland*. With echoing voice booming over drums he told a girl he never meant to hurt her; he wanted to see her again; he didn't want to be the other guy. Then he sang louder, seemingly telling a crowd times were changing; it was time for something new. "You say you want a leader . . ." Well, they better make up their mind and let him guide them to the purple rain.

At the warehouse near Highway 7, Prince had the band play the song. "Everybody was coming up with their own parts," Wendy claimed. And by day's end, they pretty much finished it. It found Prince playing charged guitar and emitting a Jackson-like "Whoo!" Near the end, the others joined its chorus.

The band was playing the song again when a woman walked in with her bike. "She was like a bag lady." She took the seat in front of them while they played. "Really quiet, very demure, really sweet."

The performance moved her to tears. "She was bawling," Wendy recalled.

Bobby Z thought its song structure and tempo almost felt like country, rock, and gospel. It had blood, sweat, tears, and soul. "You can smell the crowd in it," he said. "It's a movie, it's a hit, it's an album. It just sums it up." His bodyguard Chick was just as affected. Entering an office, he told Prince's other employees, "Wait until you hear the song he did last night. It's gonna be bigger than Willie Nelson." He kept predicting it would make Prince a superstar, and that Nelson would actually cover it. "That, to him, was a big achievement," said Alan Leeds, "that the song would have that broad of an appeal."

When Prince finally played it for them, they were just as thrilled. Dez, however, wondered if he might have spawned it. He conceded Prince was a great guitarist, but would Prince have written this kind of song without him around? "I know we influenced each other," Dez explained. They frequently discussed the rock genre. And the new ballad was "definitely reminiscent of my style." In the end, Dez decided, "I'm glad I had the chance to influence his sound somewhat."

One thing is for certain, "Purple Rain" is Prince at his most self-assured. While he spent years downplaying Jimi Hendrix as an influence, this majestic ballad finds Prince openly reveling in the free-form, long and winding sort of balladry Jimi embraced during his brief career in rock music. Huge drums proceed at a leisurely pace; Prince unveils an arsenal of riffs and high-pitched solos; his falsetto reaches stratospheric heights; his lyric—which veers from accepting a breakup to telling listeners he wants them to be saved and go to heaven after Judgment Day—is open and moving. And the strings that end the number are just as affecting. After years of fumbling with a rock sound—the discolike material on his debut, the falsetto-marred "Bambi" on *Prince,* and the plodding, canned feel of "Free" on *1999*—"Purple Rain" found Prince a style that worked— big drums, majestic guitar, and an echoing and loose conversational delivery. It also offered an unexpected alternative to the overproduced, hook-heavy ballads churned out by hair-, spandex-, and image-obsessed glam metal acts routinely appearing on MTV.

Fans descended on the downtown Minneapolis club First Avenue, which was to appear in the film. With The Revolution well rehearsed, Prince arranged to test them before a live audience, at a twenty-five dollars-per-person concert to benefit the Minnesota Dance Theatre. (They did it "because that's where we were getting our dance instruction," Fink explained.)

Since he was between tours, Prince had no "first-rate, tour-worthy technicians on payroll," Alan Leeds explained. By the time he staged his final rehearsal for the show, Alan Leeds had flown a few sound and lighting wizards into town. At the last minute, Prince asked Leeds to have a mobile audio truck near the club to record every note. Leeds obliged, accepting he "pretty much had to assume control of it all."

Alan got it there by the time the band arrived backstage; and in it, David Rivkin—his drummer's brother and the guy who helped record his debut's vocals—prepared to engineer and record. Rivkin couldn't get over how great this black truck from New York was. With no experienced road crew around, Leeds became "production manager by default," he said. Inside the club, he recalled, "it was just elbow to elbow, a goddamn sweatbox, and no one knew what to expect, 'cause Prince was gonna play a bunch of new stuff that no one had heard."

The MDT corps started things off with a *Flashdance*-inspired routine to "D.M.S.R." Backstage, Prince had his band gather around to link hands while he led them in prayer. When the curtain rose, Prince marched toward the stage "like a boxer to a ring, jabbing, feinting," Leeds recalled. By now, actor Don Amendolia had given Prince and his bands acting lessons and workouts. Local choreographer John Command (who also taught everyone their dance moves) had reshaped Prince's body so it looked toned and fit. Prince took the stage playing a purple guitar, with Wendy Melvoin replacing Dez. New to performing live, Wendy said, "I was scared to death but I loved it."

His ten-song set found Prince debuting idiosyncratic new works "Computer Blue," "I Would Die 4 U," and "Electric Intercourse." He also offered a rare cover, Joni Mitchell's "A Case of You." He floored the sweaty audience with "Let's Go Crazy" (a song so new *Rolling Stone* misidentified it as "Let's Get Crazy"). With relief, Prince watched the crowd accept its mix of fiery guitars and pop keyboard.

Then, *Rolling Stone* reported, "he encored with an anthemic—and long—new one called 'Purple Rain.'" The magazine claimed the power ballad brought the house down. David Rivkin however said the crowd had never heard any of these *Purple Rain* songs, and so when they finished playing, no one really clapped. They weren't familiar with any of it.

Either way, after his set, Loyce Houlton, a woman in her sixties who worked with the Minnesota Dance Theatre, hit center stage. "We don't have a Prince in Minneapolis," she told the crowd. "We have a king." She pulled a purple rose from her bouquet and handed it to Prince. Alan Leeds was just as pleased. "It was a great night," said Leeds. "Thank God we got it all on tape."

Prince entered his car and was about to leave when a wild fan stepped off the curb, blocking his car.

She started opening her coat, suggested that she wore nothing underneath.

But before she could, Prince winced. "No, don't do that."

He rolled his window up and drove away.

Prince didn't intend to use any of the night's recordings on the album. But while hearing the tapes later, he saw there were no technical mishaps. He could touch things up in the studio and get these versions of "I Would Die 4 U," "Baby I'm a Star," and "Purple Rain" out there. "What we did on the album was to loop a football crowd underneath," David Rivkin revealed, "so it sounded like everybody was cheering, because there was no applause."

Prince soon faced another film-related setback. He wanted Vanity to play the love interest and she was taking acting and singing classes.

One night in August, he took her to the downtown rock club First Avenue. They passed pictures of Grandmaster Flash, the Human League, The Clash, and others, then heard the disc jockey in the booth ask, what's new? Prince held up the test pressing of "Delirious," asked him to spin it, then led Vanity to the dance floor.

It was a good night, but it did little to change things between them. While Prince had half of a Vanity 6 album done, and a script with her character in it, Vanity was now telling Alan Leeds she was unhappy with how Prince treated her.

Meanwhile, Martin Scorsese was offering her a role in *The Last Temptation of Christ*. Other producers wanted meetings. All of a sudden, she was in demand—and she wanted more money for *Purple Rain*. "The movie was Prince's dream," she said. "He was bringing in everybody for very little money. You've got to pay people. You've got to be fair."

As she told it, the film's producers failed to meet her salary requests so she left. "I didn't want to be stuck in the snow at six in the morning in some camper with no place to change clothes. Who needs that?" Vanity was out.

Within days of the First Avenue show, he recorded "Darling Nikki," to be the album's shocker. Whether Prince had Vanity in mind when he yelled, "Come back, Nikki, come back!" is unknown. But Prince felt it was the coldest song he ever wrote, and perfect for the film. And though they eventually changed the film character's name from Nicolette, he kept the song title anyway.

By August 15, he was back in Los Angeles. Wendy and Lisa came by Sunset Sound to help rerecord "Computer Blue." Prince wanted something epic, to use overdubs to create something grander. Engineer Peggy

McCreary reminded him their recorders only had twenty-four tracks. "We don't have enough room."

"Make some more room."

McCreary brought in two other recorders.

They added strings and he was so pleased with the results, Lisa predicted that, from now on, he'd intersperse his "solo" albums with group collaborations.

Away from the studio, his 1999 success continued. When Warner released "Delirious" on August 18, he saw this nonthreatening, upbeat dance tune enter the Top 10 (at No. 8), and become his third Top 20 pop hit that year. Then he learned *Thriller* star Michael Jackson was, to his amazement, actually aware of him.

Between sessions, Prince heard James Brown was playing the Beverly Theater August 20. Recently, Prince had attended one of Brown's shows in Minneapolis. That night, Alan Leeds—who once worked for Brown—had asked if he wanted to head backstage and be introduced to Brown.

"Why?" Alan remembered Prince responding.

Like everyone else in his orbit, Alan knew Prince loved Brown's music. He had also seen Prince's sound checks and rehearsals frequently segue into "marathon jams on Brown tunes." As Brown's Minneapolis concert continued, Alan shrugged: Prince didn't want to meet an idol. Not only that: "Near the end of the show, I turned around and Prince had disappeared; out the side door and off into the night. It's anybody's guess why."

Still, with Brown playing Los Angeles, Prince wanted to attend. He also, Jill Jones claimed, made a few plans in advance. Prince arrived in a flashy outfit with shoulder pads and a flap open to reveal his chest. From his seat in the rear, he watched James invite Michael Jackson on stage. "Brown had known Michael since before The Jackson 5 signed with Motown," Alan Leeds explained. Michael—in trademark shades and royal blue military jacket—sang a few words ("I love you") then leaned into James's ear. "James barely knew who Prince was at that time," said Brown's former employee Alan Leeds.

But Michael did.

"Prince would like to have competed," Alan Leeds noted, "but Jackson was enjoying the biggest-selling album in the history of the music business! Jackson's success was impossible to ignore." Within seconds,

James—in a sleeveless green vest that highlighted muscular arms—told the crowd he wanted to introduce someone else. He started calling, "Prince? Prince?" He faced the bustling crowd. "Prince?"

As the crowd cheered, Prince reluctantly climbed onto Chick's shoulders. Though Prince looked mildly surprised, Jill Jones explained, "It was planned with Chick and everything." He stripped a glove off and tossed it at the audience. As he climbed on stage, James said, "You gotta do something."

A musician handed Prince a guitar. Prince strapped it on, then huddled with James for a second.

James backed away a little, watching expectantly. His band played a heart-pounding soul vamp. Prince "played some innocuous rhythm parts," Leeds recalled. James nodded along, pleased to have him there. But then Prince stopped playing. At the front of the stage, he knelt, pointing the guitar at the crowd like a phallus. Prince rose, while panting, then knelt again while hitting an odd chord. Prince rose again, removing the guitar then his shirt.

The crowd cried out.

Prince handed the shirt to a backup player then performed a few stilted dance steps. He marched over to where Big Chick waited in the crowd, raising a peace sign, clapping his hands over his head. With embarrassment, he leaped off stage and into Chick's arms. But his foot caught on a huge stage prop, knocking the fake lamppost over into the audience. Behind him, *Rolling Stone* claimed, Brown said, "Look out, Michael!" Instead of returning to his seat, where Bobby Z and Jill Jones sat "hiding their faces, Prince rushed up the aisle and out to his limo," Leeds recalled. It was a quiet ride back to the hotel.

10

DON'T MAKE ME LOSE MY MIND

AT SUNSET SOUND, PRINCE WORKED TO MAKE HIS SONGS EVEN hotter. He also began to show further interest in Wendy's twin sister Susannah. Since she had visited Wendy in Minneapolis a few months ago, he thought of her frequently. Finally, he addressed the situation the way he addressed all of the meaningful moments in his life: in song, this time with his ambitious, haunting work "The Beautiful Ones." September 20, he filled the somber ballad with cold electronic drums, dramatic synthesizers, angry guitar, and a poignant vocal that led to awful screams and rants. It was his favorite new song, engineer Susan Rogers told *Rolling Stone*. It also outlined his feelings for Susannah. He kept writing about her, Rogers said, "but that was the first one."

Before month's end, he learned another established white singer wanted to work with him. This time, engineer David Leonard said, Scottish-born Sheena Easton had asked him to relay that she was a huge fan. Easton was known for clean-cut hits like 1981's "Morning Train," "Modern Girl," and "For Your Eyes Only" (from the James Bond film of the same name). She loved *1999* and hoped he'd write something for her album. He was surprised and flattered. He liked her voice, too. After some thought, he knocked out a racy dance number called "Sugar Walls."

He was also thinking about The Time. He had started their next album *Ice Cream Castles* in March, but encountered setbacks due to firings and departures. The group still reeled. And Morris was tired of him ordering him how to dress, sing, and act on stage, Per Nilsen noted. So, sound engineer Susan Rogers recalled to Mark Weingarten, "Prince recorded every note on that record. He even laid down guide vocals for Morris Day to follow." He figured they'd get over it. They'd be in the film. This would pass.

On October 4, he arranged for the new Time lineup to play eight songs at First Avenue. Once again, he had a mobile recording unit tape the show. The crowd, he saw, was enthusiastic about their two new songs

"Jungle Love" and "The Bird." But once Morris Day finished the last song, he stormed off stage. He was unhappy with Prince's micromanaging, the band's new members, and the fact that two commercially successful albums had brought him little money. He raced past the dressing room, Jellybean told *Tones* magazine, rushed out the back door, "into his waiting Porsche with his girlfriend," and was "gone!" Confused band members stayed behind for a tense celebration. Prince decided the night's version of "The Bird" (complete with a live audience) would go on their new album.

In October, in Minneapolis, Prince saw new engineer Susan Rogers had installed a new console and fixed a tape machine in his home studio. Rogers had most recently worked for Crosby, Stills, and Nash's studio in Hollywood. But she leaped at the chance to become his new audio technician. "Prince was my favorite artist ever since the *For You* album, and the opportunity was a dream come true," she said. A call to his managers got her an interview and the job.

Since August, she had worked in his purple home on Kiowa Trail. But he threw her a curve ball, asking her to set up a vocal microphone so he could sing a few parts for "Darling Nikki." She never professionally engineered, she explained. "Next thing I knew, I was in the engineering chair."

October 24 found Prince working with Jill Jones, on her contribution to the album, "Wednesday." It had a sweet piano melody and lyrics about suicide, Jill explained.

Then, five days later, in his home studio, he tinkered with "Computer Blue" again. He and Matt Fink had created some great riffs; and Wendy and Lisa's sultry introduction was fantastic. But Prince kept writing stronger songs, and wasn't sure if there would be room for this one (since his managers and Warner didn't want another double album). And he didn't want to alienate his father John, whose old piano riff he had borrowed for the song. After years of discord, the two were actually getting along. Now John was telling people that purple was always his, John's, favorite color and about a song he wrote years ago, called "Purple Shades"—before learning Prince also favored this shade.

Vanity had left in August. They couldn't just rewrite the script, so they arranged a casting call. They wanted someone that met certain requirements, some of them physical, and auditioned seven hundred women in New York and Los Angeles. One New York woman said she auditioned, got the part, but rejected it as too pornographic. An agent for twenty-two-year-old photo model Patty Kotero arranged an audition. Kotero lived in a clean West Hollywood apartment and starred in the miniseries *Mystic Warriors*. Her parents were born in Mexico, but she called herself "a Latin-German Jew." Intrigued by the opportunity, she quickly arranged to audition in LA.

Kotero took a flight to Minneapolis to meet Prince. They went to a deli and made small talk. He asked about her experience singing, dancing, and acting. Then he fixed her with a serious look. "Do you believe in God?" He drove her around for a while, hearing her sing to a tape. Then they hit First Avenue to see if she could dance. She had passed all his tests. And with that, he gave her the part and a new name, Apollonia, after a character in *The Godfather*. He then introduced her to Vanity 6's remaining members, Susan Moonsie and Brenda Bennett, and told them they'd now be Apollonia 6 in the film, on their own album, and while touring to promote it.

With the film's start date approaching, he asked sound engineer David Leonard to fly to town to help with his studio. He wanted Susan Rogers and Leonard to move all of his equipment—including his home console—to the warehouse. He had recorded "Let's Go Crazy" during the MDT benefit concert but felt, since it would accompany a concert scene, it should feel even more like a big live performance. Rogers thought it "seemed a little crazy" since "nobody had really done that before." Producers didn't record a band live without isolating musicians from an engineer. But for four years, he had loved the echo and big sound rehearsing in large spaces provides. Despite her misgivings, Rogers and Leonard set up his equipment in the center of the cavernous space. He arrived with a new part for the song, a riff that would make it even better, he felt.

"Dearly Beloved," he said over his sepulchral organ riff and sermon: "We are gathered here today to get through this thing called life . . ." Prince got the echo he wanted, but had to deal with track leakage and electrical interference from every device in the building. "There was never any proper separation between the board and the instruments," drummer Bobby Z explained. But Prince valued spontaneity and a great performance over things like proper mic placement. He kept rolling tape and delivered his stunning new synth and guitar solo. The result had a few minor flaws, but Prince could live with them. He wanted this version on the album and in the film.

After brief prep time, Magnoli started principal photography on November 1. Prince lived twenty minutes from the Twin Cities, close to his divorced father and a sister that sang in a local gospel choir. A day before filming, during rehearsal, he told the bands to arrive at a Holiday Inn at 5 A.M. "Be there, don't fuck up," Jellybean Johnson recalled being told. The bleary-eyed band was there. By 8 A.M., Magnoli was ready to shoot. But their new bass player Rocky Harris still hadn't shown. According to Per Nilsen, Prince faced Morris. "Morris, this is costing me $30,000 an hour. What're you going to do about it? You're going to pay for it!" Nilsen quoted Prince as saying. Jesse Johnson called a replacement at home.

Despite an early start, everyone stayed on the set until six or seven in the evening.

Prince's attention to detail impressed the crew. He was always on time. He knew his lines. If asked to repeat a scene, "he always remembered where his hands were in the previous shot," said location manager Kirk Hokanson. Prince was also there, off camera, offering advice to band members. One day, they were choosing outfits for the film. New Time member Paul Peterson chose a cool black suit with pinstripes.

"Nobody's going to notice you with that. Wear this." Prince handed him an orange pin-striped suit.

"Oh, no, I don't want to wear that."

"Wear it," he said.

New to the job, seventeen-year-old Peterson didn't want to make waves. "And then they got a hold of my hair," he said. They gave him a puffed-out hairstyle he had to constantly style with a curling iron. His girlfriend took less time getting ready than he did, he said.

Magnoli started shooting exteriors downtown on November 7. That same day, Prince received a test pressing of the soundtrack. At this point, it included his fiery "Let's Go Crazy," his ode to Susannah "The Beautiful Ones," his collaboration with Wendy and Lisa "Computer Blue," his harrowing "Darling Nikki," the Jill Jones ditty "Wednesday," his power ballad "Purple Rain," the dance cuts "I Would Die 4 U" and "Baby I'm a Star," and the instrumental "Father's Song." He decided Jill's "Wednesday" wouldn't work. He cut it from the lineup and broke the news to Jones. "He told me the scene was cut," Jill recalled. "He said he was really sad about it. I really did not believe him." Jill concealed her anger while Prince blamed his managers and the director for the decision. Then he got back to filming.

Set designers turned a public street into a closed set. While Magnoli filmed Morris and Jerome walking down a street, Prince stood on the sidelines, ready to leap in and offer advice. Then it was Prince's turn to spend a few weeks in front of the cameras, riding his bike in the country, flirting with a nude Apollonia near a lake, and shoving film rival Day into some trash cans in an alley.

By this point, some say Day's growing frustration made him uncooperative. He allegedly arrived late to every rehearsal or set. Sometimes, they had to send a crew member to wake him up.

In the studio, while recording vocals for the third Time album, Morris stood in front of the mic, and matched Prince's guide vocals on the six new songs. But at the board, engineer Susan Rogers felt a palpable tension. "Morris was very unhappy and basically nonparticipating," she told author Alex Hahn. He wanted to "get the movie over with," then leave.

Prince and Morris were hardly speaking. Still Magnoli had them film another scene. Before anyone knew it, Prince and Morris were swinging fists, having a real fight. Day later claimed the media blew it out of proportion, but Jellybean told *Tones* magazine, "I had to break it up." Even worse, the weather changed before Magnoli could finish exterior shooting. They dealt with a particularly bitter winter. "The day before we began shooting, there was eighteen feet of snow and the weather plunged thirty below zero," Magnoli later explained. With the crew facing temperatures ranging from twenty-eight degrees to below zero some crew members worked through bouts of frostbite. Then it kept raining when they tried to capture pivotal scenes.

Apollonia, herself, kept filming in subzero temperatures. Between takes, a crew member rushed forward to wrap a blanket around her. Prince meanwhile started creating music she could perform in the film. On a day off, in November, he led her into his home studio. Susan Rogers heard her sing The Beatles' gentle "When I'm Sixty-four" and thought, she told Mark Weingarten, "this is gonna be a long night."

Prince had Rogers play a version of "Sex Shooter" with Vanity's lead vocals. Apollonia tried to replace Vanity's performance with her own, but Prince stopped rolling the tape. It wasn't working. They needed privacy, and so Rogers left the control room. Prince gave Apollonia a fifteen- to thirty-minute pep talk that left her sounding more assertive. "By the time we recorded it, the whole thing just clicked," Rogers also told Weingarten. "She had this campy quality to her voice that was perfect. She sounded like an actress pretending to sing."

Prince was still filming when Michael Jackson popped back into the mainstream media yet again. This time, reporters all covered a November

23 press conference at Manhattan's Tavern on the Green. Jackson joined his brothers—all in sunglasses—to talk up a reunion album and tour.

In chilly Minneapolis, Prince spent a month filming performance scenes at First Avenue, where he wanted a full house. The club was cold, Wendy recalled. "They had space heaters all around." He and The Revolution would lip-synch for the film's live-performance sequences. Two 35mm cameras would have been more than enough but they had four or five. Prince told the sound department to make the playback level as loud as a real concert. The crew spent two hundred dollars on sound suppressors, then "brought in the stacks and let 'em have it," said Playback operator Matt Quast.

Every day at 7 A.M., six hundred extras entered, ready to react to the Kid's seven numbers. During some takes, the extras cheered and danced. Some scenes called for an indifferent audience. But spirited performances, and new songs, had them cheering anyway. He'd finish lip-synching a song only to hear Magnoli call for another take. Still, Magnoli worked quickly, getting each number in a mere two or three takes.

During a break in filming, Prince made another important connection. At the time, rap music was beginning its rise. Groups like Run-D.M.C. were beginning to attract mainstream attention with their own metal riffs and aggressive lyrics. The rest of the nation was embracing the sound and accompanying culture. Producers included break-dancers in Hollywood films like *Flashdance*. In Minneapolis, New York transplants joined locals to spread the artistic movement. In fact, a local break-dancing crew called 2 Be Rude—whose Prince-like logo included a tongue standing in for the letter "u"—showed up to an audition for extras and wound up being asked to help choose people.

With The Time set to film their performance of "Jungle Love," Prince heard noise from a restroom. He led in bodyguards and saw about seventeen teenagers having some sort of party. Most created rap beats by stomping feet and clapping hands. 2 Be Rude members Damon Dickson, Kirk Johnson, and Tony Mosley meanwhile were performing their best, most acrobatic moves. "He just kind of looked at us, stood there about five minutes, and turned around and walked out," Dickson recalled. Dickson looked at Mosley. "We might be in trouble, dude." But Prince came back, walked up to them, and handed them a tape. It was already 9:00 P.M. but he wanted to see seven routines by 7:00 A.M.

Then Prince told Magnoli he wanted Apollonia 6's "Sex Shooter" in the film, too. Magnoli also filmed a performance by Dez Dickerson's new group The Modernaires. Since leaving The Revolution after the 1999 tour, Dez had formed his own interracial band. Prince also steered him to his management. After striking a handshake agreement ("no written contract," Dez recalled), Dez started his own group album, creating "epic stadium rock with radio hooks." The Modernaires believed they would soon ink a deal with Warner. Prince invited them into his film and was present the day they filmed their performance scene. "Technically, he was my manager at the time," Dez said.

Amazingly, Magnoli had all of the concert scenes done in only ten days. "We went into it three weeks behind and came out of it on schedule," co-manager Bob Cavallo recalled.

A few days before Christmas, Magnoli wrapped principal photography. The film's budget was "very small in terms of [its] results," he said proudly. He shot the entire story and even included numerous production numbers.

While cast and crew celebrated during an all-night wrap party in Bloomington, Minnesota, Prince considered his next task. He had to fly to Los Angeles to shoot more outdoor scenes in warmer weather. But the budget Warner's Mo Ostin personally provided was gone. And they still had no one to get the film into theaters. "They had their necks out and were out of money," said Alan Leeds.

Cavallo and Fargnoli asked Warner Bros. Pictures, a separate arm of the company, to invest money and distribute *Purple Rain*. "We believe Prince has much greater name value than the number of records he's sold," Cavallo felt. Warner Bros. Pictures thought his two or three million record fans might see a movie. But the managers predicted he'd attract a much larger general interest audience. "People don't know a lot about him," Cavallo explained. "He's a little mysterioso and he has a controversial image." Finally, the night of the wrap party, his managers called with good news. That very night, while everyone was partying, they had finalized the deal. Warner Bros. had financed production, which wound up going over budget, Alan Leeds explained. The studio still didn't know how many theaters would actually commit to booking the film. Warner agreed to pay $6 million upon delivery of the negative. If not for this last-minute finance, Leeds explained, "Postproduction might have been canceled."

Now Prince had both a great product and the means to finish it. But would movie viewers care?

11

EVERYBODY CAN'T BE ON TOP

DECEMBER 30, IN THE WAREHOUSE, PRINCE KNOCKED OUT A
song called "She's Always in My Hair." Over a stilted keyboard riff, raw
guitar work, and a funky beat, he sang about a woman that loved him.
Prince told ever-supportive Jill Jones the song was about her. She understood; she always asked him "to treat me better," she explained.

Either way, a nearby road crew heard its guitar riff and stopped what
they were doing. It paralyzed them, Alan Leeds recalled. That same day,
he moved on to another number with a musician he had recently reconnected with, Sheila Escovedo.

Sheila was a drummer, like her famous father Pete. As a child, she
went from wanting to play outside to playing drums, a decision her parents supported. Prince first saw her backstage at an Al Jarreau show in
1978, but they didn't speak that night. Then she attended a late 1979 concert, when he was promoting *Prince*. She saw his trench coat and leg
warmers and thought, *what is he doing?* "It was a shocker," she recalled. "But
it was cool." She went backstage to compliment his music and he told her, "I
know who you are." He asked how much she'd charge to be his drummer.
She told him. He quipped, "Well, I'll never be able to afford that." Still, they
kept in touch and now he was inviting her to Sunset Sound. She thought
Prince wanted her to play drums.

"No," he said, "I want you to sing this song called 'Erotic City.'"

He played her a track with a spare beat, catchy hooks, and electro-
pop rhythms. She reluctantly agreed. But she heard the lyrics and didn't
"want to sing the curse words." So Prince did. "We had a great time doing
it," she said. And while "Erotic City" included a few expletives, some radio
stations played it anyway.

In Los Angeles, at Sunset Sound on January 1 and 2, 1984, recording
overrode even sleep or regular meals. "He likes coffee," an engineer ex-

plained. Someone suggested a meal. "No, it'll make me sleepy." Even after long sessions, inspiration arrived. One night, he left the studio at dawn but called to say he'd resume at ten. During these sessions, he was working on the *Apollonia 6* album, revisiting his old demo, "Moral Majority."

By now, his employees back in Minnesota had moved his equipment into an old metal hangar on Flying Cloud Drive, in Eden Prairie. He wanted his own studio complex and considered this a good choice. The hangar had everything he'd need—an arena-sized rehearsal stage, a costume room, and his musical equipment—so he went from renting it (in early 1984) to buying it for a reported $450,000. He returned to town to record new music, but neighbors on Flying Cloud Drive complained about his rehearsals.

He kept working on various projects at once. First up was something for *Apollonia 6*. January 24, he recorded a duet called "Take Me With U." For this one, Sheila played a Motown-like tambourine-filled dance beat. Lisa arranged a stately string section. Her brother, David, played cello. "Apollonia couldn't sing, really," Susan Rogers claimed. "She was in the film, and he needed the song for the movie." Yet, the singer offered a performance so passionate he decided "Take Me with U" would be her lead single.

Prince meanwhile kept recording, warehousing music before having to publicize his film and album. February 4, he taped "Manic Monday," another upbeat tune with a sixties feel. With "Manic Monday," "Take Me With U" and "Sex Shooter" on the album, *Apollonia 6* looked to be his most commercial, pop-oriented side project to date.

But three days later, a Sunday afternoon, he arrived at the warehouse to find that the equipment was malfunctioning. He needed a break from all the happy pop rock. He turned off every light, ignited some candles, and recorded a religious lament with lots of piano and falsetto. After one take, he decided this piano-driven tune, "God," was done and left. "There wasn't much else to say," said Susan Rogers. Eleven days later, he recorded another downhearted ballad, heavy on the "Purple Rain" echo, called "Another Lonely Christmas." On this one, he reminisced about good times with his old girl. Only near the end did he reveal she had died. The effect was jarring.

He'd been working on *Purple Rain* since the 1999 Tour. He knew how most of the songs would sound so he wanted to start something new. But it was hard to avoid rehashing a sound, especially when you've written as much as he did. If something he created sounded familiar, he set the reel tape into a growing archive of unreleased music. "It could be I have a need to be different," he conceded.

By February 19, with *Purple Rain* not even done yet, he started the next album with a song called "Pop Life." In some ways, it revisited the elements of "Take Me With U," with Sheila playing drums at a quicker tempo and Wendy and Lisa composing and conducting a string interlude. His lyric asked, "What you putting in your nose?"

He remained tangled in *Apollonia 6*. The album included many potential hits but Apollonia herself was tired of him. He kept working to make it a strong debut but soon decided Sheila Escovedo would sound good on some of these *Apollonia 6* songs. An album by Sheila, under the raplike nickname, "Sheila E.," could do well. He could also have Warner release more music that way, engineer Terry Christian suggested. "He had so much material and he wanted to keep recording but he didn't want Warner to know what he was up to."

He told Sheila, "Why don't you do your own album?"

He kept encouraging her until she agreed.

In late February, Prince found time to attend the twenty-sixth Grammy Awards ceremony at the Shrine Auditorium. Jackson's twelve Grammy nominations dominated headlines. Everyone watched him arrive with Brooke Shields and child star Emmanuel Lewis. This time, Jackson wore a shiny sequined blue jacket with big yellow shoulder pads, a white shirt, a white glove, and huge black sunglasses. Jackson had his hair done up in Jheri curls, suddenly looking a little Prince-like.

Prince's *1999* and one of its ballads were nominated in various categories but it was definitely *Thriller*'s night. Jackson won Album of the Year. "Beat It" won Record of the Year. Sting managed to win Song of the Year for "Every Breath You Take," but Jackson's "Beat It" and "Billie Jean" were both in the running. Eventually, it was time for Best Pop Vocal Performance: Male. Prince's "1999" faced Billy Joel's fifties-styled "Uptown Girl," Lionel Richie's festive "All Night Long (All Night)," the *Flashdance* number "Maniac," and Jackson's "Thriller." To no one's surprise, Jackson won. As the night continued, Prince faced Jackson again, this time for Best R&B Vocal Performance: Male. But his *1999* ballad "International Lover" lost out again to Jackson, this time for "Billie Jean."

It was perhaps with these memories in his mind that he arrived at

Sunset Sound, March 1. Prince had a song in his head. "When Doves Cry" described a deteriorating relationship and abandonment, but instead of composing appropriately sad music, he reached for the Linn LM-1 drum machine. By now, many producers were using the Roland line of machines. But he liked this Linn's synthetic drum sound "and hung on to it for a long time, even after it was obsolete," said drummer Bobby Z. And when Bobby heard the beat he created, he felt Prince was not only "one of the very best drum programmers" out there, but that he could also "get very warm sounds out of machines." Susan Rogers agreed. "No one can program a drum machine better than he can," she claimed. "He can take a four-track machine and create a completed track out of it."

Once the beat was down, Prince quickly moved on to vocals, and a bass line. But when it was time to mix, he felt blocked. The bass line dragged it down and made it sound like everything else on the album. "They were almost done editing the movie," Prince explained. It was the last song to mix. As Prince told it, he laid his head on the console while playing a rough version. Jill Jones walked in and asked what's up.

"If I could have it my way, it would sound like this." He pushed a button, muting the bass line.

"Why don't you have it your way?"

And so he did.

McCreary's recollection was far less dramatic. "He was listening, and just popped the bass track out. And it worked out beautifully."

Either way, Alan Leeds later wrote, Prince invited Dr. Fink and Bobby Z into his car, and drove around while playing the new song. Fink was confused. He thought the album was finished. He also didn't like the song. "There is no bass."

"That's right."

"How come?"

"I tried it, it just didn't work. I just didn't like it."

The song grew on him, though, Leeds noted in print. For his part, Dez was unpleasantly surprised. Later he learned that *Purple Rain* wouldn't actually be "a true soundtrack album" containing everyone's music. Since Prince wrote "more and more music" during postproduction, Prince wanted to bump "all the non-Prince stuff" (including Dez's own song "Modernaire"). Prince never explained why, Dez added. But Prince's co-manager Cavallo soon told a reporter that it was simply an economic decision. "We were trying not to have a double record," Cavallo explained.

"It seemed obvious that we could reach more people if the price were lower."

Lisa Coleman meanwhile also believed she influenced "When Doves Cry." Prince was engaged in healthy competition with her and Wendy, she said. "He was always thinking how can I kick their ass?" The answer, she implied, was the song's pseudoclassical keyboard, harking back to her own musical background and her experience with Prince.

On March 9, Prince recorded something else for his next album: a song with a plodding shuffle beat and bouncy, calliope-style keyboard that he called "Paisley Park." It was what he now called his home studio (since he tired of the phrase "Uptown").

Prince felt he was making progress with the new album, but he had to stop to finish *Purple Rain*. On March 23, he created a new configuration of the album that slipped a short version of "Father's Song" as the middle groove on "Computer Blue." Prince also included John Nelson in writing credits. The album was nearing completion, but it still needed work.

He decided to keep the *Apollonia 6* number "Take Me with U" for himself, and made room for it on *Purple Rain* by trimming "Computer Blue" even more. By April 14, Prince had assembled the final version of the soundtrack album. Everyone involved sensed its mix of hazy guitars, arena-rock choruses, discordant melodies, upbeat chants, bitter love songs, and religious subtexts would take him to the top. Though usually his own worst critic, "Prince knew this was going to be it," Rogers noted.

On May 16, Warner released "When Doves Cry" backed with the song "17 Days." The single quickly became his first No. 1. It topped the chart for five weeks, becoming the year's biggest-selling single. *Time* noted that "When Doves Cry" was the first song since "Billie Jean" to reach No. 1 "simultaneously on the pop, black, and dance charts." And soon, the B-side was just as popular on radio playlists.

After producing three side projects as "Jamie Starr," Prince felt he had established himself well enough to justify having his own label. He had his managers negotiate with Warner, and the label agreed to distribute it, so he moved on to considering a first signing.

Recently, his bassist Mark Brown confessed that he had been moonlighting with Mazarati, a new seven-piece Minneapolis band that played funk and hard-edged rock. During shows, behind a mask, Mark called himself "The Shadow," and played bass. In his Corvette one day with Mazarati's guitarist, as Per Nilsen recounted, he worried Prince might catch him. "Just tell him!" the man blurted. "He's gonna find out anyway. The worst thing he can do is want a piece of it or tell you to stop." After Mark told him, Prince attended some of their shows. Now when Mark brought the band over to the warehouse for rehearsals, Prince joined in. He decided he would sign them to his new label once the moment was right.

June 4, Warner released Sheila E.'s *The Glamorous Life* with credits that said it was "directed" by Sheila E. and The Starr Company. Prince's name was nowhere on it, but people gossiped that Prince wrote, played on, and produced everything. At any rate, her conga-and-horn-heavy title track entered the Top 10 Pop and Black Singles Charts and stayed on the radio that summer.

With the movie complete, Morris Day moved from Minneapolis to LA. He wanted a solo deal with Warner and a career in movies. Prince was beside himself. They needed Morris to help promote the new film, and The Time's latest album *Ice Cream Castles*. Bandmates reached out and persuaded Day to join them in a video for their lead single, "Ice Cream Castles." And during this shoot, everyone was relieved to hear Day say he'd soon return for rehearsals. But back in Santa Monica, Day called Pepé Willie to claim Prince's actions were adversely affecting his plans for a solo career. Pepé flew out west for a visit.

The Time kept trying to woo Morris back, to no avail, so Jesse got his wish, according to Prince. Jesse became group leader. But Johnson already had mixed feelings about the pay and workload. And like Jam and Lewis, he wanted creative control. He, too, considered leaving.

Prince was thinking about his twenty-sixth birthday that June. After playing a show, Prince joined a crowd of guests in a sculptor's studio. Everything was purple: the plates, cups, decorations, napkins; even the big musical notes placed on a tall wedding cake. But instead of a plastic bride and groom, someone tucked a copy of the "When Doves Cry" single into its top.

That night, Prince was happy to see his mother Mattie and stepfather Heyward in the room. He also saw André Cymone and Bernadette. A crowd of locals listlessly sang "Happy Birthday." Prince assured them that he loved them but Greg Linder, music editor of the local alternative weekly newspaper *City Pages*, felt "it was an exchange in a show-biz vacuum, with a community that ignored him until he invented Prince."

A day later, Prince slipped into a black shawl and sunglasses and went to the Black Music Awards at The Prom Center. With Morris gone, Jesse Johnson led The Time in a performance of "Jungle Love." After their performance, Prince took the stage to accept an award for "Most Valuable Player" in R&B. Prince saw Mazarati take the stage and receive more cheers than The Time. "He needed someone to take the place of The Time," said a band member. Prince had his lawyers draw up a contract and hand it to his bass player Mark Brown. He'd sign them to his new label Paisley Park.

Recently, Prince had been enjoying the song "Hero Takes A Fall," from the white group The Bangles' Columbia debut *All Over the Place*. He called a band member to say, "I've got a couple of songs for you. I'd like to know if you're interested." Prince offered the Vanity 6 outtake "Jealous Girl" but they rejected it. So now, he passed them "Manic Monday." "He had a demo that was very specifically him," member Vicki Peterson remembered as Nilsen reported. Prince offered the song when Warner already had Apollonia 6's version on advance copy cassettes of their album. But The Bangles wanted it, so Prince told them to credit it to "Christopher." Then he told Warner the song wouldn't be on *Apollonia 6* after all.

The album was set for release. Warner could have blown their tops. Instead, they quietly, patiently removed the number.

In early June 1984, Prince had his managers call Lisa's brother David Coleman. David, who joined Lisa in the group Waldorf Salad on A&M, had also played cello on a few things during the past year. "We're representing Prince," a manager said. "He wishes you a Happy Birthday and he's giving you two days lockout at Sunset Sound." Lockout meant twenty-four hours of time. In the studio, David quickly recorded "Around the World in a Day," a new song inspired by the high school sweetheart from Beirut that inspired him to learn Arabic. During his sessions, David played a groove with the usual instruments. But he also used an Arabic guitar, the oud, a Darbuka drum, and finger cymbals. Pleased with the results, David passed the tape to relatives. Lisa soon played it for Prince. Its childlike sound and psychedelic flavor excited him. He said, "Oh, my God, listen to that chorus." Prince wanted to cover it. And when he ran into David at a concert, he raved. This was what he wanted to try, Prince added.

12

ANOTHER LONELY CHRISTMAS

WARNER WAS ABOUT TO RELEASE THE TIME'S THIRD ALBUM, *ICE Cream Castles*. Since Day's departure, the new Time lineup with Jesse singing had played only one show. They sat around the warehouse, growing restless. One day without warning, Prince entered and faced them all. "Morris is gone. But I'm going to start a new band, and you're going to be the lead singer." He pointed at a flummoxed young newcomer, Paul Peterson.

But Jesse Johnson didn't think having a white musician take over as The Time's lead singer would work. And so Johnson, who had been with the band since its inception, left. Jerry Hubbard and Mark Cardenas went with him. The Time was over.

But Prince was unfazed. He told the remaining members they'd still form a new band called The Family. Peterson (renamed St. Paul) would be front man and bassist. Jellybean Johnson and Jerome Benton would reprise their Time roles as drummer and backup singer. His current girlfriend Susannah, Wendy's twin, would share lead vocals and play keyboard.

Then in late June, he made another personnel decision. He attended Bruce Springsteen's concert at the St. Paul Civic Center, part of Springsteen's Born in the USA Tour, and saw black saxophonist Clarence Clemmons take center stage during many numbers. "Prince went backstage to talk with Bruce and Clarence Clemmons," said Eric Leeds. "The idea of having a horn player may have sparked something in him."

Eric Leeds played sax. And his brother Alan already worked for Prince. "He auditioned for Sheila's band and Prince heard his demo tape," Alan explained. But Eric wasn't a huge Prince fan. He was "more of a jazz head," and in no rush to join The Family. While his brother Alan spent weeks convincing him to come—recalling, "It took a while"—Prince entered the warehouse to start creating The Family's debut. Susan Rogers engineered. "He was excited and wrote the basic tracks very, very fast," she said.

June 25, 1984, five weeks after "When Doves Cry," Warner shipped the album *Purple Rain.* "Apollonia and I slept under a hotel table waiting for the reviews of [the album]," he claimed. "We were so excited we couldn't sleep. When we saw them, they were all good." *Rolling Stone*'s Kurt Loder heard echoes of Jimi Hendrix in the guitar riff that ended "Let's Go Crazy," the opening of "When Doves Cry," and the title track, which evoked Jimi's "Angel" and included "a very Hendrixian lyrical tinge ('It's time we all reach out for something new—that means you, too')."

More than just critics were pleased. Warner was delighted. It took almost four years for *Dirty Mind* to reach the half-million sales mark (it did so in June 1984). And two years for *1999*—still on the charts at this point—to sell over 2.5 million. But *Purple Rain* matched *1999*'s sales within weeks. A larger audience in fact would keep the album at No. 1 for six months.

Suddenly, Prince was in the full spotlight. Many questioned his relationship with Apollonia. But their working rapport had seen better days. He wanted her to eat what he did, she said ("often just candy and tea," a reporter claimed). She had to stop seeing Van Halen's lead singer David Lee Roth. One night, in her motel room, she found a Bible, opened to a Scripture he wanted her to study. "He wanted to make everyone clones of himself," she later told *People* magazine. Reporters meanwhile claimed she was his latest sexy girlfriend. "He made me promise I wouldn't date anyone publicly during promotion of the film," she continued in *People.* Asked if they were dating, she coyly replied, "I never kiss and tell." Another time, while speaking to *Ebony,* she said, "He loves his women but music comes first. He is married to his music and no woman can compete with that."

In July 1984, Warner Bros. invited critics and studio employees to an advance afternoon screening of the long-awaited film *Purple Rain.* The soundtrack had already sold almost 2.5 million copies. "This is serious business," *Time* noted. And Hollywood gossip said *Purple Rain* would make him a star.

Michael Jackson remained intrigued. CBS/Epic had just released the first single from The Jacksons' *Victory,* and their "State of Shock," with guest Mick Jagger, was in the Top 5. Epic had also shipped a historic 2 million copies of *Victory* to stores. Jackson made sure Warner knew he wanted to attend the film screening. Warner obliged the assertive superstar, but he ran late. At the small theater on the Burbank lot executives delayed the preview for his arrival.

Finally, Jackson arrived in sequined jacket and sunglasses. He spoke to no one. When the lights went down, he slid into a seat in the last row and watched the film through sunglasses. Finally, ten minutes before it ended (when it became an extended Prince concert), he rose and left. Outside, an entourage member asked his opinion. "The music's okay, I guess. But I don't like Prince. He looks mean, and I don't like the way he treats women. He reminds me of some of my relatives. And not only that," he added. "That guy can't act at all. He's really not very good." Jackson could only have been relieved.

Prince was also reportedly present, watching it with longtime supporter Russ Thyret of Warner in the next seat. When it ended, Thyret smiled. "It ain't *Gone with the Wind* but it ain't bad." Neither were record sales. July 18, Warner released "Let's Go Crazy" as the second single from the soundtrack and saw it become his second No. 1 hit.

Prince kept crossing paths with Michael Jackson. And while *Thriller* made Jackson pop's biggest draw, Prince's own fame was increasing. In mid-July 1984, Prince attended one of the Victory Tour's three dates in Dallas's Texas Stadium. Prince's bodyguards arranged seating on scaffolding above the crowd of forty thousand, and waited until the lights dimmed before leading him in. Near concert's end, Prince rose to leave.

A girl below saw him.

His guards knew what would happen next.

Chick quickly leaned in, whispering, "Whatever you do, do not run . . ."

"Well, he panicked and started to run," another guard recalled. Even more people noticed Prince and got excited. Suddenly, leaving the stadium became a trial. Girls went crazy. A mob tried to grab his hair, his clothing, anything. Six bodyguards surrounded Prince and shoved the frail musician toward the exit.

"Needless to say," a guard explained, "Prince never ran again."

Thursday evening, July 26, Prince left his hotel in Los Angeles. He saw flowers in a garden out front and picked one. He entered the limo that would carry him to Hollywood. Chick was near the driver up front. Alan Leeds was near him in the backseat. Prince held his flower during the tense and quiet ride. It was a big moment—the premiere of the film *Purple Rain,* and everyone knew this would make him a major star "or be one of the most embarrassing flops of all time," said Leeds. They knew the performance scenes were terrific but wondered if "the film would draw interest."

As planned, a series of limousines delivered the film's stars individually. Club owner Billy Sparks, Morris Day, Jerome, The Time, and Apollonia 6 strolled the red carpet leading to the entrance. Wendy and Lisa, drummer Bobby Z, Dr. Fink, and Brown Mark did, too. They each waved to fans, granted short TV interviews, and let hundreds of photographers snap shots. Prince's car would arrive last. When it did, security people at curbside would help him make his grand entrance.

A block from the theater, the limo stopped. The driver awaited a cue to keep driving. Leeds was ready to jump out, run ahead, and make sure everything at curbside was ready. But before Leeds opened his door, Chick turned on his walkie-talkie. Anxious, Prince asked, "What's going on there? Can we go yet?"

Chick turned. "The guys say there's a traffic jam two blocks long, more fans than the police can handle and more cameras than a photography store!"

Prince suddenly gripped Leeds's hand tightly. With breaking voice, he whispered, "Whhh . . . aa . . . tttt d-diid he saayy?" Just as stunned, Leeds tightly held his hand. "He said we're gonna have a day to be proud of and it's gonna be fun. Now let me get to the theater and I'll meet you there." Prince hadn't shown any vulnerability during the filmmaking process. Leeds was touched. But just as quickly, Prince snapped, "Yeah, hurry up over there. And don't let them mess this up!"

His mother Mattie and his stepfather Heyward Baker were in the crowd outside Grauman's Chinese Theatre. Nearing the entrance she looked at the stars around her, many of whom Prince had personally invited. Eddie Murphy (then riding high with comedic action movies) was there. Television star Morgan Fairchild was near her boyfriend, who worked as a camera operator on the film. Christopher Reeve, the big-screen Superman, told someone he was a new fan. Co-manager Joe Ruffalo had socialite Beverly Sassoon hanging on his arm. Bob Cavallo meanwhile concealed his nervousness. TV sex symbols Donna Mills and Lisa Hartman posed for paparazzi. Hartman's escort, Henry Thomas of *E.T.*, was also among the celebrities on the lilac carpet leading into the theater. Kevin Bacon of *Footloose*, Stevie Nicks, producer Quincy Jones, and John Cougar Mellencamp also attended. His mother blurted, "I can't believe all the stars."

Best of all, an MTV crew broadcast the event live. MTV video jockey Mark Goodman—who donned purple socks for the occasion—greeted celebrities as they left limousines on Hollywood Boulevard. Thousands of fans pressed against police barricades. A public address system played his interview comments.

Apollonia arrived in her transparent sequin- and feather-covered lavender gown. Lisa walked the red carpet, remembering her school days. Back then, she waited for her bus home at the stop right across the street. Dez was stunned when he arrived. "I've never seen so many flashbulbs," he said. Paul Peterson was just as amazed. "It didn't hit me how big Prince is until I got here and saw the limos, and having to stop for pictures coming into the theater, and just having someone telling me where to go."

As the purple limo neared the theater, Prince could hear screams and cheers. He left the car in his purple trench coat and with a purple flower in hand. With giant Chick at his side, Prince maintained a blank expression and marched directly inside. Fans saw he wouldn't stop for an interview or pose for their photos, and they started booing. MTV's Goodman told them, "Don't feel bad. He doesn't talk to anyone."

Inside, Prince took his seat near drummer Bobby, Bobby's wife, and Bobby's mother. About five hundred audience members had waited on long lines to buy ten-dollar tickets.

As the film began, viewers cheered various scenes. They screamed when Dez appeared on screen. In his seat, Dez couldn't believe it.

Then, when the bar manager told the Kid his music made no sense to anyone but himself, a young female viewer cried, "It does to me." Another woman yelled, "I love you." A third said, "I love you more." When the crowd laughed at jokes on screen, Prince smiled.

The film over, Prince and fellow audience members headed to the Palace Theatre, which had purple searchlights outside for the occasion. Ushers handed women purple orchids as they entered. Inside the theater, guests saw purple wherever they looked—flowers in vases, purple balloons, streamers taped to the ceiling, napkins, tablecloths. Reporters asked various guests for reviews. Eddie Murphy stopped moving through the crowd with bodyguards long enough to tell a TV audience of millions, "Prince is bad." Lionel Richie, enjoying his own string of hit ballads and MTV videos, offered similar praise and predicted, "Now everyone is going to want to make their own movie." Steven Spielberg, riding high off *E.T.*, said he didn't give reviews. Bob Cavallo meanwhile smoked a cigar in triumph.

Many of Prince's musicians excitedly listened to Harold Ramis, star of the summer blockbuster *Ghostbusters*, praise Morris Day's performance. Morris meanwhile moved through the crowd with his own two bodyguards. Jerome Benton told hometown reporter Jon Bream, "I feel sixty feet tall." Jellybean Johnson told Bream, "This is like a dream come true." Bobby Z told him, "Prince is bringing back the days of Old Hollywood." But soon, guests noticed Prince was nowhere in sight. They faced a stage, where a new Minneapolis discovery (called "an unnamed band with dancers" by one reporter) performed. Then Sheila came out and played for forty minutes. Finally, Prince took the stage. He didn't address the crowd in any way. After playing three songs with The Revolution, Prince left, and stayed backstage for the rest of the night.

By Monday morning, the numbers were in. *Purple Rain* had earned $7.7 million in its opening weekend, replacing the effects-laden blockbuster *Ghostbusters* as America's top-grossing film. At twenty-six, Prince simultaneously had a single ("Let's Go Crazy"), an album, and a movie at No. 1 on various *Billboard* and box-office charts. Prince had reached heights previously scaled only by Elvis and the Beatles.

"We looked around and I knew we were lost," Prince told *Paper*. "There was no place to go but down. You can never satisfy the need after that."

In August, *Purple Rain* and the Jacksons' Victory Tour competed for headlines in the national media. August 4 saw The Jacksons' album debut at No. 4 on the *Billboard* 200. But by August 21, Prince's "When Doves Cry" had sold over half a million copies. With *Purple Rain* electrifying audiences in theaters, and urban and pop radio embracing its soundtrack, more reporters seemed interested in covering him. *Rolling Stone*'s film review ran in August, and Kurt Loder's title said it all ("Prince stunning in 'Purple Rain'"). That same month's *New Yorker* notice ("The Charismatic Half-and-Halfs") described his "neo-Liberace finery" and praised the music, but noted that once "When Doves Cry" played over a montage of the

Kid regretting his treatment of Apollonia "we have nothing to do but listen to the words, which are not its strong point." In the *Los Angeles Herald-Examiner*, Mikal Gilmore compared it to *Citizen Kane*, adding that Prince "dominates the screen" like Brando in *The Wild One*. *LA Times* critic Robert Hilburn liked his "presence" but rejected the film as weak. *The Los Angeles Herald* declared it "the best rock movie ever made."

With the movie a sudden pop culture phenomenon, radio stations kept playing his music, fueling even more sales. In August, *Purple Rain* started outselling The Jacksons' *Victory* and Bruce Springsteen's *Born in the U.S.A.*, and *People* opined, "With his slightly sinister flash and sensuality, he provides an antidote to the eerie asexuality of Michael Jackson." There were "an unusually large number of million-selling albums," *Rolling Stone* noted. Record retailers had had a prosperous summer, and expected high sales until winter. But most successful was *Purple Rain*, which sold 5 million copies since June 13, and kept outdoing the competition "by as much as four to one."

One week in August, customers of the Record Bar, a 160-store North Carolina–based chain, bought nearly 15,000 copies. The chain's second-bestselling album that week, Julio Iglesias's *1100 Bel Air Place*, sold only 3,288 copies. Said Norman Hunter, manager of buying, "*Purple Rain* right now is our biggest-selling record of all time outside of the Christmas season."

Bruce Springsteen's *Born in the U.S.A.* sold 2.5 million copies; the Jacksons' *Victory* sold over 2.5; Tina Turner's *Private Dancer* sold around 1.3. "But the big story is Prince," said *Rolling Stone*.

In September, Prince kept dropping by Minneapolis's Met Center, to rehearse for the big tour. By now, reporters were beginning to pitch publishers on biographies about him. "It just seemed like a no-brainer to write a book about a pop genius," Barney Hoskyns noted. "There weren't many around in the eighties."

The Family album was just about finished, but Prince decided to hold it until after the Purple Rain Tour. In various studios, he focused again on the next album. And where The Revolution assumed he'd include them in songwriting, now he worked alone. After *Purple Rain*, Alan Leeds explained, "They had an enormously inflated sense of their importance to the project." Everyone knew Prince was the star, Leeds elaborated. And while fans did love The Revolution, with many choosing their favorite members, "some of us reckoned that whomever was in Prince's band would [receive] similar appreciation. It was Prince they paid to see and hear."

They resented him for, as they put it, sneaking off to studios without them. They were also griping about money. Prince was a multimillionaire now but, Mark Brown claimed, paid each band member only $2,200 a week. Some were also still smarting about the end of the tour, when he gave each member a $15,000 bonus. "It was a slap in the face," Brown felt. "We had grossed him over $80 million." Brown, however, did not blame Prince directly; he attributed these compensation decisions to Prince's management team.

At any rate, Prince wanted to record a new song without them. He had Steve Fargnoli call David Coleman again. He wanted to cover David's "Around the World in a Day." David not only let him, he was willing to bring his reels and instruments to the warehouse in Eden Prairie. On September 16, Prince met David and his musical partner—and Wendy's brother, Jonathan Melvoin—at the warehouse and played with exotic instruments, and filled his new version with a playful energy. Prince added his drum machine and voice, and changed the lyric, but kept Coleman's title and chorus. Prince liked the result and wanted the rest of the album to be just as daring.

So far, Prince was having a phenomenal year. Music fans quickly snatched up The Time's *Ice Cream Castle,* and Sheila E.'s *The Glamorous Life.* Then October 1, Warner released *Apollonia 6.* But while their single "Sex Shooter" reached No. 14 on the Black Chart and 85 on the Pop Chart, and with the album at No. 62 on the Pop Chart, and 24 on the Black Chart, Warner mysteriously decided there would be no more singles. Publicists stopped working the record. The group vanished.

The Tour was starting in November. But Prince was almost finished with *Around the World in a Day,* what he'd taken to calling his next album. Everyone expected another *Purple Rain,* but he wanted to please his core audience. The new sounds would probably sell less but he didn't care. "It keeps a roof over your head," he said of high sales in *Mojo,* "and keeps money in all these folks' pockets that I got hangin' around here!" But money and soul were different. "I wouldn't mind if I just went broke," he claimed. If he could still play heartfelt music for crowds, he'd be happy.

In Detroit, he started his "Purple Rain Tour." "And everything connected with the concert tour had to be approved by him," *Ebony* noted. Seven shows were already sold out. Opening night, the modern Joe Louis Arena held over 300 writers and photographers, some from overseas, 19,000 paying customers, about 150 guards, and Detroit police officers.

During her opening set, Sheila stripped down to a G-string bikini, twirled a drumstick, and asked, "Do you want to play my timbales?" But fans in purple interrupted. "We want Prince! We want Prince!"

After a lengthy intermission, the lights dimmed. A synthesizer chord rang. Everyone cheered. It was 9:40, and he whispered, "Detroit. My name is Prince and I've come to play with you." The curtain flew up. He stood on a raised platform, in "a Hendrixian outfit" (shiny purple jacket, white serape top, and tight bell-bottoms). Then he slid down a firefighter's pole as smoke bombs exploded and colorful confetti and the tops of fifteen thousand carnations dropped from the rafters.

The band played "Let's Go Crazy" over the largest quadraphonic sound system ever prepared for an arena show, but it sounded horrible. For a second, Prince visibly reacted. Then he kept singing and twirling in circles. What could he do?

Prince played his upbeat 1999 single "Delirious." Then, during "1999," he handed lilies to the crowd. After half of "Little Red Corvette," he stopped singing and went into the splits and slides seen in his video. But when he ran across the stage, sliding toward the microphone, a writer recalled, "He didn't quite pull it off. The mike clunked noisily to the ground." He did another spin, and fell.

The audience wasn't predominantly black or "a typical white rock and roll one," *Rolling Stone* said. It was mostly white, with camera-clutching teens that knew him only from the movie. Anticipating this, Prince tailored most of the show to them, including every *Purple Rain* song but "Take Me With U" in his fourteen-song set. He added four 1999 songs and two recent B-sides but eschewed "When You Were Mine," "Head," "Uptown" or anything from *Dirty Mind* and *Controversy*. Prince also had his most ostentatious light show yet, and many costumes waiting in the wings (annoying critics to no end). He kept imitating mannerisms of Carlos Santana or Jimi Hendrix. But music and choreography from the film brought the most applause.

During the early shows crowd reaction was "as close as anyone could get to a 'Beatles' experience," said tour manager Alan Leeds. "Surreal." Matt Fink said, "It was just insanity."

A hundred outfits had matching boots. "Every night he was breaking heels," tour manager Leeds explained. They asked an old Italian boot designer in New York, who usually did theatrical wardrobe, to make more. "The only problem is I've got a dozen boots to make for Luther Vandross," he said. "As soon as that's done, we can move to yours." An employee pulled out her American Express gold card. "Luther who?"

He was just as competitive on stage. Before anyone knew it, Prince invited the self-described "Boss," Bruce Springsteen on stage. After handing Springsteen a guitar for a solo, Prince took it away and held it over Bruce's head. While playing a few notes Prince pretended it didn't work before facing it with confusion. Then Prince relaxed his face. He played a hot riff and made an expression that told the audience, "It's fine now that *I'm* playing it."

After a show, bodyguard Harlan "Hucky" Austin told Housequake .com, Prince would arrive at his hotel. Austin would have made sure no fans were there, so he'd make an inconspicuous entrance. After dinner, he'd watch tapes, seeking ways to improve the show. His bodyguard would then leave to find a club for a surprise appearance. Prince would head there, play a show, and leave at about 4:00 A.M. By the time Prince woke up, the guard would be in the next city, arranging for another hotel, transportation, and safe travel routes. At noon, Prince's morning flight would arrive at the next city's airport. The guard would lead him to a limousine for a ride to the next hotel room. Knowing his fans might call various establishments to learn where he was staying while in town, Prince would register with an alias. At this point, Austin continued, Prince might sleep or shop. But within hours, he saw the guard again, and reached the venue for sound check. Usually, he started each Purple Rain show at eight o'clock, finished, and started the cycle again; a demanding, but monotonous schedule he kept five to six days a week.

What made it even more taxing was the fact that new melodies kept arriving when least expected. Even brushing his teeth could lead to seeing the brush shake, dropping it, and a race across a hotel room to "get to a bass guitar, quick!" as *Mojo* reported. So between shows, he began to book time in various studios. But taping led to another problem. Since he wrote and recorded so much, he sometimes caught himself trying to rehash an old hit. "You think you hit on something, right! You try to do it again."

Thankfully, Wendy or Lisa would react to these retreads by saying, "Hey, man, I've heard that. Put it away." He'd arrange to shove these tapes into a vault that now held 320 other works.

Halfway through the tour, when he reached South Carolina for three nights, he invited Eric Leeds to visit. Eric arrived the second night, and Prince immediately asked if he had his horn. The older seasoned player did. Prince had Eric get on stage and play some saxophone during his long closer, "Baby I'm a Star." At one point, Prince even ordered the band to stop playing so fifteen thousand people could hear Eric solo. He liked the sound—and respite from material and an image that now bored him—and invited Eric to stay. Wendy didn't mind—she had her guitar solo before he started singing "Purple Rain" and played for a few minutes during its break. But in Santa Barbara, right before an encore, he told the band Eric would handle this and she turned pale. "Just crushed," said Alan Leeds.

Fans kept buying tickets and wearing purple. Screaming lyrics. Cheering for the set, splits, and between-song banter. Twenty-four concerts in seven cities grossed an estimated $7 million. He earned even more from sales of tour merchandise, T-shirts, a tour book (which told fans, "U should come more often"), and a replica of the hand puppet he spoke to in the film.

The album itself passed the 10 million mark. The film grossed over $70 million in the U.S. "In some ways, it was more detrimental than good," he said in *Entertainment Weekly*. People's perception changed "and it pigeonholed me." At concerts, kids screamed simply "because that's where the audience screamed in the movie."

The unrelenting pace began to exact its toll. Backstage one night, Prince prepared for "the seventy-fifth Purple Rain show, doing the same thing over and over" for a young pop audience. "And I just lost it. I said: 'I can't do it!'" They were putting the guitar on him.

It hit him in the eye and cut him.

Blood flowed down his shirt. "I have to go onstage," he shrieked.

Prince had to escape this. "I couldn't play the game," he told *Icon*. His next album—it would change all this. He kept recording in a mobile truck. When halls emptied after some shows, he jammed with the weary band to see if anything came of it. The next album would get him away from *Purple Rain*. And he'd get it out there while this large audience—bigger than the ones that bought his earlier works—were eager to hear his next release.

December 1984, Prince was booked for a five-night stand at Minnesota's Saint Paul Civic Center. He was on the cusp, finally, of escaping the same batch of soundtrack songs, including fewer guitar solos, making things slower, losing the choruses encouraging listeners to party.

Since he kept flying to studios in Minneapolis or Los Angeles between shows, or using mobile trucks, there was only one song left to record, a rock ballad called "The Ladder." Another long and windy opus in the "Free" tradition, Prince claimed it included a chord structure his father John liked to use. Some felt the song was included as a way to improve the relationship between father and son. Since the jam session before the 1999 Tour, when Prince let John sit in with the band, they had seen him invite his father on trips; include him in songwriting credits; and keep seeking ways to involve John in his career. Now, they figured Prince wanted to claim John wrote some of these new songs to put some more money in the old man's pocket. Still, more people felt John was trying to ride Prince's coattails. Local writer Neal Karlen shook his head. "I'm not sure where those coattails would lead him," Karlen opined. He might get some money or feel proud but "he wasn't trying to rejuvenate his career or anything."

Either way, Prince taught "The Ladder" to the band during a sound check and recorded it the next day, December 30, at a warehouse. By the time he finished, Prince had taped booming echo, a fairy tale narration, striking piano, slow drums, and his girlfriend Susannah and singer Taja Sevelle's dragging backup vocals. The next day, Prince had to play the last of five shows at the Civic Center. It was Christmas Eve, so promoters made it a matinee. But Prince also had Susan Rogers load all the tapes into a mobile truck and drive over to his purple house on Kiowa Drive.

After the concert, Prince arrived to find Rogers waiting in the driveway. He recorded a final vocal, the dialog that ended "Temptation," then gathered the songs he'd recorded since January 1984. Even with Rogers helping, he didn't finish sequencing *Around* until 4:00 A.M.

"He had nobody over there at Christmas, which is typical of him," she said. "He was mainly interested in getting his record cut together."

PART | TWO
The REIGN

13

THE LADDER

PURPLE RAIN'S TWENTY-FOUR-WEEK STAY AT NO. 1 WAS THE fourth longest reign in pop album history. Further, it yielded five hit singles, including his first two chart-toppers ("When Doves Cry" and "Let's Go Crazy") His ballad "Purple Rain" meanwhile reached No. 2. *The New York Times* called him "vulgar." The *San Francisco Chronicle* said "rude and raunchy." The Minneapolis *Star Tribune* called him "an elf of a man . . . with a shock of hair that looks like it was treated with Crisco and an egg-beater." *Newsweek* saw a "self-taught prodigy." Another white writer opined that the film made him "a lot more real to people" since it showed he was more than "a strange, maybe gay, quasi-rock-and-roller, exactly the kind of entertainer whites don't trust." Yet, no one denied his amazing success. In fact, *Rolling Stone* named him Rock Artist of the Year.

He remained guarded, rejecting more interviews than most stars dream of getting. So, reporters got creative. One Saturday morning, his mother Mattie answered her door with cigarette in hand. She had earned her master's then started working (like André's mom, Bernadette) as a social worker in the Minneapolis school system. Faced with a reporter that morning, she said, "No interviews. We just don't give them." Hearing each book or article describe her differently—*Musician* said she was Italian, while Steven Ivory's book *Prince* said she hailed from Baton Rouge—she replied, "I'm from here. I've lived here all my life. I'm from Minneapolis." With that, she closed her door. His father John meanwhile told local paper the *Star Tribune* that *Purple Rain*'s depiction of him as a gun-packing wife beater was inaccurate; he never used a gun.

With the next album finished, Prince was free to attend the twelfth annual American Music Awards. But by night's end, his image had suffered even more. At the January 28, 1985, ceremony, his bodyguard told everyone "they gotta turn around because Prince's girlfriend was walking by," Cyndi Lauper recalled. It turned out to be her pal Sheila E., "and nobody was supposed to look at her. And he told that to Stevie Wonder!" (Wonder of course was blind.) Like many in the auditorium, Lauper liked and respected Prince—her debut included a cover of his "When You Were Mine"—but she thought, *C'mon, now. Now you've crossed the line.* His bodyguards also supposedly asked the group Night Ranger (the group behind such hits as "Don't Tell Me You Love Me" and "Sister Christian," and seated behind him at the awards ceremony) not to address or acknowledge him. And when Prince won three awards that night, the guards joined him on the dais while he accepted them.

Another misstep, with longer-reaching repercussions, involved his skipping a recording session immediately after the ceremony. The session was for a star-studded single whose proceeds would benefit starving people in Africa. Superstar Michael Jackson had everyone ready to record. Lionel Richie, producer Quincy Jones, and arranger Tom Bahler had already chosen vocal pairings: Tina Turner and Billy Joel, Dionne Warwick and country singer Willie Nelson, and so on. Someone pitched Michael and Prince but Michael reportedly refused. Either way, producers paired Michael with Diana Ross. When the awards show ended, a crowd of over forty stars followed producer Quincy Jones to the "We Are the World" recording session.

Prince didn't attend.

Instead, he went to Carlos 'n' Charlie, a Mexican restaurant on Sunset. And when he left at 2:00 A.M., he led Jill Jones into his car. They got inside, he said. But a photographer did, too. His bodyguard Lawrence Gibson—who stood six nine and weighed three hundred pounds—leaped forward. So did his second bodyguard, Wally Safford. They pulled the man out, but he supposedly hit his head in the car. He dropped the camera, which fell and broke. Someone called the cops.

Prince didn't show for the recording session. But at six the next morning, Fargnoli called A&M studio to ask if Prince could come lay down a guitar part. Quincy said it wasn't necessary.

February 1, in New Orleans, his concert attracted seventy thousand fans despite the media hounding him for not attending the recording session. The next day, he had a day off. In the enormous Superdome, he set up instruments and a recorder and taped "4 the Tears in Your Eyes," a moving work about Jesus and the crucifixion. In a black-and-white video, he simply sat in a chair in neat dress shirt and topcoat and strummed an acoustic guitar. His straightened hair, mascara-ringed eyes, and meek facial expressions evoked Michael Jackson. When he finished, he faced the lens and said, in deep voice, "Thank you." He sent it to the creators of the *USA for Africa* album—even rerecorded it for a video he sent to the people behind the global Live Aid marathon—in hopes of making up for his absence from the recording sessions. But reporters wouldn't let up on hounding him.

Warner would release *Around the World in a Day*, the first release on Prince's own Paisley Park Records label, in April. Until late January, only a few top Warner executives knew about it. He submitted its strange cover. Instead of a band photo, artist Doug Henders painted an image. He and band members wore funky sixties clothes and stood on a colorful landscape heavy on cloud-filled skies with bright hues. Henders depicted him with gray, shoulder-length hair and a white scarf covering a haggard face. In one hand, he held a tiny ladder. He chose this new approach, he said in *Rolling Stone*, "because I thought people were tired of looking at me. Who wants another picture of him?"

Thursday, February 21, someone telephoned Warner's offices late that afternoon to say its biggest star would arrive at the Burbank tower in forty-five minutes. Office phones buzzed. A huge crowd of employees rushed to the front lobby. Some of Prince's staff quickly descended on a fourth-floor conference room with special decorating supplies.

At about 5:00 P.M., a shiny purple limousine arrived. Prince exited it along with his father, guards, managers, and guitarist Wendy. He wore a long, purple antique kimono and striped, pajama-type pants. Prince held a single pink rose while entering the corporate tower. In the lobby, he smiled when a crowd applauded.

His entourage passed more fans in stairways and corridors. They entered the conference room, now decorated with hundreds of purple helium balloons and white streamers. Various Warner employees—*Rolling Stone* claimed there were 150 while other published reports claimed as few as 20—were waiting, including president Lenny Waronker and board chairman Mo Ostin. After a few words with Ostin, Prince silently sat on the floor near Wendy and his father and stared at the ground, holding the rose as tapes of the album played at full volume.

"Condition of the Heart" was a solo performance, a haunting ballad with moody piano, falsetto vocal, and dramatic silences. "Raspberry Beret" didn't have many overbearing guitars but its strings evoked late-sixties acid rock. He sang side one's final cut "Tambourine," over bare drums.

Side two had "America," which quoted lyrics to "America the Beautiful" with "an American Indian feel," a reporter claimed. "The Ladder" was the plodding ballad he claimed he wrote with his father. Then "Temptation" lasted eight minutes and twenty-one seconds. It started, *Rolling Stone* said, with "Hendrix-style guitar" and ended with "a weird rap that sounds like a dialogue between Prince and God."

Around found Prince abandoning the *Purple Rain* character and returning to real concerns. He sang about utopia, masturbation, loneliness, politics, and religion. Musically, Prince tapped into the sixties, but only superficially, without substance. Still, the album teems with inventive sounds that have stood the test of time: the exotic riffs on his title track; that funky beat on "Tambourine"; the giant drums and roaring guitar on "Paisley Park"; and his timeless, haunting classic, "Condition of the Heart." Some songs are too slow; many lack choruses. But despite minor flaws, *Around* stands as one of Prince's most inventive albums ever, only a step below *Purple Rain*.

It was very different from *Purple Rain* but Warner employees clapped for every song. Still, Prince felt the label didn't really like or understand it. "Everyone sort of stood up, and applauded after the record was over, and then he wasn't there anymore," said one employee. Prince soon told Eric Leeds he could tell by their faces it wasn't working. He laughed. "Well, sometimes you know right away that you're not going to reach some people but that's okay. It still was where I was at the time.'"

The world was awaiting the next Prince album. Only days remained before Warner shipped albums to stores. Warner thought "Paisley Park" (and nonalbum song "She's Always in My Hair") could work as lead single on February 27, the day after the Grammy Awards. But Prince changed his mind. He didn't want *any* single out there. Especially not one that could lead reporters to claim he wanted to distract pop fans from USA for Africa's "We Are the World."

February 26 at the Shrine Auditorium, Wendy's father, Mike, stood onstage in a black tuxedo. Tonight, they'd celebrate the success of a very special performer, he announced. The crowd at this Grammy Awards service interrupted with whoops of delight. Mike spoke through them. This next performer had taken the music world by storm, he continued. "He's always been the cutting edge of music. It gives me extra added pleasure to introduce him because my daughter Wendy is a member of The Revolution."

The crowd roared.

Prince took the stage in a light baggy shirt with fringed sleeves, and slacks with buttons running down the sides of his legs. His big hair made him resemble Sly Stone or James Brown. In front of a huge light on the dim stage, Prince did some high-pitched birdcalls and clapped his hands over his head to the disco beat. When he sang into a mic on a stand, he stumbled and hit himself in the mouth. He pretended it didn't happen, kept performing his few dance moves. These and the squeals, Jheri curls, and shrieks made him seem like a funky Jackson type.

Before long, Prince turned away from the crowd and wiggled his butt; he stood near Jerome, leaping in the air while doing the "Jungle Love" dance; then paused for Sheila's long solo. Oddly, a midget ran onto the stage. Audience members did, too. Prince's shirt was halfway off now. Other musicians, including Grace Jones, danced and had fun on stage. Prince ran into the crowd, shirtless, with Big Chick trailing; he marched out with raised arms, triumphant.

Big Chick's days working with Prince were nearing their end. Since the LA incident surrounding the paparazzo, Prince told *Rolling Stone*, Chick had been antsy, nervous he'd lose his job. Then Chick started using more coke. One day, Prince spoke to him. The guard blurted, "What are you jumping on me for? What's wrong? Why all of a sudden are you changing?"

Chick's paranoia increased. He now believed people, including Prince, were out to get him. "I started thinking he was doing me wrong, which he wasn't." Finally, Chick told Prince, "I'm tired. I've had enough." He liked Prince but had to leave.

14

INTERNATIONAL LOVER

MARCH 25, PRINCE ARRIVED AT THE DOROTHY CHANDLER PAVIL-
ion, in LA, for the fifty-seventh Academy Awards ceremony. His purple
hood, tight slacks, and high heels drew stares. And his entrance—raised
chin, blank stare—struck some reporters and photographers as arrogant.
But what could he do? Stop and tell them he was a little nervous and ago-
raphobic? Inside, he joined Wendy and Lisa near the legendary Jimmy
Stewart. Fans looked over but Prince ignored them.

Finally, they announced the category of music: Best Original Song
Score. Amazingly, Prince won. Wendy and Lisa joined him at the podium
(Wendy later joked that they looked like *The Addams Family*). Prince faced
the crowd and said he could never imagine this in his wildest dreams.

His plan, for a continuous stream of product, worked. With "When
Doves Cry," the album, and the movie he had released a new product in
each of three consecutive months. When the movie peaked, he launched
his tour. Along the way, he collected an Oscar for his score, three American
Music Awards, and three Grammy Awards. He was as proud—for having
achieved a goal—as he was terrified. "It's my albatross and it'll be hanging
around my neck as long as I'm making music," he said of *Purple Rain*.

Still, he made it through the second leg of the tour from December
26, 1984, to early April. He traveled to 32 cities, playing for 1.7 million fans
at 98 sell-out shows, finished *Around the World in a Day,* and mapped out
his next album.

Before his final show at Miami's Orange Bowl, he had manager Steve
Fargnoli issue an announcement. This would "be his last live appearance
for an indeterminate number of years," Fargnoli said. "I asked Prince what
he planned to do. He told me, 'I'm going to look for the ladder.' So I asked
him what that meant. All he said was, 'Sometimes it snows in April.'"

Reporters were bewildered. Even Johnny Carson began one *Tonight*

Show monologue with "Prince is retiring from show business." And Prince couldn't be happier. "After that things started to open up a little," said Leeds. Prince ended the tour in Miami, even as Warner filled millions of orders for *Around the World in a Day*.

With his newest album arriving in stores, Prince was already at work on his next product. It would be a film called *Under the Cherry Moon*.

After enjoying a sample script by newcomer Becky Johnson, Prince had hired her to create a romantic comedy set in an exotic locale like Miami's Palm Beach or Capri. He wanted *Under the Cherry Moon* to evoke the screwball comedies of the nineteen-twenties and thirties, which already influenced the look he designed for his side project The Family. He also wanted a love story as moving as the one he had spun on his *Around* ballad "Condition of the Heart." Lounge singer Christopher Tracy would meet and fall for rich white woman Mary Sharon, who wore miniskirts and pigtails. Then her father, a disapproving shipping magnate, would have him gunned down. Shot in the back, Christopher would fall, smile, and, with blood on his lip, say, "Hey, we had some fun, didn't we?" It was a simple, timeless story, and a sour look at race relations that he wanted in theaters within an unthinkable three or four months.

But co-manager Steve Fargnoli shook his head. Prince wanted jarring modern slang and black-and-white footage. Fargnoli didn't think it'd work.

Meanwhile, he joined other managers in relaying his strict instructions to Warner regarding *Around*. "Prince's management hasn't even let us run a plain old ad in *Billboard* just announcing that the record had been shipped to the stores," said creative-marketing chief Jeff Ayeroff of Warner. "Any merchandising in the stores is stuff they've done on their own." His campaign was refreshing but "merchandising anarchy." Warner's promotion team was just as stifled. Radio was "very enthusiastic, but we're really not pushing any particular song," said Russ Thyret. Instead, they mailed copies and let stations "pick what they like." The *Los Angeles Times* reported on the dearth of singles, videos, ads, or merchandising displays in record stores. "Either he's crazy or he's Prince—or both."

By April 22, 1985, despite the free-for-all, Warner had shipped a surprising 2.7 million copies. Fans queued outside stores each morning to buy copies. "We haven't had this much excitement in a long time," said an executive at the thirty-four-branch Licorice Pizza chain. "It's almost like in the old days, when the Beatles came out with an album and everybody got it at the same time." But the campaign confused many radio station programmers. LA station KIQQ-FM's program director said no song on the album was so outstanding they had to play it. "For now, we're going to sit back and see what tracks do well in our research studies." Influential KROQ-FM's programmer said, "We think it's going to be as big as *Purple Rain*. The only record I'd compare it to is *Sgt. Pepper's*. We're playing a cut from it every two hours." At MusicVision, a major radio promotion and research firm, executive Lenny Beer reported that Top 40 stations were "practically in shock. For once, they've actually been forced to listen to a record. It's very confusing for them."

Usually, programmers slid advance cassettes into players, heard about forty seconds of a song, and decided whether to add it. "But the Warner promo men are just handing them the record and telling them to play what they like. So they're a little bewildered—they're even calling us and asking us what to play."

The most popular tracks were "Raspberry Beret" and "Pop Life," but with neither on a single, many programmers were "very cautious about making any commitment." But MusicVision's Jon Scott remembered how *Purple Rain* had trouble with rock radio. Upon its release, about 80 percent of rock stations ignored it. "They had to be convinced," said Scott, "and it took a long time for them to see that Prince was a viable artist." His management had no comment. Prince didn't either.

Despite the unusual lack of promotion, and only ten months passing since *Purple Rain*, the new album managed to top the U.S. Album Chart. Some *Purple Rain* fans played their new copies in confusion, but producer Jimmy Jam felt a few tracks retraced some of Prince's earlier steps: "The Ladder" evoked "Purple Rain." "America's" groove was as speedy as "Baby I'm a Star."

Most American reviewers liked it, but felt "America" contained demagogic red-baiting. In Britain, most critics frowned on the cover and implied "Paisley Park," the title track, and crowd noises during "Pop Life" mimicked The Beatles' *Sgt. Pepper's Lonely Hearts Club Band* and *Magical Mystery Tour*. Prince couldn't stand what he was reading. These reviewers claimed he wasn't "talking about anything on this record," he said. Others claimed he was "trying to be this great visionary wizard." He couldn't win.

Still more invoked the Beatles—and "Strawberry Fields Forever"—though they weren't the influence. "[The Beatles] were great for what they did, but I don't know how that would hang today." What most upset him were reviews that claimed black people believed he sold out with *Purple*

Rain. "Oh, come on, come on!" he replied. He had emphasized his upbringing in a mostly white town, where he heard and played every kind of music, he explained. But now, critics were focusing on his race, rather than his music. George Clinton—leader of Parliament-Funkadelic—recently told him he loved the album. And Clinton knew more about black music than some white nerd in glasses and an Izod shirt pecking away at a typewriter.

At tour's end, Prince tried again to involve his father John in his activities. John was in his late sixties, and retired from his thirty-year job at Honeywell, but still a bit bitter about not having made it. Prince flew him out to Los Angeles, let him attend recording sessions, and even briefly considered releasing John's jazz album. Prince also bought him a new customized BMW, and handed him an early copy of *Around*, which supposedly featured John's music on a few songs and sat unopened, in the backseat of the new car. John meanwhile let him have the white Thunderbird he bought in 1966, which had only twenty-two thousand miles on the odometer.

Prince moved on from the album. He was happy about not touring for a while. "There are so many other things to do."

And one of them was music for *Under the Cherry Moon.*

April 17, 1985, only ten days after the last show, he entered Sunset Sound, with plans to create four songs that very day: "Wendy's Parade," "New Position," "I Wonder U," and "Under the Cherry Moon." Even before the success of "Little Red Corvette" and "1999," Prince had other producers reaching for their synthesizers and drum machines. But *Purple Rain*'s success inspired so many imitators he had to work hard to stay a step ahead. By the time imitators tried to mimic "When Doves Cry," he added unexpected strings to 1985's "Raspberry Beret." With imitators suddenly including strings on their works, he reached for ouds and Darbukas. Now, jazz, and The Cocteau Twin's *Treasure*, inspired him, and he would accent horns by Eric Leeds and his pal Atlanta Bliss. He mostly wrote melodies on guitar but remembered how sitting at another instrument, the drums, led to *Around*'s "Tambourine." Thus, at a piano he created the riff that carried his new "Under the Cherry Moon."

In the studio, Susan Rogers had everything ready. "I'm gonna start playing drums and when I stop, don't stop the tape," Prince told her. "Just keep going, just let it roll." He sat at the drum kit, taping lyrics to a nearby music stand. Rogers hit Record and he created one drum pattern after another. After four beats, he rose and approached Rogers in the booth. "All right, here we go. Where is my bass?" He played melodies on the four tracks and moved on to adding sounds from the Fairlight (a sampling keyboard with flute and wind sounds, voices, and hand claps that Wendy and Lisa claimed to have shown him).

He had Wendy and Lisa add backup vocals to some works, and actually let Wendy sing "I Wonder U." He credited his father for helping with "Under the Cherry Moon." After two days, he started "Life Can Be So Nice" with Sheila on drums. The next day, he taped "Others Here With Us" and "Old Friends 4 Sale."

After spending all night on "Old Friends," he wanted to keep working. He had someone call Wendy and Lisa to the studio. When they arrived, he showed them a melody for "Sometimes It Snows in April," and let them interpret it in their style. After a week, he had completed nine songs. The mood around his camp lightened. He had successfully followed *Purple Rain* with *Around*. He was already creating the next album.

He also had time to help Sheila. Fans now knew Sheila as much for her drumming as for the stilettos, paisley print jackets, huge shoulder pads, and hairspray she wore in videos. But she was bone-tired after touring for about a year and living out of a suitcase. Prince brought out "A Love Bizarre," a sax-heavy dance track he wanted on her second album *Romance 1600*. Since he left his guide vocals on it, everyone heard him sing during the chorus, squeal, then dominate the lengthy track's second half.

Work on his own next album continued. During rehearsals, tape rolled. He told the band what he wanted, since he'd already written and arranged the songs, but let them add ideas. If he liked something, he included it. "In nearly every case, Wendy and Lisa were around to provide backing vocals and input," engineer Susan Rogers noted. He also kept including Wendy's sister Susannah—already co-lead in The Family—on new songs and playing this new synth guitar that Bobby Z felt whined "like a duck." Before anyone knew it, he played them a new work, "Girls and Boys," which included its odd sound.

At the board, engineer Susan Rogers considered the songs, which would form the album called *Parade*, "some of his best melodic work."

At the same time, he started working with Mazarati, for his label Paisley Park.

April 28, he was recording in LA while Mazarati was next door with

Mark Brown and David Rivkin. Rivkin arrived in California, from Minneapolis, for a weekend of work. But in Sunset Sound's Studio C, Prince said, "You'll probably be here about a month." Rivkin had enough clothes for three days, but shopped for more. Now, Prince kept wandering into their session to check their progress, but never spoke directly to them. He heard one of Mark's songs, "Fear the Shadow," left, then returned ten minutes later with handwritten new lyrics that turned it into the gentler "Strawberry Lover." Mark's "We Did Things Our Way" inspired another ten-minute writing session and lyric sheet that changed it to "I Guess It's All Over." Prince didn't want credit for these alterations, but Rivkin noted tension. "I don't know if there was something with Mark and Prince, that he didn't want to use Prince's songs."

Then Prince wanted to write something for them. "We were very happy to have one Prince song on the album," said band member Christian. Instead, he delivered two: "100 M.p.h.," recorded in summer 1984 and "Jerk Out," a leftover from *The Time*. When singer Terry Casey rejected "Jerk Out," about a white woman and a black man, the band asked if Prince had anything else.

Prince entered another room with a portable cassette recorder and soon handed Rivkin a tape. "Do what you want with this song!"

He called it "Kiss," and presented a verse and chorus played on acoustic guitar. He told David he'd get him the rest soon. David felt it sounded like folk music by Stephen Stills. "I didn't quite know what to do with it and neither did the group."

Terry couldn't sing it. Its two minutes had no "real indication of a groove." Mark was furious, Rivkin added. "He didn't like that at all, so he walked out of the studio." Rivkin reached for the Linn 9000 drum machine and tapped out a beat. He created intricate hi-hats and copied them in a delay unit. He put the original hi-hat on another track. While playing the beat he kept cutting away to the hi-hat with delay. He added guitar chords, with echo, and had them play the same rhythm as the hi-hat. "That gave us the basic rhythm groove for the song." Mark Brown had returned, and he recorded a bass part. A Mazarati member added a piano part inspired by Bo Diddley's "Hey, Man." Casey sang the lyric, then the others added background vocals based on ideas Z remembered from Brenda Lee's "Sweet Nothings." "This is what we had at the end of the first couple of days," Z sighed. "We were trying to build a song out of nothing, piece by piece." They didn't know where it was heading but knew it was weird. Frustrated, exhausted, they decided to break for the night.

The next morning, Prince was blasting the song on a portable radio while on a basketball court. In Studio 3, he told engineers Susan Rogers and Peggy McCreary, "I'm taking that back!"

He asked their opinions. Rogers said, "Take it back. It's just great!"

Rivkin arrived, and asked what was happening. "This is too good for you guys," Prince said. "I'm taking it back." With Z near him, Prince listened to the track. He wanted something like *Purple Rain's* "When Doves Cry." "We don't need this," Prince said, turning a knob and removing the bass track. Instead, he ran the kick drum through a reverb unit. He slid headphones on and recorded his own vocal, an octave higher. With only nine tracks on the song, he got on the API console. The track sounded pretty dry and empty. Z worried that it sounded *too* stark. Rivkin reached over and sneaked a little piano in. They also applied tape delay to the guitar track. Prince kept moving faders, and he had it mixed in five minutes.

An hour later, Mazarati was playing ping-pong when the song blared over speakers. "Hey, that's the song we did last night!" They were reportedly angry when Prince said he was reclaiming the idea, so Prince added, "Of course you guys will get paid for it." They said, "Sure!" But Prince changed his mind about the song. "Kiss" was *too* strange. He shelved it.

In May, he wanted to hear how all of these strange new songs would sound on one record. While creating a test pressing of *Parade,* he had to decide. Should he really include "Kiss"? He did "as an afterthought," Alan Leeds later wrote, and probably was still not convinced it worked.

May found him using Paisley Park projects to tap into other stars' audiences. With The Family, he had targeted the Duran Duran and Wham! audience. At Sunset Sound, Prince now used Jill Jones's album in progress as a way to compete with another crowd favorite, Tina Turner. With a straight face, he sat with an acoustic guitar, and had Susan Rogers tape him singing a new work called "My Man."

Then he had to head to Manhattan, where Sheila was filming *Krush Groove,* a movie starring Run-D.M.C. He made time to call Chick. He told his former bodyguard he still had a job if he wanted it, and that he "was alone." Chick was happy to hear it and promised to meet him in the city. Prince breathed easier. With this *Krush Groove* movie involving some rough characters, it would pay to have good security.

Director Michael Schultz (of *Cooley High* fame) started principal photography on May 5, and hoped to wrap by May 31. But Sheila wasn't having an easy time of it. For one, some cast members resented her presence. They thought *Krush Groove* would dramatize the rise of Run-D.M.C. but saw producers soften it with a love story and a nonrapping outsider. "A lot of people on the set and a lot of the rappers weren't very cool," Sheila said.

Neither were street-hardened extras at the Disco Fever club in the Bronx. Sheila performed "A Love Bizarre" for cameras but heard the director yell "Cut!" Facing the crowd, Schultz said, "Look, this is a movie and you have to clap for Sheila E. We're not sitting here critiquing her."

In Manhattan, Prince waited for Chick. "He didn't show up." Even without him, Prince reached the Manhattan Center, a theater on Thirty-Fourth Street, where director Schultz quickly filmed performances by Kurtis Blow, Blow's protégés The Fat Boys, Run-D.M.C, young unknown Latin singer Chad, and Sheila. In a dim, mostly empty balcony, Prince took a seat. With raised chin, and blank, regal expression, he watched Sheila take the stage in her gray outfit. Her band feigned playing instruments, while she did "Holly Rock," a track Prince had written aimed at the rap audience, for a crowd of mostly black and Puerto Rican extras dressed like break-dancers or rappers. They didn't seem to like Prince's bongo-heavy take on the genre. But Sheila ignored the nonreaction between takes, and kept playing drums, sliding across the floor, as practiced, lying on her side and pumping her hips while panting into a microphone. Once Schultz yelled cut, extras offered weak applause. Prince quietly left the building. Young LL Cool J, whose upcoming single "Rock the Bells" insulted him *and* Michael Jackson, told a reporter, "Prince and his boys thought we were making *Sheila E. Goes to Hollywood* when the film was really about my homeboys Run-D.M.C. and Kurtis Blow."

He could have really used Chick by his side during this trip. But Chick didn't show. Then someone handed Prince the May 7, 1985, edition of *The National Enquirer*. His eyes widened. A headline read, "The Real Prince—He's Trapped in a Bizarre Secret World of Terror." *The Enquirer* quoted Chick rehashing the usual description of a lonely eccentric. But the story called his Marilyn Monroe posters a shrine; his modest home an armed fortress with a food taster, fountains out front, and a swimming pool. In short, it called Prince a fearful hermit in a self-created prison. In California, co-manager Steve Fargnoli was stunned. "The whole thing was absurd."

15

AT LEAST YOU GOT FRIENDS

PRINCE STRUGGLED TO UNDERSTAND WHAT HAD HAPPENED. Chick was still on the payroll, even after their rift. People he did business with might see this. Eventually, he learned that after promising to meet him in Manhattan, during their phone call, Chick actually hung up, returned to using drugs, and became so hungry for cash he sold this story to *The Enquirer* for a reported three thousand dollars.

Prince initially pretended to ignore it. "I never believe anything in *The Enquirer*," he told *Rolling Stone*. Someone must have inflated Chick's comments to create "a better story," he added. "They're just doing their thing. Right on for them." However, the story didn't just go away. Several newspapers ran excerpts.

Reporters were already covering former associates who claimed he dominated them all and reported on him not letting Warner promote *Around* through the usual means, his nonappearance on the USA for Africa record, his bodyguards' attack on a photographer, and why he wouldn't grant interviews (quoting an insider who claimed, "Prince does it to create controversy"). Then there was a recent TV commercial. It started with flashing purple lights and the sound of a cheering concert audience. An announcer said, "Ladies and gentlemen, in concert, Prince." The camera panned to a box of spaghetti. His lawyers wrote the company to demand they stop using his name to sell pasta. The ad's creator expressed surprise to the Associated Press. "After all, Prince spaghetti has had its name since 1912." Prince, himself, had nothing to do with that letter but saw his name dragged into that controversy. Now there was this *Enquirer* story. He had to do something.

Around was still No. 1. But talk of him selling out—ignoring his black core audience and creating softer music for a new white following—filtered into press coverage. He denied abandoning his funk roots. He never left anything behind "anywhere along the line," he claimed. *"Around the World in a Day* is a funky album. Live, it's even funkier." Then, a few reporters claimed it failed commercially, despite topping the chart. Prince said his three million customers for 1999 bought *Around* because they wanted his message. And soon he called recording *Around* before *Purple Rain's* release his best decision yet. But *Around's* departure from the No. 1 spot after a mere three weeks had Prince scrambling to film a video for "Raspberry Beret." In a blue suit covered with white cloud patterns, he showed off his new short hair and cleared his throat before performing with his interracial band.

May 15, Warner rushed the single into stores with a painted cover. On it, a moody white brunette with dark lipstick, a black shirt, and the raspberry beret held an apple. His fans liked it. So did the media. MTV premiered his clip with host Mark Goodman asking a guest what his cough actually meant. Watching at home, Prince laughed. "I just did it to be sick, to do something no one else would do."

His video helped the breezy song reach No. 2 on *Billboard's* Hot 100.

Then he scheduled an image-building interview with *Rolling Stone*. While creating a recent Wendy and Lisa cover story, contributing editor Neal Karlen hadn't bothered asking them to ask Prince for an interview. "But they told him I was an okay guy, I guess, and his people called Minneapolis," Karlen explained.

In his car, Prince had Karlen put away his recorder. He had the local writer watch The Family rehearse in the warehouse; ride with him in his car to First Avenue; visit his home and see it wasn't a shrine; and even drive over to his father John's neighborhood, where he would pick up the aging musician to celebrate his birthday with a game of pool. "He seemed very proud of his son," Karlen noted. And Prince "was probably on his best behavior his whole time with me."

During a drive, he played Karlen "Old Friends 4 Sale," his autobiographical work about friends spreading rumors and betraying him. While it played, he looked satisfied, Karlen recalled. At every turn, Prince defended himself. His home wasn't a prison. He was sending Live Aid organizers a song. He wore paisley jumpsuits because they were all he owned. "I wear heels because the women like 'em."

The interview, however, did little to stop the backlash that followed his nonappearance at the USA for Africa session.

In frustration, Prince decided to discuss it all at length on a new song.

May 24, he sang his version of events, a song called "Hello." Its lyric told everyone the photographer invaded his car; Safford and Gibson were friends, not security; he didn't give "4 The Tears in Your Eyes" to charities to improve his image; he sincerely wanted to help. He ended by saying reporters needed to get a life and leave him alone already.

But Prince had to do more. He'd be filming overseas soon and couldn't just let reporters keep turning his audience against him. With his twenty-eighth birthday approaching, he had Fargnoli arrange a concert in his ever-supportive key black market, Detroit. After a promoter there booked Cobo, a large venue that could hold twelve thousand people, most tickets sold out in less than thirty minutes, the fastest sales in arena history.

For the show, he had Mazarati open. Then he took the stage with his guests Sheila and André Cymone. Thirty minutes into the two-hour set, Wendy grabbed the microphone. "Listen, this is a very special day." She had everyone sing "Happy Birthday." With a grin, Prince grabbed the mic. "Does that mean I can come back?"

Prince was touched to see a high turnout, indicating his audience had ignored media claims that he sold out. Riding in a car with Billy Sparks, who played the black club owner in *Purple Rain*, Prince wiped sweat from his brow. He heard "Automatic" on the radio. "And we just got through playin' it," Prince said. "We don't normally play that one." He asked Sparks to call the deejay, "The Electrifying Mojo." Born Charles Johnson, Mojo routinely filled his airtime with Prince's hits, album cuts, and B-sides.

Sparks had him on the line. "Hey Mojo! Prince wants to talk to you. You got a minute?"

Prince grabbed the phone. "Hey Mojo! What's happening? This is Prince." Mojo quickly put him on the air. Prince greeted Detroit. After small talk, Mojo mentioned *Around*. "My favorite!" Prince blurted. He used the interview to assure black fans he remembered where he came from.

16

LIFE AIN'T ALWAYS THE WAY

PRINCE THREW HIMSELF INTO CREATING HIS NEXT FILM, *UNDER the Cherry Moon*. June 18, co-manager Steve Fargnoli joined him on a flight to Paris. There, they scouted locations, and met potential cast members. On the second day, new melodies arrived. After Fargnoli got him some equipment, he recorded his latest ideas. By June 26, Prince decided the French Riviera would do. The next day, he flew home to Minneapolis to hire a director. Fargnoli wanted Jean-Baptiste Mondino, a French photographer whose black-and-white video for Don Henley's "The Boys of Summer" was in heavy rotation on MTV. In the end, they picked Mary Lambert, who handled Madonna's "Borderline" and "Material Girl," and Sheila E.'s "The Glamorous Life."

Prince invited Madonna to play the rich girl. He had met her at a 1985 awards show and enjoyed her turn in *Desperately Seeking Susan*. But Madonna met with him and Fargnoli, heard about the part, and turned it down. Prince's first instinct was to cast Wendy's sister Susannah, instead. Eventually, lithe newcomer Kristin Scott Thomas got the part. He cast Jerome Benton as his sidekick Tricky. Britain's Francesca Annis signed on to play an older lover and Terence Stamp handled the disapproving father. In his Eden Prairie warehouse, he continued handing out roles, and recording the album *Parade* after a song he initially wrote about Wendy.

In early July, Warner released "Pop Life" as a single. Along with another painted cover—a gray-haired black woman crying into a handkerchief—it included a longer version that ended with him joking about his high heels. Warner wanted a video but he was too busy with the film. Even without one, the single reached No. 7 and got him back on black radio. But his heartfelt B-side, "Hello," went largely ignored, and reporters kept offering backhanded compliments. In San Diego, a *Union-Tribune* writer's July 31 column claimed he was misunderstood, mysterious, possibly a jerk, and "without doubt responsible for some of the decade's best music." Within days, the August issue of *Seventeen* opined, "In truth, it wouldn't hurt Prince—or his career—if he started acting a little less enigmatically." *Around* was one of the fastest-selling albums ever (almost three million in its first two months without advertising, promotion, or a single), *Seventeen* noted. "But let's be honest: Prince's image is tarnished, and it's his own fault." According to the teen magazine, three Grammies, an Oscar, and 1984 earnings of about $17 million "seemed to turn him into an egomaniac." He didn't attend the "We Are the World" session. "Then he snubbed new-fan Elizabeth Taylor." At her home, he wouldn't speak, pose for photos, or leave bodyguards outside, *Seventeen* claimed. He sent crystal doves in apology but she returned them. "And then there was the night of Prince's farewell concert in Miami." During the post-show party, the magazine claimed, a bodyguard shoved through crowds, demanding no one face Prince, ejecting many "uninvited guests," and ending the celebration quickly. "These incidents are only part of a distressingly long list."

Commercially, Prince was doing better than ever. His *1999* album ended a 153-week stay on the chart that led to over 3 million sales. And despite negative press, *Around* had reached No. 1, spawned two Top 10 pop hits, appeared at No. 4 on the Black Chart, and sold about 2.4 million copies in the United States. His image had seen better days but his success continued in early August, when pop radio embraced The Family's first single, "The Screams of Passion."

August 13, 1985, Prince went to see the group at the warehouse. "We're going to play First Avenue tonight," he announced. They were shocked, but they dutifully took the stage that night. The crowd knew nothing about them but that they were the new Prince group. Still, they gave a great performance. "He hugged me after the show, he was so ecstatic," said Peterson.

Three days later, Prince and Susannah flew to Paris, for some quality time, before he had to start shooting the film. As a couple, they had experienced a few difficulties. With Prince supposedly seeing other women during trips to California, Susannah wasn't thrilled. By autumn 1984, they reached a stage where they had to decide whether to remain together or split. The incident inspired his heartrending classic "Condition of the Heart." They stayed together, but he bristled when the occasional press report claimed he and she would eventually marry. Nevertheless, they weathered the storms: They lived together; he had her audition for the lead role in *Under the Cherry Moon*; she kept exposing him to rock albums from the sixties and seventies and listening to him discuss his own music; he included her in The Family, and on his own album *Parade;* and kept writing lyrics about her. Now, he had her join him overseas (although he would soon have an employee accompany her back to the States).

Since Jerome was also overseas, The Family's rehearsals stopped. Paisley Park and Warner released *The Family* on August 19, but it didn't make the Pop Chart. It reached No. 9 on the R&B Chart. With him overseas, there was little promotion. The band had to wait until Prince finished the movie. After rehearsing for months, they were, Jellybean said, "in a limbo." Paisley Park, run out of his management's office, didn't effectively promote their album. Warner didn't either, assuming Paisley Park would handle this. Lead singer Paul Peterson was livid but agreed to fly to LA for acting, dancing, and singing lessons—since Prince wanted Peterson to play a rival in another of his films. "Still making $250 a week," Peterson claimed.

Prince's managers offered The Family a contract but Peterson's lawyer said, "Don't sign it." When Peterson asked Prince questions, he remembered Prince saying, "Don't talk business to me. Talk to my managers." The group contract went unsigned but they kept rehearsing for a big Paisley Park package tour with Sheila and Mazarati.

In France, Prince and the cast tried to work with director Mary Lambert. But they felt she had an attitude. Someone—it's not clear who—fired her after only three days, Michael Shore reported. A day later, Prince told the cast he was taking over. Terence Stamp quickly left the cast. They rebounded quickly, recruiting Steven Berkoff, a heavy in *Beverly Hills Cop* and *Rambo*, but most onlookers expected the worst. The sight of Prince filming scenes in one take—to finish on time—didn't exactly inspire confidence.

In mid-September, a month into the two-month shoot, Prince remained optimistic, envisioning a nine-month world tour, his longest ever, after the film opened. But there was no band music in the film, only him alone at an acoustic piano singing "Sometimes It Snows in April." He also planned to appear by himself on the *Parade* cover.

In Nice's La Victorine studios, he had photographer Jeff Katz working hard. Katz had been there for four months and wanted something natural. Prince didn't. "It was like, 'This is my look, and this is how it has to be all the time,'" Katz explained. The huge room was empty, save for them and a tiny portable radio. After Katz filled a few rolls, Prince changed the music and posed even more. "This went on for a couple of hours, not really talking," Katz said. Finally, they got the shot.

October 2, Warner released the third *Around* single, "America." Radio response was lukewarm. But MTV wanted a half-hour special about the single's release. They also wanted an interview. Prince agreed so quickly, the network couldn't possibly fly someone over in time. Instead, Fargnoli would read him their questions in front of a video camera. By late October, The Revolution arrived in the South of France, to join him for an "America" video.

Wendy felt France had inspired in him a different, sleeker look she compared to Cary Grant. He was also happy "working with all those new people," she noticed, and wanted a hand in every creative aspect of his career. October 27, during a break, he shot the "America" video. That night, he and the band took a stage at the Théâtre de la Verdure, actually a huge tent on Nice's Promenade des Anglais. Two thousand kids watched. He directed the clip. When he finished, he had the band play a ninety-minute concert.

Next, he sat at the center of a young entourage, heard MTV's questions, and in many cases, ignored them. When one MTV question noted that critics called *Purple Rain* sexist and "a lot of people" were offended, Prince said, "Now, wait, wait. I didn't write *Purple Rain*. Someone else did." It was fiction "and should be perceived that way." Violence was an everyday thing. They were only telling a story. He didn't think they did anything gratuitous. But if they went too far for humor's sake, "then I'm sorry, but it was not the intention."

The dailies were pretty lousy. But he kept composing music. He rented Wendy and Lisa an apartment in London and they booked time in Advision Studios. He recorded their instrumental "Mountains," but tried another version with the entire band and preferred that one.

Back on the set, he wondered about his character, Christopher. He was unsympathetic so he would die at the end. Warner wanted a happy conclusion, him a changed man and part of a couple. He shot the alternate ending. "Warner Brothers insisted on him getting the girl at the end and it really worked," said a publicist. "This little asshole character that was so hard to identify with, you bonded with by the end." But Prince changed his mind. He fought for and got the real ending, a gunman killing Christopher.

By early November, Prince was almost finished with the film. But things came to a head with The Family. Peterson was frustrated. "We weren't officially signed," said Jellybean. "That was the problem. It was more like a handshake." Paul also had a very high-ranking A&M Records executive telling him, "I want you to leave Prince" and accept a $250,000 deal. "That was a lot more than $250 a week," Peterson said. Steve Fargnoli caught wind of this, and threatened lawsuits and injunctions. Band member Jellybean urged Peterson to stay, saying they'd tour in six months, and have more opportunities waiting. But Peterson wanted out. Finally, Prince reached for a phone.

Peterson told him, "If you're gonna be in charge of this band, you can't do four million other things at the same time."

"Yes, I can! I did it with The Time, didn't I?" He did it with Sheila E. and Vanity 6, too. But Peterson was unmoved. Finally, Prince asked, "What is this about? Money? You want a house? I can get you a house."

"It's too late. I've made up my mind."

Peterson quit, effectively ending The Family. "Prince was devastated," he said.

Prince angrily blamed yes-men for the departure. "I shouldn't have let him go so far away from me and out of my control," he reportedly told David Rivkin.

At the *Cherry Moon* wrap party in November, Prince saw Eric Leeds, guitarist Miko Weaver, valet Jerome Benton, and Susannah—all of whom were supposed to perform live with The Family. Afterward, over lunch in a studio commissary, Eric asked, "Well, what do we do now?"

"Why don't you just come on with us?"

"Sounds good to me!"

He made his own band twice as large but also considered what to do with The Family's dancers. He tapped bodyguards Gregory Allan Brooks and Wally Safford to help Jerome Benton form what *Rolling Stone* called "a Pips-like dance line" near him on stage. He was teaching them simple moves to perform but Matt Fink felt, "They weren't even good dancers."

Wendy and Lisa learned about the expanded lineup when they arrived to shoot a video for "Girls and Boys." And while they practiced their own dance steps for the clip, they kept complaining. In the commissary, during one break, Wendy sat with drummer Bobby Z, keyboardist Matt Fink, and horn players Eric Leeds and Matt Blistan. The black bodyguards were within earshot, but Wendy said, "Prince is out of his mind. He's ruined everything. At least you guys are musicians, but now we're just an everyday funk band. We look like a circus. Doesn't he know what an ass his fans will think he is?"

17

GOTTA BROKEN HEART AGAIN

EVERYTHING FELT FRESH AND NEW NOW THAT HE WAS BACK from making *Cherry Moon* in France. The film would soon unveil a new musical direction, and sophisticated look: an Elvis-like do with square-shouldered French-cut suits. The sense of newness extended to his home. His new place was ready—a three-story yellow number on thirty acres, with purple balconies and a tall black gate. And soon, workers would have his huge complex Paisley Park Studios finished.

His co-manager Steve Fargnoli suggested buying an existing work-place out west, but he wanted something local. He described his vision to a designer from Venice, California: a sixty-five-thousand-square-foot place that cost about $10 million; a two-story building with a white, almost cub-ist facade, pyramid-shaped skylights on towers at the main entrance, four skylights over an atrium, purple railings (and teal and taupe), a basketball court, and recording consoles taping sounds in about eight rooms. "He wanted blue mosque domes on it," Fargnoli sighed, "which we, uh, didn't get to."

Prince also turned to helping his family. He let aging father John move into his purple place on Kiowa Drive, then he checked in on his mother Mattie and her husband Heyward. The couple was happy with the modest home they shared. Mattie, who still worked for the public school system, avoided speaking with John, who didn't live that far away. Next, he checked in on Tyka.

Tyka had previously attended one of his crowded, local shows. In the balcony, she watched everyone scream for him. *I don't get it*, she thought. "I could see it if it was Stevie Wonder or Michael Jackson. But it's just Prince; he's just my brother," she told *People*. Yet, he continued to inspire her.

She was borrowing money to finance a demo and refusing his help. She, too, didn't want articles to say Prince wrote and played everything, told her what to sing, and chose her outfits. "I didn't want to be the next Vanity," she explained.

In mid-December 1985, at Sunset Sound, Prince finished *Parade*. It started with "Christopher Tracy's Parade," a noisy, bustling, string-laden work. Wendy sang "I Wonder U." Then his ballad "Under the Cherry Moon," which included his father in writing credits, again. "Girls and Boys" evoked the style of "Erotic City" and Sheila's "A Love Bizarre." "Venus de Milo," also supposedly co-written by his father, ended side one.

Side two included "Kiss," sounding like a classic James Brown groove, updated with modern studio techniques. "Anotherloverholenyohead" was just as funky, with another glossy big beat, a strong bass line that suggested Stevie Wonder, emotive strings, jazzy piano chords, a pained vocal, and what critic Jon Bream later called "hip-hop scratch sounds rendered by rhythm machines." He capped the album with "Sometimes It Snows in April," set mostly to acoustic guitar and haunting piano notes.

One day, shortly after Christmas, Prince was on the Samuel Goldwyn soundstage in LA, recording musical cues for *Under the Cherry Moon*. Brunette actress Sherilyn Fenn was also present. Prince had everything set up: speakers to the left, right, and middle; a video monitor directly in front of him; his instruments around it; a 4-track recorder rolling tape. While watching silent footage, he improvised grooves for its score.

But Michael Jackson arrived, so Prince took a break. They spoke for a while, and when David Z arrived for a soundtrack mix with a huge reel under each arm, Prince proudly asked, "David, do you know Michael Jackson?"

David was stunned. "Hi, nice to meet you."

Prince led Jackson and the bodyguards to a ping-pong table in the center of the stage. "You want to play ping-pong?"

Jackson replied, "I don't know how to play but I'll try."

Prince grabbed a paddle, handed Jackson the other. Everyone stopped to watch. They softly hit the ball to each other until Prince said, "Come on, Michael, get into it.'" Then: "You want me to slam it?"

Jackson dropped his paddle. He raised his hands to cover his face but the ball slammed into his crotch. Observer Susan Rogers rolled her eyes. When the game ended, Michael chatted with Sherilyn Fenn. But Prince paced back and forth until he left. Then he started "strutting around like a rooster," David Rivkin explained, asking, "Did you see that? He played like Helen Keller!"

By late January 1986, he had *Parade* and the movie done. Ordinarily, Prince would leap right into another project. But this time, he had no idea where to head next. He managed to record new ideas "Last Heart" and "It's a Wonderful Day" but prepared for another image-building public appearance.

January 30, at the American Music Awards, instead of the blank facial expression, outlandish outfits, and cryptic comments he brought to last year's nationally televised event, Prince wore a conservative, custom-made black tuxedo. He smiled more. He let Diana Ross kiss his cheek. He even shook hands with Huey Lewis and members of his band the News while handing them an award.

Then it was back to Minneapolis and his Paisley Park imprint. March 4, Paisley Park released *Mazarati*. The group posed for photos in the shiny pajama-style suits and big hair of The Family. They also had heels, Jheri curls, and wispy mustaches. However, Mark Brown was unhappy. Their singles "Player's Ball" and "100 MPH." didn't make the Pop Chart. *Mazarati* made it only to No. 133 on the Pop Chart and 49 on the Black Chart. Mark blamed Paisley Park for not promoting the band. Alan Leeds remembered Paisley was just starting. "It didn't have a single employee, really. Managers were administering the label out of their office. There was no Paisley label, it was on paper only." Warner was supposed to promote the album, Leeds added. "And I don't think Mazarati was a priority for them."

Prince figured Warner could get "Kiss" out there as a single. Follow with *Parade* within two months, then get *Under the Cherry Moon* into theaters in August. But a Warner A&R executive hated "Kiss." "We can't put this out," he said. "There's no bass and it sounds like a demo." Prince had Fargnoli tell the label, "You're not getting another song. That's the one we're gonna put out." The label wasn't thrilled but David Z recalled, "He basically forced Warner to put it out."

Before its release, however, Prince called David to claim Warner wanted song credits to read "Kiss" was "produced, composed, and written by Prince and The Revolution." Rivkin was skeptical but happily accepted credit for arranging. This however alienated Mark Brown, who felt he deserved this title. Either way, both accepted his decisions. Then Prince invited Wendy into his video for "Kiss." Despite her vocal opposition to the eleven-member lineup, Wendy arrived at a bare, red-lit studio, and sat on a stool. While Prince performed with a veiled dancing partner, she strummed guitar. Then, with him chasing the dancer around, and doing a few dance steps, she smiled.

February 5, Warner released "Kiss" as *Parade*'s lead single. Fans rushed to buy copies, and helped it top *Billboard*'s Black Chart and reach No. 3 on the Pop Chart. The studio started cross promoting his new film and album. *Parade* wasn't really a soundtrack, but was subtitled "Music from the Motion Picture *Under the Cherry Moon*." Warner also erected a billboard in downtown Minneapolis and arranged another *Rolling Stone* cover and an interview with *Ebony*. Shortly after its March 31 release, *Parade* sat at No. 3 on the *Billboard* 200 Album Chart. It was also No. 2 on the R&B Album Chart. Reviews, however, were somewhat mixed. While many Americans saw a carryover of *Around*'s "psychedelic" sound, most European critics praised a work of art.

Prince decided on his next project, an album called *Dream Factory*. He had created eight songs since December 1985—including a lament about Peterson's departure for Hollywood—but figured this could be a group effort with more contributions by Wendy and Lisa. Susan Rogers thought it was a great idea. "They thought of stuff that Prince could never dream of."

Instead of rejecting their "Carousel," Prince penned a new lyric, and recorded it with them in one take as "Power Fantastic." He wrote "A Place in Heaven" for Lisa and took a day off while she recorded a vocal. He started "Witness 4 the Prosecution" but let them, and Eric Leeds, complete it. Then he tapped Lisa for a short riff. At a purple piano in the studio, Lisa played music that left Rogers and Wendy—downstairs in a control room—in tears. He decided Lisa's two-minute "Visions" would open the album. Then he handed Wendy and Lisa a tape of 1982's "Strange Relationship" with his vocals, piano playing, and drums. In this one, he sang about a man that loved to hurt his woman's feelings. She always surrendered, he added. "What's this strange relationship that we hold on to?" The man couldn't live with or without her, he explained, but was beginning to recognize it was an odd coupling. "Take it and finish it," Prince told them. Wendy and Lisa returned to Los Angeles and created other parts.

Eventually, his relationship with Wendy's sister affected his work. He had bought Susannah a ring and moved her into his home. Within months, he had her leave for an apartment he found in a nearby complex. Susannah considered leaving him and the city altogether, Per Nilsen reported. During rehearsals, Wendy and Lisa Coleman felt he was expecting Susannah to be faithful while he dated other women. If he arrived at his latest warehouse in a foul mood, they suspected he and Susannah had spent the night arguing.

Then he started working alone again, taking collaborations home and adding changes without consulting them. He was also leaning more toward the sort of funk grooves he once gave The Time. After playing them his funky instrumental, "And That Says What?," he unveiled "Movie Star," a Time-like work with him speaking over odd jazz, playing an uncouth ghetto guy attending a Hollywood party. Then he addressed Susannah. "Big Tall Wall" found him over nothing but a drum machine, describing how he moved her into a nearby apartment complex and wanted her all for himself. Just as quickly, "Starfish and Coffee" said he respected her art and paid attention when she talked about childhood schoolmates. Again, he sang over a drum machine, but flipped the tape upside down, so its four-chord piano riff and rippling harp covered a backward beat as compelling as the one on Jimi's *Electric Ladyland*.

By March 15, his story lyric, "The Ballad of Dorothy Parker" came to him in a dream. He had a drink after fighting with his girl, he wrote. A blond waitress took him home and turned on the radio. While a Joni song played, Dorothy ignored a ringing phone. She made him laugh before he went home. "All the fighting stopped," he concluded.

The song described the impact their arguments had on him, but stressed that he wanted to stick it out. After hearing about the song, Susannah asked if Dorothy really existed. Did he even know who Dorothy Parker was? He left. He had to get it on tape before he forgot how it sounded.

Despite a technician not having yet installed a state-of-the-art recording console at his complex in the making, Prince had Susan Rogers meet him there, and man the board while he programmed a drum machine beat he hoped would sound like a live player, throwing in unplanned drumrolls, pauses, and ever-changing snares. His melody had keys rising and falling when least expected. His vocal matched these highs and lows, sounding warm and personal in an age of corporate rock and *Control*. As he sang, Rogers saw the console had no high end. While mixing the song later that night, he learned of the malfunction, but liked his vocal anyway.

By April 19, 1986, Prince again owned the charts. "Kiss" had reached No. 1 on *Billboard*'s Hot 100. "Manic Monday," The Bangles' lead single from *Different Light*, was at No. 2. Sheila E.'s "Love Bizarre" also charted (for its last week) along with Meli'sa Morgan's cover of "Do Me Baby."

Within days, he had *Dream Factory* done. He put its eleven cuts on a cassette and viewed this as a group effort. May 7, Warner released his next *Parade* single "Mountains" and an instrumental B-side called "Alexa de Paris." And its cover introduced his sleek new image. The black-and-white shot showed him in profile, in a black belly-baring shirt with raised collar and flared cuffs. His little cowboy hat (complete with string to slip under his chin) rode the back of his scalp, with brim pointed skyward. But the single stalled at No. 23. Fans just weren't enthused about Wendy and Lisa's cheerful horn-filled track.

Though he had supposedly finished recording *Dream Factory*, he entered Sunset Sound alone, four days later, to create an urgent, empty cut called "It." He planned to use the Fairlight sampler's limited array of orchestral hits, but also tried to see if it could sample drums. Once a big beat played, he decided against including hi-hats. With the beat tough and relentless, he added a simple keyboard riff, and freewheeling, raplike horn stabs. Some electronic drum fills and stylish guitar work added to a stark, new sound. Then he called in the band—and some of Sheila's players—to join him for a live recording of "In a Large Room with No Light."

In late May, Prince and the Revolution were ready for a surprise performance in LA. *Rolling Stone* wanted him on the cover again. Instead, he arranged for *Rolling Stone* to interview Wendy and Lisa and put them on the cover. When contributing editor Neal Karlen arrived, Prince didn't address him at all. "It was understood they would speak for him," Karlen remembered.

During their interviews, the ladies kept stressing band unity. Wendy vowed, "This band is going to be together a long, long time." Lisa nodded agreement. Backstage at the Universal Amphitheatre, Lisa added, "We don't want to leave and start our own thing, because this is our own thing. I don't feel like we're just hired musicians taking orders. He's always asking for our ideas." They were writing music for his third movie, they added; they didn't know its plot, but he vowed to tailor it to their songs. "I'm sorry," Wendy continued, "but no one can come close to what the three of us have together when we're playing in the studio. Nobody!" At this point, an aide rushed in. "Prince wants you on stage ASAP." They hopped to it.

Contributing editor Neal Karlen didn't sense any growing resentment. If anything, he felt they were part of the inner circle; Prince loved them; he was letting them share the spotlight.

They were still unhappy with the expanded lineup but joined him for another rehearsal—and variation of "Kiss," which he still felt insecure about. Prince cut the song short. "I think finger cymbals would be better," he told the band. "Now when we film videos tomorrow, we're going to drag it out so everybody will get their chance to be in it." With that, he left.

Wendy removed her guitar. Lisa unplugged from the keyboard.

"We've got a much bigger sound now," Lisa complained at some point. "And we're a lot more funk oriented, that's for sure."

Rolling Stone titled its feature "Wendy, Lisa and Prince: A Musical Love Affair." "It was a big deal for *Rolling Stone* when he agreed to pose for the cover," Karlen recalled. He donned sunglasses and a skintight outfit, stood between Wendy and Lisa, and even smiled.

But he was actually retreating from his collaboration with them. While recording a ballad called "Slow Love," he turned to Carole Davis for a few lyrics. Then June found him changing *Dream Factory* even more, replacing collaborations with solo works. Instead of finishing and releasing the album, he arranged the Hit and Run Tour, small dates in various cities. With *Cherry Moon* set for release any day now, he felt stressed. He had people claiming Wendy and Lisa inspired his new sounds, just as his Warner contract was up for another renewal. During a rehearsal at the warehouse, Matt Fink told author Alex Hahn, something upset Prince to the point where he raged, "You fucking lesbians, you're gonna rot in hell for your lifestyle!"

And, as Fink told Hahn, Wendy shouted back. "You're a fucking womanizer! You're such a prick and a control freak. You're just a womanizing pig."

Seemingly out of nowhere, Prince set *Dream Factory* aside. "He talked a lot about doing a Broadway show," Bobby Z explained. "He was writing a script and he really wanted to take it to the stage," said Eric Leeds.

———

With *Cherry Moon* coming soon, he kept trying to sanitize his image. Sheila E. thought it was a good move since reporters described "a bad boy, a rude boy," when Prince was really "an easygoing guy," as she told *People*. Lisa Coleman agreed. Current work so consumed him he ignored the darkening tone of press coverage. "He realizes it now."

Press coverage about the upcoming film remained far from glowing. He reportedly refused Warner Bros.' calls for more conflict in the script, insisting ambiance and music would entertain audiences. Some predicted the film's success would solidify his position as "a screen phenomenon." Its failure, one writer explained, might end his movie career and have critics regarding *Purple Rain* "as a fluke." This, many felt, was why he was suddenly so media-friendly. In his new home one night, Per Nilsen reported, advance word about the film reached him, and it was unfavorable. Lying on the floor, with Susannah standing nearby, he screamed that he hated the film.

Warner arranged a premiere that would mark the first time anyone apart from the studio or a San Diego preview audience saw *Under the Cherry Moon*. Sensing it had a turkey on its hands, Warner didn't schedule advance press screenings, and wouldn't say why. Yet they still believed the event would allow them to reach the film's target audience.

The *LA Times* felt this premiere represented "the inevitable marriage of MTV and the movies." The network, in fact, now seemed to be "the latest marketing tool in studio promotions." Recent weeks saw it help open Orion's *Back to School*, Lorimar's *American Anthem*, Disney's *Ruthless People*, and Columbia's *Karate Kid, Part II*. Its target audience (aged twelve to thirty-four) was "the heart and soul of the moviegoing audience," MTV senior vice president and general manager Tom Freston explained. "And it's a perfect marriage." The event gave Warner "a splashy premiere," Prince "exposure for his movie and his record," and MTV "a great promotion." But events like this were unusual for Warner. For two years, the studio had outperformed every other. Warner had also spent over $200,000 for *Purple Rain*'s San Diego premiere, the first film opening MTV covered live. Now, it rarely arranged costly premieres common in the industry. "The only time they really spend big money like this is on a movie with a music tie-in," said a high-ranking marketing executive at another major.

Small, remote Sheridan (population: 10,369) is in north Wyoming, ninety minutes from a major city (Billings, Montana, population: 67,000).

Sheridan was home mostly to "cowboys, coal miners, and retirees. Just a handful of blacks live here," according to the *Los Angeles Times*. As the ten thousandth caller in a contest sponsored by MTV and Warner Bros., twenty-year-old hotel worker Lisa Barber won the premiere and party for her economically depressed town. Barber, who entered various contests, had never won anything but "a couple of Big Macs and a curling iron," *People* reported. Now, they had to make a premiere happen in her town. Everything was more complicated and costly to arrange. They had to go to Billings for cars and limousines upscale enough to rent for the event. They also held the event at the Centennial Twin Theater, "about the last place in America you would expect to see the world premiere," the *LA Times* felt.

At MTV, Freston accepted higher costs. "Let's put it this way," he said. "We had one budget and then we had our worst-case-scenario budget in which we projected costs if the call came from Nome, Alaska. This place exceeded that budget." MTV and Warner shared the bill, which ran about $250,000, "although several put that figure higher." Barber invited two hundred close friends. Prince would bring his entourage. Another three hundred would attend. Barber gushed, "This is the biggest thing that's ever happened here. I love Prince. I saw *Purple Rain* thirteen times."

Not everyone was happy. A rancher at a coffee counter in Ritz Sporting Goods told a reporter people best knew this town for fishing lures. "We don't care about no boy who wears tight pants and struts around like a woman." The owner of an antique shop on Main Street however said, "We needed something like this to give the place a lift."

July 1, eleven days after Barber's call, a Tuesday, Sheridan was ready. A crowd at the airport held signs. WELCOME TO SHERIDAN. WE'RE PROUD OF OUR TOWN. GOT ANY EXTRA TICKETS? At the tiny airport, the crowd cheered the sight of his private Learjet. It landed and sat on the strip a few minutes. The passenger door opened. His tiny, high-heeled boot appeared first. Then he emerged in a dark silk suit. Smiling, he stepped onto a soiled twenty-five-foot red carpet, flung his black silk sport jacket over a fence to the crowd of seven hundred on the airport's one runway, then exchanged pleasantries with Sheridan's mayor, and others. Slipping into a gray-and-black limo, he claimed, "I'm going to buy a house here."

In a small cottage behind her mother's trailer, Barber didn't know what to wear. "I usually shop at Kmart." But she felt relief when his staff sent a black-and-white outfit, a hair stylist, and a makeup artist. Then she sat and waited until 6:00 P.M.

Fifteen minutes late, Prince drove a white Buick convertible with license plates that said, "Love." He wore makeup and his midriff-baring shirt. Vaulting a chain-link fence, he then knocked on the door. "Hello," he said, kissing her hand. "My name is Prince. Ready to have a good time?"

She said yeah and sat in the car.

He asked for the best radio station. Turned to it. Heard the deejay mention him. "If I had a phone in here, I'd call him."

Ahead of the car, Sheridan's female riding troupe, the Equestri-Annettes rode horses with MTV bumper stickers near their tails. Costumed cowboys also led Prince "and a glitzy contingent of stars, studio executives, and publicists to the premiere." Near the Centennial Theater, eight hundred enthusiastic people hoped to see celebrities. Jerome Benton, Kristin Scott Thomas, and Rosanna Arquette all showed up. Singer Joni Mitchell entered, unnoticed. But singer Ray Parker, Jr. drew cheers. They thought he was Lionel Richie. "We cheered for anyone who was dressed weird or who was black," said a crowd member.

Inside, Prince and Barber sat in a back row. At one point, he played with her hair and put his arm around her, she claimed. She asked how he liked it here. It was very pretty, he said. She was lucky to live here.

When he first appeared on-screen, one woman yelled, "Nice butt!" The audience kept cheering him in various scenes, but the *LA Times* recalled no "overwhelming enthusiasm for the film itself."

After the film, a local told a TV camera, "I liked it, but I didn't get it." Most viewers agreed. Another said, "It was great! Like one long rock video! But I didn't really figure out what was going on." The crowd filtered out, and Prince went to the party at the Holiday Inn. At 10:00 P.M., he climbed an enormous, specially built stage that consumed half the ballroom floor, to play forty-five minutes of funk. Martha Quinn, the cherub-faced MTV vee-jay, was hosting the post-screening party at the hotel, so about 2 million MTV subscribers nationwide saw the live broadcast. Ultimately, the packed audience seemed to find his set ("Delirious," "Purple Rain," the usual numbers) more enjoyable than the film, *People* reported. From here, he and band members mingled with locals.

Eventually, it was time to go. He made sure Barber got a ride home in a limousine.

Prince and his onetime collaborator Jimmy Jam, now a successful producer, no longer spoke but Jam thought he knew what was up. "When you're real successful and you start falling off the pedestal, you get real paranoid." People around you expressed doubt, but even worse, you "begin to doubt yourself. You think, damn, am I really what I think I am? That kind of thing." He felt something had Prince freaked out, and going through changes. Prince had done a complete about-face, promoting *Cherry Moon* with interviews. But this MTV thing took the cake. "To me, that was beneath him. Here he was sitting with this chick reporter; I can't even remember her name. . . ." He described perky on-air host Martha Quinn. "God. She made me sick. Here he's gone from not talking to *Rolling Stone*, not talking to the *LA Times*, not talking to anybody. And now he's talking to Martha Quinn? Gimme a break." It was a low point, Jam said, but he predicted Prince would regain his footing.

Reviews of his film exacerbated his stress. *People* quipped, "His movie's a smash—in Wyoming." *The New York Times* called his character a "self-caressing twerp of dubious provenance." *The Washington Post* said, "Prince begins to remind you of something your biology teacher asked you to dissect." *USA Today* noted acting wasn't his strength: "Fewer people saw [*Purple*] *Rain* for the acting than saw *Old Yeller* for the sex." It was an odd film. "Funny when it was supposed to be tragic, just plain strange when it was supposed to be funny," one critic explained. Its first weekend, it grossed $3.1 million (about the same as Walt Disney's cartoon movie *The Great Mouse Detective*).

Prince had poured his heart and soul into the film but critics kept attacking everything about it: the lack of color, the "dumb script," "atrocious acting," even the fact that he chased a white woman (when so few blacks appeared on the silver screen).

In all, it was a low point—and an unfortunate taste of things to come.

18

DON'T DIE WITHOUT KNOWING

NO MORE MUSICAL. NOT NOW. AT SUNSET SOUND, HE WORKED
to finish *Dream Factory*. One Sunday, he arrived with a lyric called "The
Cross." He started with intimate vocals and some echo. The present was a
black day and a stormy night, he sang; with no love or hope in sight. But
people shouldn't cry "for He is coming." They shouldn't die without knowing the cross. There were ghettos to the left and flowers to the right, he
continued, but everyone would have bread if they stuck it out. He described
a pregnant woman singing a sweet gospel song. "She lives in starvation,"
he noted. But the cross would solve all problems.

He kept playing loud, raucous chords then removed everything but
his hoarse voice crooning the title. Around him, everyone was amazed.
"The Cross" was a sobering antidote to the era's yuppie rock and hair
metal.

July 15, another Sunday, Prince taped another social statement. After
sampling drums with the Fairlight, he sang about AIDS, drugs, street
gangs, gun homicide, and the government focusing on space travel. He
called these situations signs that the Bible predicted would preface Christ's
return. He called the song "Sign O' the Times" (a title it shared with a
Grandmaster Flash rap single). "He had begun to see the effect of crack
and drugs on young people," said Alan Leeds. "He's not really a preacher,
but it's certainly an antidrug song."

He wrote, recorded, and mixed it during a ten-hour session, then
moved on to his 1982 idea, "I Could Never Take the Place of Your Man."
Again, a lyric seemed to echo events in his personal life. He sang about
meeting a woman in a club one Friday night. Her man left her last June,
she told him, and she kept crying because he's "gone 2 stay." He asked her
to dance, she wanted more, but he told her not to waste her time. He was
good for a one-night stand. She kept crying, asking if they could be friends.
"And I said, oh, honey baby that's a dead end." Its music included three-

chord blues-rock; jazz cymbals and a keyboard sound that evoked "When You Were Mine" as much as it did sixties garage rock. He also lengthened it with a slow groove in the middle. He tinkered with something called "Joy in Repetition," and set it aside for now.

July 18, he sequenced a final eighteen-song version of *Dream Factory* and sent it out for mastering. He was also having a cover made. A mock-up featured every band member. Each would scribble a few words to the loose free-form graphic.

Then everything changed.

Wendy and Lisa stopped by his mansion. Wendy was unhappy: She didn't like sharing stages with her twin sister Susannah, him adding a second guitarist, or the dancing bodyguards. Lisa joined her in wanting greater creative input. They reportedly demanded he treat them as creative equals. He refused. They said they were leaving.

Prince needed them for the Hit and Run Tour.

He contacted Bobby Z. The day of their flight back to LA, Bobby caught up with the women at the airport and asked them to stay. Alan Leeds also interceded, asking them to do the tour. "They were a bit disillusioned at the time," Leeds explained. "I think I convinced them that the timing was not prudent for them or Prince. That if they were committed to moving on they could strategize and time it better."

They stayed, but Prince also had to deal with Mark Brown. This was becoming a nightmare. Mark also considered sitting out the tour. Ironically, Mark felt Prince was favoring Wendy. Mark was in the band first but saw Prince work to increase Wendy's fame. Then Stevie Nicks offered him $3,500 per week. Prince convinced Mark to stay, Mark recalled. "He gave me all these hopes," the bassist said. "'You're gonna get rich next year.'" Mark had no idea Prince planned to hand each band member $1 million as thanks for *Purple Rain*.

Away from the band, he considered *Dream Factory* and the nine songs with prominent contributions by Wendy and Lisa. He removed them then decided to start over. In late July, and early August, he worked in his home studio and felt back in control. He created "Hot Thing," a lyric about meeting a young girl ("barely twenty-one") in a club. "Are your smiles for me?" he sang. As the song continued, he urged the girl to call her parents and say she'd be home late. "He was hearing a different kind of music," said Alan Leeds.

But Prince also used "Forever in My Life" to tell Susannah Melvoin he wanted to be with her and her alone. This one found him mimicking Sly & The Family Stone's cadence on "Everyday People" (from 1969's *Stand!*). However, it contained another mistake. After programming its beat, he sang his backup vocal first. Then he had engineer Susan Rogers lower it so he could sing the main lyric. He was still singing about monogamy when the softer voice burst in and interrupted. During a playback, he shrugged. He would keep it.

Prince got back to preparing for this latest European tour. They got through the one-month tour, with the expanded Revolution finally reaching Japan for their September 9 show. "We were all so tired and ready to go home," said a bodyguard. Prince couldn't get over how Wendy and Lisa threatened to quit, how he had to convince them to stay and do this Hit and Run Tour, and how they had been so unhappy and vocal. Still, the public knew nothing about this. They took the stage one more time at Yokohama Stadium. During the show, Prince deliberately smashed his guitar.

Wendy and Lisa faced each other. "It's over," one said.

Yes, it was.

After the show, he left the stage. He didn't offer his usual talk about the performance. He immediately entered a car. Tired, with towel around his neck, he sat in silence during the ride back to the hotel. Everyone sensed Wendy and Lisa were out. The next day, they flew back home.

In the basement of his new home, Prince kept recording new ideas. September 13, he started *The Dawn,* for another film musical with two rival bands. Three days later, he took a break to create something for Jesse Johnson's new album. Johnson rejected it so Prince had "Shockadelica" pressed onto a platter and sent to radio station KMOJ, which played it within days.

He returned to his own next album by creating a dark dance cut called "Superfunkycalifragisexy." Over a swirling organ, horns, and a sinister groove on Fairlight, Prince urged people to dance, drink blood, and party all night. Then he taped "When the Dawn of the Morning Comes" for his movie idea *The Dawn.* September 18, he took another break.

Producer Quincy Jones let him know Michael Jackson wanted him on his new duet "I'm Bad." Instead, Prince submitted a song. In his Encino home, the *Thriller* star heard Prince's contribution, a reworked demo from

1976, and passed. Jackson really wanted him on his title track. He even called directly to outline his promotional plan: His manager Frank DiLeo would plant stories in tabloids and both camps would hurl put-downs. DiLeo would tell *Rolling Stone* Jackson was confused since he considered Prince a great friend. Epic would release the single and video for "Bad"— helmed by Martin Scorsese—a month later, and let fans see Prince's James Brown steps, Michael moonwalking, and both trying to settle who was really "bad."

Prince considered the idea until he heard the tape Jackson sent. As with "Beat It," the song described a kid on mean streets. Only this time, a kid was back in his neighborhood during a break from private school. Hooligans gave him trouble but he sang, "I'm bad, you're bad, who's bad?"

Its slick drum machine, horn stabs, keyboards, and dark, swirling bass line didn't bother Prince as much as Jackson's opening line: Your butt is mine. "Now who's gonna sing that to who?" Prince joked on VH1. " 'Cause you sure ain't singing it to me. And I sure ain't singin' it to you . . . Right there, we got a problem." He backed out, Jones recalled, saying "you don't need me to be on this. It'll be a hit without me. It'd succeed without him."

By September 28, Prince started recording instrumental jazz. Sunday afternoon, October 1, he invited Eric Leeds to his house, played three or four tracks, and said they were for *8*, an album by a fictitious group named Madhouse. And just three days later, he finished the album. He worried that critics would pan it. "And if it comes out, I don't want it to just end up with all of the Prince fanatics," he added.

Prince arrived at Sunset Sound, October 5, and planned to record every day until his next album was finished. Within two days, he realized he had to resolve things with The Revolution. "Lisa was very vocal with him," Wendy admitted. "And I never kept my mouth shut."

October 7, he called Wendy and Lisa on the phone and told them to come over. They reached the house he was renting in Beverly Hills. After dinner, at 12:30 A.M., he played pool with them for two hours. Then he entered an adjoining room, reached for the telephone, and dialed Bobby Z's number. Bobby was great with soul and pop, but Prince was now exploring jazz. "Moreover, as the father of an infant son, he [Bobby Z] was the only parent in The Revolution, whose members are on call twenty-four hours a day," Jon Bream reported.

Once Bobby answered, Prince said, "We've been together for a long time. You're the man and you've done a great job. We're gonna be friends forever. I'm gonna honor your contract. Sheila wants to play drums with me. I think it's a good idea."

Bobby answered, "I think it's a good idea, too."

He said he was canning Wendy and Lisa, Bobby told Per Nilsen, but would try to keep Mark Brown and Matt Fink. This done, he reentered the other room and told Wendy and Lisa, "I can't expect you guys to go where I'm going to go next. I think we've gone as far as we can go. I've got to let you go."

Both had convinced themselves to stay. They were shocked. He added that he needed to start making music on his own again.

Prince approached Fink that same day. "I'm not going to fire you. You have a choice to leave or stay, and I'd understand if you didn't want to stay."

Fink thought, *Okay, if I quit, what do I do?* "I decided to keep my job."

October 16, hometown paper the *Star Tribune* reported, "The Revolution is over." His New York–based publicist Robyn Riggs told reporters Bobby would keep writing songs and producing. Lisa and Wendy had six labels and a major film studio courting them. Alan Leeds, heading PRN, the small division that handled Prince's touring, wasn't surprised by the move. "I knew it was coming," he said. "Didn't think it mattered much." When a reporter called for a quote, Leeds said band members were "growing in different directions." The disbanding would let departing members have "the freedom and the time to pursue other interests that they expressed interest in pursuing."

Warner had no comment.

Prince calmly told a reporter, "I felt we all needed to grow." They all "needed to play a wide range of music with different types of people. Then we could come back eight times as strong."

A day later, Susan Rogers was on her first vacation in three years (four days of rest in Santa Barbara). Engineer Bill "Coke" Johnson manned the board and recorded Prince's new song. Producers in Chicago at that time were popularizing "house music," stripped-down disco; Prince covered his new track beat with soul music and horn riffs in the James Brown–style and called it "Housequake."

For vocals, he revived the varispeed technique from "Erotic City," singing lyrics onto a slowed tape. When played at normal speed, his voice sounded higher, even feminine. Backup vocals were all over the place, but the song sounded like a fun house party. Prince meanwhile yelled, boasted, rapped, and sang.

When Rogers returned, he lingered on the up-tempo horn-driven dance cut to the point where she decided it was either "especially important" to him or just fun to work on. Before long, he told her he saw potential in this vary-speed voice. It could represent a character on his songs, named Camille. "He was thinking of battling with himself," Rogers explained. "He had this whole idea that Camille would be his competition."

October 27, he started *Camille*, another Madhouse-styled "side project"—and a curveball for his audience. By November 2, he was using the odd voice on "If I Was Your Girlfriend." Since March, Michael Jackson's sister Janet had reaped a fortune with her album *Control* and hit singles, "What Have You Done for Me Lately?" and "Nasty." Her producers—Jam and Lewis, formerly of The Time—had created a signature sound for her that included artificial big beats, orchestral hits, and multitracked vocals. Now, with "If I Was Your Girlfriend" Prince played a similar beat, but on live drums; with a claustrophobic bass; an organ that played convoluted minor chords; a haunting synth riff that replaced a chirpy chorus; and more than a few repeated programmed riffs.

Despite canning her twin sister Wendy, not to mention their reported bickering, Susan Rogers explained, "It was a way of asking [Susannah], 'Why can't I have the closeness you have with your sister? Why can't we be friends, too?'" He ended it with his genre-bending voice desperately begging for attention. "I want to be all of the things you are to me." Though another studio malfunction created an accidentally distorted vocal, he moved on.

In ten days, he had knocked out four pretty complex numbers: this one for his girl, "Rebirth of the Flesh," "Rockhard in a Funky Place," and "Good Love." He included a new version of "Feel U Up," from 1981, and that dance cut Jesse Johnson rejected, "Shockadelica." He also reworked "Strange Relationship," removing Wendy and Lisa's parts. The final version was also a bit Janet-like, with a memorable riff over booming drum machine. He expanded the template to include a wooden flute, sitar, some tambourine, even congas, and kept barreling forward.

Camille had no theme or concept, just the sped-up voice. To hear Prince tell it, the album explored inner conflicts and a battle between Good and Evil. He also envisioned a movie based on the character. He'd ostensibly play a guy somehow interacting with Camille, until the end when audiences saw he was actually a split personality.

By November 5, *Camille* was done and sequenced. Side one had "Rebirth of the Flesh," "Housequake," "Strange Relationship," and "Feel U Up." He put "Shockadelica," "Good Love," "If I Was Your Girlfriend" and "Rockhard in a Funky Place" on side two. Warner accepted it, issuing a catalog number and a January 1987 release date. The label also created a test pressing of the single, "Shockadelica" backed with "Housequake." But Prince wavered again, adding more songs recorded earlier that year.

Even Prince Nelson needed a break; especially after writing so many ballads with the same theme. He unwound with some Miles Davis. But two 1986 albums, Patti LaBelle and Luther Vandross's *The Winner in You* and *Give Me the Reason* really got his competitive fires burning again. Wanting to get back to his own ballads, in his own voice, he sat and wrote a falsetto-sung number called "Adore." The song featured the usual elements, but sounded warmer thanks to an electric piano (instead of a synth), and lush melodies that popped in from time to time (each of which could have carried a full song). While recording it, Prince included intertwining vocal rhythms, not to mention the "F" word.

Prince spent eight days listening to tracks he had created that year. Warner was already preparing *Camille* for release but early December found Prince combining *Dream Factory* tracks with some from *Camille* ("If I Was Your Girlfriend," "Strange Relationship," and "Housequake," all with the sped-up voice). After adding a few new works—including a twelve-minute opening suite—he was sitting on an unwieldy three-record set called *Crystal Ball*.

Warner usually balked at double albums, no less triple. Alan Leeds felt its length could inspire a backlash. Casual fans might have to pay more for the collection. Critics might attack Prince for daring to think everything on the three records was worthy of release. "Fact is, the album had a few weak spots." Besides die-hard fans receiving a deluge of new material, Leeds felt "there were few upsides."

While he moved on to the next project, his managers had to pitch Warner on *Crystal Ball*.

In December, as usual, Fargnoli met with label brass. In recent years, Fargnoli had convinced them to release demos as *Dirty Mind,* make 1999 a double album, finance *Purple Rain,* and release "When Doves Cry." Since Warner went along, and these ideas were successful, Prince felt the company would agree to *Crystal Ball.* However, by late 1986, things had changed. He was certainly talented and Mo Ostin and Lenny Waronker still felt he was an unstoppable creative force. Nevertheless, they wondered about a few of his business decisions (perhaps including a hasty decision to pull *Camille* at the last minute). Prince had also faced lower sales of each album since *Purple Rain.* Then there were media reports of unpredictable behavior, the "We Are the World" debacle, and firing Wendy and Lisa. Ostin and Waronker now reportedly wondered if Prince was another "self-thwarting" musical genius. Fargnoli, who didn't completely support the triple-album idea, either, knew there'd be trouble.

With *Parade* one of his poorest sellers, Warner balked at *Crystal Ball's* length, predicting sales would be just as low. Before long, Fargnoli told Prince, "Man, they're not going to buy this."

"You work for me," Prince answered. "You make 'em buy it."

19

WE ALL HAVE OUR PROBLEMS

CRYSTAL BALL WAS BECOMING A TURNING POINT. PRINCE WAS now ruining a very important relationship. At Warner, some people noticed. "Steve [Fargnoli] was reaching a point where he didn't need this," Warner executive Marylou Badeaux recalled. "It's not unusual for an artist to make demands of his management, but some of Prince's demands were getting more and more out in left field."

Along with *Crystal Ball* causing untold frustration, his relationship with Susannah ended. In December, she packed her things and flew to Los Angeles's San Fernando Valley to join Wendy and Lisa.

Mark Brown also left. Prince was changing his sound. "He wanted to go back to funky things, back to where he started," Mark later explained. Prince invited him to stay, but Mark considered how, despite the good times and money, the past six years hadn't offered much creative freedom. When Mark left, Prince had Paisley Park cancel Mazarati's contract.

At Sunset Sound shortly before Christmas, Prince poured his energies into a new song called "U Got the Look." He wanted to tap into the market that made a hit of Englishman Robert Palmer's "Addicted to Love" (from his 1985 album *Riptide*). Like Palmer, Prince set a familiar blues riff over a cold, artificial drum machine. He threw in lots of fake-sounding synth and shrill guitar chords. He expanded the sound with dramatic riffs and him playing a commentator during the "world series of love." But it wasn't working. Prince changed it a million times, and kept "really struggling with it," an associate recalled, but believed it was an important single. At the last minute, he told the engineer to speed the tape. His voice sounded younger. It had more energy. Sensing it would draw his white pop audience, he went with this version. But it still needed something. Shortly before Christmas, he knew what it was.

Sheena Easton stopped by unannounced to ask if he'd produce her next album. Rogers said, "He didn't feel like socializing, though." He asked Easton to play an instrument on the song. Once she did, he asked, "How'd you like to do this? Feel like singing?"

Sure.

He played it once or twice.

Easton was initially taken aback by its sexual nature, "but he convinced her to get into it, and it worked perfectly," Rogers recalled. She wished she could hear it more than twice but stood behind the microphone and in her Scottish accent reached the line: "Your body's heck-a-slammin'."

She stopped. "What the hell is heck-a-slammin'?"

Prince laughed.

"He loved to make fun of me," Easton claimed.

By December 21, Prince was adding a coda to the song, which was, Leeds felt, "as mainstream a record as any in his career."

Prince soon learned Mo Ostin, himself, was coming to Sunset Sound to hear the triple album. Fargnoli kept pressing for it but Ostin considered the economics of a triple album. How many people would pay a whopping thirty dollars? It'd be expensive to create and distribute. Even if critics did hail it as a masterpiece, there was no guarantee it would turn a profit.

Ostin arrived at the studio. Fargnoli was nearby while Prince played him all of his exciting new tracks. When he was done, Ostin said, "I respect your vision, but it just won't fly." Ostin wanted *Crystal Ball* cut to a double album. Even this in a way was stretching it (it would be Prince's *second* double album).

Prince wouldn't do it. For weeks, they bickered. "There were a lot of meetings, a lot of loud hollering, a lot of frustration," recalled Leeds. "It was very, very ugly." A few times, Prince lost his cool, screaming at Warner employees then storming out of conference rooms, Marylou Badeaux remembered.

" 'You'll overwhelm the market,' " Prince remembered them saying. "I was told, 'You can't do that.' " He felt Warner executives were overstepping their bounds. "I don't think it's their place to talk me into or out of things," he said.

In the end, Prince bitterly made the cuts. He yanked that windy title track, which ate up nearly half an album side. He named the album after his song "Sign O' the Times." He also cut "Good Love," a pop song with the "Camille" voice, and "Joy in Repetition," a soothing ballad that author Alex Hahn felt found him treading Kate Bush and Peter Gabriel territory.

But he also told Alan Leeds he "lost interest," Leeds recalled. Prince was used to hearing it only as a triple set. Now, this "incomplete work" didn't reflect his true vision for the project.

The night of December 28, in Minneapolis, Prince entered his basement studio to try something else. At a piano, he tapped out a glum riff. He spoke lyrics, pretending to ask bodyguard-turned-dancer Wally Safford for fifty dollars and sunglasses. Next, he pretended to return them, since he had no girl to impress. Engineer Susan Rogers enjoyed his vulnerable guitar, bass, and chorus. Nevertheless, he started piling on instruments. A percussion part tangled the verse, obscuring lyrics. She asked, "Don't you think it was better before, Prince? Maybe we should stop."

Instead, he added a synthesizer.

She felt he was deliberately ruining it. After recording more melodies, he said, "Now put all twenty-four channels on record and erase it."

"No, you can't do this!"

"If you don't, I will."

He'd have to. "I thought it was the greatest thing he had done," she said later. "I had waited years to hear a Prince song like this. I ached to hear him be this honest."

Regardless, he erased the tape.

In January 1987, Prince was back in his Washington Avenue warehouse, updating his baleful "Superfunkycalifragisexy." Warner got the first Madhouse single out there and "Six" went Top 10. Then the album 8 arrived on January 21, with a cover that featured buxom model Maneca Lightner in a polka-dot outfit. Prince also deemed Jill Jones's debut ready after four years, and let Cavallo, Ruffalo and Fargnoli sign Dale Bozzio (formerly of new wave act Missing Persons), Minneapolis group Three O'Clock, and Good Question. But with Prince multitasking, things at the label changed. "Warner was handling the business as far as public relations," Jill Jones recalled. But Warner wasn't providing much, she added. Then less-talented newcomers and managers came around and caused what she called "a complete feeding frenzy of the most unsavory types." Then Prince "was distracted and detached," she added. Before returning to his own album, however, he told them to sign an artist named Mavis Staples.

He was rehearsing with a new band in a warehouse on Washington Avenue. Sheila agreed to play drums for him. Then, Prince contacted her black guitarist Levi Seacer, Jr. and asked him to replace Brown Mark on bass. Next, he added new dancer Cathy Glover and dubbed her "Cat." He also had Cat pose on covers for *Sign O' the Times* singles and the album's inner sleeve. In these shots, she held his guitar, and a giant mirrored heart (his new emblem).

In February, Warner started promoting his lead single, "Sign O' the Times." For a week, the label placed ads, and a few lyrics, in left-leaning newspapers and magazines. Though eerie and not exactly upbeat, fans and reporters loved the song's social comment and sent it flying up the charts. The double album arrived soon after, on March 31, and entered the *Billboard* Pop Chart at No. 40. Critics offered unanimous praise, noting Prince effectively balanced his core and *Purple Rain* audiences. In the *Village Voice*'s year-end poll, 220 reviewers voted *Sign* Best Album, making it the biggest winner in poll history, and chose its title track as Top Single. Overseas, European writers rushed to call him a true artist.

With *Sign* rising to No. 12, from No. 40, on the *Billboard* Pop Chart its second week, Prince was busier than ever. Most afternoons he watched morning rehearsals for opening act Madhouse and his own band. Then he flew to England to rehearse for his first far-reaching European tour (which would last two months). Next, he turned his attention to a new stage set, handing Roy Bennett a picture of the album cover and saying, "Make it look like this." Bennett rose to the challenge, creating a two-level set that cost about $2 million and re-created the cover right down to neon signs flashing phrases like UPTOWN, FUNK CORNER, BAR & GRILL, GIRLS, GIRLS, GIRLS.

Prince started his tour April 28 in Stockholm. He'd be in Europe until July. He was on the road when Warner wanted a second single. "Sign" was a perfect introduction to the album. Now, he asked a few people for opinions about a follow-up, Alan Leeds told Prince.org, "but at the end of the day, he called the shots." Many said "Hot Thing," or "Adore," could work on rock, and R&B stations. "Adore" was still an album cut, not yet a single, but black radio played it anyway. They also kept playing "Slow Love" and "Forever in My Life," though neither was on a single. There was also demand for "Housequake." Many around him believed the quick party jam was an obvious choice. "So did Prince," Leeds remembered. "Too obvious." Leeds felt he missed the point. Singles were marketing tools for albums and "obvious is what the party calls for! Some wheels don't need reinventing."

Prince insisted his forlorn "If I Was Your Girlfriend" should be the second single. Warner went along with his choice. "Girlfriend" went on sale May 6, and alienated radio with eccentric music that didn't easily fit a format. The B-side, "Shockadelica," didn't help, with the feminine Camille voice, a flat discolike beat, and loud guitar. Then there was the imagery on various album and single covers. Photos actually showed a woman in a miniskirt holding a huge heart over her face. Since Cat Glover was unmentioned in credits, many believed the photos showed Prince in drag. Even his father John was confused. Once Cat cleared things up, he said, "Don't tell my son but I really thought he'd flipped out this time!" At cash registers nationwide, however, it was no laughing matter. Leeds noted that Prince's choice for second single did not sell as well as expected. "That we were touring Europe instead of helping the album in America didn't help," Leeds told Prince.org.

By mid-June, two weeks remained on the European tour. Prince quickly canceled plans for American dates. Every band member shook his or her head. Eric Leeds finally asked, "Are you out of your mind?"

"We're going to make a movie out of it instead," Prince replied.

Eric thought it might be a mistake. When sales of *Sign* slowed, Eric *knew* it was.

Still, Prince felt a movie could work. Once again, he'd direct. He arranged for a camera crew to film his final three shows in Rotterdam, Holland (June 27 and 28) and Antwerp, Belgium (June 29).

Cameras rolled when he went on stage with his ten-member band. They played his new mix of funk, rock, jazz, gospel, pop, and slow jams. Some moments, saxophonist Eric Leeds and trumpeter Atlanta Bliss stole the show. At others, he did, with solos that finally silenced diminishing comparisons to Jimi. Then cameras turned to catch Cat performing erotic bumps and grinds.

During "Hot Thing," he raced across a stage, slid between her legs, and snatched her skirt off with his teeth. Sheila E. played intricate beats and rolls. On cue, Sheena Easton came out to do "U Got the Look."

Back from Europe, Prince walked the corridors in his enormous, new studio complex, Paisley Park. By July 6, he resumed recording. He already had one film to finish but started planning another called *Graffiti Bridge*.

And this one would be different. He'd show a musician playing the sort of clubs his father once did in the nineteen fifties. He'd also try writing the perfect song, one that would cause this "rainbow" bridge to appear and take him away. He recorded songs like "No Changes," "Graffiti Bridge," and "Melody Cool," about an old sage. Then leaped into the second Madhouse album, 16, with the band that just toured with him. And this time, thanks to their input, it "was a much more organic album," said Eric Leeds.

Meanwhile at Warner, executives dealt with the aftereffects of his second single. They believed his lighthearted pop single "U Got the Look" would get things "back on track." They were right. The duet with Sheena—backed with "Housequake"—arrived July 14, and reached No. 2 on the Pop Chart. It was his largest hit since "Kiss," and the album's highest charting single (staying on the Pop Chart for twenty-five weeks). But when some detractors saw it reach only No. 11 on the Black Chart—stopping just outside of the Top 10—they whispered that the song "Girlfriend" and no U.S. tour had brought sales to a standstill. They claimed *Sign* was a failure when the album had in fact just passed the million-sales mark that month.

At Paisley Park, Prince worked on his concert film. While watching the footage, he saw there were problems with the multitrack tape. There wasn't enough separation between channels. He called the band into Sunset Sound and Paisley Park to rerecord their playing. "We played the entire show in the studio," said Eric Leeds. Sheila replayed every drumbeat.

The footage also troubled him. "It was just awful, grainy, and didn't look good at all," Rogers noted. "He realized, 'well if I'm going to do this, I better do it right' so he decided to perform the whole concert onstage at Paisley Park."

In mid-July, he invited a few hundred extras onto Paisley Park's soundstage. The band lip-synched while the prerecorded concert recording played. He filmed these performance scenes and numerous close-ups. "By the time the film was completely edited for release," said Eric Leeds, "the bulk of the shots, around eighty percent, were the ones we shot at Paisley Park rather than footage from the actual concerts themselves."

It was a concert movie, but Prince felt little vignettes with acting could add a dramatic story and his usual themes of love, lust, and the search for spiritual salvation. On a tiny set, he had cameras film Wally Safford and a Minneapolis model on a street. Prince was in the frame, too, eavesdropping on this unhappy couple's argument about trust. Before long, Prince stepped to the woman and created a classic love triangle.

While editing, Prince removed "Let's Go Crazy," "When Doves Cry," "Purple Rain," "1999," and "Girls and Boys." He left "Little Red Corvette," but at the last minute, deleted "Kiss." Then, someone decided to include his video for "U Got the Look." With the song in the Top 10, the video could potentially get general interest viewers' bodies into theater seats. Disregarding that it was on videotape, not film, and would make for a jarring change from the rest of the footage, Prince included it as a dream sequence in his story.

He finished post-production in August. The film cost about $2.5 million to produce, and included little actual live footage. "Of course he wanted it out immediately," said Marylou Badeaux. At Warner Pictures, an executive was wary, "especially after the situation with *Under the Cherry Moon*." This person told Prince, "Thank you but no thank you. Concert film, that's a summer thing. Hold it until the summer."

Prince replied, "No, I want it out now."

"Fine. Do it somewhere else."

And so he did. His managers inked a deal with Cineplex Odeon Films, the distribution side of a fifteen-hundred-screen Toronto-based theater chain.

20

DEAD ON IT

SEPTEMBER 11, 1987, PAISLEY PARK OFFICIALLY OPENED. THE first people inside saw that Prince was already recording. He planned to throw Sheila E. a big birthday party in LA. But after intense sessions for *Sign*, Susan Rogers recalled, "he just wanted to lay down some mindless jams." During this period, Prince was happy. Nothing "really dark" was happening, Alan Leeds noted. He was simply recording "very innocuous dance music." His "dream building, his facility, and his company" were all "growing by leaps and bounds."

He also spoke with Wendy and Lisa during this period. After he canned them, the duo signed to Columbia, and worked with drummer Bobby Z on a self-titled debut. When they occasionally spoke, Prince noticed they sounded hurt. He didn't know why. Their careers were fine. But they could be better. Hearing they planned a video for their moody lead single, the breakup song "Waterfall," he urged them to make a splash by "doing something like jumping off a speaker with smoke pouring out everywhere. Something." Instead, Wendy strummed guitar in a chair. When he saw it, he shook his head. "You can't do that when you're just getting established," he said. "Kids watching MTV see that and they go click." They'd change channels. "They'd rather watch a commercial."

Prince, however, was focused on his next film, *Graffiti Bridge*, which he decided was to be about a magical bridge. He had already recorded songs for it. Now he spent a few days in New York and in his Paris apartment quickly creating a first draft of the screenplay.

But his enthusiasm kept him from seeing how convoluted it was. First, a love triangle: a male character, Camille, caught between Cat and another female character that was to be played by Madonna. Then Camille's struggle to write the seventeen chords that formed "The Grand Progression." Then weird hobo characters and "Almost" (a guy whose body and face were half-white and half-black) dealing with angry cops and social problems. He couldn't wait to film scenes in which he and Madonna's character crossed that bridge, passing late jazz legends like Billie Holiday.

But in October, reality intruded again. Paisley Park released Madhouse's album 16, and Eric Leeds recalled, "Unfortunately, it wasn't that successful."

Prince didn't seem to mind. He was still knocking out songs for Sheila, but considering the film, which he had decided was his next official project. Thus, he created "The Grand Progression" and "Ruthie Washington's Jet Blues" for the film. Then he prepared for a visit from Madonna.

Recently, her third album, 1986's *True Blue*, generated five Top 5 singles on *Billboard* charts. But her 1986 film *Shanghai Surprise* (co-starring her husband Sean Penn) flopped, costing about $17 million and earning back about $2.3 million. Then her next film, the Warner Bros. comedy *Who's That Girl*, also flopped in early August.

In mid-October, she arrived in town to use Prince's studio. He offered special quarters but she moved into an upscale hotel in town. He passed her his script and after reading it, she reportedly told him it was "a piece of shit." He was shocked. Still, he continued to focus on it.

His good-natured party music "gradually took on a darker edge," Leeds added. There was something different about his approach. "Moody and hasty, for the first time he appeared truly obsessed, as if he had something to prove."

On "Cindy C.," Prince sang about feeling rejected by a high-class model in Paris. "Cindy C, play with me," he sang. "I will pay the usual fee." To clear up who he sang about, he mentioned seeing Cindy in *Vogue* and asked, "Where'd you get that beauty mark?" Sheila offered another stiff rap and Prince implied that the Cindy character was a prostitute, demanding, at full volume, to know why she didn't think he was good enough to date.

He revived "Rockhard in a Funky Place" from *Camille*, about a guy looking for sex in a whorehouse. Once he got some, Prince added, the guy could start thinking about playing guitar again. Prince soon mentioned the guy was so bummed out, he now wondered if God even existed. He left the whorehouse, to "head back to a life so tough."

Then he added September 1986's home-studio dance number "Superfunkycalifragisexy," which urged people to drink blood and dance.

Implying Cindy C. was a whore, since she didn't want him . . . describing bondage and discipline on one song . . . urging people to drink blood and dance . . . having his bandmates call each other "bitch" or "ho" . . . this was bad enough. But he had *really* alienated engineer Susan Rogers with his March 1987 creation "Dead On It," according to Alex Hahn. Over a rigid swing beat and whoosh noises, Prince rapped about driving in his Thunderbird and searching for a good song on its radio. He heard "a silly rapper talking silly shit." His next verse said "Negroes from Brooklyn" couldn't play bass like him. Rappers were so tone deaf, their singing would clear a packed house and have fans burning cars in the parking lot and complaining, "Rappin' done let us down." At the board, white engineer Susan Rogers felt this was pathetic. Where he once supported new sounds, he now attacked a new black-created form (after his involvement with *Krush Groove,* no less). "'Dead On It' was an embarrassment and proof positive that he didn't get it," she told author Alex Hahn.

Susan Rogers was sick of this music, this darkness, this recent attitude of his. "It just wasn't a good feeling in the air," she said. He finished the batch of party songs for Sheila, and then Rogers, a longtime member of his production team, ended their working relationship, finally leaving the fold.

Prince premiered his concert film in his key market Detroit on October 29. Then in early November, Warner released *Sign*'s final single, "I Could Never Take the Place of Your Man" backed with "Hot Thing." With it entering the Top 10, hopes were high for his new film. And this time, reviews were great. *Rolling Stone* called its article "Sign O' the Times: Prince Bounces Back with Bold Concert Movie," and said it restored his "luster as a formidable big-screen presence" and "blows away the haze of his last two LPs." The *Star Tribune*'s Jon Bream called the film splendid, noting the film confirmed he was "pop music's most exciting and provocative concert performer." The film opened in 250 theaters on November 20, and his fans rushed to buy tickets. But Eric Leeds believed not following up with an American tour "was the biggest mistake he ever made. It came at a very crucial time for him, 'cause he had some momentum going with the record." Prince had told the band his concert movie would compensate "but nobody went to see it." And not even *Sign*'s final single reaching No. 10 on the Pop Chart drew many more people to the album or film.

At home, Prince accepted that *Sign* hadn't done as well as he'd like. Then, Susannah was gone.

At Paisley Park, employees felt he was more demanding, always cranky. Some co-workers felt burned out. Susan Rogers had already left. Now, he told tour manager Karen Krattinger to work Thanksgiving week. She refused, she told author Alex Hahn. She was visiting family. "You are not my family," she stressed.

While at Sunset Sound, Prince figured he'd record three songs for the party he'd throw for Sheila's birthday in four days. It was December 7, and he programmed a forceful drum machine beat. With pitch-deepened voice, Prince played a man seeing his girl come home with a new coat.

The woman on his song said she bought the coat. The narrator scoffed. He called his manager Bob Cavallo a few names, threatened to slap this woman, then also accused Bob of buying her the ring she wore. He then asked which stars Bob managed. At the mention of Prince, he raved even more. "Don't you know I will kill you now?" he added. The song continued with him telling her to put that suitcase down, get in the bedroom, and don a wig he bought her. Cops arrived, he fired a gun at them, and a cop—Prince's comical impersonation of a white man—said, "Let's get the hell out of here." He named the song "Bob George" after his manager Bob Cavallo and writer Nelson George. In his office, co-manager Steve Fargnoli heard it: "I thought it was funny."

Prince kept working on the party songs, recycling his instrumental "2 Nigs United 4 West Compton."

He moved on to another "Housequake" sequel called "Le Grind," starting it by saying, "So you found me. Good, I'm glad." He was here to rock, he said, and no one would stop him.

After Madonna's rejection, Prince set *Graffiti Bridge* aside. He sent tapes of Sheila's party tracks—and other recent new works—to Bernie Grundman's for mastering, and submitted this as his next album.

Warner expected catchy songs from the hitmaker and creator of *Purple Rain*. Instead, he delivered what he called *The Funk Bible* in press releases (and in a hidden message on the record itself). To their ears, it was an album-length version of "Housequake," with frenzied backing vocals, filtered voices, shouts, samples, and party sounds. They heard Prince rant, laugh, and chant, slow or speed his voice, and sing in falsetto. After including expletives, references to a "bitch" or "ho," and mostly jams, Prince ended the collection with a feedback fade. But his voice returned to ask, "What kind of fucking ending was that?" Then he faded out again.

The collection confirmed Warner's suspicion that his marketing decisions were now alienating the public, and that he had abandoned tight songwriting. Still, some of these hooks could work on black radio: "Superfunkycalifragisexy's" swirling chorus; "Le Grind's" vibrant horn; "Dead On It" and "Bob George's" rap beats; his kindhearted ballad, "When 2 R in Love" (which seemed to belong on another album).

Prince then insisted the album include no printed title, artist name, liner notes, production credits, or photography, much like Rob Reiner's classic comedy *This Is Spinal Tap*. Despite trepidation, the label planned a mid-December release, and pressed hundreds of thousands of vinyl albums, cassettes, and compact discs for distribution. Promotional copies had a track listing and catalog number on the disc itself. The commercial version would have a peach-colored catalog number on the spine and a sticker.

Warner started sending advance copies of *The Funk Bible*, aimed at dance clubs and black-music radio stations, to disc jockeys in England. His advisers, Bream explained, were saying it could "interfere with the momentum of 'Sign O' the Times'" but Prince wanted—as usual—to audition his newest work in a club for unwary patrons.

December 1, about a week before its release, Prince traveled to Rupert's in Minneapolis. Entering unseen, he reached the deejay booth and asked them to play songs. While deejays did, he mingled with patrons and locked eyes with a brunette in her early twenties. "We had an instant attraction, but it was not necessarily a physical one," said Ingrid Chavez. The serious brunette had moved to Minneapolis to make music with a friend. When that soured, Chavez kept writing poetry. Like Prince, Chavez grew up in a religious home (Baptist in her case). As an adult, she continued to show an interest in spirituality. That night, she told Prince, "If you smiled you'd be a really nice person."

Later, facing his black album cover, Prince saw his miserable reflection. He considered how, if he died after releasing this, it would be what people remembered. "I could feel this wind and I knew I was doing the wrong thing. . . ." After a long conversation with Ingrid, they drove back to his studio complex where they kept talking religion, love, and life fulfillment. Then Prince said he had a stomachache and left the room.

He grabbed a phone. At about 1:30 A.M., he called Karen Krattinger, the tour manager he had asked to work on Thanksgiving week. During their emotional talk (according to Alan Leeds) Prince apologized for his stormy mood, and recent uncharacteristic behavior in the office. He didn't mean to be hard on her. He had trouble expressing feelings, he added, but he loved her.

Next, he called Susan Rogers, asking her to come to Paisley Park. After four years as his engineer, Rogers had a hard time leaving Prince behind. When she complied and arrived at the rehearsal room a few hours later, it was dark, save for red candles casting ominous shadows on walls. From the gloom, she saw Ingrid Chavez, who asked, "Are you looking for Prince?"

"Yes."

"Well, he's here somewhere."

He materialized from the dark. Rogers was spooked. "I'm certain he was high," she said. "His pupils were really dilated. He looked like he was tripping."

He struggled to connect. "I just want to know one thing. Do you still love me?" Startled, she said yes, and she knew he loved her, too.

"Will you stay?"

"No, I won't," she said, and left. ("It was really scary," she recalled.)

That night "a lot of things happened, all in a few hours," Prince later said. He told people he saw God. "And when I talk about God, I don't mean some dude in a cape and a beard coming down to Earth. To me, he's in everything if you look at it that way." He also supposedly told Chavez this *Funk Bible* was an evil force. Alan Leeds heard, "Some voice told him, 'Don't release that record.'"

Whatever the case, in that moment, Prince changed his approach to songwriting, and life itself. "I was an expert at cutting off people in my life and disappearing without a glance back, never to return," he said. "Half the things people were writing about me were true." He'd stop acting like such an angry soul.

Prince suddenly decided *The Funk Bible* represented rage and debauchery. "He couldn't sleep at night thinking about ten-year-old kids believing 'this is what Prince was about—guns and violence,'" Sheila recalled. "He said, 'I can't leave this on little kids' minds. I don't care if they pressed 500,000 copies.'"

He called Warner chairman Mo Ostin. Warner had over 400,000 copies of *The Funk Bible* in boxes, on loading docks, but Prince told Mo Ostin he'd pay whatever it cost Warner to cancel its release. "Prince was very adamant and pleaded with Mo," said Warner exec Marylou Badeaux. Once again, Warner understood. Ostin agreed. Warner would destroy the albums.

The incident inspired gossip in his studio complex corridors. Instead of "God," Fink said, Prince told Gilbert Davison he thought he saw Satan. Davison then, Fink claimed, told various band members. And the hallucination scared Prince. Even after ditching the album, Prince asked them to return cassettes he had hoped would teach them the songs. Prince meanwhile simply said, "I didn't want that angry, bitter thing to be the last thing. I learned from that album, but I don't want to go back." He told employees at Paisley Park that "Blue Tuesday," as he had dubbed it, had changed him; suddenly he exuded cheer and optimism. Alan Leeds felt an awakening inspired a sincere and major decision to change his focus, "be it temporarily or permanently." But Karen Krattinger believed, "It was a facade. It was evident to me that he still wasn't happy with his life." Warner meanwhile coped with fans somehow obtaining a few vinyl records and compact discs, and passing each other cassettes of varying quality. A few reporters claimed that Warner—despite helping Prince by agreeing to pull the album—had canceled it to censor Prince. Publicity director Bob Merlis finally told *Rolling Stone*, "I've seen things in print about how we were chicken, but we were committed to putting this record out."

21

THERE'S ALWAYS A RAINBOW

"AS USUAL, PRINCE'S ANSWER TO AN UNPLEASANT REALITY WAS to construct a reality of his own," said Alan Leeds. "Thus: *Lovesexy*."

He would reach Paisley at around eleven, spend an hour or two checking mail and handling business matters that required his input, then hit the studio with a song idea, a lyric he wrote last night, or an urge to improvise. By six or seven, he usually had something new, with tons of overdubs, almost done.

Now that he started *Lovesexy*, Leeds recalled, "the cloud over the studio lifted." He was nicer, happier, feeling good most times, and "writing from joy." Instead of fighting rap music, he started incorporating elements of it into his song "Alphabet St."

He also continued his newfound emphasis on image. After spending all day in Studio A, creating something for *Lovesexy*, he called Leeds's office. "Hey, come downstairs a minute. I've got something to play for you."

Leeds rushed down. He played Leeds his new work, dancing around, and emphasizing nuances by singing in his ear so Leeds wouldn't miss the important part. During the third high-volume playback, Prince shouted his concept for a video.

Leeds was impressed.

But Prince asked why Leeds's facial expression had changed.

"I can't believe you already have a video in mind."

He misunderstood again. "Alan, don't you get it? These kids today don't hear music like we do! They have to see music. That's what MTV has done. I have to think that way."

Another time, Leeds asked, "Why not throw away all the props and do a tour in a turtleneck and a pair of jeans where he and his band simply sang and played?"

Incredulous, Prince replied, "*What?* And look like *you* instead of a star? Nobody will pay to see someone who looks like an everyday guy!"

THERE'S ALWAYS A RAINBOW

The very idea of it scared him.

For seven weeks, he focused on *Lovesexy*, recording most of the songs in the order in which they'd appear on the album. After final sessions yielded a few funky things, he put these earlier. Then he included his ballad "When 2 R in Love."

March 2, Prince attended the thirtieth annual Grammy Awards ceremony at Radio City Music Hall. During the event, telecast live, Michael Jackson came out with long hair, a drooping blue sweater over a white shirt, high-water black pants and matching dance shoes. Prince had declined to appear on "Bad," but rightly predicted it'd be a hit. It recently became Jackson's seventh No. 1 single, in all, and *Bad's* second chart-topper. He watched Jackson perform "Man in the Mirror." He did a few moves on an empty stage. Four black women in black dresses, and gospel singer Andraé Crouch came out and sang. Lights landed on the huge blue-robed New Hope Baptist Church Choir. By song's end, Jackson sang to nothing but a bass drum and handclap, then called out to the crowd.

Prince, though, had his mind on *Sign*. Everyone had loved the album and called it a masterpiece. He expected it to do well tonight. As they reached Album of the Year, Prince listened with pride as they announced *Sign* as a nominee. It faced Whitney Houston's *Whitney*, Jackson's *Bad*, *Trio* (by Dolly Parton, Linda Ronstadt, and Emmylou Harris), and U2's *The Joshua Tree*.

To Prince's chagrin, U2 won.

"That was kind of a rude awakening," Prince said. Something in him sank. He felt like a failure, watching U2 go up and get the prize. Bono mentioned Prince's talent during his acceptance speech, but nonetheless the defeat deflated Prince.

The show continued.

Prince heard them announce Best R&B Vocal Performance by a Duo or Group. "U Got the Look" with Sheena lost. Then, for Best R&B Song, awarded to the songwriter, "U Got the Look" lost again.

Five other categories and no mention of Prince, even after a strong year. It was time to leave.

He couldn't get over U2 defeating *Sign*.

Back home, he tried to avoid wallowing in self-pity. Still, he says he "stopped caring about awards and all of that stuff."

Lovesexy was his most spiritual album to date. To make sure listeners got the entire message, he told Warner to put its many songs on a CD as only one selection. Thus, listeners couldn't skip from song to song; they'd have to hear it all. It was an odd move but Warner did it. Then the label decided "Alphabet St." could introduce his carefree new sound. It had crowded beats, catchy chants, and uplifting themes. They shipped it to radio. A video could help, but Prince wouldn't submit one.

Then, he changed his mind. March 20, it was snowing. It was also a Sunday. But in his Eden Prairie home, he wanted to work. Alan Leeds was at home, on his day off. Still, Prince called him. As soon as he answered, Prince said, "I want to shoot a video." For "Alphabet St."

Did he speak with Fargnoli?

No. Warner also didn't know.

Prince would pay for it. Alan could call Warner and they would.

No. He'd handle it.

"Okay, when?"

"Today."

Leeds tried to talk him out of it. No filmmakers were available. Even if they were, they'd have to rent equipment. With a snowstorm raging, few rental places were open.

"Sounds to me like that's your problem, not mine."

The call ended. Without a choice, Leeds made calls. A few directors said no. He called lesser-known talents.

Soon, Prince reached for the phone again. Alan answered.

"When are we shooting?"

Leeds reported he was having trouble setting it up.

Keep trying.

He did. A director named Michael Barnard would do it. Night fell and it kept snowing. Meanwhile, Barnard found a set owned by a cable company and a truck filled with video equipment.

Leeds called Prince to say it was on.

At eleven, Prince was on the set with Sheila and Cat. Barnard filmed him against a blue screen. The result looked slipshod and cheap. During postproduction, Prince had Barnard add text phrases that cruised across the screen, including a one-frame subliminal message that said, "Don't buy *The Black Album* [his unmarked *The Funk Bible*]. I'm sorry." Then: "Ecstasy."

Upon its release, April 23, the single for "Alphabet St." stalled at No. 8.

Warner rushed the video out but Alan Leeds shook his head. All of the stress involved with creating this catchpenny clip. "All this for a song that was probably beyond saving."

A week before *Lovesexy*'s release, Prince attended Michael Jackson's show in Minneapolis. After seeing Jackson moonwalk, and sing and shout, Prince proudly told him he was heading in a hopeful, new direction. But with the release date approaching, controversy surrounded *Lovesexy*'s cover by Jean-Baptiste Mondino. On it, Prince sat naked, atop a giant orchid, against a white background. *Rolling Stone* predicted, "Prince may have to pay a price" for it, and noted a few major record chains refused to order it. Many that did, stocked copies behind their counters. With reporters describing the painted photo more than his new songs, he was livid. "If you looked at that picture and some ill come out of your mouth, then that's what you are. It's looking right back at you in the mirror." That may be but Walmart refused to order copies. And at the Handleman Company, the country's largest record distributor, company head Frank Hennessey said, "Most of the accounts we service are family-oriented stores, and the cover is not one that you would consider to be an integral part of the family relationship."

Either way, Warner got the new album into stores on May 10, only a few months after he had withdrawn *The Funk Bible*. Critics offered mixed reviews. Though *Rolling Stone*, in June, gave *Lovesexy* 4 out of 5 Stars, *GQ*'s writer Stephen Fried felt the cover showed "Prince as a scrawny little Adam in a Garden of Eden." Jon Bream felt the most shocking thing about it was that it held no surprises, though he mostly approved of Prince's new direction. Many European critics loved every note. But it divided his core audience. Some liked *Lovesexy*'s riffs, hooks, and lyrics. Others frowned on overblown production, upbeat ballads, and self-righteous lyrics.

Lovesexy was self-aware and life affirming. It was also overproduced in spots. Part of Prince's spiritual reawakening meant abandoning some rock material and sanitizing a few themes. Productionwise, *Lovesexy*'s drums sound artificial. His interlocking riffs were as innovative—entering when least expected, and usually in another key—as they were, at times, distracting. Many lyrics were only vaguely spiritual, and as escapist as anything on *Around* or *Parade*. *Lovesexy* wasn't as ambitious or diverse as previous works. In spite of these limitations, it remains one of his most experimental—and consistently entertaining—works.

In print, Prince defended *Lovesexy* as "a mind trip, like a psychedelic movie. Either you went with it and had a mind-blowing experience or you didn't." Judging from sales, most didn't. *Lovesexy*'s low sales kept it out of the Top 10, making it his least successful work since 1981's *Controversy*. Sitting at No. 11, it fueled talk of his career being over.

22

I AIN'T GOT NO MONEY

"EARLY 'EIGHTY-EIGHT WAS THE FIRST TIME WE FELT FINANCIAL pressure," said Alan Leeds. But in Europe, *Lovesexy* sold 1.9 million copies, topped album charts in many countries, and emerged in many nations as his biggest-selling hit since *Purple Rain*.

Prince kept planning a show that brought fans a god-fearing message and newsworthy spectacle: handing designers sketches for bright stage costumes with lots of polka dots, sending contracts to specialist dry-cleaning stores in various cities, hiring an entourage member to hand-wash clothing in case something went wrong with the specialist dry cleaners, having four wardrobe assistants under the stage to ensure band members changed costumes within seconds, and using the tour program to explain his shelving of *The Black Album* (the name most had now taken to calling *The Funk Bible*). He also spun a fairy tale fable in the program about his *Graffiti Bridge* character Camille giving in to his hateful, competitive dark side and about wasting time and energy creating "something evil," to silence critics and express "hate 4 the ones who ever doubted his game." He tacked on an upbeat moral. If readers killed their own "spooky electric" sides, they would experience "lovesexy," a fancy term for a joyful loving relationship "with the heavens above." Considering the path he took to arrive at this album, the fable seems surprisingly apt.

After six months, he was still staging rehearsals and unveiling a costly new idea each day. "He wanted water fountains and a moat around the stage," Leeds recalled. Longtime set and lighting designer Roy Bennett, co-manager Fargnoli, and John McGraw pitched ideas. Then Bennett helped create his most ambitious and spectacular stage set ever. It cost about $2 million, and included a multilevel circular stage, see-through curtains, and a hydraulic brass bed. But the process dragged on. "Prince kept adding things and saying, 'Can I have this?'" Bennett recalled. Bennett added a swing set, a small basketball court, and his car, which alone cost $250,000, Bennett recalled, "as much as the entire *Sign O' the Times* show! But Prince wanted to have this car."

Prince worked around the clock: videotaping morning rehearsals, working in the studio until four or five in the morning, and watching the rehearsal videos when he got home before dawn. Then he dressed for another rehearsal.

He and his band practiced for months. But they spent only three weeks on full production rehearsals. Trying to determine what caused lighting problems consumed two more weeks.

He was handling another problem, too. Somewhere along the line, relations with New York's Howard Bloom Organization, the publicity team Prince had signed on to help expand his audience, had soured. Bloom kept trying to promote Prince, though he had given only one in-depth interview in six years. Prince sat in on meetings, but Bloom hadn't seen him in two years, since the campaign for *Under the Cherry Moon*. Now, employee Robyn Riggs was handling Prince's publicity but hadn't seen him since mid-May.

Recently, they tried and failed to get Prince the cover of *Rolling Stone*. "That had a lot to do with it," said Bloom, talking of their soured rapport. They got him the cover of *Vanity Fair's* upcoming September issue despite him not giving an interview; but it wasn't enough. In mid-June, Prince had Warner senior staff publicist Liz Rosenberg fly to Minneapolis to discuss his publicity.

Two weeks later, Prince reached a stunning decision. Riggs was still working on his forty-concert European tour, which would start in a week, but he fired The Howard Bloom Organization. "It happens in this business," Bloom told reporter Jon Bream. They had a good eight-year run—in a business where acts usually changed publicists once each year.

His tour was starting in days, but they were still trying to work out problems with the lighting. Inevitably, they ordered an all-new system from another company, which installed it within a day. But they had to reprogram the entire show. "Within three days, the stage set and everything was shipped off to Paris for the tour start," said set designer Roy Bennett. "So we had to do the first show as a dress rehearsal."

Opening night, July 8, in Paris, France, Prince had other things on his mind. His designers had already included phrases and colorful graphics on everyone's clothes but he approached wardrobe director Helen Hiatt. "Can you write 'Minneapolis' on the sleeve?"

Hiatt did it an hour before showtime.

Warner arranged more publicity. Major magazines shipped reporters to the show. MTV and BET wanted to televise part of it. But Warner's Bob Merlis arrived to find Prince wouldn't let them film anything. People claimed he was angry with a French media outfit running an unbecoming photo of him near a better one of Michael Jackson. Either way, MTV's Kurt Loder vowed to fill on-air time with disgruntled journalists. Prince reversed his decision but during his two-hour show for seventeen thousand fans at the Palais Omnisports de Paris, Bercy, BET's video crew was left literally out in the rain, hoping someone would let them into the venue.

Prince attended a party Warner threw after the show. Warner publicist Liz Rosenberg led some journalists over to his post near a buffet table, but Prince decided reporters wouldn't be able to interview his band after all. By curtailing all access, Alan Leeds explained, Prince wanted reporters to have no choice *but* to cover his music. The move, however, backfired. *Musician's* writer tried to ask Bob Merlis why Prince and Fargnoli reneged on the promised interview. Merlis had no idea. Fargnoli stalled the writer and left. The writer approached Fargnoli the next night after Prince's second show in Paris. Fargnoli left even quicker. The writer tried again. Fargnoli claimed they hadn't promised the interviews.

The writer went on to contact twenty associates. Hearing most wouldn't speak on the record, former bassist Mark Brown said, "That's pretty typical. The guy doesn't want anybody to know about him." Then Jimmy Jam explained nonparticipants either respected Prince's privacy or had "some sort of fear, if they're pursuing a career, that he can ruin it if they say the wrong thing."

For his part, Prince had moved on to thinking about his next single. He told Warner to put his ambitious "Glam Slam" out next. The label agreed. But then Prince changed his mind a day before Warner shipped copies to stores. This time, label executives ignored him. Record shops had received copies and were about to start placing them on shelves.

He told Warner to pull it, sensing it'd tank. Unfortunately for him, he was right. "Glam Slam" arrived on July 11, Bream explained, "and it completely missed the mark." Radio stations ignored it to the point where it didn't even make *Billboard*'s Hot 100 Pop Chart.

Prince's European tour continued, and so did the costs for a staff of ninety. As he played Milan, Italy, his payroll grew to include hundreds of employees. He also paid for over fifty trucks lugging his equipment, props, and wardrobe. There were four hair and makeup people. And too many outfits. "That's how excessive things were in the eighties," Eric Leeds quipped.

The tour continued, with high overhead. Prince reached London in late July. At the Chelsea Harbor Hilton, his valet wanted the usual baby grand piano in Prince's room. A promoter said they couldn't do it. His valet said, "There's got to be a way. It's the Presidential Suite."

"The only way we could do it is if we got a crane and lifted it over the balcony."

"Do that."

And so, to satisfy Prince, that's precisely what they did. They lifted it three floors, and removed it the same way. Prince would have his piano during his month in London. "In those days," the valet told the Minneapolis *Star Tribune*, "you didn't want to cut corners."

In every venue, the three-level, seventy-by-eighty-foot stage was usually in the center. But during his show, he felt exposed. It was a circular stage. "He had nowhere to go, nowhere to hide," said Bennett. Forever in the spotlight, he had to perform every second. Even worse, everyone saw his reaction when something went wrong. Then, at certain points, the band had to cram into a tight space under the stage and change clothes. Along with about twenty employees, the space held various props and equipment.

Every night, Eric Leeds bumped his elbow on the same bed in a corner. Eventually, he asked, "Why is it here?"

Head of wardrobe Helen Hiatt laughed. "Eric, 'Dirty Mind.'"

"What about it?"

"The bed is in 'Dirty Mind.'"

The next night, when he started "Dirty Mind," Eric turned and saw the contraption rise into view. "We had been on the road a month with this show, and I didn't know!" he said. "That's when I realized that I didn't have a clue what this show was about. I was just playing my part."

Between dates, in August, Prince kept flying back to Paisley Park to record more songs. Once he finished, his assistant Therese came in to transcribe lyrics. But one week during a visit, he was sick and told people he couldn't sing. Still, he made his weekend session last forty hours, without breaks for meals or sleep. An engineer asked, "Do you want headphones to get the lyrics?"

"What lyrics?" his assistant said. "He's not supposed to be singing. He's got strep throat."

On the road, Prince also called engineer Chuck Zwicky at Paisley Park. He wanted Zwicky to enter the vault and mix a few songs. "I think I did 130 songs that had never appeared anywhere."

Prince was trying to bring his fans a show with the vitality and excitement they had come to expect from him. But everywhere he went, it seemed, Michael Jackson, coincidentally or not, was on his heels. In October, Prince arrived in Manhattan to play two nights at Madison Square Garden. A day after the first show, October 2, Michael Jackson played the New Jersey Meadowlands Arena, the first of three nights and enough to inspire *The New York Times* to call it a potential "trans-Hudson battle of the bands."

The media had promoted the two as pop's biggest stars. They described a rivalry similar to the one between the Beatles and the Rolling Stones, casting Jackson as the innocent and Prince as the bad boy. As usual, Prince ignored it. He and Jackson were friendly backstage and had discussed working together. But their two tours would—if all went as planned—continue to keep meeting up with each other on the road. After Madison Square Garden, Prince was to play the Washington area. Jackson would arrive there within days for three shows. Jackson would then play Detroit from October 24 to 26. Prince would play Long Island on the twenty-fourth, then reach his key market Detroit on October 30, to play two nights. Then, in November, Prince would play Los Angeles on the fifth, seventh, and eighth. But Jackson would arrive on the thirteenth, and play the next two days, and then November 20, 21, and 22.

But Prince didn't worry. Their shows were similar in that both presented choreographed dance routines, programmed lights, extravagant costumes, special effects, flags adorned with peace symbols, even simulated gunplay—but as performers, they were completely different. Jackson was clean-cut and humble, asking his audiences for permission to step to another part of the stage. Prince took control from the moment he stepped into view and didn't let up. Jackson and his professional dancers did the same routine every night. Prince changed things up, adlibbing, changing his set list, rearranging his hits. Jackson played traditional G-rated pop and ballads while Prince ran through rock, jazz, swing music, soul, bygone Blues, even raw hip-hop. Jackson kept two spotlights on him, and stopped songs so he could freeze during a dance move—stooping over like a robot, getting on his tiptoes—and hear fans applaud. Prince started call and response routines, chiding fans if they did not sing loud enough. Jackson's lyrics emphasized terror, loneliness, and love; Prince interchanged medleys of ballads with funk numbers.

Prince kept dividing the Lovesexy show into two parts. The first featured risqué hits. As the band did short versions, he played sassy Camille, and interacted with Sheila, Cat, and keyboardist Boni Boyer. In his mind, this part presented a message about sexual temptation. But at his keyboard, Matt Fink shook his head. "I was always unhappy with doing the medleys." People wanted full songs.

During "Anna Stesia," while the band noodled on instruments, Prince sat and preached to the crowd, sometimes for ten minutes. "It was overkill. I thought it was a big waste of time, and the audience didn't get it." During the second part, Prince had the band play entire songs but still tried to push a message about salvation, asking crowds if they believed in God, saying God was in everyone.

Prince knew it was an odd show but he felt the first part was what they expected and the second was where it was at.

Backstage, Prince had *Purple Rain*'s director Albert Magnoli ready to shoot a documentary. He had replaced Fargnoli as his closest confidante. Where co-manager Fargnoli once followed his instructions to the letter, he now disagreed with a few questionable ideas. For instance, he didn't believe in *Graffiti Bridge*. "Fargnoli was saying, 'You shouldn't do this, that was a mistake,'" Warner's Marylou Badeaux remembered; and Prince was shouting, "You don't believe in me anymore!" Then Magnoli entered the picture, she added, whispering in his ear, playing to his insecurities. "Everybody knew Prince was influenced by whomever had his ear and Magnoli told him what he wanted to hear." Without warning, Prince tried to fire Fargnoli. Bob Cavallo, who usually ran the firm in LA, joined Prince on the road to smooth things over. Prince stayed with the firm, for now, and arrived back home, where *Lovesexy* had faded after less than three months on the charts. American concerts didn't instantly sell out.

Wednesday, September 14, at the Met Center in Minneapolis, Prince wore his white suit with the black polka dots and "Minneapolis" on his left sleeve, and entered the white Thunderbird. He drove it onto the 5,600-square-foot, three-tiered theater-in-the-round stage, circled it, then got out. Despite his antics in Paris, Warner flew various radio programmers and contest winners to town. A crowd of Warner employees—planning a third *Lovesexy* single, "I Wish U Heaven"—also arrived by jet; along with reporters from *Time, Newsweek, The New York Times*, the *Philadelphia Inquirer*, and TV's *Entertainment Tonight*. Prince ran through excerpts of past hits, but his sellout crowd of 13,500 seemed bored with them.

Later that night, he attended a party in Paisley Park's parking lot. They would have invited the six hundred guests inside but actors in Muppet costumes rented the soundstage for a show rehearsal, so employees set eight spinning searchlights outside, filled tents with Lovesexy posters, and covered the asphalt with synthetic flower petals.

He saw his mother Mattie in the crowd. At 2:20, he mounted a stage and smiled. "Now we're going to wake up the farmers across the street." Soon, he poked fun at Madonna, including a few bars of "Material Girl" in one jam. His mother cried, "This is his best concert ever. That's because it's free; improvisational." At 3:45, he wrapped things up. He had to be back at the Met Center in seven hours to let Jean-Baptiste Mondino film a video for "I Wish U Heaven."

Prince had turned the once-pithy number into a ten-minute suite. The first portion stressed a dance beat. The middle included new lyrics that evoked "Housequake" and Brian DePalma's *Scarface* ("Say hello to my little friend . . ."). The finale found his "Jamie Starr" voice from old *Time* albums claiming his beats were "so fine." Its B-side held a raunchy Camille song—"Scarlet Pussy."

September 20, Warner released "I Wish U Heaven" with a cover that showed his soft-lit face—not facing the viewer, paler than usual—and a strange tiny hand in the backdrop. It managed to reach No. 18 on the R&B Chart but tour costs weighed heavily on his mind. Shows in Chicago, Detroit, and New York City sold out quickly but Jon Bream predicted he'd play Western states "if only because his business advisers hope to recoup its $2 million production expenses."

Sensing *Lovesexy* had run its course, Prince worked to make *Graffiti Bridge* a reality. In California, he showed his managers a twenty-page document detailing his idea for the movie. He then passed it to Cavallo. Cavallo saw elements of *Purple Rain,* which he enjoyed, then cheerfully said, "This is a good idea. Let's get you with some hip young screenwriters and make this happen."

Prince fixed him with a look of confusion. "We don't need any screenplay. This is all we need."

Cavallo said this was a treatment. It needed to be developed.

No it didn't.

Cavallo rose and shook his hand. "I don't think I can do it."

Prince left the office, but this discussion was far from over.

23

A SPACE TO FILL

BY DECEMBER 5, PRINCE SAW *LOVESEXY* FINALLY REACH THE 500,000 sales mark. Instead of leaping right into another album, Prince planned to take 1989 off. Warner didn't expect, or want another album until Christmas. "All parties had decided that it didn't make sense for Prince to put out a Prince record for some time," said A&R executive Michael Ostin. Warner now believed he was "confused and a little frustrated" about his career since *Purple Rain*, and actually causing lower sales with oversaturation. "As brilliant as he is," Ostin added, "the audience has a hard time keeping up with him." But another opportunity came his way by month's end.

Director Tim Burton was filming *Batman*, a big budget darker interpretation of DC Comics' Caped Crusader. And one of his stars, Jack Nicholson, was a Prince fan. Burton was, too, playing Prince tapes in his car while driving to the studio. While creating his rough cut, Burton temporarily set "1999" and "Baby I'm a Star" over two party scenes. Eventually, Nicholson urged him to hire Prince. In December, Prince was elated to hear both wanted him to remake the songs for the film. Neil Hefti's "Batman" TV theme was among the first things he learned to play on the piano. At Warner, executives didn't mind. *Batman* would let him record a new album without it being a Prince record. "Being attached to something with this kind of buzz; that could only be a positive right now," said Michael Ostin. *Batman* could potentially boost U.S. interest in him. Gary LeMel, president of Warner Bros. Music, was even more enthusiastic. With the Joker in purple spraying purple poison gas in a museum, and his gang driving purple cars, LeMel said, "Prince's involvement was fated."

But Prince and his managers butted heads again. He wanted to back out of Japanese dates, they believed, to work on *Graffiti Bridge*. But the shows were already booked and customers had bought tickets, Fargnoli explained. "He could have been sued [for up] to $10 to $20 million. If you don't show up, you pay for it." Fargnoli felt it was another example of Prince wanting to "satisfy his creative urge" but not making "intelligent business decisions."

For Prince this was the last straw. Until now, he and his managers had enjoyed a lucrative relationship. Immediately after Warner steered them his way, Cavallo and Ruffalo sent employees to help Prince with day-to-day chores so he could concentrate on recording his music. They promoted one of these helpers—Steve Fargnoli—to a full partner and helped with *Dirty Mind* (persuading Warner to release his home demos), *1999* (convincing the label to release a risky double-album from a relative unknown), and *Purple Rain* (helping him secure financing from Warner chair Mo Ostin). His managers also helped him talk Warner into releasing *Around the World in a Day* despite minimal promotion; helped scout locations and handled preproduction chores for *Under the Cherry Moon;* pitched Warner on his triple-album version of *Crystal Ball*. And they said nothing when reporters arrived in Paris during the Lovesexy Tour and he suddenly decided to cancel interviews with band members.

Now, Prince wanted to create *Graffiti Bridge* and offer it the same thin support. He allegedly planned to cancel shows in February that were already booked. And, while his creative choices—and offstage antics—surely contributed to lower album sales and less interest from music fans, Prince seemed to think the blame belonged to the firm.

In early January 1989, he shocked people by firing his Los Angeles–based managers. When Prince also fired his accountant and business manager, the media, including the Minneapolis *Star Tribune,* started calling it a housecleaning. Even more surprising, he tapped film director Albert Magnoli as his new manager. At *Billboard,* black music editor Nelson George said, "It's amazing that he would make that move. I don't know what to make of it."

Prince also ended his eleven-year relationship with attorney Lee Phillips. He hired Ziffren, Brittenham, Branca to represent him instead. People around him believed that, after the Lovesexy Tour lost money, he unfairly blamed his managers, attorney, and business manager. Rather than admit he'd been imprudent, hadn't paid enough attention to "the financial aspects of the business," be it "record-making, touring, or running a studio—it was easier to blame everybody," said Alan Leeds.

————

In mid-January, Prince took the Concorde to London for a private screening of *Batman* footage at Pinewood Studios. The Gotham City set awed him. He watched Burton film a batcave scene with Batman (Michael Keaton) and female reporter Vicki Vale (Kim Basinger). After meeting both, and getting on well with Basinger, he viewed thirty to forty minutes of Burton's rushes. Leaving the screening room, he told an associate, "I can hear music. I hear the music in these scenes."

Burton wanted one or two songs, but, in characteristic fashion, Prince canceled a vacation in Paris and returned to Minneapolis for a week of recording. Then, after a two-week tour of Japan in early February, he returned for more frenzied, around-the-clock sessions.

New manager Albert Magnoli remembered his "instantaneous affinity" for *Batman*. Warner was also, an insider claimed, paying over $1 million in fees and advances for the album. A month after seeing *Batman* footage, Prince played Burton eight songs, most synched to footage. Burton was overwhelmed. "He was way ahead of me," he said. "Vicki Waiting" was first. Once called "Anna Waiting," after a pal, it was moody and intense. He played "Rave Un2 the Joy Fantastic" and his instrumental "The Batman Theme." He also played "200 Balloons," another flat beat and guitar work in the "Shockadelica" mold; and the dense and indecipherable "Electric Chair." Burton rejected the theme, "Rave Un2 the Joy Fantastic," and "200 Balloons," but accepted the others.

Producer Jon Peters rethought a number of the film's elements, including the score. Originally, Prince was to compose "for the dark characters only," Peters said. Now Peters wanted more glossy Prince music. On the set, Prince watched Burton try to make the film he envisioned when he accepted the assignment. "There was so much pressure on Tim," Prince recalled, "that for the whole picture I just said, 'Yes, Mr. Burton, what would you like?'" Yet, he quickly responded to producers' calls for more music with "Trust" and "Partyman," lightweight ditties that nevertheless struck Warner executives as some of his best stuff in years.

Then, undeterred by rejection, he returned to "200 Balloons," replacing most components with sampled film dialogue, new beats, a variety of riffs, and a new title ("Batdance"). In the end, Tim Burton included six of nine tracks in his film: "Partyman," "Trust," "The Future," "Scandalous," "Vicki Waiting," and "Electric Chair." But he swapped instrumentals for the last two and rejected "Batdance," "Lemon Crush," and "The Arms of Orion," with Sheena Easton.

That summer, he put other projects on hold. He was working on *Batman* and, Eric Leeds remembered, "had to hurry up and finish—he was in overdrive getting that done." At the time, he didn't plan to promote the *Batman* soundtrack, his new publicist Jill Willis explained, "but then it was somewhat abruptly decided that it would be publicized—and the project could be 'worked.'" Once Warner mastered the record, Prince started work on the "Batdance" video. With Magnoli, he dreamed up a corny plot: He'd appear as himself and a dual personality called Gemini that resembled a cross between Batman and the Joker. They hired fifteen dancers and choreographer Barry Lather. But Warner didn't want any movie footage in this clip, preferring to reserve it for the true soundtrack, Danny Elfman's score, which would arrive in August.

USA Today's Edna Gundersen titled a supportive article "Batdance to fly on MTV." June 20, MTV gave it a big video premiere. Then Warner released the nine-song *Batman: Motion Picture Soundtrack* on June 23 to effusive praise. *Rolling Stone* and other critics called it some of Prince's most commercial work in years. Even better, *Batman* returned him to the U.S. charts. "Batdance" reached No. 1 on *Billboard*'s Hot 100. And while *Batman* fans debated whether "Partyman" was the film's most unforgettable or jarringly inapt moment, the album sold a million copies in seven days, making it one of the fastest sellers in history.

Publicly, Prince's image was as sterling as it had ever been. *Rolling Stone* opined that at decade's end, five years after *Purple Rain*, its influence, and his own, were incontestable. He was one of only two artists (Bruce Springsteen was the other) to place four albums in their *100 Greatest Albums of the Eighties* list. "And perhaps more than any other artist, Prince called the tune for pop in the Eighties, imprinting his Minneapolis sound on an entire generation of musicians, both black and white."

That autumn, according to Alex Hahn, Kim Basinger came to see him. They talked of collaborating on *Graffiti Bridge,* and she helped with a treatment that had a few people laughing behind Prince's back. "It was about a guy who goes on a search for God," one reader said. "God turned out to be a blond who seemed a lot like Kim Basinger." Still, he remained proud of it. He had Basinger's moaning on an eighteen-minute mix of his *Batman* ballad "Scandalous," and continued to try to involve her in his professional activities.

During a visit to the office of Warner executive Lenny Waronker, he was visibly stunned to see that Basinger accompanied Prince. "She's sitting in front of me," Waronker recalled. "She has her legs crossed." Prince passed Waronker the cassette. After five or six minutes of seductive moaning, Prince tapped his shoulder. "That's good enough." Warner executives agreed. November 28, they released a four-minute-and-twelve-second edit as a single called "The Scandalous Sex Suite."

At one point, he wanted to release photos of Kim Basinger to the press. By this point, new publicist Jill Willis saw, "Prince had both good and bad ideas." He'd become frustrated with her "or anyone who didn't agree with his suggestions or ideas," she explained. Even so, she resisted any idea she thought lacked sense and refused to deliver messages she felt "were crazy or irresponsible or damaging to his reputation or his relationships." When Willis didn't immediately rush to send the Basinger shots to media outlets—instead, she contacted her representatives to get their opinion—Willis recalled that Prince ranted and raved about her disobeying his instructions.

But Basinger supposedly got bored with sitting in the studio. She flew back to Hollywood. "She's a sore subject around here," said Craig Rice, Paisley's facility director. Prince redesigned *Graffiti Bridge* without her.

In LA, Prince had Albert Magnoli join him at a meeting with Morris Day, Jimmy Jam, and Terry Lewis. Various Time members had approached Warner with their own film project. One member told executives, "We want to do another record and a movie." They had a screenwriter, but wanted Prince's help with the music, believing his participation would make it a true Time album. Prince meanwhile wanted to see if they could come together for *Graffiti Bridge*. Nothing was truly resolved during this talk. A few band members refused to participate in a band reunion. But Prince kept barreling forward as if they had, even going so far as to begin planning yet another Time album for which he would write all the songs, play every note, and lay out precise blueprints for how vocals should sound.

As preproduction continued, however, Magnoli had doubts about the script and Prince's plan to film it all with cheap sets on his soundstage. And so, rather than be involved with a project that could prove disastrous, Magnoli left the project. Prince tried working with manager Arthur Spivak but their chemistry didn't seem to mix, publicist Jill Willis recalled. They stopped working together just when he wanted to create a new film then tour. "He needed someone to act as his manager and put it all together," Willis noted. Anonymous sources told reporters his early treatment amounted to gibberish. "That was just a real rough thirty-page treatment I wrote with Kim," Prince said. "*Graffiti Bridge* is an entirely different movie."

Before long, Prince learned two management firms, Stiefel Phillips and Lippman Kahane, were in talks with his attorney, Gary Stiffelman, and his business manager and accountant, Nancy Chapman. Based in LA, Arnold Stiefel and Randy Philips represented clients like Guns N' Roses and Rod Stewart, among others. Stiefel had also been involved with various films, including Bette Midler's *The Rose*, and the Talking Heads' *Stop Making Sense*. They promised a deal for *Graffiti Bridge* when "no one else wanted to touch it," Marylou Badeaux recalled. In the end, Stiefel and Philips received the "twelve-month management consultancy contract," Jill Willis remembered, before Prince actually met them. Prince told people not to refer to them as "his new managers," Willis continued. The management team meanwhile got him the film deal.

They sold it to Warner Bros. Pictures as a Prince musical. "He's positively perceived at Warner Bros. Pictures," Stiefel reported. "We presented the idea at the end of the day on a Tuesday and got the go-ahead by Wednesday morning."

But the story also changed. Now, as in *Purple Rain*, Prince would play the Kid. But this time, a dying friend left him and Morris a club called Glam Slam. Morris felt The Time's funk sets were earning money while the Kid's offbeat music and Janet Jackson–like dance routines were turning people off. So the two bands battled over the club's direction.

Prince met with The Time. "The next thing we knew, there was *Graffiti Bridge*," said Jimmy Jam. "It became his project, and we were just kind of the bit players." Prince agreed to let them co-write and record new tracks for a revised album called *Pandemonium*. They agreed to star in the film. Warner was happy. The Time album was suddenly scheduled.

The Time cleared red tape and schedules, and arrived at Paisley Park to play Day's band and henchmen, and record new songs, without him. But they didn't discuss touring, or anything but *Graffiti Bridge*. "We'd like to see all that happen, but nothing happens if you push it," said Jam.

With Warner and The Time on board, Prince moved on to casting other parts. Ingrid Chavez, he decided, would be the romantic lead. He hired the twenty-five-year-old to play Aura, the Kid's spiritual guide. "Kim Basinger had become Ingrid Chavez and Patti LaBelle had become Mavis Staples," said Arnold Stiefel. Next, Prince recruited singer Jill Jones. But while flying to Minneapolis, Jones read the revised script and saw Prince had fused Kim Basinger's role to Jill's and handed it all to Ingrid. Her new part was a smaller rehash of her walk-on role in *Purple Rain* (another woman whose musical ambitions he stifles). She tore the script up, hurled pieces around the cabin, then fled to the bathroom. Her assistant darted down an aisle, saying, "That number 58 page there, in your fettuccine, can I have it please?" Jones thought, if she weren't already on the plane, she'd go home.

24

PARDON ME FOR LIVING

PRINCE STARTED WORKING ON THE SOUNDTRACK FOR *GRAFFITI Bridge*. Unlike with *Batman*, he worked slowly, creating a two-disc compilation from tracks he created over the last few years. Instead of rock guitar, however, he filled it with drum machines, synthesizers, and samples. Some sessions, he stopped playing a new idea and faced new engineer Michael Koppelman, a fan since *Purple Rain* and new to town. "You like that sort of shit don't you?"

Usually, Koppelman said, "Yup, I do."

He'd then play something completely different.

Another time, he and engineer Tom Garneau were recording with a TV monitor on, which was usually the case. When an ad for the group 10,000 Maniacs aired, Prince pointed at them, and sneered. "Do you like these guys?"

Garneau replied, "Actually, I like them a lot. I thought it was one of this year's best albums."

With a smile, Prince said he really liked them, too.

"Who knows what that was really about," Garneau quipped.

As sessions continued, Prince created "Tick, Tick, Bang," a glossy keyboard over Jimi Hendrix's opening beat on "Little Miss Lover." He added "The Question of U," a catchy pop melody with numerous vocals, overdubs, handclaps, and abnormal grooves. He reworked a four-song sequence from an early version of *Dream Factory* and filled The Time number, "Shake," with a big rock beat, sampled bass, and pop keyboard evoking Question Mark and the Mysterians' "96 Tears." The only new material was "New Power Generation," "Round and Round," and "Thieves in the Temple."

At the same time, Prince, never satisfied to have just one project in the works, started creating tracks for his next album. Songs came when least expected. And sometimes, they came back. This seemed to be the case with "Diamonds and Pearls," a ballad that recycled part of a melody from Sheila E.'s fast-paced "Romance 1600." Another time, Prince was in front of a mirror when lyrics for a song called "Cream" arrived. In the studio, he created a pop rock track that evoked T. Rex, The Cars' "Dangerous Type," and The Time's "Shake." Then he sang, smoothly, asking a woman to "get on top."

During one of these sessions, he told his new nineteen-year-old drummer Michael Bland, "Play the break like on *Fresh*, like how he goes over the barlines on 'In Time.'"

Bland asked, "What's *Fresh*?"

"Oh man, you haven't heard 'In Time' on *Fresh*? You've got to stay after school."

Fresh was a Sly & The Family Stone album, one of a dozen works he had his housekeeper bring to Studio A. For three hours, Prince played Sly's music and Graham Central Station and analyzed every note.

Another day, Prince entered a studio and saw his bassist Levi Seacer, Jr., working with a thickset singer named Rosie Gaines. She was helping Levi create a demo for the Pointer Sisters. After she stopped singing, Prince quickly invited her into The New Power Generation. She wanted to be a soloist. "Join up with us," he replied, "and I'll put a record out on you."

He soon had her singing "Diamonds and Pearls" with him.

January arrived, and Prince still needed someone to sing "Round and Round." He considered Tevin Campbell. Warner executive Benny Medina and Michael Jackson's former producer Quincy Jones discovered the eleven-year-old grade school student in Texas and had him sing two songs on Jones's *Back on the Block*, an all-star album for Jones's Warner-backed Qwest imprint. Prince reached for his phone. A kid answered. "Can I speak to Tevin?"

"This is Tevin. Who is this?"

"This is Prince."

Prince asked him to come to Minneapolis to sing "Round and Round" for the soundtrack, fit him into the cast as Mavis's son, then—as a concession to a label executive—let Junior Vasquez, who remixed stuff for Madonna, work on "Round and Round," the first time an outsider touched his tracks. Then Vasquez's remix somehow became the album version of the song, engineer Tom Garneau recalled.

Finally, Prince ended sessions with "Thieves in the Temple." He entered the studio one day with the complex number done in his head. "We recorded and mixed it in one marathon thirty-hour session," engineer Tom Garneau recalled. After Michael Koppelman spent fifteen hours at the board, Garneau took over. It was grueling, he recalled, but "strangely enjoyable being part of the process."

A day after finishing it, Prince leaped right into filming its video. Prince started filming *Graffiti Bridge* February 15. The first day, Stiefel flew in from Los Angeles. Minutes before shooting, Stiefel visited Prince's dressing room and saw him in an outfit that reminded Stiefel of *Flashdance.* "When are you going to change?"

Prince stared blankly. "I'm not. This is what I'm wearing. What's wrong with it?"

"What's wrong with it? Everything."

Stiefel left.

Within minutes, a bodyguard approached on the soundstage. "He'd be more comfortable if you weren't here."

Stiefel asked, "You mean here on the set?"

"No. Here in Minneapolis."

Warner had Peter MacDonald working out of an office outside the main courtyard. MacDonald had worked in the business for over thirty years, operating the camera for Bob Fosse's *Cabaret* and Barbra Streisand's *Yentl;* directing *Rambo III;* executive producing Stallone's *Tango & Cash.* Now, he claimed he was merely an executive producer, not a potential backup director. "The idea is his. The script is his. The music is his. It seemed like a good bet to put him in charge."

On the soundstage, Prince had work crews re-create the Seven Corners of the 1950s—a local intersection where seven streets ran into each other, and jazz musicians like Prince's father John Nelson played sets in the area's many nightclubs, hoping to become famous. Extras meanwhile dressed as hipsters. It all resembled old Gene Kelly musicals. "Yeah, cheap!" Prince quipped. "Actually, that's okay. It's like how we did *Dirty Mind.* But man, what I'd do with a $25 million budget."

As director, Prince handled every problem thrown his way. But the biggest seemed to be his vow to deliver "a different kind of movie. It's not violent," he continued. "Nobody gets laid."

At one point, it was working out. "We're already two days ahead of schedule," MacDonald reported. "That's probably because he doesn't sleep." But he kept bringing new songs to the set and shoehorning them into the film. "When he comes in humming," MacDonald quipped, "we all know we're in trouble."

From the sidelines, Alan Leeds remembered *Purple Rain* brilliantly capturing an era. "Most importantly, it was a film produced and directed by professionals." He had qualms about the new one, though. Prince could be a great director and producer if he'd "study and learn the craft." Instead, he hired a crew that unquestioningly followed orders. He made lighting a scene take even more time by improvising changes on the spot. He kept arguing with MacDonald and trying to cram eighteen or nineteen musical numbers into a thirty-six-day shoot. "It's been a challenge to stay just behind him," MacDonald soon explained. "His energy: It never seems to run out, unfortunately. I'd like for him to get tired a bit more often so we can go home."

There were other obstacles. His final week of shooting, CBS started filming a TV movie in town. Some of his crew left for that project. Then he couldn't always find equipment or facilities. On the last day of shooting, Benny Medina was still at Paisley Park. Head of Warner's black-music division in Burbank, Medina was the top executive handling his albums.

As usual, Warner wanted to promote at least three singles to radio before the film's release. Medina needed to know what the first single would be. He wouldn't leave until he got an answer. Without one, Warner wouldn't be able to start pushing the music.

If he wrapped principal photography today, Warner would book the film in fourteen hundred theaters by August. Knowing music drew people to movies, Medina wanted to release a Time single to black radio in April, trailers to theaters after Memorial Day, a Prince single in June, a second Time single in July, and scenes from the movie in both acts' videos. Prince felt it was a great plan, just the sort of high-powered promotional push he felt his work deserved.

In March 1990, after thirty-six days, Prince completed principal photography. Instead of his typical unbridled confidence, he told a reporter he'd survive if *Graffiti Bridge* flopped. "I can't please everybody," he said.

That month, Sinéad O'Connor's cover of The Family's "Nothing Compares 2 U" was all over pop radio. Her producer Nellee Hooper had ignored Prince's pianos, and overdubs, and emphasized a mellow drum-beat, minimal keyboard, and her piercing vocal. Reporters preferred her version to The Family's original and most of Prince's own recent work. And O'Connor's manager, Steve Fargnoli—now running a new London-based agency, Pure Acts Ltd.—bragged, "She is not someone who is driven by a pop career or pop sales." She was exciting. "She's willing to take risks because she's not trying to protect anything . . . such as a record ca-reer. She'll do what interests her."

Despite having written the shaved-headed singer's hit, Prince still heard anxiety from the Warner executive visiting his complex. Prince was asked to delay the *Graffiti Bridge* album so his five-million-seller *Batman* could sell more copies, and not jeopardize sales of both albums.

Prince ignored this and threw himself into rehearsing for another tour. His new managers organized it quickly. But they didn't tie it to the new album. If anything, it would let Prince capitalize on overseas popu-larity and generate revenue.

In April, he was still rehearsing when he heard forty-nine-year-old Chick had died of heart failure on April 2.

After leaving in 1985, his former bodyguard sank so low he sold his lawnmower to buy coke. But he kicked the habit, becoming an evangelist, who lectured in schools and prisons. Now, he died without life insurance. Prince agreed to help Chick's widow Linda and his six kids by playing a hundred-dollar-a-ticket concert at Rupert's Nightclub.

That night, six hundred people showed up. His mother Mattie sat near Chick's widow and kids. More than just a benefit, Prince used the show to test-market his upcoming tour set.

His shirtless silhouette opened with a brief eulogy and "The Future" (one of four *Batman* songs). He told everyone the show was for Chick, who was "looking down, smiling." His new dancers joined him on Rupert's small stage, to perform steps that evoked some by then-popular Bobby Brown. Prince did a few signature hits. "Alphabet St." included part of Rob Base and DJ E-Z Rock's current rap hit, "It Takes Two." New singer Rosie Gaines covered Aretha's "Respect." He introduced "Purple Rain" by saying Chick usually played air guitar when Prince was on stage playing its solo. He dedicated this performance to Chick and filled it with fiery Jimi-like solos.

Besides "The Question of U," his set list held plenty of old hits. Prince rearranged their elements but longtime fan and writer Per Nilsen still felt he should set them aside for a while. "After all, Prince had played them on all of his four European tours since 1986." He played more old songs then threw in "Nothing Compares 2 U," popularized only a month ago by Sinéad. In the end, he raised about sixty thousand dollars for Chick's family. And *Rolling Stone*'s David Fricke felt, "This was the kind of Prince gig you don't get to see much anymore: no fancy props or heavy sacred-sexual shtick, just hit songs, dirty dancing, whiplash funk, and blowtorch guitar."

Prince finished his first cut of *Graffiti Bridge* on April 19. Warner saw a rough cut and felt the story was unintelligible and it looked amateurish. The studio nevertheless arranged a screening in the Pasadena theater where *Purple Rain* pulled in its second-highest grosses. But three or four unruly viewers kept making wisecracks. After the screening, people kept saying it sucked. "It was all mixed up," Ingrid Chavez recalled. "There wasn't much of a story there." The characters were unsympathetic, she added. He was improvising on the set, following gut instincts. "But when it came to putting it together, he realized he needed to structure it a little bit better." His manager Stiefel however defended it. "Never have a screening in Pasadena," he said. "The film was not ready yet. The sound was wrong. It was too early." Either way, Warner Bros. Pictures said it needed editing. But his new managers Arnold Stiefel and Randy Phillips had a tour ready to start.

Warner enlisted Steve Rivkin, brother of Bobby Z and David Rivkin, to edit the film, still wanting to open in fourteen hundred U.S. cinemas on August 7. Prince wanted to postpone the tour to finish the film but couldn't: Money was at stake. The tour kicked off in Dublin on April 27, but he wanted to stay in the loop while he toured Europe. He kept receiving videotapes of edited scenes, dictating changes by telephone, and moving dates around to buy time in the editing room.

His summer tour of Europe and Japan would build anticipation for his film and album *Graffiti Bridge*. Instead of a show as structured as the Lovesexy Tour, he wanted something as loose and unpredictable as a party. In Spain, he took the stage with blinding lights—ten feet high— spelling his name. When he reached "Purple Rain," the lights rose. He started playing the guitar. Everyone in the crowd pulled out their lighters. "It was a real golden-oldies thing," an observer noted. But he played only one verse and the solo. He then lingered at a piano, with long, winding melodies that led to an austere "Nothing Compares 2 U."

He reached Germany, where he'd play July 22 to 29. And after one show, everything changed.

Prince was backstage in his dressing room when a security guard brought him a videotape. The guard received it from a Puerto Rican man standing near the back door. The man was still out there with his family. Prince watched the tape, which showed a short, shapely beauty dancing.

He told the guard to go get them.

PART | THREE

The RETREAT

25

LOLITA

THE GIRL'S NAME WAS MAYTE GARCIA. SHE WAS SIXTEEN, AND born in America to middle-class parents. Her father was a pilot in the military, stationed in various countries. Her mother, an academic and linguist who loved dance. For eight years, Mayte had danced, first ballet, then belly dancing in Cairo. At some point, a dance-related injury led to forced recuperation and voice lessons. Now, she was studying ballet again, near the family's current home in Frankfurt, Germany. Recently, her family had attended Prince's show in Spain, and her mother enjoyed the Arabic feel of "Thieves in the Temple." Since then she kept telling Mayte, "You have to make a tape of your dancing and send it to him."

Five minutes after seeing the tape, Prince watched the guard lead her and her family in. Face to face, she thought, *Wow, he's really—small!*

He complimented her moves. She mentioned she could flip coins on her stomach. He called in band members to watch. Soon, he had to leave. But he asked her father if he could keep in touch. The man said sure. While leaving, a band member reportedly joked, "There's your future wife."

August 10, near Switzerland, Prince nursed a cold. But the show had to go on. He rested and swallowed Sudafed then marched into the dressing room on time. After the band's last-minute huddle, costume designer Helen Hiatt slipped a huge crucifix necklace around his neck. Then Gilbert Davison said, "It's raining."

Prince squinted. "It's raining," he mumbled. He still did the show for damp and screaming teens.

Between shows, Prince and the band crammed into Olympic Studio in London to tape "Walk Don't Walk" and "Daddy Pop." Then, they reached Japan, on August 30. For the next two days, he booked time at Warner Pioneer Studios in Tokyo and recorded his mellow "Money Don't Matter 2 Night" and the similarly breezy "Strollin'." To his relief, the band worked quickly, finishing basic tracks in one or two takes.

―――――

By the final concert on September 10, over a million people had bought tickets to see his tour. "Considering Prince didn't have any new product on the market or any recent hit, the figure is incredible," critic Per Nilsen opined. Once the show ended, he led the band to the borrowed multitrack recorder in his backstage dressing room. He taped his drummer's beat, hummed, and added melodies, and called it "Willing and Able." Then he led them through recording an album side's worth of basic tracks.

Back home, Gilbert Davison was working on another movie tie-in. Davison had been his bodyguard since 1984, when Gilbert left a local community-college computer program. Now, he was turning the former hat factory at 110 North Fifth Street into a two-story nightspot named "Glam Slam." Prince's *Lovesexy* single had been one of his biggest flops, failing to enter *Billboard*'s Hot 100 in 1988, but Prince was using the title in his upcoming movie, and now, this new club.

As for who financed its creation, one published report claimed twenty-seven-year-old Davison collaborated with club owner Ruth Whitney in December 1989, and owned 90 percent after investing over $1 million. "He has no financial interest in the club," Davison said of Prince. Another report claimed Paisley Park provided most of the $2 million. What's clear is that Davison worked on its look while Prince toured Europe and Japan. Now, Prince's likeness was on some of the plaster cast masks on columns surrounding the dance floor. They had workers dye the thirteen-hundred-square-foot maple dance floor black. Everything was black, gray, and industrial, right down to the artificial rivets that resembled scrap metal.

Employees created displays featuring guitars, old stage costumes, and neon signs from the sets of *Sign O' the Times* and *Graffiti Bridge*. They even rolled Prince's bike from *Purple Rain* to a spot behind a fence. The in-house shop on the first floor stocked Prince-style outfits, cheap T-shirts, and fifteen-hundred-dollar leather jackets with fractured local license plates on back. In a rear stairwell, artist Sotera Tschetter covered walls with graffiti, Prince-like slogans, song titles, and lyrics to "Elephants and Flowers." With local authorities prohibiting the hanging of a sign on the historic building, they slipped their huge neon "Glam Slam" display in a front window.

Davison hoped to sell three-year memberships to the second-floor balcony. Here, people could, for three to five thousand dollars, lean over and see the stage or dance floor. But he reserved a booth in the rear—with one of the best views of the stage—for Prince, who bragged, "Glam Slam's gonna kick ass. It'll be one of those joints that's remembered!"

Rumors about the film soon appeared in print, as did predictions it would fail. "I don't mind," Prince replied. "Some might not get it." They said the same about *Purple Rain,* dubbing it unfit for release, he recalled. "And now I drive to work each morning to my own big studio."

But it was a concern. In addition to shows and recording new songs, Prince worked on the film. Warner delayed its release from summer to November. In dressing rooms, he used VCRs and telephones to oversee dubbing and editing. He now suggested, "One of these days, I'm going to work on just one project, and take my time." A few nights later, he assembled his near-finished film. "People are going, 'Oh, this is Prince's big gamble,'" he said. Fast-forwarding a video of his rough cut, he added, "What gamble? I made a $7 million movie with somebody else's money, and I'm sitting here finishing it."

July 17, 1990, he had Warner release "Thieves in the Temple" as the lead single. On it he sang over a break-beat familiar to almost any hip-hop fan—Lowell Fulsom's "Tramp." Bream called it "the least striking first single from a Prince album since 'Uptown' from *Dirty Mind* in 1980." Warner quickly planned to follow up with "Round and Round," now-thirteen-year-old Tevin Campbell's cheery song over the same drum pattern heard on the break-beat "Ashley's Roachclip," once heard on Soul II Soul's hit "Keep on Movin'."

By August 20, Prince was in London, for twelve nights at Wembley Arena. His crinkled dime-store notebook held ideas for twenty-one new songs. But during a sound check, he heard dancer Tony Mosley rap, and asked Tony to write something. Tony delivered a dance rap called "The Flow." During the next show, Prince let Tony perform it during his *Batman* number, "The Future." Tony wondered how Prince's audience would react. But they seemed to like it. Prince asked Tony to write more.

August 20, he was still editing *Graffiti Bridge* during the tour. But Paisley Park and Warner released the album of the same name, two months before the movie's premiere. While promoting the album, he assured one reporter it was "just a whole bunch of songs. Nobody does any experiments or anything like that."

In frustration, he saw reviews describe his trendy music and ignore his heartfelt messages. For their part, his hardcore fans knocked *Graffiti Bridge* for aping the trendy new-jack swing sound. Rap fans meanwhile ignored the break-beats he sneaked onto songs, and even the Jimi Hendrix sample on "Tick, Tick, Bang."

An employee in Minneapolis faxed the latest notices to his suite at England's Wellington hotel. His eyes landed on one in *The New York Times*. He couldn't believe it. In disbelief, he reached for his phone at 4:48 in the morning and called the *Rolling Stone* reporter down the hall. "Hi, it's Prince. Did I wake you up?" He wouldn't call this late if he didn't have interesting news. The *Times* notice stunned him. "They're starting to get it. I don't believe it, but they're getting it!" Maybe he was wrong about the mostly white rock intelligentsia. "They're starting to get it," he repeated. *The Times* hadn't exactly praised his lyrics. If anything, Jon Pareles wrote, "Verbally, he's no deep thinker; when he's not singing about sex, his messages tend to be benevolent and banal." But Prince felt "they're paying attention." Sounding amazed, he ended the call.

In the end, *Graffiti Bridge* reached No. 6 on the Pop Chart but failed to sell a million copies. In trying to recapture the *Purple Rain* magic he had offered listeners dozens of catchy melodies. He also improved his rap sound; made his lyrics more accessible than those on *Lovesexy*; and employed his usual quality production. The results were a mixed bag, though the album includes winners like his prog-rock ballad "Graffiti Bridge," his classic "Thieves in the Temple," and his popular, slower work "The Question of U." Despite the presence of too many aging vets, second-tier acts, and trendy sounds, *Graffiti Bridge* was better (if less successful) than *Batman*, and rougher than *Lovesexy*.

He wouldn't tour the States. Warner was investing big money in Paisley Park Records, he claimed, so he wanted to "put in some serious time behind the desk." He leaped instead into trying to save the film. By now, reporters were claiming he desperately wanted to return to the old *Purple Rain* heights by creating this quasi-sequel. *Entertainment Weekly* reported it had "already been totally overhauled twice" and would arrive in November, "if it is ever released at all." He had promised to tour the States that fall to promote the seventy-two-minute album but wouldn't even finish this current European jaunt.

After rescheduling a few final shows, Prince flew to Hollywood to spend four days editing. By now, two cuts by Warner Bros.' editors did leave everyone—him included—unhappy.

Prince had filmed performances for every song. He cut four and trimmed two others. Warner still sent it back for reediting. Now, Prince spent a week reshooting scenes in Hollywood. He shot transitional scenes since, as Ingrid Chavez had noted, it was confusing before. The new scenes created an "adorable story," she added. "Before, you couldn't get into the characters." He kept editing into fall, eventually removing thirty minutes and production numbers set to songs already heard on the soundtrack album released in August. He kept tinkering with it until October 1990, when he deemed it finished. He had done what he could. Warner, still not pleased, considered a direct-to-video release (embarrassing since viewers feel straight-to-video meant a studio had deemed something unfit for theaters).

November 1, *Graffiti Bridge* opened nationally. Originally, Warner wanted *Graffiti Bridge* in fourteen hundred U.S. theaters on August 7. Now, it opened at only seven hundred. The ads read, "The story only Prince could tell. Music only Prince could play." With him listed as screen writer, director, composer, and star, reporters wondered if the oft-delayed film was any good. Rumors claimed the film, about two nightclub-owner musicians disagreeing over music, needed repairs. "It has gone through the normal process," said *Bridge* producer Arnold Stiefel, Prince's manager. "It has changed in postproduction as much as any film."

The negative buzz continued. As with *Under the Cherry Moon*, Warner Bros. decided not to screen it in advance for critics. Said *Los Angeles Times* movie critic Patrick Goldstein, "I've gotten no indication that Warner Bros. has any high hopes for this beyond the normal Prince following. That's large in record-industry terms. It's relatively small in movie-industry terms."

The New York Times described Prince dancing in spike-heeled boots and shiny hip-high leggings, and joked "Prince is nearly ready for Broadway." But the plot was feeble. Characters solved problems by singing and dancing. He filmed himself "in Christ-like poses." His acting and directing were "roughly equivalent to his aptitude for presidential politics."

Entertainment Weekly gave it a "D-minus," and added that comparing it to rock videos "would be an insult to videos: The movie can barely muster the energy to get from one shot to the next." This critic zeroed in on his self-pitying stare, and female characters receiving "the usual shabby treatment," shoves, insults, and apathy. "*Graffiti Bridge* is a sad fiasco," it added, and the only good song was The Time's "Shake!" This was the first time Prince seemed to "be preaching to a world that has left him behind."

The Washington Post's Richard Harrington felt the film should immediately be bronzed and sent to "Hollywood's Hall of Shamelessness, where it might draw bigger crowds than it's likely to at movie theaters, once word gets out about how thoroughly execrable it is." Harrington claimed it made *Under the Cherry Moon* ("a Golden Turkey honoree just a few years back") look like *Citizen Kane*. "We are talking major disaster here." He noted that Prince directed, starred in, wrote the script, and scored the film. "This may be four hats too many." His thin plot suggested "that the music came first, the script last." There were too many "poor-pitiful-me close-ups"; his wardrobe resembled "Kim Basinger castoffs"; the dance numbers looked seriously dated, "as if *Graffiti Bridge* had been shot in 1984, right after *Purple Rain*." And of the white feather that floated during various scenes: "One suspects it has escaped from Prince's brain, much like the film itself." *Graffiti Bridge* bombed at the box office. The film left theaters after grossing only $4.2 million and effectively ended Prince's film career. But at Paisley Park, Prince refused to admit it flopped. Ingrid Chavez remembered him blaming the world for not getting his vision.

26

RELEASE IT

FORBES SAID PRINCE EARNED $20 MILLION IN PRETAX PROFIT IN 1989. *The New York Times* reported Paisley Park was quite solvent. "We're doing okay," Prince said.

This would change. After managers Stiefel and Phillips left in 1990, Prince decided he had the perfect replacement. During his Nude Tour in Europe, Arnold or Randy had frequently called Jill Willis to relay messages to Prince. "I think Gilbert was in the same position," Willis said of Prince's main bodyguard. Soon, she and Gilbert were fielding calls from his attorney Gary Stiffelman, his accountant Nancy Chapman, and various Warner executives. "Prince might speak to Mo Ostin, Lenny Waronker, Russ Thyret, or Benny Medina but that was it," Willis recalled.

Prince invited Willis and Davison to his home and asked Willis to become his manager and run the company.

She said she'd consider it if Gilbert were involved. Former head of security Davison meanwhile had been working with him on the Glam Slam club not to mention a screenplay. They had a history, Willis added. "He seemed to be the one person Prince trusted." The topic next arose when the duo traveled to Manhattan for the film premiere of *Graffiti Bridge*. There, business manager Nancy Chapman and attorney Gary Stiffelman asked both to accept positions as President and Executive Vice President. They did. "But there was more to the 'job' than just managing Prince," Willis added. "He had nearly one hundred employees and there was no one running the ship."

At Paisley Park, co-manager Davison ran the company, handled damage control, and sometimes advised vendors to disregard Prince's expensive requests. "They say, usually after the fact: 'You can't listen to what he says,'" said set designer Blaine Marcou. But once Prince heard someone had dismissed a request, Paisley Park's CFO Jenifer Carr explained, he simply wrote a check from a private account and bought what he wanted.

People around him claimed not matching *Purple Rain's* success and seeing acts like MC Hammer, and white pop rapper Vanilla Ice, outsell him had Prince frustrated. He even asked Alan Leeds, "Do you know what it's like to sit here and see these people on the charts who do nothing but talk?" Prince resented hip-hop's ease in selling records, Leeds remembered. "In his mind, if emcees couldn't sing or play an instrument, they didn't deserve hit records. I'm sure he would deny this today, though," Leeds added.

But when MC Hammer rented one of Paisley Park's studios, to record music for a footwear ad, Prince said, "I like his stuff a lot." He even let Hammer deliver his religious lyric "Pray" over the beat to "When Doves Cry."

Then he started his own next album. But he had an unexpected new influence. Robert Clivillés and David Cole called themselves 2 Puerto Ricans, a Blackman, and a Dominican on their 1987 dance-hit "Do It Properly." In 1989, as the 28th Street Crew they created an album for Vendetta/ A&M Records. Now, as C+C Music Factory, they covered a speedy drum machine track with sampled guitar chords playing a dance riff, a rap by then-unknown Freedom Williams, with thickset Martha Wash singing, "Everybody Dance Now." In late 1990, C+C Music Factory's lead single "Gonna Make You Sweat (Everybody Dance Now)" topped *Billboard's* Hot 100 and R&B Singles Chart. Their album *Gonna Make You Sweat* was on its way to selling a Madonna-like five million copies.

From the start, Prince loved their sound. Prince identified with rap's hard edge and "other pop music like 'Everybody Dance Now,' which came out during that time," engineer Michael Koppelman told Housequake .com. Engineer Tom Garneau agreed. "I think he was chasing that trend."

The song was soft for hip-hop, dismissed by most genre fans as a diluted form, but Koppelman explained, "He worked hard to make parts of *Diamonds and Pearls* 'hard' like that."

Prince was doing "tons of sampling" those days with "the Publison, a very odd, early sampler," Koppelman added. They mostly used it, however, to sample and rearrange his own recorded tracks, Garneau recalled. "We'd pick up a vocal or a lick and he would fly it around all over the song."

He was working hard to emulate contemporary black music. He also told people he liked rap, and that he, himself, had profoundly influenced this genre with his spoken-word break in "Controversy." People shook their heads. "I remember Prince saying something to the effect that he had invented rap," Koppelman told Alex Hahn.

His other engineer Tom Garneau meanwhile thought Prince "came to rap way too late. I considered it boring by the time he was doing it."

Prince had dancer Tony Mosley writing raps. "When I came into this I realized that Prince has a lot of hard-core fans who don't give a damn about rap," Tony explained in *Musician*. At the same time, people in hip-hop didn't "give a damn about Prince." Tony wanted to sound "straight from the 'hood" but Prince swiftly requested a more "worldly aspect." Just as Tony was getting used to these simple dance-raps and Hammer-like chants, Prince suddenly asked for a "Gil Scott-Heron thing on black-on-black crime, cops, and the community," Tony recalled in *Details* magazine. "I think black awareness is really taking an upturn today and he really wants to be a part of that," he added. Tony delivered, but returned to his neighborhood and saw pals dismiss Prince as a pop sellout. "It's been rough," Tony eventually said, "but I knew it would be like that."

Prince hadn't attacked rap with "Dead On It," so much as what it had become, Tony explained. During the early 1980s, Prince had heard acts like Grandmaster Flash and the Furious Five address social ills with "message-raps" (a subgenre named after one of their hits, "The Message"). But during the mid-1980s, rap moved in another direction. Rappers weren't "saying anything but, 'Yo, baby! Party all the time! I got this, I got that,'" Tony explained. This was when Prince used his song to denounce shallow sentiments. But socially relevant artists like KRS-One, and Chuck D— who set their hits to James Brown samples—had him eager to record more rap.

Still Prince kept recording corny raps like "Jughead," about a new dance step. His engineers wondered what happened to the old Prince. For his classic "Sign O' the Times," Prince had required only six tracks. Now, many new songs had forty-eight or more, tons of drums, loops, and basses. "It was a bit frustrating to see what I consider to be a very talented musician fucking around with a lot of trendy crap," Michael Koppelman said.

January 21, 1991, Prince was ready to play Rock in Rio II, in Brazil for $500,000 (the same amount as headliners Guns 'N' Roses), the *Jornal do Brasil* reported; he had decided on short notice to do the show. But his keyboardist Fink was producing another project. Fink had to submit it on time. Fink asked Prince's managers to find a replacement for the show. Prince had invited young local keyboardist Tommy Elm to play a warm-up show at Glam Slam, and decided Elm could handle it.

At Maracana Stadium, nine shows would start at 6:00 P.M. and run until 2:00 A.M. Brazilian acts would open for Guns 'N' Roses, George Michael, Santana, and INXS. MTV would air portions February 9. Green laser lights covered a crowd of 100,000. Giant monitors broadcast the events onstage. The crowd danced, waved arms, lit matches, and sang along to every hit chorus. Santana's set went over well. Between sets, seminude ladies danced near inflatable animals while a band played carnival music.

Prince ran two hours late. He got onstage with his hair standing up, his beard carefully sculpted, his collar points raised, and his shirt unbuttoned to the navel. His image—three stories high—appeared on the giant video screens. He started his set with a cool funk riff. Then he began swiveling his hips and claiming this was the hot new dance, "the Horny Pony." Sections of the crowd yelled *"Viado! Viado!"* (Portuguese, *Entertainment Weekly* explained, for "faggot"). After the show, he decided to buy the TV rights back from MTV.

Back home, he decided that Tommy Elm should stay, taking Fink's spot in his New Power Generation and a new nickname: Tommy Barbarella. Fink meanwhile wondered what just happened. He had been with The Revolution since its earliest days. He said nothing when Prince expanded the lineup (circa *Parade*). He remained with Prince even after Prince fired most other members—even as each new album found him straying further from his bestselling *Purple Rain* image and sound. He absorbed Prince's putdowns during recent rehearsals (including one reportedly hurled in front of Fink's parents). Fink stayed even when, as he told Alex Hahn, he felt Prince was suddenly favoring the band's black members.

"There was no personal phone call, no loyalty," he said. "His attitude was 'You didn't drop everything you were doing for me, so see ya!'"

Prince now worked on designing their look, asking designers to create what amounted to pajamas with lapels. He also publicly extolled his new band's virtues. But new singer Rosie Gaines explained, "We were his first black band, and our thing was to help him get his black audience back, because he had lost that."

Prince's public image suffered in late January 1991 when Fargnoli's client Sinéad O'Connor told *Rolling Stone* about her alleged December visit to his rental home in LA. "He continually said that he was going to beat the shit out of me," she told *Rolling Stone*. He also kept her from leaving, she insisted. According to her, he sent his limo driver away, leaving her without a ride home at 5:30 in the morning. When she cried, he laughed. Her big mouth got her in trouble again, she remembered him saying. "He's jealous. And he did say to me that he wished I'd never done his song. . . . I think, frankly, that that song saved his fucking ass," she added. "He was in serious financial trouble until that song happened." When *Rolling Stone* called to ask if he really did this, Prince said, "That never happened. I have no idea what she's talking about."

Prince resumed work on his next album. For eighteen months, he had been writing new songs. No vault material on this next one. By February, he felt he had it. He put a song called "Horny Pony," debuted in Brazil, back in and created another configuration. It was a strong album. But Warner executives again arrived at his studio complex to ask him to delay a new album.

Warner really wanted some sort of greatest hits compilation to remind people of his talents, especially after the disappointing *Graffiti Bridge*.

Prince proposed a big boxed set with four or five discs of unreleased material.

Warner felt its retail price would be too high and proposed a more manageable two-CD set, with one disc containing the never-released *The Black Album*.

He didn't want it out there.

Warner agreed that they'd accept another Prince album but they pleaded with him to hold off for some time. By releasing one annually since 1979, he had glutted the market, they explained. He didn't agree, but he didn't cause another scene. He considered *Diamonds and Pearls* done, but kept rewriting lyrics, remixing music, and putting things back in. Engineer Koppelman said in the *Star Tribune*, "I think he was purposely not putting it out—or was being forced by his record company or whatever. But he's got to constantly work, so we just kept working on it."

27

GIRLS AND BOYS

AT PAISLEY, IN MARCH, PRINCE ALSO STARTED A POP RAP ALBUM
by a white woman named Carmen Electra. Her real name was Tara Patrick, and he had sent someone to invite her to his rented house in Beverly
Hills after seeing her dance in the LA club Spice. He told her he was
starting an all-girl band. Could she sing or dance? She said sure. He had
her audition immediately. He kept his face impassive, even as she left that
night. He was already spending more of his time on the phone with that
Puerto Rican girl Mayte from the tour, after all, according to the British
Mail on Sunday.

But he called within a month to offer her a recording contract. She
quickly flew to Minnesota, moved into his home, and agreed to change
her name to Carmen Electra (which he chose after showing her the 1954
musical *Carmen Jones*).

Now, when he recorded music, he looked over and saw Carmen taking everything in. Before she knew it, he told her to record his new song,
"Carmen on Top." He had bassist Levi and rapper Tony help fill her album
Carmen On Top with ho-hum beats and James Brown samples. He had Carmen speak lyrics over "Good Judy Girlfriend" and two James Brown samples. "Go On (Witcha Bad Self)" featured Brown's "Say It Loud, I'm Black
and I'm Proud." "Just a Little Lovin'" used Brown's introduction from
"Make It Funky" ("What you gonna play now?"). A sample from Brown's
"Fun" sat near the familiar Run-DMC quote, "Awww yeah."

On a Wednesday night, around 9 P.M., Prince was steering his classic
T-Bird toward downtown. He was driving quickly when he saw a curve in
the road ahead, "It was close to his house," his spokesperson Jill Willis
explained, to justify what followed.

Prince suddenly lost control of the car. His hands gripped the wheel
tightly, but it was too late. In shock, he felt the car shake. He couldn't see

the road through his windshield anymore—the car had left the road entirely. It was airborne and for a second, the world looked sideways. It flipped in midair, then suddenly, everything shook. He felt a jolt as the car landed on the ground.

Prince was still breathing. His nose hurt a little. He had banged it on something. But he could move. The car behind him stopped. His friend, driving it, got out and ran over to the wreck. Prince crawled out of the car. Eventually, cops rolled up. They heard what happened and didn't issue any tickets. They towed the car away, Willis noted; "probably" destroyed.

But Prince himself somehow avoided any serious damage. "He was fine," Willis said. "He walked away unscathed."

Seemingly undisturbed by the accident, Prince continued to focus on his career. He grew impatient. Warner had asked him to wait but he wanted *Diamonds and Pearls* out there already. Indignant, he flew to Burbank and persuaded them to release it. But then he insisted they ship it with an expensive, hard-to-manufacture hologram cover (an image of him staring through a string of pearls while two women rub his chest). Warner agreed to this, too, but advised him to promote this one more. They also delayed its release from mid-September to mid-October.

Prince knew this was a pivotal album. And if he didn't, print reports kept reminding him. *Lovesexy* hadn't sold. *Batman* did, thanks in part to a hit film and popular superhero. He connected *Graffiti Bridge* to another film, but both products flopped. *Diamonds and Pearls* was a genuine Prince album. If fans rejected it, they were rejecting him.

In spite of these pressures, he was proud of the album. He carried a CD of it with him and blasted it in his car. "Instead of buying a tape, I make music," he told *Details*. Usually, he cued up his dance-rap "Push," but on sunny days, he drove to his mild-mannered "Strollin'." "I don't listen to any of my old music, you know," he said proudly. (Heath, 1991)

One Friday in May, however, Waronker called from Warner to say the urban department didn't hear a single for radio. "Maybe I could take so-and-so [song] and turn it around," Waronker remembered him saying in the *Star Tribune*. But he caught himself. "It's a marketing problem. You guys deal with it." Still, he considered what Warner was saying. As with *Batman* and *Graffiti Bridge*, he went to Paisley Park, on May 10, to record another song for a lead single. This new work "Gett Off" seemed to describe an encounter with a woman in his home. He told her he didn't serve ribs, then asked her to move closer to him so they could copulate. Its metallic drumbeat and high-pitched flute evoked Public Enemy, then he added metal chords and a sneering rap. That Monday, he called Waronker back. "You've got yourself a new baby." Waronker loved "Gett Off," saying, "It was an amazing new track."

Prince was also working on Ingrid Chavez's debut, *May 19, 1992*, envisioning another disc with spoken-word poetry over his music. For good reason, she now wanted to sing. After appearing in his film, she helped Lenny Kravitz and André Betts write and record Madonna's 1990 chart-topping dance hit "Justify My Love." Ingrid saw the mix of styles result in big sales. But while creating "Elephant Box" and other songs, Prince wanted whispering and talking. "He had recordings of her reading her poems," Koppelman, now main engineer, told Housequake.com. "He let me try one and 'Winter Song' resulted."

Prince liked it.

"Can I do another?" Koppelman asked.

"Sure."

Koppelman produced "Candledance," but needed a guitar solo. While recording, Prince kept playing hazy riffs. Sensing a shift in the mood, Prince lowered the guitar and asked, "You aren't going to use any of this, are you?"

He didn't plan on it. "He hadn't been hitting it," Koppelman remembered. "Right after that he played a great solo which we kept."

With Ingrid in LA, and his plate already full, Prince told the producers to hit the studio "and mess around," Koppelman recalled to Housequake.com. They created "Hippy Blood." The next day, during her meeting at Warner Bros., Ingrid played executives the song. "They loved it," said Koppelman. "Prince had not yet heard it." Eventually, he did, and liked it, Koppelman recalled, but he had a vision for this record. "So a bit of a spat broke out 'cause Ingrid wanted to sing some more songs and Prince had the spoken-word idea." Warner meanwhile wanted some "Justify"-like singing. Prince argued with her and Warner then disowned it. After producing five songs, he handed Koppelman and Levi the reins. New works like "Spiritual Storm" mixed poetry with catchy singing. Koppelman recorded and mixed "quite a lot of it," he said.

Prince moved back to his own work, planning a video for "Gett Off." Young director Rob Borm, trying to get his new production company

Point of View Films off the ground, was saying, "Hire me. I'm young. I'm hungry. I can make you some money," according to the St. Paul *Pioneer Press.* Prince gave Borm a break, and had Gilbert Davison tell Borm, "Prince wants his yellow suit in it, and he wants his yellow car in it, and he wants it to look a little like *Caligula,*" the 1980 film. Borm tried to keep the two-day shoot within the Warner-approved $220,000. Prince liked the stunning, surreal "fall-of-Rome set." Inevitably, Davison told Borm, "Oh, by the way, there's probably going to be quite a few changes to the concept." It needed more erotic imagery. He also used this video to introduce new dancers Diamond and Pearl (Robia Lamorte and Lori Elle Werner) to his audience. On the set, costs reached a staggering $1.3 million over seven days. Prince was finally done. Borm figured with Paisley handling the seven-figure overrun, he wouldn't have to fear creditors.

Predicting success, Prince then created four more clips, including an eight-minute-long "orgy/club mix" that had him blindfold Diamond and Pearl and lead them from Paisley to his yellow house. "Violet the Organ Grinder" showed him in chains near four women covered in gold paint. "Gangster Glam" purported to show the "erotic behind-the-scenes" during a day at Paisley Park.

Prince wanted "Gett Off" out there as soon as possible, and threw a 9:16 version on an EP, near his pop-rock number, "Cream," "Horny Pony," and his mellow "Money Don't Matter 2 Night." But right before its release, for reasons unknown, either he or the label cancelled the EP. He wanted his music—and perhaps advances—released faster, and disagreed with Warner's assertion that fans couldn't handle more than one album a year. As a kid, he rode his bike to a record store to buy a new James Brown single "every three months," he claimed. And no one called Brown too prolific. Warner however had reasons for delaying releases. "The third single from the previous album would bump into the first single from the new album," said Bob Merlis. The promotion department couldn't handle him competing with himself. Some promoters felt, " 'Okay, we love the guy but can we have a break?' "

Undeterred by the cancellation of the EP, he threw "Gett Off" on a limited-edition twelve-inch in time for his thirty-third birthday. The morning of June 7, clubs and radio stations received a strange-looking record in a white jacket covered with purple handwriting. Prince had pressed up about fifteen hundred copies. Warner and Paisley Park knew nothing about it but deejays played the rap-styled "Gett Off." He created an edit for a commercial single, yanked "Horny Pony" from *Diamonds and Pearls* and included the new song. Warner rush-released the single and scheduled *Diamonds and Pearls* for release soon after. Yet, Prince couldn't ignore that, locally, pop and rock stations had ignored it. Only KMOJ-FM, the urban radio station run on donations, played it, and even this outlet, a writer noted, was more likely to play the Fresh Prince's rap.

Despite little disagreements, Prince was generally happy with Warner. "I mean, when *Diamonds and Pearls* came out, he played on the roof of the Warner Bros. building and was very proud of the relationship," said engineer Tom Tucker. He played a private concert for Warner, one in their Burbank parking lot and another at their Warner-Elektra-Atlantic convention in Chicago. "He was walking around and saying hello to people before his performance," said Warner vice president of publicity Bob Merlis. It was impressive, Merlis noted, but also precisely what artists should do with people that could promote products. "Setup," Merlis explained, "is everything in the music business. He's got everything."

Prince also played the Jack the Rapper Convention for R&B industry professionals in Atlanta. He packed his bags for a mid-August stop in Manhattan, to play MTV's private tenth anniversary party at the Ritz (on Monday, August 19). The crowd included influential music and television executives. Richard Harrington of *The Washington Post* wondered if this "was a canny move or desperate." After disappointing projects ("notably the *Graffiti Bridge* soundtrack and film"), he needed friends in high places and couldn't find "any on the radio side." His mix of old hits and six new songs showed "flashes of brilliance, vocally and on guitar," but his dancers felt "two or three years out of style." He undermined credibility by emphasizing the visual. "And if the *Under the Cherry Moon* and *Graffiti Bridge* movie disasters taught Prince anything, it's that he should forget playing to the camera and just play the music." For weeks, people around him considered Harrington's suggestion. An anonymous source near Prince said, "It's what he should have done for every one of his albums."

Steve Perry, who once wrote a *Musician* cover story about him, felt it was smart marketing to perform at the MTV event, but the new music was desperate. "It's flailing after something not grounded in artistic motives. For the first time in his career, he's not sure what to do artistically; he's acting out of market impulses."

In early September, Prince played TV's *The Arsenio Hall Show,* the first guest to perform five numbers. Then September 5, he traveled to the Universal Amphitheatre in LA, where Arsenio was hosting the MTV Video Music Awards. The ceremony found the network celebrating its tenth anniversary, and changing the name of its Video Vanguard Award to the *Michael Jackson* Video Vanguard Award. As a slew of acts performed and accepted astronaut-shaped trophies, Prince waited backstage, with big hair and sculpted five o'clock shadow. When it was time, he took the stage in his yellow meshlike jumpsuit and started singing "Gett Off." Then he turned around, and shocked the entire audience. His yellow pants had huge openings over each buttock (soon dubbed "peekaboo pants" by *The Dallas Morning News*). Even Bream wondered whether this was the act of a skilled promoter or a "desperate, fading superstar." Ultimately, Harrington answered his own question in another writer's article. "This soft-spun Prince," he said, "I don't buy it."

28

WATCH THEM FALL

PRINCE NEEDED *DIAMONDS* TO HIT. BUT AFTER *GRAFFITI BRIDGE*, he wouldn't rely only on Warner's publicists. Jill Willis and Gilbert Davison suggested he turn to Jackson's former manager Frank DiLeo to help Warner promote this new one. As Willis saw it, DiLeo could "guide us through some of the areas where we both lacked experience such as radio promotion." Warner employees included DiLeo in promotional efforts. Warner was also still excited about Ingrid Chavez's album and predicted success when it arrived on September 21, 1991. Executives chose "Hippy Blood," "Heaven Must Be Near," and "Elephant Box" for singles and club remixes. "There was a lot of excitement about it but by the time it came out it kind of fizzled and the record did not do well," said co-producer Koppelman. Turned out, Prince was right about this one.

"Gett Off," though, was another story. The single debuted at No. 66 on the *Billboard* chart but dropped twelve places its second week, even as another song he helmed, Martika's "Love . . . Thy Will Be Done," rose from No. 57 to No. 45 during its third week. *Billboard*'s Club Play Chart had "Gett Off" at only No. 21. Critics were frowning on him singing about "twenty-three positions in a one-night stand" then mentioning some. *Entertainment Weekly* chose this moment to remind readers that only two of his seven albums since *Purple Rain* sold 2 million copies. "Two of his last three, *Lovesexy* and *Graffiti Bridge*, have yet to reach the 1 million mark." The biggest Prince song in years, they added, was Sinead's "Nothing Compares 2 U."

Once again, Warner got things back on track by quickly releasing "Cream" as a single on September 9, 1991. More radio stations added the guitar-heavy pop song to playlists than any other single that week. Even better, it became his fifth U.S. No. 1 single.

Warner released *Diamonds and Pearls* October 1, but at *Controversy*, the British-based fanzine Prince had mentioned in liner notes, editor Eileen

Murton said, "Many of the fans think he's selling out." Eric Leeds agreed. For years, peers expected him to call the tune "but then there came a time when he began to listen to rap and other stuff, and said, 'I can do that, and I can do it better.'" Eric felt the new CD's best moments returned "to who he really is. It's not cutting edge, but at least it's true."

Riding high with his latest chart-topper "Cream," Prince started October by recording "Sweet Baby," a gentle number heavy on cooing, and far from the crowded dance-rap he had lately been creating. That same month, at Larrabee Studio in LA, he recorded another ballad called, "Insatiable."

It was while working on his next album that he saw the media suddenly crown Michael Jackson the King of Pop. Like Prince, Michael Jackson saw rap and metal rising, and worked to deliver new work that looked and sounded modern without alienating his core audience. Jackson had filled half of *Dangerous* with songs that mimicked early hits. The other songs featured rap producer Teddy Riley's trademark new jack swing, James Brown rhythms over drum machine swing beats.

But what got Prince's goat was how Jackson tried to promote his video for lead single "Black or White." In late October, Jackson let Fox, BET, and MTV know, if they wanted his "Black and White" video first, they had to call him "the King of Pop." The song was a rock-tinged dance cut that urged racial unity and included Guns 'N' Roses' guitarist Slash. But Jackson's video was a bit raw. Jackson had director John Landis, back from *Thriller*, direct scenes of Jackson dancing in an alley, without music; shaking his feet, adjusting his hat, and splashing in a puddle; leaping onto a car with a crowbar, to smash windows, and scream. Then, still on the car, Jackson tap danced while holding his crotch. He pulled his zipper up. He screamed, "Ho!" Near a puddle, he dropped to his knees and tore off his T-shirt. He threw a trash can through a store window and screamed so loud, the sign on a hotel fell off. Then Jackson morphed into a dark panther and left the scene.

November 11, a week before Jackson's video premiered, MTV executives sent on-air staff a memo on letterhead telling them to call Jackson "the King of Pop" at least twice a week for the next fourteen days. "Fox and BET are already doing this," it added. Prince laughed and reached for a pen, planning, as he sometimes did, to respond to a real world development with a new lyric.

———

Warner saw Prince's latest album *Diamonds and Pearls* become his biggest hit since *Purple Rain* and its four Top 30 hits attract the mainstream media and casual music fans. With a nationwide American tour, he could get back up there with Madonna and Michael Jackson. But Prince was unmoved. He flew to Paris, for a quick trip, to create more ideas.

By December 1, Prince returned to the studio with new songs for a concept album. For the next few weeks, he had the band help record complex numbers like "The Sacrifice of Victor," "And God Created Woman," and "Arrogance." Along with these, he added May 1991's "Blue Light," September's dance-rap "My Name Is Prince," and his recent "Sweet Baby" to the lineup. At one point, he slapped an old title from 1988, "The Max" onto a new work.

At home at night, Prince banged on a piano, sang, and taped ideas on a portable radio. The next morning, he carried the device to the studio. He already knew how he wanted things to sound but let the band suggest ideas. After playing a new tape, they recorded together and things happened quickly. After creating one intricate melody, he turned and asked everyone present, "What do you think U2 will do when they hear that?" The awards show defeat was still on his mind. But after comments like this, he got back to work on some of his most complex arrangements to date. "We cut entire records in a day, sometimes," said one player.

For "3 Chains O' Gold" he wanted classical to lead to rock, funk, and more classical. After cutting the basic tracks, he let Tommy Barbarella add riffs. Then Levi added bass. Engineers also took a turn. Finally, he would enter the studio, sift through their concepts, and choose the best, then add his final touches to certain works. He wanted similar changes on "Love 2 the 9's" so its airy groove gave way to heavy hip-hop. For "7" he mixed an odd but catchy groove, a break-beat (Lowell Fulsom's familiar "Tramp"), some Egyptian musical references, and backup vocals from a singer named Jevetta Steel. When Steel asked what it all meant, he only smiled. Then he heard Levi Seacer, Jr. singing something while walking around Paisley. In an elderly tone, Seacer joked, "You sexy motherfucker!" One day in Studio A, Prince created a melody on piano. Seacer added notes. Prince threw in soulful horn blasts. "Within half an hour we had an arrangement," said drummer Michael Bland. Prince had Seacer perform the hook "into a shitty old SM 57," engineer Michael Koppelman recalled, and got the new song, "Sexy M.F.," done in one take.

It was an even further departure from his usual style than "Gett Off."

But it reflected what Prince saw during his frequent hangout sessions at Glam Slam. "There was a dance troupe there, and the sexier the dancers, the bigger the revenues and the noisier the crowd," Prince told *Interview* magazine. He also saw they loved a record called "Bitch Betta Have My Money." "When you hear something constantly, you can get swayed by the current. I was swayed by hip-hop at the time." At the same time, his band's evocation of old James Brown convinced him to abandon sampling.

Outside of the control room, Prince put a "For Sale" sign on a tall pile of electronic equipment.

29

MY NAME IS PRINCE

MAYTE KEPT INSPIRING LOVE SONGS. EVERY TWO DAYS, SHE told the *Mail on Sunday* online, he would call her at home to chat. It was intense, having him stay in contact, but she didn't bother telling friends, assuming they wouldn't believe her anyway.

For his part, their talks led to fantasies and dreams he channeled into lyrics. "I Wanna Melt with U" seemed to describe a point in time in which they would finally—once she was of age and they were together—have safe sex. "The Continental" also alluded to her. In it, Prince called for a woman to flip quarters on her belly (something she mentioned she could do when they met at his show overseas). As the lyric continues, she tells him, "If I flip 'em on my stomach, will you marry my ass?" And his response would be, "Yeah man." By song's end, he added that he'd show her how couples should have fun.

Even "Sexy M.F." seemed to be for her. To be his wife, he sang, a woman had to be peaceful. He didn't want fights; he wanted real love. And though his desire to wait confused her, he said he wanted "the whole 9," her body and mind. He ended this one by saying he was usually into physical relationships. "But I had to change my state of mind for this behind."

Prince was as ever private, and those around Prince assumed these were simply components for his concept album's fictional story. But they can be seen to present his life as an open book. And since Mayte's arrival, he continued to involve her even more in his professional life and Art.

Away from the band, everything was "all work," Mayte noted.

They rehearsed and recorded, and while others called him a demanding boss, she felt they brought his anger on themselves.

Prince meanwhile liked Mayte's optimistic attitude, unflagging support, truthful nature, and willingness to take professional advice. He liked how she danced—and her body, his eyes frequently drifting down to a posterior he would soon describe in songs. There was her voice, too. He felt she could handle a solo album.

Before anyone knew it, Prince had Mayte sitting near him some nights in his booth at Gilbert's club, or joining him on the dance floor. Now that things were heading south with Warner, he began to slowly entertain a different vision of his future: one that included her—after she turned eighteen, of course—by his side as a companion, a recording artist, and a supportive soul mate.

However, before any of that could happen, he wanted Mayte in his new epic video for "7" and onstage during an operatic show, in which he rescued her from a royal family while dodging annoying reporters.

He remained happy with his band, though its members knew things could change in an instant. "With Prince you can only take one day at a time," drummer Michael Bland told *Q Magazine*. "You never know what's gonna happen. He's been known for hiring and firing folks so quick, just out of nowhere, just uninitiated." Sure enough, before Christmas, he got into it with engineer Michael Koppelman. During his three years with Prince, Koppelman had played some of the music on "Blue Light" and worked on half of Ingrid Chavez's debut. Prince had scheduled a Carmen Electra session for Christmas Eve, engineer Tom Garneau remembered hearing. Koppelman couldn't do it. He was, Koppelman explained, "deathly ill, and Prince wanted me to cancel a trip home for Christmas!" He boarded his flight, Koppelman wrote on lolife.com, so Prince fired him.

Koppelman left, feeling Prince really made a mess of things. His company once had tons of energetic talents. Now, he fired many for air-headed reasons. Prince meanwhile was a "dysfunctional 'leader,'" who failed to build a successful label and studio. "He also put out album after album of shit and a couple of ridiculously bad movies," Koppelman later opined.

Engineer Tom Garneau couldn't disagree. "Being his own manager and career advisor, he made many bad decisions. Too many clubs opening. Too many 'girlfriend video shoots' on double-time Sundays. No one was saying no to him. This led to his well-publicized cash flow issues."

———

Unmoved by the shift in personnel, Prince turned his attention to his label Paisley Park. It could really use a hit, and he felt he had one in new discovery Carmen's album. He helped create seven of her eleven songs. She was gorgeous and photogenic. Her dance-raps were as good, if not better, than any by chart-toppers MC Hammer and Vanilla Ice. He kept sending Warner assorted versions of her debut *Carmen on Top*, but label staff rejected the tracks and vocals as weak. He ignored them, writing more songs and planning a big-ticket clip for her song, "Go-Go Dancer."

In March 1992, he filmed a video for her title track and hoped a strong promotional push would make a hit of her album. At Paisley, he told staff members his latest marketing idea. "Prince wanted to drop eight-by-ten publicity photos of her from a helicopter over major cities," said Jill Willis. It would have made a splash but Willis told him "it would be too big of a liability if someone were to get hit in the eye by a falling eight-by-ten."

They paid for commercials on MTV but the network barely played her video. Then in April, their ad in *Rolling Stone* backfired. As in the film *The Idolmaker*, Paisley Park showed her face, and nothing else. She was hot, it was undeniable; but most people didn't understand what was happening—the ad didn't mention her name or album. Many insiders felt it was another wrong move.

But Prince knew what he was doing. Everyone would know who she was when he had her open his European concerts in July, and released her album.

That summer, reporters from *Spin, USA Today, Playboy, Musician, Request*, and the *Sunday Times of London* visited Paisley Park Studios. He gave most a hard time. "There's not much I want them to know about me, other than the music," he claimed.

The latest tour, for *Diamonds*, started April 3, 1992, and would run until November 25. As usual, he staged another costly spectacle: a lit Milky Way backdrop, plasma lamps, and two giant statues with huge bosoms. He rode a glass pod into view, played "Thunder," and rushed around walkways, podiums, three male dancers, eight musicians, his dancers Diamond and Pearl, and a four-piece horn section. One critic noted his young new protégé Mayte's ballet dancing was "rather spoiling the futuristic theme," but it continued.

During the tour, he groomed Mayte for stardom, designing her look by tearing pictures out of magazines, especially those with fashions by

Vivienne Westwood, and Versace. The tour continued, with thirteen huge trucks lugging 200 tons of equipment, twenty wardrobe cases with 1,000 costumes, and an entourage that numbered 137 and included his chef.

A month into the tour, back home, Alan Leeds did some thinking. It was, he explained, "time for a change." Prince's ideas for alternative marketing and records that bypassed Warner and the industry were fresh and challenging. But many ignored his legal obligation to Warner and the funding they provided Paisley Park Records, "not to mention a contract!" as Leeds noted.

Late one night Leeds told his wife, "You know where this is going to end up?" Playing Sundays in a purple church in Chanhassen. "People will be dressed in ruffled shirts, looking like it's the eighties, watching him preach and play 'Purple Rain.' "

At his desk at Paisley Park, he gave it his best shot. But Prince's differences with Warner infected everything the label was trying to do. Prince kept racing through projects and thinking, "That's done. On to the next thing." Warner felt he wasn't creating competitive records to turn the label around. With both sides harboring "very real frustrations and agendas," Leeds said, "I could see it was never going to work." After seven years as his tour manager, and three running the label, Alan Leeds decided it was time to leave the fold.

At the same time, Jill Willis recalled, "Gilbert became more and more involved in running Prince's nightclub, the Glam Slam, and so he was in the office less and less." Prince had various underlings tackle projects, whether they were qualified or not. If one couldn't handle a chore, he quickly assigned it to another. Before long, Jill Willis recalled, many of these individuals approached her or Davison to "discuss whatever request had been made."

Prince was on the road but wanted to get "Sexy M.F." out there as soon as possible. In a studio, his engineer Tom Garneau used an Akai S1100 Sampler to create a clean version, "replacing every instance of the word *fucker* with a Prince scream," Garneau explained. As with "Gett Off," Prince leaked the song to clubs and radio stations early. Leeds called the latest giveaway of a gold vinyl pressing the "1992 Birthday Surprise." Then Prince kept touring. In June, after midnight during another show, he mysteriously played "Happy Birthday" on guitar. Apparently, no one remembered it was his thirty-fourth birthday.

———

At Warner, publicists started mailing promotional advance copy cassettes of Carmen's album *Carmen on Top* to the media. Her twelve-inch single "Go Go Dancer" was in stores, but only small network Video Jukebox Network played her clip. Still, he had her opening European concerts in fringed bikinis. She had a band, a birdcage, and a dressing table on stage. "She bumps and grinds like there's no tomorrow," a woman reporter explained, "but I don't think anyone's going to take her seriously, despite the subMadonna 'strong woman' stance."

Halfway through the tour, Warner executive Benny Medina flew in to catch a few shows. During a sound check, Medina approached to say four tracks had to go: "Power From Above," "Carmen on Top," "Go Carmen Go," and "Powerline."

In fact, her album needed new songs and remixes. Prince's reaction was uncharacteristically responsive—and swift. He fired everyone in her band and tapped Sonny Thompson, Levi Seacer, Jr., and Michael Bland to play behind her during two London shows, her last of the tour. He also recorded two tracks at Olympic Studios in London in June 1992, with most of his band as guests. Reportedly, British-born female rapper Monie Love appeared and he put her on the payroll as a songwriter. He also spent some of his time at Olympic knocking out "Goldnigga," "Black M.F. in the House," and "2gether" for a controversial album by the NPG.

Now that he had finished his new album, he had to choose a name. He liked artist Elizabeth Schoening's creation "Love Symbol #2." It looked like the symbol he included on *Purple Rain*'s cover, a mix of the male and female symbols. Since it wasn't a "work made for hire," he got the copyright "by written assignment," and decided to call his next work simply:

At first, he wanted to start with live band numbers, "Sexy M.F.," "Love 2 the 9's," and "The Morning Papers," but then he decided his solo work "My Name Is Prince" would be first. The song started with samples from his classics "I Wanna Be Your Lover," "Partyup," and "Controversy." His lyric described his contempt for the trappings of fame, then seemed to respond to

Michael Jackson's claim of being "The King of Pop." Prince rapped, "You jumped on my D.I.C.K." He implied this target was an imitator and a simpleton. Prince would bust him like a pimple. "You must become a Prince before you're King anyway." Around him, some band members reacted to his decision to have this start the album by shaking their heads. The other way was better, they felt, but they said nothing.

30

MONEY DON'T MATTER TONIGHT

WITH COMPANIES ALL TRYING TO OUTDO EACH OTHER, SUPER-stars and huge multinational conglomerates were negotiating "status deals" for recordings, films, TV shows, videos, books, clothing lines, "and sometimes even their fragrance lines," Bream explained. Early in 1992, Michael Jackson signed with Sony and Madonna signed with Warner "each for about $60 million." Sony U.S.A.'s vice chairman Michael Schulhof described Jackson's deal as economic for Sony. Madonna's six-album agreement included a label and movie company.

Gary Stiffelman of Ziffrin, Brittenham, and Branca had already negotiated huge deals for the Rolling Stones, Aerosmith, and ZZ Top. Negotiations with Warner had lasted "at least a year," Alan Leeds remembered. And there had been much in-house disagreement on the priorities of the deal. The new deal in fact was part of the reason Leeds left, he explained. Prince, however, wanted a deal to happen. And in late August, he kept in contact with Stiffleman during every round of negotiations. Prince also kept pal Davison, President of Paisley Park Enterprises, in the loop. In the end, reporter Jon Bream wrote, "Prince wins."

Prince's deal was "reportedly the biggest ever signed with a single entertainer," even though he didn't sell as many records as Madonna or Jackson. It extended a preexisting five-album 1986 agreement by one album. He'd deliver the first under new terms on October 20 and receive a royalty rate of about 25 percent (about $2 per record sold). And—if this album sold 5 million copies—a $10 million advance for his next one. These numbers, *Daily Variety* noted, would "place him at or near the top of music industry artists." But Warner's financial risk was actually minimal.

Though *Diamonds* did well with its No. 1 single "Cream," preceding works sold nowhere near 5 million. Even if he sold enough to merit a $10 million advance—triple, Bream claimed, what he used to get—it was actually just an advance against sales, "like a loan." Still, the deal could inspire him to write hits again, and let shareholders see a big name stay on the roster.

Besides his individual contract, the deal expanded Paisley Park Enterprises's presence in Los Angeles. His label's roster included acts like Rosie Gaines and Carmen Electra but he reportedly received $20 million to reorganize it, and an office on a studio lot in Burbank. He also created a second label called ✦ to release singles filled with "cutting-edge street music." Employees called the hieroglyph "the Love Symbol," but a spokeswoman stressed this *wasn't* Love Symbol Records. Warner also agreed to name him a vice president; a position one person claimed Prince wanted in order to acquire stock options.

Prince's deal extended to his publishing. With Warner/Chappell Music, he formed a new company to discover and promote young songwriters. His existing company, Controversy Music, signed new administration agreements in North America and internationally. An insider valued the publishing side alone at close to $40 million, but no reporter verified this.

Warner would keep sending annual funding for this and other joint ventures but had no interest in his films. Executives told his attorneys Prince could negotiate elsewhere for movies, videos, TV shows, books, and merchandise. Despite this, Prince was thrilled with the deal. After stories about other recent pacts, Alan Leeds recalled, he "wanted the headline of a $100 million deal."

The industry was abuzz. Reporters implied he'd automatically receive twice what Madonna got ("the reported $5 million") under her Time Warner deal. *Daily Variety* quoted his representatives claiming "several joint ventures" would guarantee income of over $100 million. A *Los Angeles Times* lead paragraph read, "Eat your hearts out, Michael Jackson and Madonna."

Warner was not happy with his staff publicly claiming it was a one-hundred-million-dollar agreement. Prince himself said it was nothing like this. Regardless, the claim continued to appear in various news reports. "If you're saying that our deal with Prince makes him more market driven, I don't see it that way," Merlis added. "It's always good to sell a lot of records." If anything, Prince had always been "Prince-driven," he noted. "The contract doesn't change that."

———

Shortly after signing the deal, they reportedly disagreed about the new album's lead single. Warner wanted his moody and ambitious "7" but he insisted on "My Name Is Prince." This one was a lighter work, an up-tempo accessible dance-rap that seemingly told self-crowned "King of Pop" Michael Jackson, "My name is Prince, I don't wanna be king."

He got his way and quickly planned another image-changing video. He had Kirstie Alley, formerly of the high-rated NBC hit *Cheers*, play a TV news reporter filming a segment outside of Glam Slam. She claimed there was a riot in the club but cops were letting Prince shoot a video behind the building. From here, he took his spot in an alley decorated with burning trash cans and fiery orange, yellow, and red lighting. He wore a strange cap. On its brim, pearl-like beads drooped and covered his face. His black band surrounded him, like a gang. Dancers splashed in puddles—as in Jackson's clip—and swung fists toward one other. Prince wore the hat while singing, dancing, slamming into walls, and writhing on the floor. At clip's end, he raised the cap to flash his face, but faced the ground.

MTV premiered the clip on Monday, September 28. The single arrived in stores the next day. A *Chicago Sun-Times* headline soon asked, "2 Passé & 4-Gotten?"

At Warner, promoters were in a bind. They had just released *five* singles from *Diamonds* in seven months. They sent ⚥ singles to radio, but many stations wouldn't play them since their listeners were still tuning in for *Diamonds*. Now, he delivered a pretentious genre-bending rock opera that attacked the very media Warner hoped would raise sales. Even so, Warner got the new album—the first under the new deal—into stores on October 13. However, from the start there were problems. Not even publicists knew how to pronounce its title. Since the cover provided no phonetic clues some reviews called it *Androgyny*, others *Untitled; The Village Voice* called it *Prince XV*. Other critics just called it *The Love Symbol Album*.

⚥ reached the Top 10 of the U.S. Album Chart, but Prince felt it should be doing a lot better. Then, when it was obvious ⚥ would slide out of view after sales of about 1 million in America, Prince wondered if publicists even bothered promoting singles they felt he shouldn't release. He decided that was the case, and that Warner could somehow promote ⚥ until it *became* a hit. "Look, I don't blame the guy for being disappointed," Bob Merlis told a reporter. "We were disappointed. But whose fault was it? The company who had just paid top dollar to get the guy?" Warner made a good-faith effort to market his ambitious, untitled work, Merlis continued. "Would it have done better on another label with another approach? No. I don't think so."

He had already hid his face in that "My Name Is Prince" video. Now, on the Paisley Park soundstage, he slipped into a domino mask (like that of Robin the Boy Wonder; black with openings for his eyes) and kept spending nights—his peak creative period—working on a video for "7." Though he usually sped through videos, he lingered on this one for four months.

The soft-lit set resembled his album cover's science-fiction setting. Once cameras rolled, shadowy men in suits stepped forward. With a wave of his hand, a masked Prince sent lightning to strike them down. He filmed himself in an old stage costume—similar to his *Dirty Mind* period—trapped in a tall test tube, clawing to escape, with lightning finally doing him in. Prince added scenes of children dressed like the new him, and Mayte, walking hand in hand in a parade. Then another old Prince, in a different outfit, the yellow *Parade* suit, and hairstyle, tried to escape the fatal test tube and fell. The real Prince—the one in the mask near Mayte—kept singing and watching his old images perish.

After this, he traveled to Puerto Rico for a short break. There, he experienced another revelation. This time, he considered recent developments in his career. Warner still wanted only one album a year, to release a single, an album, and more singles and reach the old *Purple Rain* heights. If something sold 5 million, they'd advance $10 million for the next. But during board meetings, he tried to persuade them to release an album—and perhaps an advance—every six months. They ignored him. Another time, he offered to leave and someone said, sternly, too, that he couldn't. He answered, "Excuse me? What did you say?" He shook his head. By the time an album reached stores, he had finished a second. When he toured for the first, a third was ready to go.

His name had lost its personal resonance. His Pop gave it to him, but people now used it to describe—or denounce—what he called a media-made persona. Millions of people all thought they knew who he was. But their perceptions were false. He was tired of defending himself. Constantly hearing "Prince is crazy."

Let me just check out, he thought.

Changing his name could accomplish a few things. He'd leave the negative image behind. Be free of it. Start over. Save himself. He'd also "get out of the contract." Take the first step toward emancipation from "the chains" binding him to Warner. But what would he call himself? Nothing conventional.

Finally, it came to him.

Back in Minneapolis, he told dancer Mayte, "I know what the symbol on the album is now. . . ." He wouldn't tell her until the end of the tour. She asked again and promised to keep it secret. "Well, I can't say just yet, but I'll give you a hint. My name isn't Prince."

November 17, 1992, Warner released "7" as a single with a still from the video on its cover—him in that black domino mask, with young Mayte seemingly about to kiss him. The B-side included "2 Whom It May Concern" and various mixes of the A-side. It soared to No. 3 on the Pop Chart. But even with its "Tramp" sample, most rap fans ignored it. "7" reached only No. 61 on the R&B/Hip-hop Chart.

With ♀ not doing anywhere near as well as *Diamonds*, Prince suddenly resented the deal he just signed. The label didn't want more than one Prince album a year. Nevertheless, he told *The New York Times*, "The music, for me, doesn't come on a schedule. I don't know when it's going to come, and when it does, I want it out." Then he claimed they wanted commercial rap—despite the battle he waged to have "My Name Is Prince" introduce this new album. He claimed when he sat to write something he could already picture Warner executives asking, "How many different ways can we sell it?" He was trying to appease them with trendy slang and current sounds, he claimed, but the big deal wasn't working. They had different priorities, he said, and "those two systems aren't going to work together." Relations had cooled to the point where executives no longer stopped by his recording sessions. Now, he felt trapped. *City Pages* editor Steve Perry felt it was Prince's own fault. "He wanted his cake and to eat it, too." He wanted to be pop's best-paid performer and to circumvent red tape and major label protocols. "And you can't have it both ways."

He kept trying to promote ♀, agreeing to an episode of *ABC in Concert*. But his people, not ABC, created it. Instead of a performance, the usual fare, he filled the episode with music videos, footage of band members praising him, scenes of them touring Japan, and part of a concert. He highlighted the album's best moments, but shortened many songs so the audience wouldn't hear any hip-hop. The network aired an hour-long version in mid-December with little promotion. Then it divided it and aired it on two separate nights. It did nothing to move ♀ sales closer to the much-needed 5 million. And he wouldn't tour. "Nothing's scheduled at this point," New York–based publicist Michael Pagnotta said. "Right now, everyone's focusing on the new single '7.'"

31

TAKE MY FAME

IN FACT, HE WAS ALREADY TRYING TO MOVE ON. JANUARY 2, 1993, Prince rang in the New Year with a session that yielded rock numbers "Endorphinmachine," and "Dolphin," the mood piece "Dark," and "Laurianne." He was taking another break from the dance-rap and Warner, working with playwright David Hwang (*M. Butterfly*) and envisioning a play based on *Ulysses*. He kept recording, knocking out other dark works like "Papa," "Pheromone," "Space," "Loose," and "Poem."

He was also gearing up for Tara Patrick's album as Carmen Electra. While their romantic involvement seemed to cool once Mayte entered the picture, Prince remained optimistic about Electra's chances of attracting a large Madonna-like audience. Since recording new tracks in London, he had remixed her album and named it *Go Go Dancer*. But with ♀ arriving in stores in October, Warner delayed *Go Go Dancer* until February 9, 1993.

After spending over $2 million on a video, promotional campaign, and an enigmatic but ineffective *Rolling Stone* ad, her album, now self-titled, arrived in stores. Relations were tense. Warner seemed less interested. The work reportedly received the bare minimum as far as promotion. Prince saw mixed reviews. *Billboard*'s critic was enthused but most others were incredulous. Derisive reviews didn't inspire more work or sales. *Carmen Electra* flopped even as Prince struggled to raise sales of his own ♀. He went out there to promote it, even singing four songs during his February 25 appearance on *The Arsenio Hall Show*. Then he did his in-store show and record signing for over one thousand fans at Atlanta's Turtle's Rhythm & Views (signing most items with ♀).

The Act I Tour could raise sales. He'd play consecutive dates in smaller theaters and halls of about one thousand to five thousand seats. But Warner's Bob Merlis said, "Promoters are looking hard at this tour to see what he can do. They've always been a little gun-shy in this country about booking Prince dates, but I think they're heartened by what he's doing this time." Merlis likened it to "a 'brand relaunch,' although I hate to use a term you'd read in *Ad Age*."

Five months after its release, ♀ was stuck in the middle of the charts and hadn't sold 2 million in North America. So he worked to endear himself to fans. At Fort Lauderdale's Sunrise Musical Theater, March 8 and 9, he was casual with a sold-out audience of four thousand. He joked with the band, played guitar in the aisles, did a stage dive, and shouted "Can't nobody fuck with my band." He followed "My Name Is Prince" with eleven of sixteen songs from ♀.

The pop market still wasn't responding.

The *Chicago Sun-Times* called its April 4, 1993, report, "Prince—What Happened?"

He reached San Francisco.

On April 10, he met with *Vibe*'s Alan Light. His camp had contacted Light over a year ago after he enjoyed Light's *Rolling Stone* review of the opening night of his ♀ album tour in 1993. But Prince wanted to get a sense of who Light was, Light explained, "and that went on through several sessions before his team finally decided it was time to sit and talk on the record."

He wanted Light to fly to San Francisco one weekend. "This was actually the weekend between my last day at *Rolling Stone* and my first day at *Vibe*," Light remembered.

In a theater in San Francisco, he sat in an empty audience section watching his band warm up. Light sat in the next seat. "We talked quite a bit, but of course it was pretty loud in there," Light explained. Prince then rose to his feet and invited Light onto the stage with him. He had the writer nearby while he played guitar and keyboard. "He'd play a bit and then say a few words to me." He talked about Earth Wind & Fire, Mavis Staples, and some of the older acts he worked with at Paisley Park. Then he began to issue pronouncements. After playing a solo, he asked Light if he saw how hard it was to be able to play anything he could imagine. He was friendly, trying to feel Light out, but still wouldn't let the writer use a recorder. "He also made it clear that he didn't want me taking notes," Light added. "So I would kind of hide in a corner or duck into another room and scrawl as much as I could remember."

After the sound check, he let Light come to his show that night and mentioned his name on stage. Then he met with him in a roped-off section of a club called DV8. "That's when he ordered glasses of Port for us," Light remembered.

Handing him a glass, Prince told him Warner didn't know a new album was finished. "From now on, Warner only gets old songs out of the vault. New songs we'll play at shows. Music should be free, anyway."

One Thursday, Prince played the 7,500-seat Universal Amphitheatre in LA. It was the final stop and according to reviewer Jon Bream, his worst show in twelve years. Friendlier, warmer than ever, Prince kept entering the audience, inviting people onstage to dance, giving fans in the front row high fives. He tried to stage his rock opera to music from ✤ and soon joined the band in tearing off an actress's skirt. After playing old hits, Prince started a long-winded jam built around the chant "rock the house." The crowd demanded an encore, but he said, "I'm sorry, but Prince has left the building." Before they could react, he was back.

But he meant what he said. ✤ was only at No. 93 on *Billboard*'s Top 200. Not even Warner's release of his lame "The Morning Papers" helped. Neither did touring and high-fiving fans in the front row. The album had sold about 2 million in the United States but he needed 5 million to get the next big advance. Recent concerts sold out but the album hadn't reappeared in the Top 10.

Prince stopped in at Warner Bros., a source recalled, to meet with chairman Mo Ostin and president Lenny Waronker and express "dissatisfactions and frustrations." Then, April 27, he had Paisley President Davison call Ostin and Waronker in Burbank to say Prince wouldn't deliver any more studio albums. That night, the ambush continued. A New York–based publicist sent reporters a press release headlined "Prince to retire from studio recording." Instead of new studio works, he'd honor the rest of his six-album deal with old songs from his library of "five hundred unreleased recordings." This way, Warner could release new Prince albums "well into the twenty-first century," while he focused on "alternative media—including live theater, interactive media, nightclubs, and motion pictures."

The Associated Press called Warner offices in Burbank for details but no one answered. "This is the first I'm hearing of this," someone in Warner's Minneapolis office told the Minneapolis *Star Tribune*. John Dukakis, business manager of Paisley Park Records in California, said, "The press release speaks for itself. In the coming days there will be more comment." His management company wouldn't take questions. Warner didn't officially comment but an unnamed insider said, "People were laughing." At

Time Warner–owned Atlantic Records, Senior Vice President Danny Goldberg remarked, "Anything he says you have to take with a grain of salt."

Eventually, Warner referred everyone to Paisley, where even his spokespeople couldn't explain it. "The reason no one wants to comment is that no one knows," said an unnamed associate. "There's no information. . . . Who knows what he's gonna do? Only Prince knows." A spokeswoman there said, "No one speaks for Prince." She referred everyone back to the press release, released by his publicist. The announcement made Eric Leeds chuckle, and think, *Okay, here he goes again.* Eventually, Eric Leeds publicly said, "Prince is a very mercurial fellow. He could change his mind tomorrow." He figured Prince might not like something in the new deal "and he's saying, 'Well, let me play hardball with them for a minute.'"

When people heard Prince worked with his band the next day in an LA studio, many predicted this retirement would be brief. "I can guarantee that if he comes up with another 'When Doves Cry,' the first thing he's going to do is go to Warner Bros. and say: 'Release this. Tomorrow,'" said Eric.

His brother Alan agreed. Only three things in life were certain, he joked. "We're all born, we all die, and Prince will make another record one of these days."

First manager Owen Husney meanwhile felt, "It's very reminiscent of the recent death of Superman in the comics, only to have him reemerge three months later in six or seven different characters."

More people spoke of isolation and yes-men leading him astray. "He goes from his indoor garage at his house to the underground garage of Paisley Park through the secret stairs to the studio," said an associate in town. "Then he's chauffeured to his own club, where he sits in his private guarded area." Not interacting with people, including bandmates, showed in his music, some claimed. "Prince has gone from leading to following," said another associate (anonymous due to a gag clause in Paisley Park contracts). "He's following trends, not making them."

Either way, his announcement left fans and associates alike baffled.

32

UNSPEAKABLE

PRINCE WASN'T DONE WITH RECORDING. BUT HE WAS TRYING TO shift gears. He had in mind an album called *Come*. He combed through old recordings again. He reworked November 1991's "Race." Then, he included seven of ten songs from his proposed *Ulysses* production. He added the songs "Papa" and "Solo." March 1994 found him creating the album's only new work, "Letitgo." And hoping to recapture the magic of "Gett Off," Prince had Eric Leeds play flute.

He also had young dancer Mayte dash off a letter to the fanzine *Controversy* in which she claimed the "7" video—which featured lots of kids and showed Prince killing off old images—had changed him.

The letter ended with her saying he was happier than ever. "And free. And loving! He finally kissed me!" Then her postscript said, "The truth is that I had help writing this letter. I can't say from whom—but his name isn't Prince."

Publicly, he claimed to have disbanded the New Power Generation. But he still had Sonny and Michael Bland stopping by to help with his songs.

While taping backup vocals for "Pheromone," he muttered, to himself, "That was cool, wasn't it?" Then: "Who can outsing me? Nobody! Good answer."

Mayte watched, assuming this was part of his process.

When he finished sequencing the new songs, he played them for Mayte. "What are you going to do with this new music now that you have retired?" she asked.

"I'm going to give it to my friends."

She looked confused, Mayte explained in her letter. He just laughed.

She realized he missed the days when no one knew who he was. "Now everyone knows him. And they think they know what he's gonna do," she explained in print. He had the band rehearse only these new songs and told people it felt like a new beginning. He looked forward to rocking a stadium with only new songs.

In May 1993, another *Ulysses* number, "Pope" found him presenting more hip-hop music. Over another speedy dance beat, he rapped about his superiority as a rapper. He was like a pontiff, he claimed, while presidents worked in lame governments and had no true power. It was a strong theme, but he softened the song by including Mayte's chirpy singing on the chorus.

When he finished this round of recording in May 1993, the proposed album's title track had over-the-top lyrics about oral sex and slurping noises. "Pheromone" had whispers and half-spoken vocals. "Solo," with *M. Butterfly*'s David Hwang, was simple and spare. "Papa" darkly suggested he (or a character he played) had experienced child abuse. But it sounded dreary and colorless. Warner executives rejected the album

At the same time, he worked on the New Power Generation's debut, *Gold Nigga*. The album had eleven songs and five skits. There were also short instrumental bits. They finished recording in late June 1993. He had concealed his heavy involvement and creation of most song ideas by crediting the band with producing, arranging, and performing everything. But he had copyrighted the songs through NPG Publishing, which he owned.

At Warner, executives faced strange song titles like "Goldnigga Pt. 1" (and 2 and 3), "Guess Who's Knockin'," "Oilcan," "Deuce and a Quarter," "Goldie's Parade," and "Call the Law."

Instead of tight songwriting, *Gold Nigga* offered Tony's raps over loose funk riffs, chants, and horns. One song was about a car. Another echoed Wings' 1976 hit "Let 'Em In." On a third, Tony said, "Fuck the record company, there's too many ways for them to stiff us." The title track attacks labels for cheating black men and urged black artists to "Get up, stand up, stand up for your rights." "2gether" encouraged black people to work together and stop the "black on black genocide." Hearing few hits, Warner rejected the album. His drummer Michael Bland told the Minneapolis *Star Tribune* that he felt he had dragged them into his feud. *Dude, I didn't sign up for this*, he thought. *I just want to go out and rock, eat some steak, wear funky clothes, and watch a little Nick at Nite.*

Now, *Gold Nigga* was rejected. With the label also owning his name, and the music associated with it, Prince felt even more like "a pawn used to produce more money."

But he had a way out. For months, he had let a few people in on a secret. He'd talked about it for three or four weeks, executive vice president Jill Willis recalled. "I hoped for his sake that he would eventually let it go." Everyone worried the media and public would disapprove. But he didn't care. It was his way out.

♀

That symbol that had appeared in his work for years.

It's who he was.

His name.

Battling Warner could last for years. And he might not get out of his situation without observers thinking he was acting like a child. Still, he set his jaw and had New York publicists create the press release.

Suddenly he relaxed. It was all over. When people attacked Prince, they'd no longer be addressing him. "I'm telling you," he said, "the pimples go away, all the stress in your system leaves."

On his thirty-fifth birthday, the release announced, "From now on, Prince will be referred to as ♀, the combination symbol for male and female which also served as the title for his most recent multiplatinum album." He was also "separating from the NPG," it claimed, though he actually had plans for their solo album.

They faxed a copy to his European publicist Chris Poole, who told *Q Magazine*, "He's finally gone mad." Poole called Paisley Park to make sure this wasn't a joke. "They said, No. He's serious. Put it out."

The next day, photographer Jeff Katz flew into town. At Paisley Park, he told the receptionist, "I need to talk to him." Usually, she'd page him. Now, she said, "We haven't figured this whole thing out." She wasn't sure how, specifically, to address him.

"How do you get in touch with him?"

"We just wait 'til we see him in the halls, and we run and grab him."

His band and management didn't know what to call him, either. "After a while, everyone settled on 'boss,'" said keyboardist Tommy Barbarella. That or "Hey, man."

The announcement got Prince his most press in years. "My name is the eye of me," he told *USA Today*. It had no sound, but looked beautiful; made him feel good and offered escape from Prince's baggage—not to mention "massive ego." In fanzines, and on Web sites, his die-hard fans calmly discussed it, accusing outsiders of being narrow-minded.

As reporters kept inquiring about the name, a publicist said, "There is no pronunciation for it." Disc jockeys "just have to deal with it. They just have to explain what the symbol looks like." When MTV referred to him, they showed his ♣ with a sound effect, *"boingg."* His publicist joked ♣ may be starting a trend—sounds instead of names—but from a promotional perspective, it was no laughing matter.

"Everyone was baffled and upset," said Warner's Marylou Badeaux. "On top of everything else, now there was this. I couldn't see how it would be a positive." Paisley Park soon mailed reporters a bright-yellow floppy disk with the ♣. "That way, art departments everywhere can print ♣ by just pushing a button," George Kalogerakis wrote in *Vanity Fair*.

33

UNDERTAKER

HE STILL OWED WARNER FIVE ALBUMS. HE COULD GIVE THEM that much vault material whenever they wanted. Then, as ♀, he could release new stuff on a smaller label. It'd be a dream come true, to finally release as much music as he created. "I just wish I had some magic words I could say to Warner's so it would work out."

During one meeting, a Warner executive said, "We don't want any more Prince albums."

"That's the name on the contract," he answered.

"That's not the name people know you by now."

If he was going by ♀ they wanted ♀'s new work. But he said, "You didn't sign him."

Claiming he'd stop playing old Prince songs added to Warner's frustration. Mo Ostin, Waronker, and other top executives and attorneys met to discuss his "retirement," his refusal to submit new music, and his name change. He was retaliating for *Gold Nigga*, they felt, hoping to use "alternative media" for new projects while handing them old stuff. Some in the room called it breach of contract. But—thanks, some said, to Russ Thyret—they wouldn't take immediate legal action. If anything, they were relieved. For once, he wasn't in their face, asking them to release more music. They could also create a stopgap Greatest Hits collection.

That summer both sides retreated from a potential legal battle. They told Prince about the Greatest Hits collection. He reluctantly supported it. Though his Paisley Park Studios vault held about five hundred unreleased songs, project producer Gregg Geller of Warner Bros. didn't use many. Warner filled it with classics like "When Doves Cry" and "1999," and rare single B-sides. But Prince soon stepped forward to offer four unreleased numbers: his new song "Pink Cashmere," his late-eighties ballad "Power Fantastic," his smooth new dance-rap "Pope" and his fifties-inspired new rocker "Peach," most of which featured playing by the New Power Generation. He even threw in his live version of "Nothing Compares 2 U," with Rosie Gaines, recorded during an invitation-only Paisley Park event with revamped music.

Some reporters claimed Prince was discarding a celebrated trademark. But Prince felt when the lights went down in a concert hall, and he spoke into a microphone, "it doesn't matter what your name is." Jokes and references to "Symbol Man," "the Glyph," and "What's-His-Symbol" crept into stories. As did accusations this symbol was part of a renegotiation strategy or scheme to escape his contract. Prince claimed he was just drawing a line in the sand. "Things change here." He was seeing which media outlets respected him. And if something frustrated him, Prince remembered that Muhammad Ali saw reporters and fight fans call him Cassius Clay for years. Privately, however, Prince knew this decision was shrinking his audience even more.

"It was the worst period of my life," he later told Salon.com. "I was being made physically ill by what was going on." But he had started on this path and couldn't give in. He had to keep putting on a brave front. He told another writer at Paisley Park, "Here there is solitude, silence. I like to stay in this controlled environment." People were saying he was out of touch. Fine. He'd create twenty-five to thirty albums and "catch up with Sinatra so you tell me who's out of touch." Detractors could say what they want. "One thing I ain't gonna run out of is music." A magazine wrote that fulfilling his Warner contract with vault songs while releasing new ones somewhere else as ♣ didn't "hold much promise as a legal theory." And before Prince knew it, the media had a new name for him. After a British journalist described him as the Artist Formerly Known as Prince, others adopted the phrase. It seemingly ridiculed his decision but American newspaper writers used it, too. So did TV stations. He frowned. "I'm not the Artist Formerly Known as Anything. Use my name."

By July 1993, he wanted to release a song as ♣ on another label. Warner chairman Mo Ostin said no. They could find a way "but they're afraid of the ripple effect, that everybody would want to do it," Prince felt. But Warner wasn't the only problem. It was the entire industry. "There's just a few people with all the power." After declining to play the MTV Music Awards "suddenly, I can't get a video on MTV, and you can't get a hit without that." He earned respect for Pearl Jam, who recently decided not to film any more videos.

Unable to release music as ✿ , Prince decided to cram new music into other media. August 21, he premiered *Glam Slam Ulysses,* a play that offered a modern take on Homer's *Odyssey* in his new Glam Slam club in Los Angeles (his renovated club). The production cost several hundred thousand dollars and included twelve dancers, and thirteen new songs. But the *LA Times* called it "silly." Once it flopped, Prince kept moving these new songs from one project to another.

Around him, people felt Prince was wasting money on what insiders called "things of little or no commercial value." These included the erotic stage version of *Ulysses,* a cheaply packaged "poly-gender fragrance" called "Get Wild," stage sets and rehearsals for tours he never took, and videos. If someone told him "no," he grew exasperated. A business manager urged him to spend less, and he told her, "I don't need a mother."

Alternative media could also mean movies. So Prince agreed to provide songs for director James Brooks's latest film. The fifty-three-year-old's debut as writer-director, 1984's *Terms of Endearment,* won three Oscars, including Best Picture. His 1987 film *Broadcast News* frowned on network news stations and infotainment. His latest, *I'll Do Anything,* was a father-daughter story with Nick Nolte, Tracy Ullman, and other cast members singing songs. Prince handed Brooks all-new works called "Wow," "Make Believe," a title track, "Don't Talk 2 Strangers," "My Little Pill," "There Is Lonely," "Be My Mirror," and "I Can't Love U Anymore." He offered two others, "The Rest of My Life" and "Empty Room," but Brooks rejected them early in production. (By August 1993, Brooks had finished the film. Columbia Pictures held the first test screening. "Audience response was calamitous," *Time* reported. "One hundred people walked out, and opinion cards showed they hated the songs.")

September 7 and 8, Prince was in London, with Rob Borm, director of the "Gett Off" video, filming his shows. But just as Prince was about to take the stage, according to Bruce Orwall in the St. Paul *Pioneer Press,* Borm asked about the $450,000 Paisley Park still owed him for the "Gett Off" video. "You should know better than to talk to me about money, especially before a gig," Prince snapped. Prince went onstage to perform but his attorney and business manager soon delivered similar lectures. Facing angry creditors, Borm called his own attorney for advice. The lawyer advised Borm to pull his crew, come home, and start negotiating for payment. The tour ended by September 1993. And back home, Prince finally dismissed the New Power Generation.

That same month, there were changes at Warner. A corporate realignment plan now had Prince's longtime supporter Mo Ostin reporting to Warner Music Group chairman Robert Morgado instead of the company's top man, as Ostin had for years. Fearing a loss of autonomy, Ostin resigned. His departure inspired more resignations and realignment plans, leaving the world's largest record company nearly paralyzed. Still more acts and executives learned Ostin was leaving, and planned their own departures as soon as contractually possible.

Prince, or ♀, was a lousy talent scout, other Warner executives in Burbank decided. Paisley Park Records had costly penthouse offices in Century City, California, and a staff of nearly twenty, but had changed top executives three times in one year. Prince reportedly never stepped foot in the place. They saw Prince authorize overgenerous projects like sending a film crew to Egypt to shoot footage of Carmen Electra he allegedly never even released. Then Carmen's album flopped. By the time Paisley released new albums by Mavis Staples and George Clinton in late 1993, Warner's interest had faded. They faced the facts: The label wasn't profitable.

Warner decided to salvage what it could, working on the three-CD greatest hits set. They claimed the ♀ album sold 3.45 million copies, Bream said. Believing he had little interest in the collection—especially now that he was ♀—the label kept working on a package that would include digitally mastered versions of his hits, and a Herb Ritts portrait on the cover (Prince in sleek outfit, with pomaded hair and singing into a mic). But after his tour, Prince kept trying to get involved, submitting six new songs and offering his choice for liner notes. Warner, already behind schedule, agreed at Prince's urging to hire his former employee Alan Leeds. Prince, in fact, personally called Leeds on the telephone. But to ensure no further delay, *Uptown* explained, the label actually paid Prince to stay uninvolved.

Despite the name change, Warner felt people were most interested in his activities as Prince. Instead of the usual price—$16.98 or $17.98—Warner priced the collection at $49.99. They filled the first two discs, *The Hits 1* and *The Hits 2* with hit singles, B-sides, unreleased tracks and, thanks to him, two new singles, "Pink Cashmere" and "Peach." They also accepted liner notes in which Alan Leeds claimed the new symbol might actually start a new phase that, in fifteen years, would result in enough new hits for another collection. Warner arranged to sell *The Hits* volumes as separate discs, then got the singles "Pink Cashmere" and "Peach" into stores by September.

The label also promoted everything with a *Billboard* ad. But it infuriated Prince. Along with smiley faces, dollar signs, and other icons (including his ♀), a sentence read, "Just don't call him Prince, OK?"

Critics praised it as almost four hours of phenomenal music.

Jon Bream wrote it should get Prince elected to the Rock and Roll Hall of Fame as soon as he was eligible. But Prince's die-hard audience complained about the absence of *Parade's* "Girls and Boys," *Sign's* "Housequake," and "Batdance."

Prince himself complained about Warner's ad in *Billboard*. A week after it appeared, his own *Billboard* ad also presented an array of symbols, and it implied that the company restricted his output. Fans saw how even a promotional campaign could devolve into a public battle. *The Hits* single "Pink Cashmere" quickly left the Pop Chart. "Peach" didn't even appear. The set peaked at No. 19, sold about 3 million copies in the U.S., and struck many as another failure.

Prince spent October 1993 working on an aggressive album called *The Gold Experience*. His new songs included "Now," "319," "Shy," "Billy Jack Bitch," "Gold," "Acknowledge Me," and "Ripopgodazippa." He wasn't breaking any new ground with it, but *Gold* was fun, playful, and teeming with potential hits. Some, in fact, judged it as his most marketable work since *Diamonds and Pearls*. Since he'd be crediting this to ♀, he revisited the Prince album *Come*—the songs from January—and made a few changes. He moved his rock-flavored songs "Interactive," "Endorphinmachine," and "Strays of the World" to the ♀ album. He divided "Poem" into skits and presented what was left of it as "Orgasm." He also added a new work called "Letitgo," and an eleven-minute title track.

Some of *Come's* best moments were on *Gold*, credited to ♀. He wanted to change *Come* even more, but he submitted *Come* and *Gold* to Warner at the same time and said release both the same day. This way, ♀'s *Gold* (which held his more commercial works) could compete with his Prince album. Warner didn't like his first *Come*. It now had few commercial songs. Its tracks were also dark, dreary, and dull. Sensing he was eager for a battle, executives accepted both albums. But they rejected his plan for two albums in one day.

But the problems weren't over yet. They disagreed when *Guitar Player* planned to include his new song "Undertaker" in an issue, free, "to remind people that, hey, I'm actually a guitar player, too." He created a thousand copies of this "picture CD" *The Undertaker*, and sent its cover to a printing company. Somehow, Warner learned of it and, according to *Uptown*, asked him to destroy every copy. He laughed. He simply wanted everyone to hear his long solos. "But Warners wouldn't let me."

By now, he even blamed Warner for his rock opera's poor showing. But what really started the problem was when he introduced the topic of owning his masters, the actual reels that held his performances. He agreed to the contract, and earlier ones, but felt he recorded the albums in his own studio, and should own the tapes.

No dice.

Changing anything or giving him his masters would open floodgates. It would change how major record companies did business.

"He genuinely was hurt," said engineer Tom Tucker. He didn't know he didn't own them. He either didn't ask his managers and lawyers or they didn't tell him. He assumed they were his. He learned otherwise. "He really changed then," Tucker continued. "At that point, he took control. He started signing the checks, literally."

Relations with Warner continued to sour. One day, Prince claimed, "some suit at Warners told me I no longer 'had it.'" The next day, he sat, thought about Mayte, and wrote a ballad, "The Most Beautiful Girl in the World." He filled it with sound effects: harps, chirping birds, and dripping raindrops. But Warner accountants questioned a single that wouldn't precede an album. His new CD wasn't due for four months. This wasn't on it. Why launch a costly promotional campaign? Warner rejected the song.

He was almost relieved. He contacted independent national distributor, Bellmark, which had huge chart hits the previous year with Tag Team's dance-raps "Whoomp! (There It Is)" and "Dazzey Duks." Soon, he and Bellmark president, Al Bell, were talking. Bell, once at Stax Records in the sixties, had recently worked with Mavis on her album for Paisley Park. Now, Bell would help with the single.

In December 1993, ads in several national magazines showed an obscured photo of Prince. A caption read "Eligible bachelor seeks the most beautiful girl in the world to spend the holidays with." Interested parties should send photos or videos to Paisley Park. Ads in *People* and *Entertainment Weekly* mentioned people could order advance copies by calling 1-800-NEW-FUNK (though the service charge exceeded the cost of the record). Reporters rushed to ask Warner's opinion. "He is able to do this with our consent," said Bob Merlis. "He is still a Warner Bros. artist and should he do an album, it will be for us."

34

WHAT'S THIS STRANGE RELATIONSHIP?

BY NOW, THE MEDIA WAS CLAIMING WARNER WOULD RELEASE two albums—*Come*, by Prince, and *Gold*, also by Prince—on the same day in April or May, frustrating Warner to no end. "I got the feeling they kind of wanted to be rid of him," said Neal Karlen, who knew people at Warner. "They were waiting for another 10 million seller, and it wasn't coming." Before executives knew it, he was asking them to release even more music. When they didn't immediately rush to release his single "Love Sign," he told himself he'd throw it on a compilation album, *1-800-NEW-FUNK*, named after the phone number customers would call to order copies.

The Warner situation entered its next stage. With Prince about to release music on another label, Warner reconsidered its stake in his label Paisley Park Records. No Paisley record or ancillary release—save for Prince albums and the 1990 Time reunion—had topped charts. Paisley hadn't broken an artist in years. But Warner had still invested about $5 million as a partner. Finally, Leeds remembered, Warner told him, "We've supported you and we've never ever said no to something you wanted to do; so when are you going to come with something that will help subsidize that?'" It was "a generous attitude to have," Alan Leeds felt, since Prince had delivered works by George Clinton and Mavis Staples that Warner vice president Bob Merlis reported had sold 175,000 and "less than 100,000," respectively.

Warner hadn't bothered releasing Staples' work in other countries. Clinton's *Hey Man . . . Smell My Finger* vanished just as quickly. As usual, Prince insisted that bad promotions were to blame.

By February 1, Warner decided to end its deal with Paisley Park Records. Both companies announced the sudden closure. Clinton, Staples, Rosie Gaines, Tyler Collins, and Eric Leeds all lost their deals. Warner stopped pressing Clinton's album. Prince lost his spot on Warner's board. Merlis publicly said, "It's a mutual agreement. When I say, 'It's mutual,' it's not face-saving. I think he wants to make his career happen."

As usual, Prince blamed the other side. "All we do as artists is make the music. I didn't think I'd have to be marketing the records, or taking them to the [radio] station."

He focused on the ♀ single—arriving in mere days—as reporters began to claim his empire might be too expensive to maintain.

As promised, the video debuted during the Miss USA Pageant, featuring women from the ads. Then, February 14, Valentine's Day, NPG/Bellmark released the single, his first as ♀. MTV aired the video that night and the song rose on *Billboard*'s Hot 100, from No. 3 to 2 then 1. Using the 800 number, customers paid $3.95 for a cassette, a dollar more for a CD, and other prices for special versions (remixes and different packaging). The handling charge however was $3.25 while shipping ran either $5 (for four- to five-day delivery) or $9.50 (for a two- to three-day rush order).

Without Warner now, he turned to an international network of independent promoters (including the UK's two-man outfit Grapevine). And according to him, they did a better job. "I was number one in countries like Spain and the UK where I never had a number one single before."

He was reportedly spending heavily on promotion, but it was worth it. The single was his most commercial hit of the decade. Still, the media remained divided on how well it was actually doing. One reporter claimed it "sold enough to cover its modest overheads" and that a "spin-off EP" did well. Another said it sold a million copies in the U.S., but its price ($1.85 wholesale) "virtually ensured it couldn't make money." Either way, Prince was hot again. And though Warner claimed he was glutting the market, the single enjoyed a long Top 10 run. More than ever, Prince felt justified in placing the blame on others—not his material—for all his previous low sales.

March 11, he submitted *Come*, his album as "Prince," only to hear major label executives say it needed work: a better title track, stronger numbers and, supposedly, the song "The Most Beautiful Girl in the World." He allegedly refused to hand them that ♀ song. Five days later, at another VIP party at Glam Slam, he played a few songs from his other new album *Gold*, including "Billy Jack Bitch" (about a local newspaper columnist), his fuzzy "Days of Wild," "Now," and a theatrical new ballad, "Eye Hate U."

In May, Prince was off to Monte Carlo for the World Music Awards, not to mention interviews with Britain's *Q*, Germany's *Max*, and America's *Vibe*. Everyone panicked, however, when a poster for the awards called him Prince. Someone quickly drew his gold ♀ over it. "If he'd seen that," said a relieved employee, "he might just have turned around and gone home."

In the front row, Prince watched Whitney Houston accept a World Music Award for "I Will Always Love You," 1993's most popular record. "I don't care," she said to him from the stage, "I'm going to call you Prince." In his seat, he smiled weakly and nodded. His performance at an after-party thrown by Prince Albert of Monaco kept him in the headlines. And supportive rock writers kept mentioning Warner's release of *Come* approaching in July.

He kept money coming by opening a shop in North London and doing good business with Prince memorabilia. But he had gone through four publicity firms in only nine months. In Europe, he continued to maintain that a spiritual change inspired his new name, ♀. But while leaving a posh hotel one night, he heard fans outside scream "Prince!" He lowered his head, smiled, and entered a waiting car, clearly not minding that they used his given name.

Still, he *had* to continue with the ♀. "He genuinely thought that by changing his name he could get out of his Warners deal," European publicist Chris Poole told *Q Magazine*. At one point he told Poole, "If I'm not Prince anymore, they can't hold me to my contract." When Poole asked if he'd discussed this with his attorneys, Prince said, "Hah. Lawyers." But when the *Daily Star* called him insane, Prince vented. "Why are they calling me mad?" Poole replied, "What do you expect? You do these things and don't explain yourself properly." Prince said he'd do interviews. But he wouldn't let anyone tape or write anything. This way, he'd be able to discuss Warner. "But if there was no record of the conversations he could always say he was misquoted," Poole explained. "Which drove Warners mad."

He was eccentric, Poole added, but not careless.

One night at midnight, he was in white silk clothes and full makeup. He was using half brother Duane's room for an interview. Duane, now his head of security, had led him into the junior suite. Again, Prince banned recorders, notepads, and pens. Sitting near the writer on a bed, he said, "I don't say much." After he evaded a few questions, he and his interviewer heard a crackling noise escape the huge TV nearby. Nodding at it, Prince said, "It's a sign. It's a sign that we should go to my room." He raced for the door.

Duane asked what was wrong.

"A sound came through the TV. It's a sign."

"Nah, you probably just sat on the remote control."

He returned to the interview but exploded when the writer asked how he thought others perceived him. He shrilly answered, "Are you normal? Are you normal? Is that what you're asking me? Do I think I'm normal? Yes, I do. I think I'm normal. I am normal."

Next up was *Vibe*'s Alan Light, again in an opulent overseas hotel. After meeting Prince in San Francisco one night a year or so ago, Light had returned to New York City the next day and called Prince's publicist Karen Lee. "And she said he was happy and I should just sit tight and we would see what would happen." Months later, Prince's camp invited Light to Paisley Park.

Light traveled to his studio complex but later called this the weirdest part of trying to arrange the interview. There, Prince had him spend the day watching him rehearse new songs. Only at the end of the session did he offer Light a brief greeting. To this day, Light is "still not sure what that was all about. If he wanted to talk then changed his mind; if there was one specific thing he wanted me to hear . . ." Light had fun "but I didn't really get the point." They met one more time in Manhattan before Prince sent word "in late spring of 1994 that he wanted to commit to an interview," Light explained. "But the only time and place we could schedule was in Monte Carlo, when he had to be there for a few days for the World Music Awards."

Once again, Prince let Light glimpse the man behind the image. "When you sit and talk to him, his voice, his whole demeanor when you're with him one-on-one is so different from the 'space alien vibe' he usually projects in public," Light noted. If anything, he was surprisingly normal.

But in Monaco he continued to promote his dramatic image. One day, he changed his outfit three times. "And that was a day without a show!" Light quipped. "Talk about always being on." Then he left his hotel to attend the awards show. He let Light accompany him. "And there was this wild throng of people out front screaming and grabbing for him," Light said. The writer wound up becoming a link in the line of security guards blocking the path Prince used to reach his limousine. "And it was terrifying," Light said. "When you really confront just how insane people are around stars like him, it is such a reminder of how unreal their lives are."

After a few conversations, Prince decided it was time to speak. This time, he hoped to use their interview to convince Warner to reconsider his plan for two albums in one day. He brought out two CDs with hand-drawn art. "And he did play me the two discs, or at least highlights from them," Light recalled.

First, he played Light *Come,* by Prince. But he skipped between tracks. "It all sounds strong—first-rate—but he seems impatient, like it was old news," Light suggested. Next, he introduced *The Gold Album,* his first ♩ collection, and let songs run, played air guitar, even played at the piano. Light saw "he was more excited about these songs." That "he was so into this music, he wanted to hold it back from Warner" until they came around to the "kind of distribution and strategy" he wanted. In print, Light wound up judging the Prince album as more commercial but "also more conventional."

Back home, in mid-May, Prince created another version of *Come.* He included the revised title track that Warner wanted and "Letitgo." He then momentarily lost himself in further improving *Gold,* removing his thrashing rock dirge "Days of Wild" and the fake reggae of "Ripopgodazippa" (part of which appeared in that flop *Showgirls*). After further tinkering, he submitted the newest *Come* to Warner. Even with an eleven-minute title track, it was his shortest work since *Batman.*

Warner executives still felt it was mediocre and lacked a hit single. They agreed to accept it, but only if he included "Shhh!," a new song he had performed during his February 13 Paisley Park show. He wouldn't.

Warner executives again found themselves at an impasse. Rather than lock horns, they relented. "Letitgo"—the only new work—was far from his best, but enough for a single.

Prince insisted that they credit the album to "Prince: 1958–1993." They said fine, and asked him to make a video for "Letitgo." He refused. Instead of complaining, label executives cobbled one together with footage from his older clips.

By June, a contractual clause—allowing him to shop nonmusic ventures elsewhere—meant he could release a new product. So on the

Tuesday he turned thirty-six, small independent Graphix Zone unveiled *Interactive*. Despite public claims of being restrained, Prince filled the CD-Rom with three full-length videos ("Diamonds and Pearls," "Gett Off" and "Endorphinmachine"), fifty-two songs (old and new), some 3-D computer animation, a virtual tour of his home studio, and a karaoke setting for "Kiss." Reviews sang its praise and sales topped sixty thousand copies. That same month, he released even more music away from Warner, crediting the "Love Sign" single solely to Nona Gaye—suggesting only Gaye was behind its actual creation, that he—as Prince or ♀—was uninvolved—and having its label note it was for promotional use only. And more music was on the way, if all went well: an opera, a blues album, an album he'd give "for free, like air," and—never far from his thoughts—*The Gold Album*.

At Paisley Park that summer, Prince, ever inspired, suddenly wanted to work on something new. He paid David Rivkin to move a project to Los Angeles to make room. Instead, David, who used Paisley so much he rented an office, moved out. "They didn't seem to give a shit if I was leaving or not," David told reporter Bruce Orwall. "They just said, 'If you're not going to use this office, can we use it?'" Despite fewer customers and less incoming revenue, Rivkin saw that Prince was still spending several hundred thousand dollars on new recording equipment. He was ignoring financial problems, Rivkin added. Devouring newspaper and magazine reports hadn't inspired him to avoid past financial mistakes. "I don't think he ever did reform his practices," Rivkin concluded. "It happened so fast in the beginning for him that it's always been 'easy come, easy go.'"

Now, Prince worked on three projects: something for his small Bellmark-backed NPG label, something for Warner, and something for the future. By August 12, Bellmark was shipping his compilation album *1-800-NEW-FUNK*.

Warner meanwhile planned to have *Come* in stores four days later. The cover said it all. He was in black clothes, by an ominous gate and a crumbling gray house (actually a church in Barcelona). The skies were black. A nearby caption credited *Come* to "Prince: 1958–1993." Then, elsewhere, he wrote, in reverse, "This is the dawning of a new spiritual revolution." It was supposedly his final recording under the name. Warner shipped it on schedule. Fans, for their part, didn't know what to make of the cover, the "1958–1993," and the morbid photo. It was, they were to assume, a posthumous work.

Segments of his audience were willing to buy anything he created; *Come* managed to reach No. 15 in the United States.

But reviews were reproachful. Most described a "blatant contract-fulfiller." One claimed *Come* held vault outtakes. *City Pages'* Steve Perry described the "1958–1993" caption as Prince's "most public fuck-you" yet, and in poor taste after Warner "spent two years helping convince people he is now ♀."

Warner saw a few radio stations embrace "Letitgo," and *Come* debut at No. 1 in the United Kingdom. There was still hope, but instead of promoting his creation, Prince focused on pushing *1-800-NEW-FUNK*. When he did promote *Come*, Prince called it "old material" (despite having recorded it during sessions that yielded some of what he now called *The Gold Experience*). Warner executives shook their heads. *Come* emerged as Prince's lowest-selling album to date, struggling to sell even 500,000 copies. Still, even this commercial letdown didn't stop him from asking Warner when they'd release *The Gold Experience*.

At the label, Mo Ostin's replacement Danny Goldberg had installed a new regime, and Prince decided to tweak the team at Warner by filming a video for his *Gold* number "Dolphin," in one take. Over an upbeat melody and guitar solo, Prince sang about independence, and sticking to your guns. But a special effect superimposed the word *slave,* in reverse, on one cheek. Prince had an independent publicity firm leak the video to reporters.

By September 3, reporters worldwide had rushed to cover the video—and the word—creating articles he hoped would show Warner there was interest in his work.

It was time to negotiate for the release of *The Gold Experience*. And before meetings, he wrote the word *slave* on his face with mascara. But he wasn't angry, he told *Icon* magazine. He just wanted to unnerve people he viewed as adversaries. On one occasion, he entered a room, and took a seat. An executive said, "It makes it real hard to talk to you with that on your face."

"Why?"

Silence ensued.

Prince knew he was playing the race card. And the term "worked perfectly," he said. "It changed the dynamic."

Close associates however frowned. "You're the only slave that owns the plantation," Alan Leeds told him. "It was all silly," Leeds added of Prince's crusade against the label.

He ignored it. At Warner, Bob Merlis quipped, "If he's a slave, he's one of the best-paid slaves in the world."

Negotiations continued, but Paisley Park's employees and vendors were just as frustrated. "He talks about himself being a slave to Warners," said wardrobe director Heidi Presnail. "Hello? Let me knock on your door. We don't work for free."

He and Warner reportedly reached a verbal agreement to get *The Gold Experience* out a week before Christmas 1994. But *Uptown* claimed smaller Tommy Boy Records would handle its domestic release, while East/West covered other nations. But they never put it in writing, according to *Uptown,* and Prince rejected the plan once he learned Warner wouldn't count *Gold* as one of four albums he still owed.

He kept publicly claiming Warner was enslaving him and his music.

Many in the media ignored Warner's side, claiming the year-old *Gold* album held some of his best music in years. Others quoted like-minded artists who praised him. *Musician* called him one of several industry "revolutionaries" challenging the status quo. Bob Merlis, however, told a reporter, "If he had a string of hits, we wouldn't be having this conversation."

October 13, 1994, the "battle" reached a new low. Prince's publicists issued a press release denouncing Warner for not releasing *The Gold Experience.* "Fans may never hear what is being called his finest album to date," it claimed. And "he now feels that his much publicized $100 million deal may have just been a way to lock him into 'institutionalized slavery' with Warners." Prince had had enough, it continued. He just wanted to submit four albums and leave a stressful situation.

His New Power Generation retail store in Minneapolis also distributed the message about *Gold.* Customers received full-color flyers that claimed: "Release Date: Never!" Then, "Do you want to see it liberated from Warner Bros. Records?" If so, vote "Yes" and write Warner.

NPG Records then spread the word online. It inspired more media backlash. His publicist insisted, "*The Gold Experience* likely will never be released."

But Warner's Merlis said it wasn't true. "Yes, we would like to put out the next Prince or symbol-person album. And we will, once he delivers the masters."

Another Warner executive remembered Prince "at least three times" backed out of deals he negotiated for its release. Regardless, Prince kept playing *Gold* songs during shows and sending people to negotiate with Warner.

He claimed otherwise but it was apparent that his fortunes were dwindling. Sales dipped lower with each new release. *Come* was another flop. The name change made him a national joke. He kept attacking Warner for not releasing *Gold*. Now, he needed it out there as soon as possible. An unnamed source told *City Pages*, "He needs cash. And the way to get cash is to tour. So he needs to do that soon, and he didn't want to tour behind *Come*, which has already disappeared from the charts. He wants to tour behind the *Gold* record, but he's got to get it out there first."

35

OLD FRIENDS FOR SALE

EVENTUALLY, PRINCE SENT HIS ATTORNEY TO NEGOTIATE A DEAL. Despite the provocative "Dolphin," *slave* on his cheek, press releases, and the album's potential to create more poor sales and "market saturation," Warner was still willing to discuss *Gold*. By October 25, Warner agreed to give $4 million up front. They would release *The Black Album*—the album he canceled in late 1987—in November, and have *The Gold Experience* out by February or March 1995. He'd also record a soundtrack to a future Warner film, *Uptown* added. But *The Black Album* wouldn't count toward fulfilling his contract. The three would count as two toward the four left on his contract. "He's releasing that only to strike a bargain for the release of the other record."

And so, years after it was recorded, Warner announced *The Black Album* would arrive right before Thanksgiving. *City Pages's* Steve Perry felt it was a good move. The well-known work could sell at least 500,000 copies and bring both sides "a step closer to freedom from each other." Yet, Prince sabotaged even this, saying Warner should only make it available from late November to January 27.

Advances, publishing royalties, and fees for producing others still earned Prince $10 to $20 million annually. He also had a number of companies under his control. But his campaign against Warner and freewheeling spending habits were beginning to have an impact.

Paisley seemingly ignored bills, Bruce Orwall reported. The company suddenly halved fees owed to makeup artists or hairstylists. "There's a lot of little guys out there," Julie Hartley, production manager, told Orwall. One friend had "to borrow money from his mom to pay his mortgage" due to nonpayment.

Gary and Suzy Zahradka, the St. Paul couple that made the elaborate canes he carried to French fashion shows and Monte Carlo, waited almost six months for their $4,500 payment, then sued Paisley in November when it still wasn't received. They settled quickly, but other creditors reported slow payments. Northwest Teleproductions in Edina saw Paisley stop sending payment on a months-old debt in the tens of thousands. Collection calls baffled employees. "Mostly, we just meet with the frustration of employees over there," said company president Bob Mitchell. High turnover in middle management meant people that commissioned the work were gone.

In California, recording studio the Record Plant had been grateful that Prince spent $500,000 annually on a crew and that his company always paid on time. But that summer, a $150,000 bill went unpaid for five months. Inevitably, Paisley called for a master tape. Record Plant owners said pay the debt and they would send it. Paisley paid that very day.

Jim Mulligan of local company Videoworks worked on a project for Prince that spring but waited months for his $1,400. He began a relentless collection campaign: faxing an invoice each morning; calling the accounting department; leaving voice mail; then faxing the invoice twice a day. After six weeks, he called one morning and told the voice mail he wanted his check at the front desk that afternoon. He got it. "I never talked to an actual human being," he said.

With the company firing every key executive or the executives resigning, Orwall noted, creditors didn't know who to badger.

For ten months, local film producer Rob Borm tried to get Paisley to pay its $400,000 debt. He settled for $315,000, about seventy cents on the dollar. Since his company relied on Paisley for 90 percent of its work, he had Point of View films declare bankruptcy with about $5,900 in assets and $135,000 in debts. With more creditors complaining, Randy Adamsick, president of the Minnesota Film Board, said, "People haven't gotten paid, it's absolutely true."

The New York Times blamed Prince's lack of business acumen for his financial disarray. *Forbes*'s analysis was simpler: He quarreled with Warner, accusing executives of "enslaving" his music when they simply wanted him to honor the terms of the contract. Once Warner closed his office and label, he "retreated to Paisley Park, where he has nearly ruined himself with self-indulgent spending, including $6 million a year to keep the studio running."

Forbes noted that in 1994 "he spent about $4 million to rehearse his band and build stages for a concert tour he never made." Another $2 million went to nine versions of "The Most Beautiful Girl in the World," all released independently. "It sold only about 700,000 copies." He filmed about thirty videos a year, with many costing "up to $500,000 apiece, and never released them." He did this despite the fact that he did not tour overseas or in the States, and earn the usual money, that year.

His campaign against Warner alienated even hard-core followers. "He's losing a lot of his fans," said Nathan Wright, whose local 900 line offered Prince information. "A lot of his fans are tired of it. It's like a gigantic game that only he seems to know the rules to."

Prince confronted production assistant Julie Hartley on a soundstage, and accused her of misrepresenting the cost of his stage prop the "Endorphin Machine." Then he fired her and ordered all but two members of a film crew out. "Now here's the shot," Prince told those remaining. "I want the bed to get up and fly over me to there."

Fired employees told the *St. Paul Pioneer Press* he wasted huge sums on his stage show "Ulysses," and overblown sets for tours he never took. Meanwhile, his $2 million-plus chain of Glam Slam clubs in Miami, Los Angeles, and Minneapolis struggled to remain open "amidst bitter bust-ups with ex–business partners."

By October, even Davison left, *The Dallas Morning News* reported, "After a dispute over who actually owned Glam Slam." With Davison gone, Prince's immediate reaction was to install stepbrother Duane Nelson to head a five-person downsizing committee. Duane's committee sent pink slips flying. "What they told me is that I was being fired on a cutback and they were eliminating my position," wardrobe director Heidi Presnail said. Soundstage manager Mark "Red" White, with Prince for a decade, left when things were "a little behind financially." Paisley was slow to pay vendors, he conceded. "But, God bless him, he paid for a lot of mortgage payments in this town." They fired chief financial officer Carr.

Even his Glam Slam West club—opened without Davison in early 1993—wasn't doing well. On November 19, 1994, the *LA Times* wrote, "Perhaps it's a Sign O' the Times, but the once-radiant Glam Slam has lost its luster." The *Times* noted it had "quickly come to resemble Sodom—after the fall." The walls were "in disrepair," bathrooms were "unkempt," and the club operated "with a skeleton crew." This was fine for "any number of seedy punk or rock clubs," but not "Glam Slam, the home of performances by Prince, himself, as well as nearly every popular R&B and hip-hop artist." The attitude around the club, the *Times* felt, was "more depressing than exhilarating."

———

In seven years, bootleggers had already sold over 250,000 CDs or vinyl copies of *The Black Album*, and passed more around on cassette. Its ten tracks were already old hat to his core audience. But Warner still released the album with the original artwork on Tuesday, November 22, 1994. "We are accommodating the artist's wishes," said Bob Merlis. "He signed an agreement to let us do it. We've wanted to put it out for years."

But Warner wouldn't release any singles. They placed a humorous ad promising amnesty, and a new official copy, to the first thousand people who mailed in their bootleg copies. With Prince not filming, they filled a video for "When 2 R in Love" with lyrics flashing across a black screen. The day of its release, label employees in Burbank even wore black clothing, and respectfully shut off office lights for fifteen minutes.

But in print, Prince's spokeswoman Karen Lee fueled anti-Warner sentiment among his hard-core following by claiming Prince still didn't want *The Black Album* out there. "He's thoroughly pissed off about it. He had to sign an agreement—I can't go into why—but contractually, he didn't have a choice." Prince felt he wrote that album when he was a different person, she added. He was angry, and didn't ever want it out. "And here we are back in the record-company politics again, and he doesn't have a choice." Merlis said, "All I can tell you is that October 25, he signed an agreement letting us put it out."

Yet his representative Karen Lee continued to imply Warner somehow mistreated Prince. "Before they agreed to release *The Black Album*, he owed four albums, and he still owes four albums."

A Warner executive said Prince let them release it, "so clearly he's able to do business with us."

Either way, Prince made it available for only two months. Once again, his work divided critics. One felt *The Black Album*'s release couldn't hurt since *Come* "was one of the biggest duds of his career." Others appreciated hearing the pre-rap Prince. *Time* felt, "*The Black Album* is far too stark and angry to restore him to his previous place on the charts," and didn't have "the same quality as his best work." Still another reviewer wrote, "It's nice to have the album to complete collections, but its time has clearly passed." *The Black Album* also sold poorly.

November 24, 1994, at the MTV Europe Music Awards ceremony, a presenter had a problem with the ♀. Prince asked for specifics. "He just said there is a problem," Prince recalled. "The truth is that there is no problem. I made it known very publicly that that was my new name. If people do not use it, they are insulting me. I don't understand that insult. I don't play the race card, but it seems to me that, in this case, you can't get away from it."

In late November, publicist Karen Lee quietly cleaned out her desk and left. "It's time for a change, time to move on." Levi Seacer, Jr., the former band member running NPG Records, and Lee's boyfriend, quit at the same time. When severance payments stopped, several people hired attorneys. By year's end, most negotiated final settlements with Prince's company (as did the couple that made his canes).

Prince's December 13 performance on the *Late Show with David Letterman* was strange enough, since his lightweight "Dolphin" had impenetrable lyrics like, "If I came back as a dolphin, would you listen to me then?" But at his desk, the popular host faced a cheering studio audience and introduced him by saying his next guest was one of music's most talented and influential performers. "The song he will be doing for us tonight is from, uh—" Letterman lifted a gold CD case—"this CD right here, uh, which is entitled *The Gold Experience*. And I'm told that this particular CD will never be released." The host shrugged, causing someone in the audience to laugh. "So it makes perfect sense that he's here promoting it tonight." The crowd roared as Letterman asked the crowd to "please welcome—" He reached over for a prop on his desk, then raised a huge black ♀ to the camera. "The artist formerly known as Prince," he said.

Prince walked out in his short Jackson-like hairdo, with the word *slave* on his right cheek. He had an odd black shirt with gold patches on it and played a ♀-shaped guitar. He ended the performance by pretending to die. People dragged him off the stage as part of what an observer dubbed "a mock suicide."

New Year's Eve arrived, and Mo Ostin's contract officially expired. But Ostin would stick around, as a senior consultant to Time Warner's chairman until August 3, 1995.

During this period, Prince told Warner he would deliver master tapes for *The Gold Experience* if they released his single "Purple Medley." This track was a mix of old Prince hits he hoped would remind listeners of how many classics he created during the previous decade. Especially since his antics had fans leaving in droves. Warner agreed to put the song out—along with a B-side filled with more portions of old hits—even though it wasn't accompanying any album. It was just a random mix with some hits sampled, some replayed, and all flying in the face of his claim to want to leave "Prince" behind. Still, he wanted to perform the new song publicly, and got his chance when Dick Clark, founder and executive producer of the "American Music Awards," invited him to the televised ceremony.

During the three-hour show, held in January 1995, Madonna, Little Richard, and Queen Latifah all performed. There was a tribute to Led Zeppelin. But Prince was the big draw. Before every commercial break, the announcer promoted him to ABC viewers, "Still to come, superexcitement from the artist formerly known as Prince and his twenty-five-member dance troupe." Presenters doled out twenty-two American Music Awards. Prince, however, received the most prestigious, the one for Merit, given during past ceremonies to such industry legends as Irving Berlin, Ella Fitzgerald, and Michael Jackson. Dick Clark also praised his talent, influence, and record of accomplishment (fourteen million albums sold).

Come time to perform, Prince executed "The Purple Medley." Twenty-five dancers roamed the stage. Clips from his videos and films filled huge video monitors. An unseen band played parts of his hits "When Doves Cry," "Kiss," "Baby I'm a Star," "Diamonds and Pearls," among others. An announcer then claimed Prince left the earth on June 7, 1993, that they would now see the artist formerly known as Prince. He revealed himself from his hiding spot in the crowd of black-clad dancers. After lip-synching to his unreleased *Gold* songs "Billy Jack Bitch," "I Hate U" and "319," he slid through dancer (and sometime lover) Mayte's legs. After the performance, he accepted an award from Nona Gaye. He waved it, and pulled a note from a pocket.

Removing the gum from his mouth, Prince thanked—individually—every bandmate he ever had as Prince. He thanked his influences Muhammad Ali, Martin Luther King, James Brown, Santana, Sly, Joni Mitchell, Miles Davis, and Jimi Hendrix. He added, "I'd like to thank Dick Clark for allowing me to put Prince to bed." Then he answered media claims of financial disarray. "It's all cool. Peace and be wild!"

Prince left the stage but soon returned for the finale, a tenth-anniversary re-creation of the star-studded "We Are the World" session led by producer Quincy Jones and singers Kenny Rogers and Harry Belafonte. Prince was at the center of the singing, swaying celebrities this time, surrounded by Nona Gaye and Jones. But when Jones held a microphone in front of his mouth, inviting him to sing, Prince pulled his Tootsie Roll Pop out of his mouth and held it in front of Jones's mouth. "Both smiled, neither sang," Bream noted.

Warner hadn't released it, but Prince simply couldn't wait any longer. He took *The Gold Experience* on the road with his $250,000 "Endorphin Machine," a huge stage set with various gold-painted structures including a big phallus-shaped object, a birdcage with elevator, a clitoris, a coiled contraption, and a womb (actually a two-story space with mixing board, dressing room, and red curtains that drew one comparison to covers on cheap sci-fi paperbacks).

February 20, Prince fired the next round against Warner. At the BRIT Awards, the British Phonographic Industry's annual equivalent of the Grammys, Prince and a publicist sat in their $350 seats a few feet from Warner's official table. He had "Slave" on his right cheek and ignored the Warner contingent. This was more than enough, but while accepting his award for Best International Male Artist, Prince told the audience, "Prince best, *Gold Experience* better. Get Wild. In concert: free. On record: slave. Peace."

Chairman Danny Goldberg wanted to meet in Los Angeles to discuss the relationship Prince had publicly called "institutionalized slavery" before scheduling *The Gold Experience* or NPG's forthcoming album, *Exodus*, for release.

By March 3, Prince had approached five powerful Los Angeles entertainment lawyers to negotiate a release from his contract, the *Los Angeles Times* reported, and they all turned him down. His image continued to suffer. "I want people to think I'm insane," he said. "But I'm in control." He wasn't before he became ♀, he claimed. "I didn't know what was happening beyond the next two albums." Now he knew exactly how they'd sound. "I'm not playing anyone else's game. I'm in control. I don't care if people say I'm mad. It don't matter." A writer asked, if sane, why change his name? For a new mindset, Prince explained. "I don't want to destroy the mystique by revealing everything."

During one talk, Prince said he had planned this transition for at least eleven years, even including an early version of the ♀ on the side of the sleeve to *Purple Rain*. He kept including it and soon had Paisley Park Studios—where he could actually create his music—open for business.

Now, he was exploring other distribution methods. And if he had to, he'd make like Pearl Jam, "just turn up at radio stations, and play the people our music."

But Prince was trying to get *The Gold Experience* online. Fans would hear his music, he vowed, "whether it be through duplicating cassettes, or if we press up ten thousand CDs after the show and charge five dollars each, just to cover costs you know?" The ideas struck many as odd, but Prince felt he had already created an infrastructure that bypassed existing multinationals. "That's what the live show is about," Prince admitted. "I've done it! And if you look around at the fans, so many of them are waving signs with the new symbol. It's such a beautiful sight."

Despite his complaints about Warner, the label released his "Purple Medley"—and its B-side "Kirk J's B-Sides Remix"—March 14, 1995, and wasn't that surprised to see it fare poorly. Nighttime radio ignored it. It didn't make any airplay charts. It made it to No. 84 on the Hot 100 and No. 74 on the R&B/Hip-Hop Chart, then vanished. It did better in the United Kingdom, reaching No. 33, but was far from a hit over there, either. And though Warner released the song, *The Gold Experience* tapes he promised to deliver in exchange for this release *still* had no release date.

The truth was that, at some point, Prince gave up on waiting. He had started his next album. "For this one, I started with the blueprint of three CDs, one hour each, with peaks and valleys in the right places," he said. But instead of vault material, this new *Emancipation* would have all new songs handled by his new publishing company Emancipation Music and ASCAP.

In 1994, he had recorded "The Plan" and "Somebody's Somebody." Now he kept adding songs. Every day, he brought a new idea to the studio. He played every instrument but let Kirk A. Johnson help. A dancer during the Purple Rain Tour, Johnson now handled a few beats. With Prince focusing on what he'd actually record, and in what order, Johnson filled a drum machine with patterns that evoked current hip-hop, R&B, or the drum solos on obscure records compiled on the twenty-five volume series of "break-beat" albums from which many rap producers drew their own samples or loops. Prince could easily have handled this part himself but didn't like setting up equipment. While plugging wires in, or adjusting sound levels, a song idea might leave.

Prince focused on writing commercial R&B. And he didn't fill his button-down beats with too many sounds. If anything, these new songs sounded as satiny, and uncontroversial as works by Chicago's R. Kelly, Boyz II Men, Toni Braxton, Mariah Carey, or Whitney Houston. He already had enough for an album, but kept working without a view toward ending. "We'd cut three or four songs in one day," Johnson recalled.

Then in mid-May, Prince flew to Los Angeles to play at Glam Slam. While out there, he also planned to meet with Ostin's replacement Danny Goldberg. Before the meeting, he wondered if Goldberg would understand him and his music. To everyone's surprise, the meeting resulted in a positive agreement: If Prince stopped disparaging the company publicly, Warner would release NPG's *Exodus* and *The Gold Experience* on September 12. After the meeting, Prince told reporters he wasn't bitter or angry. If anything, Mo Ostin let him release "The Most Beautiful Girl" as ♀. "And I will love that man forever because of that." And Warner? "I'm content with them." He even backpedaled about why he wrote on his face. "I'm not a slave to Warner Brothers. It's not there to embarrass Warners. Why would I do that? You gotta understand that. I don't need to. It's not about that. I'm not angry with them. It's just there as a reminder."

But in June, he ruined things with an interview in South Beach, Miami. He left a car and quickly entered that city's Glam Slam to film a video. Staring straight ahead, with "Slave" written in marker on his right cheek, he sat with Carolyn Baker, a Warner vice president of artist development, and two NPG members. Juli Knapp, director of operations, introduced him to an *Esquire* writer as "the artist formerly known as Prince."

During the interview, he told the writer his slave side would release *The Gold Experience*; his semifree side would credit *Exodus* to NPG; and his new self was already working on a big hidden album called *Emancipation*. The latter, the writer noted, "would be his first album when he is free— maybe fifty new songs." Then he'd reemerge and speak to the press. His heart, "and perhaps his best work are in *Emancipation*," the writer added. "This album is a big surprise to people at Warner. No one seems to know about it."

Some Warner employees were already complaining in the corridors about the *Gold* number "Pussy Control." They felt the title was vulgar and suggested changing it before stores decided not to stock it on their shelves. But then, *Esquire*'s special autumn issue—with Prince on the cover—made the rounds. That he bewailed his contract and mentioned a fifty-cut *Eman-*

cipation album he'd unveil after his departure had top executives saying he had reneged on a promise they alleged he had made to stop disparaging Warner in public, according to Alex Hahn.

And so, without warning, Warner decided to take a firm stance: They wouldn't release NPG's *Exodus*.

Prince was reportedly shocked. The cancellation came at a time when, Mayte's bodyguard Arlene Mojica said, "We kept getting complaints from local tradesmen about bills not being paid."

In September, Paul Verhoeven's *Showgirls* opened in American theaters. Warner let Verhoeven use Prince's *Gold* numbers "319" and "Ripopgodazippa" in the MGM/United Artists film, but not on the soundtrack album.

Four days later, Warner released *The Gold Experience*, which may have pleased Prince, but it was a Pyrrhic victory. His first album as ⚥ had sat on a shelf since spring of 1994. It included his usual mix of randy R&B ("Billy Jack Bitch," "P Control"), upbeat rock ("Dolphin," "Endorphinmachine"), slow jams ("I Hate U," "Shhh"), and a guitar-driven power ballad in the "Purple Rain" tradition ("Gold"). But Prince had little interest in promoting it.

Critics mostly approved, describing his most reasoned, commercial and melodious work since *Diamonds*, but *The Gold Experience* sold just 530,000 copies in North America. And its release didn't end his protests. When he bowed out of a scheduled appearance on *Saturday Night Live*, people accepted Prince had moved on. In his wake, some claimed he released *Gold* only to move one album closer to ending his contractual obligation.

36

SOMETIMES IT SNOWS IN APRIL

THAT WINTER, PRINCE WAS WORKING ALL NIGHT. HE WOKE AT four in the afternoon when the sky was dark, and never saw sunlight. Someone would drive him over to Paisley Park, where he likely worked on his mega-album, *Emancipation*. He wouldn't return until seven in the morning. He skipped meals, employee Arlene Mojica recalled, some days consuming only a cup of rice. "Often nothing for three days." He was also withdrawing into his personal relationship with young dancer Mayte Garcia.

Prince continued to include her onstage—she danced and simulated fellatio—and on songs like "Pope," another half-hearted dance-rap seemingly trying to compete with acts like Eric B. and Rakim. They spent their days and evenings together—and she had supported his decision to change his stage name (going so far as to sign a longwinded essay about it sent to fanzine *Controversy*). Now, trying to distance himself from Warner and his past few works, Prince began to work with Mayte on a solo album. Though people in his camp later said this was more his idea, not hers, Mayte went along with it, heeding his calls for more Prince-like vocals on songs like "The Most Beautiful Boy in the World" (a Spanish answer to his own recent hit).

In November, he had released her solo album, *Child of the Sun*. She hoped to promote it, but he had other plans for the young performer. He proposed marriage in mid-December. Mayte accepted, and soon flashed a huge diamond ring to friends. Prince meanwhile looked forward to a big wedding in Paris.

But even these developments couldn't drown out the thoughts of Warner.

Danny Goldberg had left the CEO position at Warner where he had only recently been installed. Prince's old associate, Warner Bros. Records vice chair Russ Thyret, replaced him. It sounded like a promising development, but Prince was annoyed. And with good reason: "Mr. Ostin began the yearlong run of executive departures and dismissals at Warner Music when he resigned last August," *The New York Times* explained. Since Ostin's departure, Warner had created Warner Music U.S., a unit to administer their three American labels. Then, in June, Warner brought in Michael Fuchs, chairman of HBO, to supervise Warner Music U.S. According to *The New York Times's* Lawrence Zuckerman, Fuchs fired Doug Morris, who ran Warner Bros. Records and two other domestic labels, by July. Now, Goldberg was the latest to leave, and the company promoted Thyret. Fuchs himself told *The New York Times*, "There is no longer a Warner Music unit." Prince felt these time-wasting label mergers and the "revolving door of executives" were like "musical chairs or something."

So Prince leaped into creating a special with VH1 to express annoyance with Warner. In this thirty-minute show, he sat in Paisley Park, taking over VH1's airwaves. Just as a network host introduced a Madonna video, a bandmate shoved two wires together, causing the screen to fizzle. His ♀ appeared, followed by a video he created for NPG's *Exodus* (which Warner, as a de facto retaliation for his bad-mouthing of the label, had cancelled). If they wouldn't put out his music, he'd find a way to do it himself, his special seemed to suggest.

This wasn't enough. By December 22, he had Paisley Park issue another statement, officially notifying Warner that Prince wanted to leave due to irreconcilable differences. Warner couldn't successfully promote certain acts due to an unstable business environment and high turnover on the supervisory level, it claimed. A Warner executive publicly called the release one in a line Prince hoped would sway public opinion in his favor. Thyret meanwhile was already dealing with more executives resigning, and other major acts expressing unhappiness (including R.E.M.). "I'm not interested in getting into any side controversies that will distract me from moving this company forward," he said. This included, he felt, Prince. Thyret decided that if Prince was so unhappy with the relationship, Warner would end it.

It must have been a surprising turn, but Prince had his mind on other things. He was planning his wedding, and writing a string-heavy collection of pieces called *Kamasutra*. He also played shows in Japan, and recorded a song for Mayte, and *Emancipation*, called "Friend, Lover, Sister, Mother/ Wife."

In February 1996, Prince and Mayte wed in a south Minneapolis church. The twenty-two-year-old walked down the aisle. He looked into her eyes as he slipped the five-carat wedding ring onto her finger. They flew to Hawaii for a honeymoon, and three weekend concerts at the Neal S. Blaisdell Center Arena. He carried her across the threshold of their room. Two months earlier, Mayte had told a reporter she didn't want to have a kid yet, but in the honeymoon suite, a crib was among the presents Prince offered. They both cried. She knelt near him and they both prayed.

Then they did a show where Mayte danced for the last time.

Prince wished he could have more time off. But he had to end things with Warner. He was seeking a lawyer. Meanwhile, Mayte bought a pregnancy test from a pharmacy, employee Arlene Mojica recalled, and learned she was pregnant. Prince was delighted and, in characteristic fashion, began writing about it.

He was knee-deep in *Emancipation* when his advisers suggested he meet Londell McMillan. A dynamic young attorney raised in Brooklyn's Bedford-Stuyvesant neighborhood, McMillan had once offered to work for him. Feeling the thirty-year-old was too young, Prince's advisors rejected him. But after several other attorneys couldn't resolve the situation after months of negotiations, his advisers suggested he give McMillan a shot.

So Prince had him come to Paisley Park.

Prince had started out trying to change the state of music. He wrote too many classics to count. He played almost every kind of music imaginable. But he started doubting himself, he told *Rock & Folk* magazine. While writing, he'd ask himself, *Do I really have the sound of the day? Will this be a hit? Shouldn't I be using the latest slang in these lyrics?* He started reaching for samples; ordering his band to imitate C+C Music Factory; rapping to fit in—ruining everything he worked hard to build. "I really felt like a product and then I started turning in work that reflected that," he said. He was also repeating himself, rehashing old hits, "doing my best to fulfill my contract."

Now, he knew where he wanted to go, but needed direction. "I looked up and L. Londell McMillan was there," Prince said in *Interview*. Their discussion of "what we as black people are supposed to represent during this time period" inspired Prince to hire McMillan to be his sixth attorney since 1978.

———

As winter receded, Prince was talking change. There was no color at Paisley Park. Only the same white walls and gray carpet he had ignored while stopping by to record seemingly every day for fifteen years. Facing artwork on a wall, he thought, *pfft. That's out of here.* "Those pictures got to go," he said aloud. He wanted colorful, alive. Prince must have been considering his impending parenthood. He wanted employees to bring their own kids to a kid-friendly workspace, complete with a carousel, educational playground equipment, and a twenty-four-hour day-care center. He also wanted primary colors with soft, oversize furniture, stars, and zodiac signs.

He also planned personnel changes. He had employees return their keys to Paisley Park. Now people had to ring the buzzer. One evening, someone did. Mayte, barefoot and pregnant, answered and let keyboardist Ricky Peterson in. "It was the sweetest thing," Peterson said. Then Prince descended a flight of stairs by the front door in big bunny slippers. "Come on in," Prince said. "He was so happy," Peterson remembered. "I've never seen him happier than when she was pregnant."

And in the studio, he expressed this joy on his big album.

Marriage made him more focused. Songs came a lot easier. The whole album would be about love. He could already picture the finished work. And while he'd protest the 1992 Warner deal on one or two numbers, he would end these angry works on a positive note.

It was the most exciting time of his life. Instead of rushing, he constructed the album and did what he felt. He left a familiar sample from George Clinton's "Atomic Dog" on "Style." Another time, he put a guitar on the floor and based a song on its feedback noise.

Before long, he wrote about Mayte on his piano ballad "Let's Have a Baby" (an account of their wedding night). He described a sperm making its way toward an egg on "Conception," and told Mayte he wanted to include their unborn child's in-utero heartbeat over the beat. "It was a hard decision," Prince said. "But Mayte prayed on it, and then she said it was cool." Midway through its creation, he decided its theme was too heavy. He changed a few things and offered the lighter "Sex in the Summer," about guys seeking girls on a hot summer day.

He covered Joan Osborne's "One of Us" because he wanted to hear God's name on the radio. He updated "Goodbye," an idea from late-1991 sessions for ♔, but changed his mind, setting it aside in favor of his lengthy

"The Holy River." And moments like these reminded him of why he was doing any of this.

Without Warner, nothing stood in his way. No one looked over his shoulder. "Nothing was remixed, censored, chopped down, or edited," Prince explained to *USA Today*. Where he might have pulled "1000 Hugs and Kisses" and "She Gave Her Angels" from Warner albums because he feared executives would frown on religious subject matter, he now openly mentioned God; he made his midtempo piano hymn "The Holy River" one of his longest tracks; and he didn't "worry about what *Billboard* magazine will say."

By this stage in his career, implying that Warner demanded dance music, rap-ready sounds, and contemporary slang on his recent commercial turkeys had become part of his rhetoric. Nevertheless, left to his own devices, Prince hurriedly included all three on some of these new works. He dabbled in many styles, but delivered what many other R&B contemporaries (and West Coast rap producer Dr. Dre) had been doing for years. His vision for pop and R&B on the first disc, ballads on the second, and dance music on the third was impressive—and the sort of structure he seemed to need—but he wasn't really breaking any new ground. His epic and resonant ballad "The Love We Make" is one of his more powerful, effective, and engaging songs of the 1990s and one of his best lyrics ever. But he then returned to slapping R&B riffs over sedate beats, forging songs that weren't as bad as *Come*, but that lacked the energy, innovation, and daring generally associated with Prince albums.

Warner released the Spike Lee soundtrack to *Girl 6* on March 19. The compilation of old hits included Prince's newer creation "Pink Cashmere." But he focused on the future. By early April, his publicists issued a release that said "glyph is about to assume another name: Dad." *People* reported on it, calling a short news item, "Little Red Bassinet."

That same month he summoned his New Power Generation band to his enormous studio complex, and finally dismissed them. The payroll clerk called individual employees to meetings and canned them, too. "Last week he even laid off his longest-term employee, Paisley's chief engineer, with Prince for twelve years," reporter Jon Bream wrote. When he was done, Prince reportedly trimmed his payroll to a receptionist, two people to run his day-to-day business, a personal recording engineer, and outside accountants. He agreed to rent one of his two main studios but stayed in the other, working on the perfect album to celebrate his marriage and the impending birth. Soon, he stopped renting the second room. Remaining employees called clients to cancel sessions.

Director of operations Juli Knapp-Winge explained Paisley was heading in a new direction, preparing for twenty-first-century challenges and aggressive corporate goals. A new staff would enhance advances they made "corporately, operationally, and creatively." They regretted losing talent, but were "excited about the new direction," looking forward "to an exciting and aggressive future for Paisley Park." Prince also closed his New Power Generation store in Minneapolis, according to Jon Bream. When people called 1-800-NEW-FUNK, a recording said, "We are currently restructuring our shipping department." The tape steered callers to a 612 area code number but another machine answered there, too.

Warner Bros. Records wasn't angry with Prince. They just felt Prince needed to understand that the label could not just release everything he spewed. "That way of thinking can come from living isolated like he has in a place like Minnesota," an executive explained derisively. There, Prince was shy, secluded, and surrounded by "a small group of people around him who never told him anything he didn't want to hear." So Prince continued to believe he was right. "He wanted his freedom so badly," this executive added. "He was really tortured."

For almost four months, Warner had been willing to negotiate with his new lawyer, McMillan. "We were prepared to go to litigation," McMillan told a reporter, but they didn't since all parties were sincerely interested in, and eager to reach, a deal that would benefit the company, and Prince himself.

His 1992 deal called for six albums. ♔, *Come,* and *The Gold Experience* were three of them. Warner released the soundtrack to Spike Lee's *Girl 6* and *The Black Album* but they reportedly didn't count. Prince still owed Warner three albums of new material. Thyret, many said, gave him a break. Warner would let Prince leave if he submitted two. But he'd have to let Warner release the two albums, and two more compilations of material he recorded while under contract. Warner would also hold onto his back catalog and pay lower advances on royalties.

With an agreement taking shape, Prince took a break from *Emancipation* to create one of the final two albums of new material for Warner. He wanted the first, *Chaos and Disorder,* to sound better than recent works. He searched tapes of things he created at Paisley Park, looking for spiritual subtexts and the sort of loud guitar playing that had carried him to the top. He started finding short, catchy numbers that highlighted the guitar skills that fans saw onstage but rarely heard on albums.

He added his May 1993 blues-rock creation, "Zannalee." Then "Chaos and Disorder" and "Right the Wrong," both created on the same day during sessions for *Gold*. "Chaos" discussed how social mores were changing for the worse. "Right the Wrong" was about race and reparations. He also decided his epic "The Same December," from 1994, should appear. His more recent tapes held February 1996's "Into the Light" and "I Will," both with spiritual messages that would be right at home on *Emancipation*. The only misstep was "I Rock, Therefore I Am," taped in March, and about identity. Its chunky rock riffs, Tony's old raps, and Rosie's singing all sounded stale. His eighty-six-second "Had U," was a better choice. Set to nothing but dirgelike strings and classical-style guitar, it found him bitterly describing a relationship two words at a time. After outlining his happiness at the onset, his emotions during various stages, and his ultimate disappointment, he ended with the phrase "Fuck you," causing many listeners to believe this slow, epic work was directed at Warner. This was more than enough, but Prince still felt the album needed something more. So he booked time at South Beach Studios in Miami and flew most of his old band down there in early April. Here he remembered someone saying Van Halen recorded its debut in a week. "That's what we were going for—spontaneity, seeing how fast and hard we could thrash it out," he explained. In Miami, he achieved his goal.

He taped a delicate work called "Dinner With Dolores" that described a strange, unpleasant interlude with what sounded like an aging hard-core fan. Musically, he set it to balmy jazz-tinged melodies and gentle guitar that revived the soft rock style of "Money Don't Matter 2 Night." Then with Bland on drums, and old mentor Sonny Thompson on bass, he plugged in his guitar and played catchy sixties-styled pop-rock on "I Like It There." This one offered chugging metal bass and upbeat singing, a frenzied solo in the middle, and his shift from rhythm to lead.

When it ended, he breathed easier. Ten days' work led to a noisy, forty-minute rock collection that worked. But it also drained him and dredged up painful feelings. It was nearly over. The album, Warner, all of it. "That whole album is loud and raucous," he said later, "but it's also dark and unhappy."

By April 18, he returned home. He had a lot on his mind: the recent album *Chaos, Emancipation*, the firings at Paisley Park, the end of his relationship with Warner, not to mention impending fatherhood. But he dressed and left the house to hit the studio. He had to create the second album of new material for Warner.

No one worried when he didn't come home that night. But then he didn't stop in the next day, either. Or that night. Or the day after. Finally, April 21, Mayte traveled to his complex. She entered the studio and couldn't believe her eyes. Prince was lying there unconscious, according to reporter Stuart White. Near him, there were reportedly four empty wine bottles and a pill jar. "Oh my God, he's dead!" she screamed. Her twenty-six-year-old bodyguard Arlene tried to rouse him. Prince muttered a few words. Arlene rushed ahead to tell Fairview-Northdale hospital he was on the way. Mayte helped him into a car and got him to the emergency room. There, nurses quickly started an intravenous drip. A doctor called Mayte and Arlene over and asked if it was a suicide attempt.

All they knew was he had been missing three days. "We don't know how long he'd been drinking or how many aspirins he'd taken," Arlene told Stuart White. "But he'd clearly vomited and that may have saved his life, bringing up the tablets. He told the doctor he'd taken drink and pills to stop heart palpitations," she added.

It was later revealed that in recent months he had been feeling heart palpitations. Whether stress caused them is not clear, although Prince— offstage, in some creative decisions, and even in scenes during his semiautobiographical *Purple Rain*—showed he was prone to worrying. Author Alex Hahn noted that the pains had Prince questioning whether he was experiencing heart problems. Either way, it had certainly been a stressful time. Almost as stressful as the period preceding his creation of *Dirty Mind*, during which, he openly admitted, he had sought escape in wine, women, and song. After a long winter spent working on *Emancipation* and getting used to a new life as a happily married monogamist, Prince faced a springtime filled with layoffs at his studio complex, complications with his wife's pregnancy, a never-ending stream of negative press, and suspense over his representatives' negotiations with Warner Bros. executives in Los Angeles. From the references to wine in various song lyrics— including *Chaos*'s "Zannalee," and his *Emancipation* number "The Holy River"—it seemed Prince had decided to bring a few bottles of the stuff with him into the studio. Now he was in a hospital.

That night he woke with a start. "What am I doing here?"

Arlene, sleeping out in the corridor right outside his room, ran in.

"What's going on? Get me out of here!"

He yanked the drip from his arm, leaped into a wheelchair, and told Arlene to drive him home. There he continued getting two albums ready. He and McMillan had to meet with Warner out west.

37

SEE YOU IN THE PURPLE RAIN

FOR YEARS, PRINCE AND VARIOUS MEDIA OUTLETS HAD DRAGGED Warner through the mud. "We never were angry," said Bob Merlis. "We were puzzled. He evinced great unhappiness at being here." The issue wasn't content, but quality. Warner also wanted him to adhere to his contract. "He had artistic control. We didn't want to stifle his creative spirit." But he wanted to release more albums than his contract called for, each for a sizable advance. He wanted a different contract that went against good business practices. "He made a habit of it, and we accommodated him to the best of our ability," Merlis added.

"It was better for everyone that it ended. . . . He's happier, and we don't have to fuss and fume with him anymore."

In Los Angeles, Prince sat with McMillan and Warner executives to hash out a termination agreement. It was April 26, and he had the two new albums with him. He handed Warner *Chaos and Disorder* and the compilation, *The Vault: Old Friends 4 Sale* along with artwork for both. For *Chaos*, instead of something as elaborate as *The Gold Experience*, he and his designer Steve Parke supposedly threw a crude photo collage together with a home computer and a color copy machine one afternoon. A panel showed a syringe full of money. Blood dripped from its tip onto a Polaroid of a reel-to-reel machine and "racks of master tapes." A heart sat in a toilet, various boot marks all over. His teary-eyed face was on the label of a broken vinyl platter. Five photos showed awards, gold records, guitars, and a secret vault. A matchbook had a burnt match. The title *Chaos and Disorder* was in red. The cover also included burning roses with a razor blade, a Bible with his initials "P.R.N." burned into its cover, a credit reading all songs were composed by ♀, and an off-putting disclaimer ("originally intended 4 private use only, this compilation serves as the last original material recorded by [The Artist] 4 Warner brothers records"). The other album, *The Vault: Old Friends 4 Sale*, was a turkey. But Warner executives had no say in what the albums contained. A Warner executive called it a "take it or leave it" presentation. Several high-ranking executives were livid: Much of this stuff was beyond pedestrian. Still, they accepted the albums to end this. And Prince surprised them by agreeing to shoot a video for "Dinner With Dolores."

Warner promoted *Chaos and Disorder,* by "⚥." The album arrived in stores Monday, July 8, 1996. Critics were quick to attack. *Rolling Stone's* review called it as sour and jagged as its cover. "At its best, the record sounds like a collection of polished demos." Or worse, a bad Prince impersonator. Whether "his record-company battles" distracted him or he ran out of ideas was unclear, their critic added, but "it's been a while since (The Symbol) has really had anything important to say in his music." And it didn't matter what he called himself, *"Chaos and Disorder* is the sound of the man repeating himself badly."

Prince ignored this review and others. With critics trashing *Chaos,* he was already turning his attention to *Emancipation.* He had spent a year working on the new set but saw light at the end of the tunnel. One day, he wrote three new songs and worked on recording two of them, Prince told the London *Times.* He was tired when he ended this recording session at 5:00 A.M., but coffee helped.

Later that day, he slipped into a tailored black suit and met in Manhattan with *LA Times* reporter Elysa Gardner in his only U.S. interview for *Chaos.* He held no real grudges, he said. "I was bitter before, but now I've washed my face. I can just move on. I'm free."

On July 10, Prince did his first of two TV appearances in support of the album. Monday night, with "Slave" again on his right cheek and glitter in his hair, he sat at a piano on *Late Show with David Letterman* and played "Dinner With Dolores," *Chaos's* first single. Before leaving the stage, he said "Free TLC," supporting the female trio that sold 9 million copies of *CrazySexyCool,* but wanted to leave their current label, according to Gil Kaufman of Addicted to Noise. The next morning, on the street outside the *Today* show studio, he again played "Dinner," and "Zannalee," also on *Chaos.*

He maintained that problems with Warner hadn't affected his income. "I'm not in financial straits and never will be." But they hadn't improved it, either. *Diamonds and Pearls* was his last true hit. *The Gold Experience* couldn't sell 500,000 copies. That year's *Girl 6* soundtrack sold less than

100,000 copies, according to SoundScan. He could use a hit but *Chaos* wasn't selling. Not even the TV appearances helped. Its embarrassing sales of only 140,000 in the United States were the worst of his career. After a month on the *Billboard* 200, *Chaos* rose only to No. 26. The album didn't even enter the R&B Chart, and left the charts entirely a week later.

After turning his audience against Warner, and refusing to promote *Chaos* with a tour, or more appearances and interviews, Prince blamed the failure on the label's "chaotic and disorderly" promotion. Warner's Bob Merlis calmly said Prince could now "make a new deal with another record company. We've come to a point where we feel that if he's happier somewhere else, we don't have any beef with him."

Now, Prince exuded uncharacteristic uncertainty. "After I'm free from Warner Bros., it'll either be very quiet or very exciting. But it won't be in the middle. It'll be extreme. Life, I mean. It'll all be extreme."

Prince finished *Emancipation* and could use a break, especially with Mayte about to give birth. But he had to find a label to release it. Sales of his last few Warner albums were shockingly low. Reporters claimed he was bankrupt and crazy, Prince remembered in *Rolling Stone*. He'd have to use the ♀ until his final deal with Warner—related to publishing—expired on New Year's Eve 1999. His new hairstyles and fashions couldn't raise sales. "People stopped caring years ago, other than a shrinking base of fanatics," Alan Leeds said.

When a *Rolling Stone* writer arrived at Paisley Park to hear the new album, Prince had pregnant young Mayte nearby for support. And instead of his usual haughtiness, Prince asked, "We still all right? Let me know when I start boring you." He leaped off the arm of a couch and raced to the CD player. He replaced his slow cover of "Betcha by Golly Wow!" with the rock-flavored "Damned if I Do." He said, "I'm bouncing off the walls playing this."

When he wasn't promoting the new album, he helped allay Mayte's fears about the baby. In July, she traveled to Manhattan with her bodyguard Arlene Mojica, and Arlene's sister Erlene, hired to be the baby's nanny.

But an unexpected physical pain led to the Mojicas rushing her to an emergency room. During a subsequent telephone call to Prince in Minneapolis, the Mojicas informed him of the hospital visit and he allegedly suggested that nerves were probably to blame. Upon her return from Manhattan, Mayte scheduled an appointment for a sonogram. At North Memorial Hospital—about eighteen miles from Prince's Paisley Park complex—Dr. Leslie Jaeger performed the examination and said the child had "an abnormally large head and could possibly be born with deformities." Mayte was shocked. She was also retaining water. The doctor referred her to a specialist and advised that Mayte have a full chromosome test performed, to determine the problem, and either terminate the pregnancy or "go ahead and have the child," Arlene claimed.

Prince received the news just as Londell McMillan told him EMI-Capitol Music Group was interested in distributing *Emancipation*, and wanted to move quickly. Prince had met EMI's Chairman/CEO Charles Koppelman six years ago, when he stopped by Koppelman's SBK Records to pitch some artists. Nothing came of those meetings but the elder Koppelman still wanted to meet. Thus, Prince welcomed EMI executives to Paisley Park for a brief meeting on September 18.

Before, Prince told *Hello!* magazine, he had never wanted to discuss anything but his music with reporters. Now, his inch-thick global marketing plan included sales targets, promotion strategies and plans for interviews, press conferences, radio and TV ads, and a worldwide tour that could earn as much as $45 million in ticket sales. He even considered distributing albums at his shows. "Maybe we could put a sampler on every seat," he joked. "Or give them the whole thing, and build it into the ticket price." He could also have 1-800-NEW FUNK (his direct-selling hotline taking about seven thousand calls a month) sell it.

A three-CD set like *Emancipation* was risky but Koppelman was impressed. After ten days of quick negotiations, EMI started preparing a contract. NPG Records would officially release *Emancipation*. Prince would receive no advance. Instead, he'd submit a finished album and pay Capitol-EMI a cut for every copy it created. They would manufacture and distribute the album, and help promote and publicize it. He meanwhile would keep his masters, receive a larger cut of profits, do his own marketing, and continue to sell other NPG albums on his Web site The Dawn Experience.

One late September day, Mayte again visited North Memorial Hospital. Much of what follows is based on the Mojica sisters' comments to reporter Stuart White of *News of the World:* A female doctor had the Mojica sisters call Prince—it was an emergency. When he arrived, the doctor said, "Your wife is having contractions." The doctor wanted to prescribe magnesium to delay them. Prince needed a second to take this in, the sisters remembered. He wanted a private moment with Mayte, to see how she was doing. But the doctor complained about his delay. "This is bad news," she said. "We have to deal with it."

Mayte was trembling now.

Unfortunately, the Mojicas recalled, he signed a release form and led his wife out of there. He sat near his wife in a limousine. He had barely had time to hear what was happening. After rolling a few miles, he had his driver stop. This was all new to him. He was reeling. He asked Erlene Mojica, the nanny, for her suggestion.

Erlene suggested taking her to another nearby hospital.

It was a good idea. At the new hospital, the Mojicas led her inside. Prince sat out in the car, knowing that if he entered, hospital employees would be distracted. Before he knew it, one of the Mojicas rushed out. He leaned forward, eager to hear the news. Another doctor was saying Mayte needed magnesium.

She went back in while Prince waited. Then the woman returned and said the doctor had injected Mayte. Another trip away and back: the contractions slowed. But the hospital would keep her there.

This was all happening as Londell McMillan was arranging a deal for *Emancipation*.

Prince was worried about his wife, missing her as she remained in the hospital. But still he packed for his October 10 trip to EMI's Manhattan offices. He said nothing about his personal problems while playing executives more music. The next day, they finalized the deal.

Back home again, he had to balance his personal life—making sure Mayte was okay in the hospital—with preparations for the next step in the wooing of EMI.

October 15, chairman Koppelman, Vice President Terri Santisi, distribution president Russ Bach, and label president Davitt Sigerson arrived in Minneapolis by corporate jet. Local EMI employees and key personnel from Best Buy, Musicland, and Target also arrived at Paisley Park.

Prince was not sleeping well these days, according to the St. Paul *Pioneer Press*. Still, he slipped into an orange suit for a scheduled listening party, including uninvited reporter Jon Bream. He entered a control room and started previewing *Emancipation* songs. At one point, he felt they didn't like one song. He turned it off and removed this disc from the player only to hear the crowd shout "More! More!" Behind a glass in the control room, he put the CD back on, then took a series of bows. After a dozen songs, some in full, others fragments, he said, "This is my most important record. I'm free, and my music is free." An ovation followed. Facing his audience, he asked, "Any questions?"

No one spoke.

He said, "Jon, I see you back there. I'm sure you have some questions."

Bream, invited by a Best Buy official, did indeed. How long would this deal last?

"Forever, I hope."

Once most of the guests left, Prince handed two EMI executives a few songs. They rushed to catch a flight to Phoenix, Arizona, where they would audition them that night for accounts at a fall conference held by the National Association of Recording Merchandisers.

That night, Prince couldn't sleep. Dawn finally arrived. He dressed and got over to the hospital, where doctors prepared to perform a caesarean on Mayte eight months into her pregnancy.

They were about to start the operation. He was outside of the room. A doctor told him to slip into special surgical clothes.

Prince was present for the birth. His son. But almost as soon as Mayte had given birth, nurses quickly took the child out of the room. Nurses transferred the boy to the adjoining Children's Health Care Hospital and placed him into an incubator, Stuart White reported.

Then, a doctor delivered the news that would transform their relationship—and their lives: Their child was born with the rare Pfeiffer syndrome 2, Stuart White noted, which could cause the skull to harden before it should, thereby compressing the brain, and potentially causing retardation and other problems. As days passed, the frightened couple heard even more bad news: Their child had water on the brain, and intestinal and eye problems.

"Prince was crying," Arlene Mojica recalled. In a hall, he openly sobbed, "I'll bring anyone from anywhere . . . whatever it takes and whatever it costs, to help my child."

As the week continued, the Mojicas told White, he and Mayte reportedly saw their child undergo surgery on his left eyelid.

Then doctors performed a colostomy.

The child remained connected to a ventilator.

Doctors proposed yet another operation.

Some considered removing the child from the ventilator to see if he would be able to breathe.

It was the most difficult challenge Prince had ever faced. He told Erlene this wasn't what he wanted for his child. Mayte remained hopeful, even as doctors hinted at another, impossible choice: to spare the child needless suffering.

Prince tried to be strong for Mayte. To spare his son further pain. Erlene recalled he told her, "We have to convince Mayte to let the baby go. We're not having the tracheotomy." He led Mayte into a room to tell her what doctors told him. She started weeping. When he emerged, Erlene asked if he would be there when they removed the baby from the machine. He had barely had time to process this latest development.

Still, she remembered him saying, "No. Just let me know when it's done."

October 23, 1996, at about seven thirty in the morning, the Mojicas dressed the infant in all-white clothing. Every fifteen minutes, the doctor checked his heart and blood pressure. Prince was nervous. He was hoping for the best, as always. He reached for his telephone, Erlene remembered, to ask Arlene, "Is it done?"

Arlene said not yet.

He called again.

At 8:45, the phone rang. He rushed to answer. Arlene delivered the bad news. His son hadn't made it.

Prince hung up. He was numb. Prince had memorialized his short life in a song, in which Prince included his ultrasound heartbeat, written when he thought everything had turned out all right. And at Paisley, the playground he built, so they could play together, remained, a painful reminder. He barely noticed when Erlene Mojica entered the room hours later, carrying a small urn. "Sir, I have the baby."

"Give it to me later," he replied.

Even as magazines started rolling out interviews he gave during the pregnancy, he and Mayte coped with their loss. For three weeks, he slept only three hours a night.

More than ever, he could use a break. But still he worked to honor his commitment to EMI. At the same time, he filled a video for "Betcha by Golly Wow" with kids' faces, and a scene in which he and Mayte embraced in a hospital room. Then he rushed to add special effects—a rainbow and a falling star—thirty-three hours before its premiere on VH1, MTV, and BET. "I didn't have enough time but I'm real proud of it," he told a reporter in the editing room.

At home, he and Mayte reacted differently to the tragedy. "Losing a baby is a terrible thing," she told reporter Judith Woods. It could make couples closer or drive them apart. "In our case the latter happened." They didn't fight or have dramatic fallouts. Instead, his bereavement inspired the already industrious musician to bury himself even deeper in work. Where he had planned a break after *Emancipation* he now reached for an acoustic guitar and wrote short, lonely works like "The Truth," "Don't Play Me," and "Comeback." He considered building a children's hospital on vacant lots across the road from Paisley.

Publicly, he continued to honor his promise to promote *Emancipation*. Mayte was by his side November 12, when he greeted hundreds of reporters at his complex and played a concert for MTV cameras. That night, a sea of fans followed the couple from room to room. Some reporters wondered aloud about his newborn son.

At midnight, he took the stage in purple and black, and had his latest band seemingly play to backing tapes. Then he staged his first informal news conference for two hundred people in Studio A. He let photographers snap shots for thirty seconds and admitted Warner helped him out. "They built this place for me," he said. "I even invited them to come tonight." But he still didn't own Prince's music, he quickly added. Eventually, one writer asked why he was suddenly so open.

"I've got a record to sell," he answered.

Prince was ready for reviews. "People will say it's sprawling and it's all over the place. That's fine. I play a lot of styles." To his surprise, reviewers offered nearly unanimous praise. November 19, people rushed out to buy copies, and *Emancipation* debuted at No. 11 (and No. 6 on the R&B Chart).

Two days later, he was on *Oprah*. Women watched in record numbers. But even Winfrey's seal of approval couldn't stop *Emancipation* from dropping twenty-seven spots, to No. 38, its second week in stores.

At home, Mayte told Judith Woods, she wished he would spend more time with her, help her cope with feelings of loss. Instead, he kept to himself, adding lonely acoustic works to *The Truth*. He planned to finish this for EMI, then tour for *Emancipation*, as promised. He wanted to move past the tragedy but reporters wouldn't let it go.

Prince maintained his composure while facing questions about his personal tragedy. Mayte joined him for a mid-December appearance on NBC's *Today*. Mayte was "very friendly, but guarded," Robyne Robinson explained. Prince meanwhile was turning to the Bible for comfort. "And they were very guarded because of the baby's death. It was sort of a bittersweet time." The television appearance found them confirming the child was born with a health problem.

In early January, *Emancipation* slid to No. 72 after selling only 316,000 copies. Radio stations kept playing his album cut "Betcha by Golly Wow!" But EMI executives wouldn't put it on a single. Instead, January 13, they released "The Holy River" for Top 40 and rock stations and "Somebody's Somebody" for urban-contemporary.

People gossiped about low sales even as he arrived at the Manhattan club Life for a private party. It was February 28 and EMI's Koppelman threw the party to celebrate, quizzically, the double platinum sales of *Emancipation*. "Not bad for someone whose career was supposed to be in the gutter," Prince said. That night, he saw the crowd included rapper LL Cool J, Michael Jackson's former producer Quincy Jones, Smashing Pumpkin's Billy Corgan, shock rocker Marilyn Manson, Jon Bon Jovi, actors Kevin Spacey and Chris Rock, even TLC's T-Boz. These stars and more watched Koppelman hand Prince a plaque and call this commemoration "a historic event both for the industry and for our relationship." He added that *Emancipation*'s 2 million sales in just thirteen weeks made it "one of the best-selling multiple CDs of all time." Prince was proud. So was EMI, which quickly created trade ads bragging about *Emancipation*'s sales. But *Entertainment Weekly*'s "Platinum Bombshell: Why Record Sales Numbers Don't Add Up" asked "was the claim 2 good 2 B true?"

The RIAA and SoundScan tallied sales differently, it explained. The RIAA offered "less exact" figures by reporting the number of albums that labels claimed to have shipped to retailers and clubs, or sold through mail order. SoundScan meanwhile conducted weekly tallies of actual retail sales. Then, a little-publicized RIAA quirk had double albums count as two separate units when it came to Gold and Platinum awards, so long as both discs' combined running time was at least 120 minutes. With Prince making sure his three-CD set lasted exactly 180 minutes—one hour per disc, he said—*Emancipation* only had to ship 666,666 copies to be certified double platinum. Thus, the RIAA had *Emancipation* down for 2 million sales while SoundScan showed it sold 460,000 copies by early April, "quite a long way from 2 million, though not all that bad for a higher-priced triple-CD set." An EMI spokeswoman said, "It's up to the RIAA. They make the rules, not us." But *Entertainment Weekly* felt she was "passing the buck," and called the label's claim of double platinum sales a "king-size discrepancy."

Prince continued to tour for the album, and to earn good money thanks to his larger percentage of royalties. He again brought fans another memorable stage set, gold Chinese lions and white palm trees surrounding his enormous ♀. But instead of faithful *Emancipation* numbers—and thoughts of the pregnancy and tragedy—he held his ♀-shaped guitar and played "Purple Rain" in a haze of violet lights. *The New York Times* loved it, saying he made clear "what low standards we've set for rock and pop concerts in the nineties." Soon, he pulled even more *Emancipation* songs from the set list, replacing them with Prince classics.

Prince was still promoting the album when EMI experienced major trouble. London-based owners EMI Group P.L.C. decided to shutter two New York–based imprints. Regrettably, EMI Records was one of them. EMI Music Chief Ken Berry called this "the final step" in reorganizing the North American music operation, and a way to save EMI Group between $80 and $100 million a year in expenses and salaries. At Virgin and Capitol executives were allowed to bring EMI acts to their labels, if they so chose. But no one mentioned Prince or *Emancipation*.

PART | FOUR

The RETURN

38

INTO THE LIGHT

AS CEO OF NPG RECORDS, PRINCE OVERSAW A STAFF OF TWENTY-five. But he didn't view himself as a businessman. He hated the word. "It's not a business, what I do." Still, he was good at it. Critics claimed his music wasn't as hot anymore, but his shows got him onto *Pollstar's* list of top-earning tours. Playing midsized venues with little promotion and no booking agent also brought in a bigger cut of profits.

EMI was gone, but Prince had already made headway on his next offering, *Crystal Ball*, a four-CD collection of vault recordings. He figured he'd create about two thousand five hundred copies with special packaging and sell them directly to fans at his Web site. He claimed it would cost a whopping fifty dollars due to expensive manufacturing costs but admitted his label NPG would get "the bulk of that money" after paying the manufacturer. "And distribution is just a postage stamp." Once he had the set mastered, he started taking orders. But he wouldn't send any out until he received 100,000 payments.

His next move was even stranger. Though EMI Records had folded, he still had his acoustic work *The Truth* pressed. He planned to sell it over his 1-800-NEW-FUNK telephone line. But Mayte said he should just give it away, free, to people that helped this business grow. He announced he'd hand 100,000 copies out, then expanded this to include anyone that contacted his phone line or Web site.

"It's a pretty slick idea," he observed, "because the phone has been ringing off the hook."

Mayte helped again when he planned a tour with acoustic instruments. Instead of focusing on his appearance and stage show, he had planned a more intimate performance to suit the mood of *The Truth's* sobering sound.

But Mayte suggested he give his core audience what they expected:

the electric instruments, flashy costumes, old hits in familiar recognizable form, and dance moves and party songs. This was what filled the coffers.

And so he changed the plan.

Then Prince considered a new stage set. He wanted something spectacular—a huge dream set shaped like his ♀ and sitting in the middle of huge arenas. But there was no time to build it. He decided instead on an empty stage. Next came booking shows. No middlemen. He'd do it himself, and start in relatively small fifteen- to twenty-thousand-seat venues.

Another change was the set list. An internal voice said, *Play where you are now*. But while surfing the net—something he allegedly did frequently—he saw fans wanted "Little Red Corvette," and "Kiss." Despite claiming he wouldn't under his new name, he filled the set list with old Prince hits. "Even 'When Doves Cry' we play again," he soon told MTV.

But he also kept an eye on the future. By September 30, fans had ordered eighty-four thousand copies of *Crystal Ball*, at fifty dollars a pop. Between concerts, he announced he'd press one hundred thousand copies. "Keep the orders flowing," he added. "We might reach two hundred thousand!" Tower Records' chairman Russ Solomon quipped, "Pearl Jam rides again." Then more seriously, "The Internet is a hard way to do business." But Prince's next move shook up Tower even more. After considering how Best Buy, Musicland, and Blockbuster sold the most copies of *Emancipation*, Prince let Minneapolis-based Best Buy, a consumer electronics chain with 285 stores in 32 states, stock a four-CD version in stores. Tower's Solomon frowned on the deal. "We wouldn't strike one, and I would resent it if another chain struck one," he said. But Musicland and Blockbuster also agreed to stock *Crystal Ball*.

In the end, *Crystal Ball* sold 250,000 copies without a video or radio play (about 100,000 domestically). At Warner, he would have received maybe 20 percent of this money after the label deducted "recoupable" expenses for recording, marketing, and tour support. Now, he earned anywhere from 80 to 95 percent. He settled into his new life as an artist and executive, and soon felt the hardest part of his day was writing checks.

Booking a show was easy. He called a few radio programmers, said he'd reach town in a few days, and bought a five-thousand-dollar ad. "That's my idea of promotion."

He would call the guy from Best Buy or Target and play them a record. *Oh, you like it? How many you want?* "That's distribution."

Joe Kviders, general manager of Tower Records in Chicago, said,

"The Artist is bungling it." But Best Buy senior vice president Gary Arnold said whenever he met Elton John, Elton always wanted to hear about Prince. In fact, everyone in the industry was watching Prince these days, "because he's breaking ground," and controlling his product when the business was "basically being run by five major corporations," Arnold explained.

But selling *Crystal Ball* online and directly to Best Buy angered many distributors (middlemen that earned money by carrying records from labels to stores), *Details* magazine reported. He invited music retailers to Paisley to hear a new album, *Newpower Soul,* hoping they'd hear its ten tracks and order copies from its official distributor NPG. He told them they could have copies for ten dollars, one attendee told *Details,* with a suggested markup to $12. 99 in stores. A few balked at an unrealistic price. "I mean, how can anyone make money on a three-dollar markup?" These discs didn't "magically go from Minneapolis to a store in New York," he said. "There's just not enough money for everybody in the middle." Some retailers played hardball and got it for nine dollars, he claimed in *Details.* A few even got it for eight. "If I were a retailer who paid full fare and found that out, I'd be pretty hacked off," said the distributor.

This same distributor also claimed he wanted cash on delivery for *Newpower Soul,* and agreed to the industry standard of a sixty-day billing period, this person continued, in *Details.* But twenty-five days after delivery, he allegedly changed his mind and wanted payment within thirty days, asking, "Can you shoot us a check next week?" "He has no clue how the industry operates," this person continued Attorney Londell, however, told *Details* that some retailers received discounts for buying in bulk, but other accusations were "absolutely not true." Their pricing system, he stressed, was "absolutely consistent and standard."

He hired independent distributors for *Newpower Soul,* but some retailers were still smarting. One felt it was "a pure ego thing, running a label without really knowing how," and that he was as unsuccessful fighting the industry as Pearl Jam in their fight against Ticketmaster. Yet, BMG—parent company to labels like Arista Records—agreed to distribute *Newpower Soul,* credited to the New Power Generation, worldwide.

Prince had NPG Records release *Newpower Soul* on June 30, 1998. And while it was supposedly a group album, only he was on its cover. *Rolling Stone* complained that stiff rap and "clunky hip-hop and stale jamming" had now ruined another recent work. Other critics complained it was bankrupt of ideas and contained nothing they hadn't heard in the past. Still more claimed it had fewer hit singles because he couldn't write them anymore. "Well, that's what they said before 'The Most Beautiful Girl in the World,' too," he said. And right after *Purple Rain,* "and I had ten hits after that. And *Lovesexy* was supposed to be a failure."

Newpower Soul did about as well as *Chaos,* reaching No. 22 on the Pop Chart, and No. 9 on the R&B Chart. It sold 138,000 its first months of release (low compared to earlier work but more than *Chaos and Disorder* for Warner). In the past, he would have worried. Critics and hard-core fans may not accept it but he had different priorities right now. They kept claiming he'd never match "the success of such and such, but I'm not on that road. . . ." He was happily receiving most of the $140 million an album and tour grossed. In the past, he claimed, "I'd get at most $7 million." Though *Newpower's* sales were nothing to brag about, the larger cut of profits meant this album alone earned enough for a magnificent, white and peach-bordered villa in Marbella, on Spain's Costa del Sol.

He arranged another tour to promote this work, and Chaka Khan's *Come 2 My House,* which he'd soon release through NPG. But disaster struck again after his September 27 show at Atlantic City's Marina Theater. That night, a fog machine covered the floor with moisture, MTV reported. Opening act Chaka fell but wasn't hurt. Then he took the stage. Midway through "Delirious," he strolled down a ramp on stage. His shoe caught on a piece of equipment and he tripped. In Cleveland, before his next show at CSU University, a doctor diagnosed him with a torn ligament.

And so on October 2, the tour was off. But he quickly announced a new record called *Roadhouse Garden* by his old eighties band, The Revolution. Like *Crystal Ball,* this album *Roadhouse* would compile unreleased tracks.

With the year 1999 approaching, reporters kept invoking the good old days. Prince had to tell a reporter, "I know that people want to talk about the past. But we're not at *Purple Rain* anymore." He and the band didn't act or dress like that anymore. "If you talk about that, the next thing you know, people start writing things like The Revolution is going to reunite!" Sure enough, writers claimed it would happen. Before he knew it, he and Wendy Melvoin were speaking on the phone, for the first time in years. But when she called him Prince, Wendy told Steve Appleford, of Yahoo Music, he said, "Ohhh, don't call me that."

"I'm so sorry," she remembered replying. "I'm not used to this. I'm not really sure what to do. Please forgive my clumsiness in the situation." They moved past it. He said he'd send old vault material she could update for *Roadhouse*.

Warner meanwhile reacted to growing fan and media nostalgia by reissuing his 1982 hit "1999" as a promotional single for radio stations. But reporters kept bombarding the label with questions, to the point where Bob Merlis said, "Never has the simple servicing of a seasonally appropriate song generated so much press attention."

Warner simply wanted to do radio stations a favor. With the year 1999 approaching, many stations would want to keep the song on the air; they'd need copies; they'd realize this and start calling, clogging voice mail. Warner pressed CDs and sent them out to various stations. But that was it. They wouldn't do anything else to promote "1999" during the next twelve months. Everyone already knew the song. If they wanted it, they could get it on the 1999 album or a greatest hits collection.

But Prince wasn't satisfied. He was now "faced with a problem. But 'pro' is the prefix of problem, so I decided to do something about it." On his site, he wrote that he'd release a new remastered version on his own NPG label. Subsequent messages hinted he might even remake the entire album.

On the surface, it seemed as if Prince simply wanted to tweak his old label. But it was actually a canny business move. By this point, licensing songs to commercial advertisers and television and motion picture creators had become a more lucrative proposition. Most commercials and TV shows now included pop songs, instead of jingles or themes. Some labels were making $20 million annually through licensing, before handing the artists any money. Artists generally went for it—since they signed deals that agreed to split licensing fees with a label that released a song, and agreed to avoid remaking their songs until five years after their deals expired. Now, many older artists saw a way around it. With the ban on remakes having passed, they could rerecord a song, own the new version, and license it for ads or films without having to hand their old label a share of profits. Once Aerosmith offered automotive giant General Motors a remake of their signature work "Sweet Emotion" for one of their ads, other artists rushed to studios to create remakes—and then to ad agencies on

Madison Avenue to sell them. For artists it was a great deal. And many music publishers were just as delighted. These firms could strike licensing deals faster—without having to wait for label approval—if they were dealing with a songwriter directly, and a remake for which labels held no rights.

Rolling Stone, which put him on its cover five times, frowned on the idea, but Prince was within his rights. Warner owned the back catalogue but he could legally rerecord any Warner song so long as the original had been in stores for five to seven years. And in fact, according to *The New York Times,* he had already re-created "significant portions of his catalog." Then Prince casually dropped a bombshell. He actually possessed the old master tapes. "I don't own 'em. But I got 'em."

In the studio, he worked on *1999: The New Master,* seven new versions he hoped would lure fans away from Warner's reissue. He planned to release the CD on NPG Records, and sell it in stores and on his site. Into December, he kept posting sour comments about Warner Bros.'s reissue of "1999." In one, he wrote that despite having created the song, its rerelease would benefit Warner, who owned the master tape. And Warner would keep taking the "bulk of the profits" until "this absurd concept is challenged." But someone at Warner finally said, "It's our right to do this, and we're doing it. But we don't begrudge him anything. He's a free agent; he can do what he wants."

During this same period, he and Mayte traveled to Spain. December 12, they met with reporters and announced they had annulled their marriage. Prince told *The New York Times* they both studied documents they signed in 1996, "and there were a lot of things in there we didn't like." But Mayte told Judith Woods it was his decision and one she accepted with reluctance. "I never wanted to be a divorcée." The conference found them claiming they'd only be apart until Valentine's Day 1999 "when they plan to remarry," MTV noted.

Back in Minneapolis, Prince continued to claim they were a couple. "We pretend it didn't even happen," he said of the marriage. "Like a lot of things in life I don't like, I pretend it isn't there and it goes away."

But Mayte soon packed her stuff and moved to the house in Spain. There, she wondered if she should change her name. "I didn't want to be forever known as Prince's ex-wife." She decided against it.

In Minneapolis, meanwhile, he was touchy about rumors that claimed he kicked her out. During one interview with the Minneapolis *Star*

Tribune's Vickie Gilmer, he raised the subject. "I implore you to realize that I'm perfectly healthy and happy. My wife and I, you can see nobody's kicked her out."

In mid-January, Prince was still releasing albums to his fan club. He was still in business with Warner thanks to the publishing-related deal he signed in 1992. And he still wanted the master tapes for his Warner albums, starting with *For You*. On his Web site, he posted an open letter to Madonna, who remained one of Warner's top draws. Eccentric, florid language described a dream in which he saw her at the Grammy Awards, and asked her to help convince Warner to give him the masters. She didn't respond.

He wanted the year 1999 to be "a time for reflection." But he kept recording. Instead of the usual four or five albums at once, *and* side projects, he focused only on *Rave Un2 the Joy Fantastic*. In June 1998, he had taken the first steps toward creating *Rave*. He wanted a "very memorable album" to take listeners back to the days when they could remember and sing along with great songs. He wrote catchy hooks and intricate drum machine patterns, balanced genres and styles, and hoped to draw new fans while satisfying calls for what Per Nilsen called "the risk-taking that characterized much of his eighties work."

In February, he released *1999: The New Master* on NPG. Most critics ignored the work. Fans did, too. But he was still thinking about his master tapes. By April 15, 1999, he publicly claimed that he had no choice but to rerecord the seventeen albums he recorded for the label between 1978 and 1996. "I wanted to buy my masters back from Warner Bros. They said no way. So I'm going to rerecord them. All of them." He smiled. "Now you will have two catalogs with pretty much exactly the same music—except mine will be better—and you can either give your money to WB, the big company, or to NPG. You choose."

Instead of doing this, however, he moved forward with plans to return to a major label. He had done well for two years, pitching albums to retailers and selling three to online fans. But major labels could get him on radio, back in the mainstream media. In New York, he wanted a label to release *Rave* and let him keep the master tapes.

He was making the rounds in Manhattan when his lawyer Londell McMillan met with Arista president Clive Davis to discuss unrelated matters. When Prince's name came up in conversation, Davis asserted that he hadn't had "the right record" for some time.

McMillan noted that Prince was in New York, with a few new songs from a new album.

They quickly arranged a meeting.

Prince drove up in his limo.

Davis left the building, approached the car, and got in.

In the car, he played the aging executive four or five pop- and rock-oriented tracks, such as "So Far, So Pleased" and "Whatever U Do, Wherever U Go." Davis liked what he heard. These were just the sort of hits Prince needed.

Even better, Davis said he'd let him own his masters. "I almost get misty when I think about it," Prince said. "It was really like being reborn. There is no ceiling now, no limits. I can see the sky."

At this point, Prince wanted only ten tracks. But Davis's praise made him feel he had in his hands his biggest hit since *Purple Rain*. Davis's enthusiasm inspired more sessions and his new ballad "The Greatest Romance Ever Sold."

Davis loved this one, too.

Then he even included the name "Prince" as producer. But in spite of the presence of his Linn drum machine and analog Oberheim synthesizer, and the production credit, most tracks had nothing in common with his eighties hits. Prince avoided excessive overdubs or melodies and filled some songs with the modern beat–heavy R&B of *Emancipation*. Either way, by May 20, he had a fifteen-track album sequenced and ready to go. He told one source it revived the style of *Sign O' the Times*.

Davis quickly scheduled "The Greatest Romance Ever Sold" as lead single. Instead of the dissent over singles shown at Warner, Prince rolled with it. Davis, after all, boldly predicted the song would be "number one all over the world."

Warner meanwhile chose this moment to release *The Vault: Old Friends 4 Sale*. It was late July, three years since he handed them the album and the messy-looking cover (a shot of a spiky-haired Prince in purple shirt and matching skintight slacks and heels, straddling a chair). At Warner, Bob Merlis told a reporter the delay in releasing it was "just a marketing judgment. . . ." They waited until they felt audiences might want something like this.

Prince complained, even though Warner had the contractual right to release three compilations of music he recorded for them. As Warner prepared his ballad "Extraordinary" for release as lead single in mid-August, Prince reminded everyone he had no love for Warner. He had a spokesperson say he didn't care when Warner released this work; he wouldn't promote it; it didn't mean they were cool again. "It was the last thing he delivered to them, so it was like, 'This is what I owe ya, see ya,'" his rep claimed.

39

SILLY GAME

AS PLANS FOR THE ARISTA RECORD UNFOLDED, PRINCE WAS NE-
gotiating with Clive Davis. Some published reports claimed Davis had
Arista advance $11 million—a million more than Warner. Reporters rushed
to call it his return to a major. Former employee Alan Leeds shook his
head. "Sugar daddy once, sugar daddy again," Leeds said. "Based on the
kinds of deals he's made lately, he seems more money-driven today than
he was when I was working with him. I mean, Arista steps up with a deal,
and he runs like a thief to get it. He wasn't broke."

His hard-core fans were just as stunned. But Prince offered a written
statement. "I believe I had to get out of the recording industry for a while
so that I could reclaim my artistry and become empowered by it again."
He didn't like labels trying to own masters or offering long-term contracts. "Both of these problems are nonexistent in my agreement with
Arista."

He continued to stress that *permanently* leaving the industry was
never his plan. And this wasn't the standard deal with a long contract and
the usual boundaries for what each party would or wouldn't do. "People
are looking for drama in it. It's for one album."

Davis, riding high after guitarist Carlos Santana's comeback hit *Super-
natural*, felt a guest-crammed Prince work could do just as well. But Davis
didn't play *Rave* for anyone at the label, or seek any opinions, until he
signed the deal. When other Arista executives heard the album, they
weren't as impressed. Davis praised it to the skies, but they felt he stuck
them with a turkey and a difficult sell.

August 24, 1999, Warner's compilation *The Vault: Old Friends 4 Sale* arrived in stores. Warner credited it to Prince, not ♀, and promoted it as a
"noteworthy musical event." Some critics liked its jazzy sound—it had no
funk or dance material—but most felt the thirty-nine-minute work was

uninspired and mediocre. Prince had already included a disclaimer in liner notes that read the "enclosed material was originally intended 4 private use only." Now, he disparaged it on his Web site. He wrote that a Warner insider heard the test pressing and told him it sounded "like a Contractual obligation" (sic). He typed that its songs were "indeed very old." He dismissed "dated tracks," Per Nilsen reported in *Uptown* magazine. Then he told a *Rolling Stone* reporter, "The compilations don't concern me. They're some songs from a long time ago—that's not who I am." Despite his attacks, *The Vault* appeared at No. 85 on the *Billboard* Pop Chart and No. 33 on the R&B Chart. It also sold 140,000 copies in the U.S., about as much as *Chaos*. But a day later, MTV announced his deal with Arista. Arista publicists also let media outlets know they'd have *Rave's* lead single—that "Greatest Romance" ballad—out in September.

With *Rave* recorded, he moved on to its cover. His artist Steve Parke would once again handle art direction, photos, and design. For the cover shot, Prince slipped into a tight royal-blue bodysuit. He now had a goatee and a trendy new haircut—short, thin dreadlocks tinted blue. But he adopted his usual pose, standing in profile.

Davis predicted *Rave* would be a hit with pop and R&B/urban stations. But other Arista executives weren't so sure. It didn't have much R&B. In response, he went back and created his passionate work, "Man 'o' War."

Prince traveled to Manhattan on Thursday, September 9, to introduce female trio TLC at the MTV Awards, and entered Electric Ladyland Studios the next day. Only a few days had passed since female rapper Eve's solo album *Let There Be Eve . . . Ruff Ryders' First Lady* arrived in stores, but he had her add a verse to his dance song, "Hot Wit U." But even with her signature put-downs and praise, the song still felt like generic club rap in the post–Dr. Dre mold.

One Saturday night, Arista introduced *Rave* at a listening party in New York for its sales force and the international media. Arista would release the first single, his ballad, "The Greatest Romance Ever Sold," September 22. He'd also film a video. "I will be touring to promote this album—definitely," Prince added.

During interviews, Prince predicted his ballad would be a big hit that "cut through everything on radio."

Programmers wouldn't be "afraid to play it."

But upon its release, the song landed at No. 63 on the Pop Chart and

No. 23 on the R&B Chart. It didn't enter *Billboard*'s Top 75 Airplay Chart. If anything, it stalled the album's sales.

Prince continued to promote *Rave* with more interviews, even appearing on live talk shows he generally avoided in the past. For his interview, *Bass Player*'s Karl Coryat asked to bring a stenographer. "Apparently, no problem." But Prince saw her in Paisley Park's waiting area. "Okay," he said. "But that hasn't worked out too well in the past." In a studio control room, he slammed the door behind Coryat before the stenographer could join them. "I like to start by feeling out a person through conversation," he began. "When we talk in here, it's your word against mine." The walls were completely soundproof. "I prefer it this way." Within minutes, Prince asked, "Why do you want a witness, anyway? This isn't a deposition." He smiled. "Are you a spy? Who sent you here? What did you do before you worked for this magazine? Are you working for someone else? Did somebody put something in your ear?"

Despite these counterproductive antics, Prince called this the best time of his life. "It's been a great year for me." He saw the single climb to No. 18 on the Pop Chart and No. 8 on the R&B Chart. Arista released *Rave* on November 9. Some critics described it as being one of his best albums in the nineties. Some judged the music as tame. Fans debated whether there were too many slow songs and rehashes of earlier hits. Some even claimed the R&B sound aped what Dr. Dre and others had been doing for years. At week's end, he saw *Rave* debut at No. 18 "with just under eighty-four thousand units sold in its first week," MTV reported. Within days, he tried to spur sales by announcing "Rave Un2 the Year 2000," a concert he'd tape at Paisley Park then air on pay-per-view on New Year's Eve. Then, he quickly had publicists claim the show would mark the last time he ever played his hit "1999."

He also wanted to shoot a video for the ballad. But before he could, Davis said he needed to do a few promotional appearances in Europe (where BMG—the company that owned Arista and authorized the $11 million advance—was located). He told Arista the video should come first, along with an American tour. In the end, the video was set aside. Prince packed for an overseas flight.

The RIAA certified *Rave* Gold December 12 (though Arista might have shipped, and not necessarily sold, 500,000 copies). But that month, sales were slow. Pop radio barely played "The Greatest Romance Ever

S I L L Y   G A M E

Sold." He filmed a TV special believing it would raise sales and looked forward to a second single and a tour in late February.

Some people around Prince urged him to team with Santana for shows. But after a while, low sales got to him. He abandoned these plans. Suddenly, almost as soon as it had begun, relations with Arista soured. Both sides were bitter. He blamed them for not properly marketing his music. Arista felt he gave up on it prematurely; he wasn't cooperating. Their differences made it even harder for *Rave* to make a commercial comeback. Once again, people felt a new album couldn't bring Prince back to the old heights. Even his fans felt he was starved for a hit.

By late January 2000, Prince met with Davis to discuss the album. Davis had told him "The Greatest Romance Ever Sold" would be number one worldwide. It didn't happen. Now, he wondered what happened. Davis was just as disappointed, with the music and the artist—he felt Prince was retreating from their arrangement. "I thought you'd be different from what I've read about you," Davis reportedly told him. "Everyone warned me."

Arista asked him to deliver an edited "Man 'o' War" and a "Hot Wit U" remix. Prince handed them in, but didn't film videos. With the label suspecting he no longer cared, there was gossip that Prince was already pitching Epic Records—Michael Jackson's longtime label—on his next album.

Rave's Gold certification didn't change the general impression that he had passed his peak. Still, black music executives continued to embrace him. Thus, in early February, he heard he'd been crowned "Artist of the Decade" at the fourteenth annual Soul Train Music Awards in Los Angeles.

In March, print reports claimed—despite Gold-certification by the RIAA—that *Rave* had sold only between 350,000 and 425,000 copies in the United States. It was more than *Come* and *The Black Album* but less than his EP *1999: The New Masters*. He was livid. Like *Emancipation*, *Rave* yielded no outstanding hit. No one talked about it. Again, he blamed a label. "But I'm not mad at these guys," he told David Schimke of *City Pages*. "I mean, what else is Clive Davis gonna do? He can't sing." His unhappiness spilled onto his new site, NPG Online LTD. In one post, he accused Davis and Arista of allowing *Rave* to fail on the chart.

He wanted to get in there himself and raise *Rave*'s sales. He decided to create a remix album, to be released by his own label. While Arista—he claimed—kept letting *Rave* slip further down the charts, he revisited the songs. Facing its fifteen cuts, Prince quickly removed "Strange But True" and his disco cover of Sheryl Crow's "Everyday Is a Winding Road." He also remixed a few other numbers. Most sounded as they did on Arista's version. But "The Sun, the Moon, and Stars" now had ocean sounds, the hidden track "Prettyman's" music returned from a fade out, and "Tangerine" lasted forty seconds longer. "Baby Knows" now had a male singer and yells, his title track had a technobeat and new vocal, and "Undisputed (The Moneyapolis Mix)" sported a new vocal (and rap). Then he threw in a new rock ballad, "Beautiful Strange," that urged listeners to look within for "the light" that "forever glows." He decided to call this version *Rave In2 the Joy Fantastic.*

But on March 9, before releasing it, Prince decided to "give Mr. Davis time to make good on his promise to deliver a couple of real hit singles to 'the top of the charts.'" And "as soon as a single is 'locked' at radio (Arista's job, not NPG's), a video will be shot and a promotional campaign put into effect," he added.

Despite public posturing, however, Prince kept working behind the scenes to try to raise *Rave*'s sales. That same month, Gwen Stefani and No Doubt were enjoying success with their single "Ex-Girlfriend." No Doubt was to release *Return of Saturn* in about two weeks, and Prince wanted "So Far, So Pleased," and Gwen's singing, on *Rave*'s next single. He also wanted to film a video that could draw all those No Doubt fans to his work. But he needed permission from the group and their label Interscope. He reached out to Gwen and her managers and waited. And waited. And waited some more. By March 20, his new site let fans know he was still waiting. In the end, Interscope didn't grant the necessary permission.

Then he learned, in a repeat of the upheaval he witnessed involving his chief proponents at Warner in 1995, that Arista had ejected Davis from his position. With Davis gone, reportedly forced out due to his age, Prince was able to save face by saying he would discuss future projects with Davis's successor, young, black R&B producer L.A. Reid. But "any previous agreements with Clive Davis and NPG," he added, "were null and void."

By April 29, 2000, Prince had more and more fans subscribing to his online fan club. Each month, he planned—in exchange for their membership fees—to upload new songs, videos, and an hour-long radio show, not to mention the new version of *Rave*. He was selling them the same songs again, but told fans it was his response to Arista's "lackluster way" of promoting the first one.

His former label Warner was also keen to repackage some of those old songs. They contacted Prince's lawyers a few times to see if Prince would help create a second greatest hits collection. At first, Prince reportedly agreed to be involved. If anything, he wanted to submit a few new songs. But while Warner was willing to raise his royalty rate, they couldn't reach a deal.

Warner had Gregg Geller, a staff project producer, keep compiling his biggest hits from 1979 to 1992. It would be called *The Very Best of Prince*, a phrase that seemed to suggest recent albums presented something else.

Prince moved on to inviting fans to an upcoming weeklong celebration of his forty-second birthday. Fans that paid seventy dollars would be able to tour Paisley Park and see him play two arena concerts. At his complex, employees made sure everything was in order. His twenty Gold and Platinum albums were on display. The bike from *Purple Rain* was, too. They'd open doors at ten each morning. Every thirty minutes, until 5:00 P.M., employees would lead fans on a tour of his studios, offices, the wardrobe department, and the soundstage.

In his personal life, things moved on as well. With his and Mayte's annulment, he attended Bible study classes with his twenty-three-year-old assistant Manuela Testolini. He soon promoted her to become his personal assistant. Before long, she was designing the candles he stocked in his dressing rooms before shows. She would go on to create a company called Gamillah Holdings, Inc. and serve as its president.

That same month, May, he announced that another contract—this one professional—had quietly expired. Back in 1992, he had signed a deal for his publishing. Despite Warner closing his label Paisley Park in 1994, and letting him go as an artist in 1996, this deal remained in effect. He hadn't discussed it at all in public.

But on May 16, he invited reporters to a sports club in New York. Forty-one-year-old Prince appeared with auburn-tinted hair and in a white turtleneck. At a mic, he said he was "reclaiming" the name "Prince" and putting the ♀ aside. "On December 31, 1999, my publishing contract with Warner/Chappell expired," he revealed. Now, his real name was free of "all long-term, restrictive documents." He kept reading his prewritten speech. "I will now go back to using my name instead of the symbol I adopted as a means to free myself from undesirable relationships."

Someone interrupted to ask what he'd do with the ✚.

"Well, it's an internationally known logo now, so . . . I haven't really given it much thought." Then he got back on track. He'd never change his name again "because I won't be under a restrictive long-term contract again.

"I'm in a really great mood right now."

One journalist called him Prince.

"'Hi, Prince,'" he repeated. "That sounds great. I haven't heard that in a while."

After seven years, he'd return to his real name. He'd still use the ✚ as a logo, and on album covers, and keep playing his ✚-shaped guitar. But his years as ✚ had affected his career. *The Tonight Show* host Jay Leno echoed sentiments held by many when he told a camera, "He should change his name one last time to the 'artist who formerly sold albums.'"

But he and other detractors hadn't seen the last of Prince.

40

IT'S GONNA BE LONELY

PRINCE FINISHED AN ALBUM CALLED *HIGH* IN LATE SUMMER BUT let it sit. It presented the usual mix of come-ons, calls to the dance floor, and nonspecific revolutionary rhetoric. But a better idea arrived, for another rock opera. And he wanted to challenge himself. He had gotten somewhat lazy in recent years—using the same bland samples and mellow rhythms on *Emancipation*, *Newpower Soul*, and even *Rave*. He wanted warmer acoustic sounds and an epic story involving warring clans, mind control, liars, bigotry, and a biased media.

He started recording most of *The Rainbow Children* that fall. As usual, he wrote most of the music himself. But he was more creative on guitar, bass, and keyboards. His grooves were more confident so he didn't crowd every track with the usual dense production. He included seventies keyboards, jazz, gospel choirs, R&B, show tunes, and spoken word. There were more guitar solos than usual and a tribute to Gilbert and Sullivan. His booming, decelerated voice interrupted to provide long-winded and bewildering narration. And now that he was reading the Bible more, a few overt, unapologetic spiritual messages.

His title track found him singing that the "Rainbow Children" were "flying on the wings of the New Translation," the Bible favored by the Jehovah's Witness church. "Muse 2 the Pharaoh" hinted death was better than slavery. "Family Name" tackled how whites replaced African slaves' surnames. As the album continued, he sang that the Banished Ones, his villains, invaded the Rainbow Children's compound. They surrounded it with a Digital Garden, his metaphor for the media. The good guy, the Wise One, performed "an invisible deed" and sent these goons running back to their home, Menda City. Then the Rainbow Children went "door to door," like Jehovah's Witnesses, to ask others to help dismantle this Digital Garden and bring about the "everlasting now."

He was working on these religious songs when he had an opportunity to reunite with The Revolution. Former Revolution Drummer Bobby Z, keyboardist Matt Fink, and bassist Mark Brown had just attended his forty-second birthday party, and jammed with him onstage.

Now, major concert promoter SFX was offering lots of money for a few shows.

Wendy had every band member interested, she claimed. But Prince refused, she added. By August 11, *Entertainment Weekly* reported on the failed reunion.

That autumn, Prince planned a "mini road trip dubbed the Hit and Run Tour," MTV explained. He had a new lineup for his New Power Generation and pitched the Bravo cable network on a documentary. Nothing came of their talks so he moved on to trying to find a label to release *The Rainbow Children*. And despite complaints about Arista's "lackluster" promotion of *Rave*, as he put it, MTV claimed he was "deep in negotiations with Clive Davis's new J Records, according to a source close to the talks." But nothing ever came of these alleged meetings, either.

Prince finished *The Rainbow Children* by early April 2001. A facility was mastering it, prepping it for release, but he was already working on another album. This batch of songs was mostly about relationships. At the piano, Prince stomped a foot, creating a backbeat, and exhaled into the mic. "U're Gonna C Me" had him pining for an ex. "Young and Beautiful" urged a young girl to remain abstinent since "they only want your virginity." "Here on Earth" expressed gratitude for a great relationship. "Objects In the Mirror" described a couple brushing their teeth during a postcoital moment.

He also threw in a cover of Joni Mitchell's 1971 work, "A Case of You." He had played it during the 1983 First Avenue concert filmed for *Purple Rain* but spent a career ignoring fan cries for a recording. Now he dedicated it to his father, John.

Then he offered "Avalanche," a jarring departure with cracking falsetto that called President Abraham Lincoln a racist, and claimed the late music industry legend John Hammond signed black artists to unfair deals. His closer, the instrumental "Arboretum," went from classical to easy listening. Then Prince taped himself rising, walking away, and shutting a door.

One Nite Alone was a respite from the overproduced trendiness of his recent albums. At piano, he offered gentle, moving works that told simple stories of love, loss, and life. The songs didn't break any new ground—everyone had heard him at piano on haunting classics like "Condition of the Heart"—but his fans were especially happy to see him release music that didn't include tons of face-saving backup vocals, excessive melodies, rap beats and slang, or ponderous album concepts.

Prince kept working on albums he'd release on his site or with smaller labels. He also kept touring. On the road, there were some teens and fans in their twenties, but "most looked desperate to fend off middle age," one reporter noted. Some men wore bright rayon, wrinkled linen, and battered shoes. Women in paisley-patterned skirts wobbled on thick heels. "It was a *Star Trek* convention for over-the-hill hipsters," a writer for *City Pages* noted. Regardless, Prince pulled fans onstage to dance during encores. He had the largest cult audience out there and could live on this fan base. And he did just that, said Steve Perry, former editor of *City Pages*. "That's what these many recent tours are about." Prince had no new records or songs to promote. But people in various cities wanted to see him. Perry felt Prince still deserved to be "in the pantheon with James Brown and Louis Armstrong. But among those guys, I can't think of anyone who suffered a more precipitous fall in a shorter period of time."

June 6, Prince had publicists fax media outlets an invite to the next day's press conference at Paisley Park. It said he'd field questions about his weeklong "Prince: A Celebration" and his forthcoming *The Rainbow Children*. Only one national reporter showed up, a stringer from *Newsweek*.

Publicist Stephanie Elmer told twenty or so writers that there were no advance copies of the album. They should limit questions to topics in the release. Prince wouldn't discuss religion. But if he did, they'd eject anyone with follow-up questions.

Prince entered. He was clean-shaven with feathered, shoulder-length hair. He wore a velvet red shirt with translucent sleeves, matching pants and boots, and a thick chain with a diamond-emblazoned "NPG" (New Power Generation) medallion.

He spoke for ninety minutes. He kept saying he wanted to "put the focus back on the music," then digressed. Without interruption, he grew impassioned. But follow-up questions made him withdraw and mutter, "no comment."

Before long, he did indeed talk religion, a subject many had become curious about. He said he loved Psalms. But then, *City Pages* reported, he said the Bible outlined "very clear roles" for men and women. "Twenty-first-century women do not want to live by a role," he continued. "They want to say to men, 'Let's switch our roles.' But things don't work that way. You have to know your role and make it work. It's the same thing with the music industry. You have to find the good roles that work and go with them."

After the conference, he shook hands with departing reporters. *Pulse's* Erin Anderson, last in line, asked if they could someday sit and talk religion. No better time than the present. They talked for thirty minutes. But Anderson told *City Pages*, which reported the events of the conference, that she felt interrogated. At times Prince listened "but for the most part I felt like he wanted to hear himself speak." When she left, she considered throwing her Prince CDs in the trash. She couldn't play them anymore. "It's like watching a train wreck. He's working himself into eventual obscurity."

He moved on to focusing on his birthday party. His mother Mattie attended, despite health problems. She and her husband Heyward continued to live in a home Prince bought them in the late 1980s. She had finally retired (after twenty years of social work in local schools). But she had also undergone a kidney transplant. "She didn't stay long, but he introduced us and had us sit together," said an attendee. Prince saw his father John there, too. And he couldn't help but reflect on their knotty relationship. They had reconciled by the time Prince toured for *1999* and John joined him, Wendy, and Lisa during a sound-check jam. Prince also included John in credits for "Computer Blue." He let him have the purple house on Kiowa Trail. He bought him a custom-made purple BMW and had him fly to Paris and Los Angeles and, as author Liz Jones wrote in *Purple Reign*, Prince gave John royalties for songs like "Around the World in a Day," "The Ladder," *Parade's* "Christopher Tracy's Parade" and "Under the Cherry Moon," and even his *Batman* ballad "Scandalous."

But they had fallen out again by 1996, so John missed the February wedding to Mayte. They were still at odds when Prince went on *Oprah* that November. But John still lived in Prince's old purple house. He had health-care workers watching over him. And royalties brought in checks. Prince also made sure his wardrobe department kept John in nicely tailored suits. But when he saw his aging father at his big celebration at Paisley Park, Prince sensed the end was near.

After the party, Prince faced fallout from his comments at the press conference. Someone showed him Melissa Maerz's June 13 *City Pages* column, which began, "This is a story about control." Maerz ridiculed his many "spiritual transformations," quoted his comments, and claimed he had a "general scorn for feminist women."

Within a day, his publicist had called Maerz.

Prince wanted to see her.

Maerz could do it tomorrow.

It had to be that night at nine.

At the appointed time, Prince entered the small conference room at Paisley Park. He exchanged niceties, and sat by Maerz on a couch. She began to write in a notebook, Maerz recalled, but Prince said this was off the record. Their thirty-minute talk went from friendly to confrontational, Maerz felt, and ended abruptly. "It became clear to me that the only reason he invited me out there was so he could have the last word. It was a total power trip."

Again, Prince was planning a tour. But the Warner Catalog Group chose this moment—when his next album *The Rainbow Children* was about to arrive—to release *The Very Best of Prince* on their label Rhino Records. The seventeen-track album featured everything already included on 1993's *The Hits* volumes, along with his *Diamonds and Pearls* number "Money Don't Matter 2 Night." But nothing from after 1993.

As planned, his Prince: A Celebration Tour would end August 5 in Anchorage, Alaska. But after a July 6 show in Canada, at the Montreal Jazz Festival, Prince spent four days thinking things through. Then he suddenly canceled the last sixteen dates. Industry gossip called it a deliberate reaction to Warner's second greatest hits collection. His press release said, since Warner owned his masters, he would have earned "virtually no money" from the album. The tour would have provided free promotion for Warner's product. Some industry workers disagreed. Even without the tapes, every sale would bring Prince money for being the artist and songwriter and for his involvement with publishing rights.

The Very Best Of Prince landed at No. 66 on *Billboard*'s Pop Chart. But rather than support it, Prince had New York–based publicity firm Susan Blond, Inc. steer any reporter that called for comment to his NPG Music Club Web site. There, fans in a chat room blasted his former label. But at unauthorized, independent fan site Prince.org, people frowned on the cancellation. "Whether he wants to admit it or not," one fan wrote,

"Prince has been well compensated for those hits. I know this is easy for me to say, but I wish Prince would just get over it and focus on what he can do now that he's free."

On August 25, 2001, Prince received bad news. His eighty-five-year-old father John died in Minneapolis. The cause of death was never publicly revealed. The news threw Prince for a loop. He had just seen John at the big celebration. Now he was gone. Then Prince saw his mother Mattie arrive at John's funeral, in a wheelchair. Her health was failing, too, he saw. Then, on a mid-September day, as Prince was still coming to terms with the fact that John was gone, an airplane crashed into the World Trade Center.

41

THE DAWN

THE NATION WAS SENT REELING BY THE SEPTEMBER 11 ATTACKS.
America was on its way to war. Many celebrities wondered if it was appropriate to release upbeat products on a shell-shocked populace. Studios
delayed a few motion pictures. Radio stations stopped playing a few songs.

For Prince, it was a time to refocus on his positive new album *The Rainbow Children*. His first "Prince" project in years, it contained heartfelt personal music and bold religious themes. Instead of pop hooks and traditional
song structure, Prince filled this latest rock opera with funk and jazz.

As an executive, Prince was just as excited about finally being free of
all contracts. "I'm the record company now," he said. And during this new
phase, he would clear seven dollars from every ten-dollar CD, rather than
the pennies he said a traditional contract might bring. October 16, Prince
avoided fan criticism by letting NPG Music Club members have the album
first, via download. But with Arista now out of the picture, he worked to
find a label.

November 20, *The Rainbow Children* arrived in stores with Red Line
Entertainment handling distribution. Prince decided against singles or videos, insisting it stand on its own, remembered for its sound and story. What
reviews there were compared it to Weather Report and Steely Dan, critic
Per Nilsen recalled. But critics were torn. Some rejected its odd music and
lack of hit sounds. One called it an "arcane, for hard-core-fans-only album."
Many hard-core fans were just as torn about its quality. Some were delighted. They preferred this mature, experimental, noncommercial Prince.
But others judged the melodies and ideas as dull, with Per Nilsen opining
"the actual songs illustrate the continued lack of fresh inspiration in Prince's
songwriting." In the end, few people spent money. Sales of about 130,000
kept *The Rainbow Children* out of *Billboard*'s Top 100 (his first album since
1978's *For You* to not appear).

By December, Prince was recording yet another new record, *Xenophobia* ("fear of strangers"). Its jazz and systematic titles (all began with the letter X) evoked his Madhouse days. So did its title track, a riff created in July 1987 for Madhouse's *16*.

But with Mattie ailing, Prince set the tapes aside. According to the *Daily Mirror*, Mattie told Prince she wanted him "to become a Jehovah's Witness, as she had been for most of her life, and to see him married."

Prince did indeed propose to Manuela Testolini, and she accepted. They had known each other for three years and those close to Prince noticed the bond that was forming between them. He had let her start designing products for his NPG brand. After Prince recorded a song called "Gamillah" for his canceled album *High*, Manuela had formed a company with the very same name (Gamillah Holdings, Inc.). With Manuela around, Prince seemed more confident, less hesitant to discuss religious beliefs in public, and ready to finally fire most of the bodyguards that kept the outside world, and overzealous fans, at bay.

Still, the upcoming private ceremony surprised many close to Prince, who hadn't seen him so committed to anyone since Mayte, but were well aware of his free-wheeling tendencies. They traveled to Manuela's hometown, Toronto, and looked at a few houses. On an upscale, tree-lined street called the Bridle Path, they both loved a gray stone mansion that had been on the market since September. The property was also "a five-minute drive from Mani's parents' tiny apartment," the *Daily Mirror* explained. Gamillah Holdings—the new company where Manuela worked as president—forwarded a $1.3 million down payment.

New Year's Eve, they married in Hawaii. "It's all a bit surreal," one UK-based fan opined. "She was just a fan who posted a couple of messages and then suddenly she was working at his Paisley Park recording studios . . . and then she was his wife." She was also eighteen years his junior.

The next morning, New Year's Day, Gamillah Holdings started making payments on the $4.1 million mortgage for the mansion in Toronto. Work crews arrived soon after to perform renovations.

Prince found that he liked it in Toronto. It was cosmopolitan, diverse, filled with great music, eateries, and nightclubs. Winters were milder. But fate soon returned him to Minneapolis: His mother Mattie was now in a hospital.

Away from fans and the media, Prince had always maintained a loving relationship with her: He invited Mattie to shows, film premieres, and events at his studio complex. Since she'd retired, Mattie's health began to slip. She underwent a kidney transplant. But she still accepted invitations to functions at his studio complex, and even his wedding to Mayte. And even as her health worsened, Mattie continued to be a sounding board for ideas, to offer consolation and support, to listen to him describe personal and professional woes. Most recently, she had attended John's funeral in a wheelchair. Along with kidney problems, she was suffering from arthritis. Now, doctors thought her condition serious enough to hold her at Fairview Southdale Hospital in Edina.

Prince and Manuela soon arrived at Kingdom Hall, the temple for Jehovah's Witnesses, in Chanhassen, Minnesota, just west of Minneapolis. They were reportedly there for a private baptism ceremony. Only 167 parishioners were present. A small pool was ready. With knee-length robes over swimsuits, they entered the water and, in so doing, became full members of the church, satisfying Mattie's alleged hope. For church elder Ronald Scofield, any baptism was exciting. "But this was exceptionally exciting because it was someone who has made a lot of changes to their life." The congregation had seen Prince study the Bible and undergo dramatic change. "It's something to be very proud of."

But on Friday, February 15, just six months after John Nelson's death, eighty-year-old Mattie died at Fairview Southdale Hospital in Edina. Prince was stunned.

Away from his career, and the public, he had privately relied on both parents for support, advice, even company during hard times. With both gone, those around him worried how he'd react. "They really kind of kept him together emotionally," local newscaster Robyne Robinson said of his parents.

Prince reacted the way he had to all of his life's challenges: through song. He entered a nonverbal jazz phase. Whether he did it to somehow honor his father, or because he couldn't muster the energy for his usual come-ons or his more recent optimistic piety is unclear. But recording instrumentals allowed Prince to express himself, and work through his loss.

He planned the One Nite Alone With Prince Tour, to start in Saginaw, Michigan, on March 1, and end May 4, in Vegas. But he'd perform on an emptier set. He'd emphasize music over fashion. He'd play what he wanted. He also looked ahead to a live album. On March 11, in Indianapolis, recorders taped four songs. Twenty days later, in Washington, he captured "Rainbow Children." More relaxed, and confident, Prince told the crowd, "For those of you expecting to get your *Purple Rain* on, you're in the wrong house!" Then: "If you drove up here in a 'Little Red Corvette,' you might be surprised at what you find!"

April 4, in Lakeland, Florida, he added his religious love song, "1+1+1 Is 3." Five days later, in New York, he recorded even more. As the tour continued, he kept jousting with his hard-core following, and his past. One night, while introducing his 1982 rock ballad "Free," he quipped, "Ain't none of us free." Another time, Per Nilsen reported, his rendition of "How Come U Don't Call Me Anymore" seemed to evoke Alicia Keys's recent cover. When it ended, Prince said, "I don't want to leave you worrying about some stupid fool calling you up on the phone. This is how we want to leave it." "Anna Stesia" followed, urging people to believe in God. Where he generally eschewed releasing live work, these tapes inspired him to plan a three-CD set that ran over three hours.

In May, the NPG Music Club started offering albums. May 14, *One Nite Alone . . . Solo Piano and Voice by Prince* was the first. Club members dutifully ordered CDs then hit the boards to praise it as tender and honest. Just as many judged the album as forgettable compared to old, personal favorites. They complained that "Young and Beautiful"'s chorus sounded like his earlier classic, "Little Red Corvette." "Have a Heart" and "Objects in the Mirror" seemed to share a melody. "Pearls B4 the Swine" sounded more like *The Truth*. "Somewhere Here on Earth" used the same whining synthesizer as remixes for his ballads.

December 17, 2002, the live album arrived with jewel cases; a fifty-six-page full-color booklet with quotes from fans, newspaper critics, and band members; various photos; and a small poster of Prince on guitar. He also gave club members the original *One Nite Alone . . .* and a disc of after-show gigs. While they started the usual debate over a new work's merits, Prince leaped back into *Xenophobia*, changing its title to the less disputatious *Xpectation* and not even planning a retail release. Instead, he uploaded the jazz album to his music club on New Year's Eve 2002, making him one of the first major recording artists to opt for this sort of distribution.

Within three days, he sent his fan club *C-Note,* another online-only MP3 album credited to Prince and the New Power Generation. He had taped these five instrumentals during sound checks for his recent One Nite Alone Tour, and named the album after the initials for their individual titles ("Copenhagen," "Nagoya," "Osaka," "Tokyo," and "Empty Room").

By February 6, he had knocked out basic tracks for another jazz album called *N.E.W.S.* Saxophonist Eric Leeds and his band helped create four instrumentals ("North," "East," "West," and "South") that each lasted fourteen minutes, and presented two or three ambitious melodies. When everyone else left, Prince stayed in the studio, adding guitar, keyboards, and drums. By the time Prince finished, the album evoked the best of his bygone Madhouse. After crediting everything solely to Prince, he tried to line up a traditional release in stores.

Away from work, in mid-March, Prince moved forward with plans to destroy the old purple house on Kiowa Trail. John had spent his final years there, with health-care workers watching over him. Now, Prince wanted it gone. He also thought about Tyka, his only sibling of the same two parents. Along with financial woes, *City Pages* reported forty-three-year-old Tyka now had a serious drug habit. For years, Tyka had occasionally used drugs or drank. But now, her habits reached epidemic proportions. She didn't even want to live anymore, *City Pages* added. After handling some bills, Prince urged his little sister to seek treatment. He helped get her into a rehab clinic called Hazelden. When Tyka left, she was clean, sober, trying to take it a day at a time. She relapsed once, but got back on the horse the next day and remained sober. Before anyone knew it, Tyka celebrated ninety days clean. "It's the longest I've been sober and drug-free in years," she told contractmusic.com in September.

By June 19, Prince had released *N.E.W.S.* on his site. Most critics ignored it. Mainstream listeners barely knew it existed. Some club members felt a few sections were tiresome, his James Brown tributes had devolved into formula, and that Prince should probably end this current jazz phase. But many industry executives were amazed, calling its mix of jazz-rock, Eastern melodies, and classical, some of his best music in years. "Regrettably, distribution of *N.E.W.S.* was limited and it didn't reach beyond Prince's core audience," Per Nilsen remembered. "In fact, the music media hardly noticed the release."

That July, his thought-provoking, cathartic jazz phase continued. During David Sanborn's show at the Hollywood Bowl, Prince stood on the sidelines, watching keyboardist Ricky Peterson—once considered for

The Revolution—play with Sanborn's band. After a song ended, Prince gave him a big hug. Peterson thought, *What? This is unheard of.*

Prince told him, "Man, it sounds really good."

Peterson felt the old Prince would never have been so effusive. "Geez, man, maybe you *are* turning a corner."

In late July, Prince was preparing his music club's first DVD for release within a month. But then he confused members with a group e-mail. "Help the cause!" it said, before asking readers to search their collections for "anything with a WB logo that was unofficially released during Prince's tenure at that label."

This was followed by a list of items he hoped to receive, including singles from 1999 and *Purple Rain* released by such companies as Back 2 Back, 2-on-1, and BackTrax; compact discs; boxed sets; even home videos.

These were all sold as imports, in Europe and Japan, the letter mentioned; meaning someone cut Prince out of rightful royalties and payments; and readers should send them to "The Ways of the Pharaoh," a post office box in Vermilion, Ohio. Since the e-mail didn't mention a reward or reimbursement, some of his hard-core fans went online to complain. At the unauthorized Prince.org site, one wrote that he bought these in a shop and legally owned them "and Prince wants me to send them back free of charge. Fool."

Others expressed similar sentiments, so Prince elaborated on his site. "Not long ago, an unauthorized version of the concert film *Sign O' the Times* surfaced online," a message explained. "Supposedly originating in Brazil and distributed by WEA International, this DVD is not something that was approved by Prince or any of his affiliates." Prince tolerated most bootlegging, the message continued, but it crossed the line "when Prince's [former] record company . . . gets in the mix." They needed these items "to show a federal court the actual truth of this age-old rift between artist and label." MTV soon created a story about the e-mail, titled "Prince Wants His Music Back . . . Now."

42

A CERTIFIABLE LEGEND

THE ROCK AND ROLL HALL OF FAME INDUCTS MUSICIANS twenty-five years after their debut. Since 1986, the hall had inducted 201 artists and industry figures. Seventy-five record executives, lawyers, managers, journalists, and musicians had started the induction process by meeting to discuss potential nominees in spring. After whittling down choices, they created a ballot with about twenty names.

In early September, the Rock and Roll Hall of Fame mailed ballots for the year's nominations to fifteen hundred industry workers and inductees. Now they waited to see which five to eight names received the most votes. On Monday, September 15, a spokesperson for the Hall announced Prince was among the names up for consideration on the ballot.

In spite of this undeniable endorsement, various media outlets continued to debate whether Prince was a has-been. Industry experts felt he'd sell more albums with a major label. People also suspected his beef with Warner, the "Slave" stunt, and other antics had alienated label executives and the mainstream media, not to mention fans. His work wasn't on radio, MTV, or other outlets.

But Prince had a plan.

In September 2003, Prince hired veteran music publicist Ronnie Lippin. Raised in Brooklyn, she had worked as head publicist for MCA Records. After her stint at Elton John's Rocket Records, Lippin arranged publicity campaigns for RSO, the label that released the hit soundtracks *Grease* and *Saturday Night Fever*. In 1989, Lippin arrived at her husband's The Lippin Group to work with Mark Knopfler, Eric Clapton, and Brian Wilson. Lippin knew that a major comeback "doesn't just happen." But Prince told her he'd be more flexible with the industry, regain his audience, and aggressively work to get back on the mainstream radar. "It is far from a casual process, and Prince is the primary force driving everything," she explained.

———

Part of a comeback meant the right album. Now that he got all of his bolder ideas out of his system with the jazz albums, Prince started creating new songs while in Mississauga, Ontario, a four-and-a-half-hour drive from Ottawa. And the distance from the American music scene, or industry, he felt, made the album that he created, called *Musicology,* unlike anything on the market. If anything, he used his lyrics to denounce what popular music had become in his absence. "Making music about alcoholism," he frowned. "Is that the one topic? Is that it?" If he grew up on that music, he wouldn't be here.

In the studio, Prince considered changes back home, and alluded to the ongoing war in Iraq, and government surveillance during his ballad "Call My Name." "Cinnamon Girl" described an ethnic woman's life in the U. S. during wartime. He also mentioned social ills on his broody, Sly-like "Dear Mr. Man." But most of the album was undemanding: "A Million Days" offered heartfelt balladry. The title track and "Life 'O' the Party" called fans to the dance floor and mentioned producer Dr. Dre and Missy Elliott. "What Do U Want Me 2 Do?" dabbled in beat-heavy R&B and sounded a bit like Michael Jackson's *Off the Wall* number "I Can't Help It." Prince played instruments, reveled in influences, and emerged with twelve songs that ran only forty-seven minutes. What resulted from the recording was a collection of songs that was far from groundbreaking, but appealing enough to get him back onto pop radio.

Prince also continued to visit his complex in Minneapolis, where cynics now claimed his marriage and faith were marketing tools. But even Cheryl Johnson—the local reporter who called herself C. J. and reported on his personal activities for the Minneapolis *Star Tribune*—believed religion had changed him for the better. "A lot of credit is being given to Manuela," she told another writer. "Both his parents died recently, too." Their deaths were "the last barrier to realizing that you, too, will die." Prince was warmer; spiritual; monogamous. In the past, with other women, he "got bored quickly," Johnson noted. "The traumatic death of his baby changed all that. It affected him in a big way." Still, people in Minneapolis kept saying, in jest, "It looks like they finally got the medication right."

One day in early October, according to *Entertainment Weekly,* Prince knocked on the door of a suburban home in Eden Prairie.

When a white man answered, he introduced himself as Prince Nelson, and entered with his band member Larry Graham. The homeowner's wife thought: *Cool, cool, cool. He wants to use my house for a set. I'm glad! Demolish the whole thing! Start over!* Instead, they started "in on this Jehovah's Witnesses stuff," she remembered.

She interrupted him. "You know what? You've walked into a Jewish household, and this is not something I'm interested in."

"Can I just finish?" Prince answered.

Graham pulled out a tiny Bible and read scriptures "about being Jewish and the land of Israel," the woman recalled.

They left a pamphlet and got out of there after twenty-five minutes. "He was very kind," she said of Prince.

Outside, Prince and Graham reentered a black truck where a woman—thought to be Manuela—waited. Prince left without knocking on other doors. He realized that he had just tried to "convert a Jewish family hours before the start of Yom Kippur, the holiest day on the Jewish calendar," *Entertainment Weekly* explained.

Prince returned to planning what he called his "World Tour 2003/2004." He needed a break from the image, meetings with distributors, scalding reviews, and interminable fan expectations. And his father was still on his mind. Before leaving for the tour, Prince reflected on this in a video for "Musicology." He had the clip include a light-skinned kid playing him at age ten; and a stand-in for his late father (originally to be played by popular comedian Steve Harvey).

After announcing he'd release a seven-disc boxed set called *The Chocolate Invasion*, that compiled downloads from his site's first three years, Prince flew to China, where local officials hoped his performance during the three-week Hong Kong Harbour Fest could lure tourists back after a SARS epidemic.

October 16, at the Tamar site in Admiralty—a huge outdoor lot surrounded by skyscrapers and overlooking Victoria Harbour—Prince led the band through rehearsal. Promoters barely advertised the show but the next night, October 17, he played all of the old hits. As he had many times since 1995, Prince claimed these shows marked the final time he'd perform them. Thus, instead of segments in medleys, he offered full versions. And despite claims of resenting *Purple Rain* typecasting, he featured seven of its songs. (Only "Computer Blue" and "Darling Nikki" were absent.)

While onstage, Prince also got to hear how this latest band handled numbers from *Prince, Controversy, 1999, Parade, Sign O' the Times, Graffiti Bridge, Diamonds and Pearls, The Gold Experience,* and *The Rainbow Children.* But his inclusion of "I Feel For You" (popularized by Chaka Khan), and "Nothing Compares 2 U" (made famous by Sinéad) inspired some to suggest he was trying to make money on the nostalgia circuit.

The accusation that he was coasting on past hits arrived just as he was preventing VH1 from celebrating one of them. The network was creating a special called *True Spin: Prince 1999,* with everyone from Jill Jones to Lisa Coleman singing his praise and discussing his past work. "But at the eleventh hour Prince wouldn't allow use of the song so it was shelved," said photographer David Honl.

Even *The Wall Street Journal* said he looked "like a has-been" at this stage. His name change sealed his reputation as erratic, they suggested. Battling Warner had also affected his stature and sales. "He was furious that the company, following standard industry practice, refused to cede ownership of the master recordings for his albums going back to 1978," the *Journal* continued. They also noted his claim that Warner didn't effectively market older work.

It was two months ago that the Rock and Roll Hall of Fame announced his name was on the ballot. He considered how they must view him: complaining about major label Warner for a decade; refusing interviews; hurling accusations at record companies, radio stations, industry trade journals, and even MTV; accusing executives of being racist or greedy. He didn't get too excited about being included.

By November 20, the votes were in.

John Mellencamp, on the ballot for the first time, didn't receive enough votes. They passed over five other first-timers. But they named Prince to the Hall of Fame, the only honoree inducted during his first year of eligibility. Bob Merlis, on the nominating committee, said his induction was "automatic." Prince was everything people could want in a rock star. "Iconoclastic, great guitarist, great dancer, enigmatic, a rebel, everything—and he makes great records."

Someone told him the Hall was inducting him. "I didn't feel anything at first," he said. At Paisley Park, reporters' calls went unanswered. Los Angeles publicist Lippin said he hadn't sent a statement. But she was ecstatic. Most inductees were happy anyone remembered them so many years after their last hits. But his induction would smooth his transition into a bankable "heritage act" stage of his career, where a loyal, older following, not into downloading, would keep buying products. Bobby Z meanwhile said, "It's not a surprise; he deserves it. From the first day I met him in seventy-five or seventy-six, I could see it immediately: He had a magical gift. One in a billion!"

43

EVERYTHING AND NOTHING

THE BAND WAS READY FOR AN AMERICAN TOUR. PEOPLE KEPT talking about the Rock Hall induction. Soon, even old white women approached in public to congratulate him. He didn't think they even knew he existed. He realized how important this was; the industry was essentially calling him a legend. Though his excitement grew, he said little about the honor in public.

Meanwhile, his second wife Mani had become a close aide. She chose artwork for his studio's walls; developed products for an ambitious new NPG Home brand; supported his decision to upgrade his two studios, and add two more; and agreed that interns should work here in exchange for lessons about every aspect of the music business.

They were just as united away from work. When her sister was marrying a businessman in Calabogie, a village outside of Ottawa, Prince joined Mani at the ceremony. Local residents stared in disbelief as they observed the couple emerging from a gleaming limo, but her family extended the usual warm welcome. Then they joined eighty other guests at the Dickson Manor ski lodge. He would also have her join him on the road, and hire laborers to finish adding a big gatehouse, a fence, a tennis court, and a pool to their home on Bridle Path.

By this point, Prince was self-managing. If someone called his publicist for an interview, Lippin might have them call Prince's guitar technician, Takumi Suetsugu. If Prince weren't busy, Takumi would then let him know who wanted what. This was how Prince learned that television producer Ken Ehrlich wanted him to perform a duet with pop-star Beyoncé Knowles during the 2004 Grammy Awards. The invitation was nothing new, Prince explained. Every year, they invited him onstage. Usually, he declined. But he'd soon be meeting with major labels, to pitch them on *Musicology*. He also had a tour to promote. The exposure could only help. Instead of declining, Ehrlich noted, "he was ready for a major return to the scene." But on one condition: "That he open the show."

February 8, 2004, onstage at the Staples Center in Los Angeles, the breast pocket on Prince's suit jacket held a yellow handkerchief. He wore his signature elegant, white ♀-shaped guitar. Violet lighting covered everything onstage as he began with "Purple Rain," filling the opening of the song with screaming solos. By the second verse, Beyoncé had emerged in a short pink skirt. To the next chorus, she added her passionate vocals. Live horn players joined them then for "Baby I'm a Star," then the festive riff that started Beyoncé's hit "Crazy in Love." They capped the set with "Let's Go Crazy," and an onstage fireworks display.

At least one observer, Jon Bream, felt he upstaged the twenty-two-year-old (who would end up dominating the awards of the evening).

As the ceremony continued, N.E.W.S. was a nominee for Best Pop Instrumental Album, Prince's first nomination since 1996 (when *The Gold Experience* and "Eye Hate U" competed for R&B Awards)—this in spite of the fact that satirical magazine and Web site *The Onion* named it the "least-essential album of 2003" and sales showed a meager twenty thousand copies after nine months. It faced Jim Brickman's *Peace*, Kenny G's *Wishes*, George Winston's *Night Divides the Day: The Music of the Doors*, and Ry Cooder and Manuel Galban's *Mambo Sinuendo*. Prince lost out to Cooder and Galban. Still, critics raved that his duet opener stole the show.

Former Revolution band member Wendy Melvoin told the Minneapolis *Star Tribune* that she called Prince's guitar tech to say the original Revolution and his ex-girlfriend Susannah wanted to attend a party he was throwing at West Hollywood's House of Blues (an informal gig before his well-rehearsed run of arenas). They hadn't really spoken since the failed Revolution reunion attempt in 2000. Someone called drummer Bobby Z, she continued, to say he and the old band could attend, but only Bobby would get in free. Wendy thought, *What the hell is this?* Still, they went. (And no one had to pay.) But it was hard getting in. They felt a little ignored, especially in light of their history with the man of the evening. They watched stars like Steven Tyler and Beck walk in effortlessly. Eventually, someone led them to another room, but "there wasn't a seat for us and we all just had to stand there." During his show, Prince called various people onstage, but not his former bandmates. Wendy thought, *Well, that's it.*

Then Mani came up and introduced herself. Wendy said tell him thanks for the tickets and good-bye.

After the party, however, Wendy's phone rang. According to her, Prince's guitar tech said, "Prince would like you to come down to the recording studio and rehearse with him on acoustic guitar for a benefit he's doing for *The Tavis Smiley Show*."

What the hell is this? Wendy remembered thinking.

But she went, and she saw Prince to be "remarkably kind and open." He gave her a huge hug, she explained, and let her sit in with the band. For two hours, he taught her the song. The next day on the set, Wendy said of Prince, "He was the guy I knew when I first met him. He was the guy who spent the night at my and Lisa's house on our pullout bed." She held, kissed, hugged him, and kept repeating she loved him.

Hundreds of reporters squeezed into Prince's press conference at LA's El Rey Theatre. As usual, Prince claimed this new tour marked the last time he'd trot out the hits. "Our last tour was based on the music from *The Rainbow Children*," he claimed. Now, he'd get to hear his new band play his early work "in a newer way." With that, he called them out for "Kiss," "Sign O' the Times," and other classics.

Meanwhile, he continued to approach major labels with *Musicology*. And with the media lauding his duet at the Grammy Awards and reporting he'd soon play the Rock Hall ceremony, getting meetings was easier. He figured a major could handle *Musicology*'s distribution while he toured and promoted the album with interviews.

Many reporters still frowned on his decision to write "slave" on his face during the 1990s. But during meetings, he noted one advantage of having done so: Label executives entered talks knowing they wouldn't own anything; that any deal they struck had to be advantageous to him, otherwise he could release music on his own label and keep the majority of profits. "Maybe at one time they could get Little Richard for a new car and a bucket of chicken," Prince joked. "We don't roll like that no more." Now, he was the content provider. They couldn't exert pressure. They had no power over him. He felt confident enough to tell executives at competing labels that he wanted *all* of their companies to release *Musicology*—"the notion being," he explained, "that the pie, the market share, should be shared by all."

Away from meetings, Prince actually hoped to find just one distributor excited enough to get out there and promote his work. After working five to six months on it, he didn't want to "give it to somebody to mess up in two weeks" with shorthanded promotions.

Prince also wanted to sell it online, charging ninety-nine cents per song (or seventy-seven cents for fan club members). Then he considered giving it away. "The thinking behind that being the people who buy concert tickets have been with me for over twenty years. So it's just my way of saying thanks."

While making the rounds, Prince reportedly met with Bruce Lundvall, head of Blue Note (enjoying success with piano-playing newcomer Norah Jones). "We talked for about an hour," said Lundvall. And what he said about the industry was "pretty profound. I don't think you can ever count this guy out."

Ultimately, Prince's lawyer negotiated with Columbia, where Sony Music U.S. president Don Ienner was eager to work with Prince. But Ienner noted, "There are certain things we don't talk about. Obviously, he doesn't feel the same way about us as he does about [his old label]." Prince called for industry reform. Ienner didn't necessarily agree with everything he said. In the end, they signed a deal for Columbia to manufacture, distribute, and market *Musicology* domestically.

Ienner was pleased. Publicly, the executive predicted people would "respond to it as a twenty-first-century Prince record." Prince was just as happy. "I feel at peace," he said. "I knew it would take time, and I had to deal with a lot of ridicule. But this feels like peace right now." He'd receive no payment from Sony but had full ownership of the album. He would receive $7 from every $10 sale. And online sales were his so he let NPG Music Club subscribers have it first; charging $9.99 for a download, a discount compared to the CD's "suggested retail price" of $18.98.

At her desk in Los Angeles, publicist Ronnie Lippin booked him on *The Tonight Show with Jay Leno* for February 26. Then, March 3, Prince was on the syndicated talk show *Ellen*. But not as "part of some master strategy," he said publicly. Ellen asked if he'd perform and he said yes. Print reports kept describing a comeback, and at his NPG Music Club site, Chicago-based webmaster Sam Jennings said sales were "steadily growing." But *Rolling Stone*'s editor Joe Levy differed, saying people respected Prince "for the work he did twenty years ago."

He hadn't "had a radio hit in ten years," the *Star Tribune*'s Chris Rie-menschneider explained, but fifteen days before his first *Musicology* show, arenas in five of thirty cities were 75 percent sold out.

As he had for five years, Prince had to decide what hits to exclude. There wasn't enough time to play everything fans wanted so he retired "a good portion of them," he explained. But when a reporter asked if this was *really* the last time he would play certain hits, he said, "Well, it is called the 2004ever Tour. And time is forever," he quipped.

"So this probably isn't the last time?"

"Probably not."

44

PLAY IN THE SUNSHINE

MONDAY NIGHT, MARCH 15, 2004, PRINCE ARRIVED AT THE WAL-
dorf Astoria for the nineteenth annual Rock and Roll Hall of Fame induction ceremony, a fifteen-hundred-dollar-a-plate event that attracted a
thousand industry professionals and artists, many in black tie and linger-
ing on the red carpet out front. Novelist Tom Wolfe, cast members from
HBO's *The Sopranos*, Lenny Kravitz, and Hall of Fame members Robert
Plant, Robbie Robertson, George Clinton, and Bruce Springsteen were
among those present that night.

For his part, Prince arrived in a white suit that had one long tail and
one short. He was the first to perform that evening. He played a strong-
willed medley: his rock-fueled party song, "Let's Go Crazy," his sobering
"Sign O' the Times," an instrumental refrain from Sam and Dave's "Soul
Man," and his irreverent "Kiss." His guitar solo had the normally staid
crowd on its feet. Reporters saw Mick Jagger execute his signature stilted
dance moves. Yoko Ono (in silver-lamé jacket and big sunglasses)
bounced. Soon, most of the crowd was dancing. And when his ten-minute
set ended, they gave a standing ovation.

Prince was the first artist of the night to be inducted. It began with a
video tribute, with sound bites from rare interviews. Then rap duo Outkast, recent recipients of an Album of the Year Grammy, took the stage.
Andre 3000 and Big Boi openly discussed loving Prince's music, both as
kids and now as best-selling stars.

Their introduction was followed, at Prince's request, by twenty-five-
year-old Alicia Keys (Best New Artist at the 2001 Grammy Awards). By
this point, she had covered "How Come U Don't Call Me Anymore," and
joined him for a few art-show parties in midtown Manhattan. She took
the podium and, reading from a TelePrompTer, said, "There are many
kings: King Henry VIII, King Solomon, King Tut, King James, King Kong,
and the Three Kings. But there is only one Prince." By defying rules and

restrictions he had created music "so superbad that he makes us feel super-good." He was an inspiration "that generations will return to until the end of time."

With introduction complete, Prince took the dais, where he shook hands, gave hugs, and set his award on the floor. Everyone in the room had witnessed his ups and downs. The tragedies and the triumphs. The media and his own audience's attacks on him. The skepticism that greeted his unveiling of ideas—ideas that now helped many of them earn more money in this business.

Prince faced the crowd, opened a red book, and said, "All praise and thanks to the most high Jehovah. Thank you, Rock and Roll Hall of Fame. This is definitely an honor." When he first started, Prince continued, he was most concerned with freedom: Freedom to produce, play every instrument, and sing what he pleased. "And after much negotiation, Warner Brothers Records granted me that freedom and I thank them for that."

For two minutes, he thanked artists that inspired him for "a journey more fascinating than I could ever have imagined." Then he said, "A word to the wise: Without real spiritual mentoring, too much freedom can lead to the soul's decay." He told young artists: "a real friend and mentor is not on your payroll." The crowd applauded. A real friend and mentor would care for their soul, he added. "I wish all of you the best on this fascinating journey."

Then, with the crowd applauding, he rejoined Mani at their table. Her black outfit with white trim matched his white suit and black shirt. Nearby, Anita Baker and Larry Graham offered congratulations. Then Keith Richards approached for a few words.

Prince soon had to leave the hall. The four-hour ceremony was at its halfway point, and he had to change for his next performance.

While others were inducted (Traffic; the Dells, Bob Seger, ZZ Top, and *Rolling Stone* founder Jann Wenner) Prince slipped into a black suit, red hat, and matching shirt, preparing to make history again.

By the time he left backstage, Tom Petty and Jeff Lynne had posthumously inducted former Beatle George Harrison, who played in their eighties ensemble the Traveling Wilburys. Prince went out and joined them, and Lippin's other client Eric Clapton, for a show-closing rendition of the Beatles' "While My Guitar Gently Weeps."

Prince was sharing the stage with some of rock's most distinguished guitar players, but his solo stunned every guitarist in the room and stole "the entire evening," Alan Leeds recalled. "But his arrogant slamming of the guitar at the end was tasteless and disrespectful to the other artists on the stage with him."

His cocky attitude was "rock and roll," but in light of the circumstances—that the song was a tribute to the only recently deceased George Harrison—many viewed it as not only disrespectful to others on-stage but to Harrison's memory. "It should have been enough to let his guitar solo speak for him," Leeds felt. "It was the one time he should have been a team player." It wasn't, Leeds added, "very grown up."

Either way, the media again described Prince's performance as the highlight.

David Bowie had no problem with the performance. "I'm always floored every time I've seen him live," Bowie said. "There's very few people to touch him."

Back in Minneapolis, Prince finalized plans for his tour and made time to join Mani at Bible study class. The couple also performed field ser-vice, door-to-door visits to local residents with church elder Ronald Scofield and security guards in tow. One day, Prince left the limo in a tailor-made suit and trademark heels. He walked up to one of the modest picket-fenced homes on this street, knocked on a door, and waited. A resident opened and looked shocked.

"Would you like to talk about Jesus?" Prince asked.

From the sidelines, church elder Scofield nodded with pride. "He uses the scriptures very well," Scofield said, and he was growing spiritually.

Prince continued to refine his set list for the road. He wanted crowds to hear new songs and ideas but accepted that "Let's Go Crazy" had be-come "like a piece of Americana in a way." But he was through with the old act. He also toned down the crowd-pleasers. "That's not me anymore."

Times had changed. As a young man, he did what no one else was doing with these lyrics "and I knew that would get me over." He offered "Darling Nikki" when television's most risqué show was Dynasty and saw critics equate it with "porn" due to its lyric about "masturbating." Today, Dynasty looked "like The Brady Bunch" and there were no more envelopes to push. "I pushed it off the table. It's on the floor. Let's move forward." And with parents bringing kids to shows, he didn't want to perform any-thing these adults would find difficult to explain on the way home. "I'm not trying to be obscene to anybody." He also remembered a 1992 tour. The band played "Sexy MF" with "seventy thousand people yelling that at me, and I don't need to hear that anymore."

In addition to the set list, he decided to run with an idea he first considered in 1994. He'd give every ticket holder a free copy of *Musicology*; build its cost—about $9.99—into the ticket price, then report every ticket sold as an album sale *Billboard* had to count on their charts. "See, if I sell four hundred thousand tickets to my shows, that would make me number one on the charts before I even release a CD into record stores. You feel me? Then Norah Jones is gonna have something to worry about." Tour promoter Randy Phillips was amazed by his level of thought. "Prince is ahead of his time and thinks outside the box."

Prince started his tour March 27, in Reno's Lawlor Events Center. Movie theaters in thirty-one cities broadcast the show live via satellite, with high-definition projectors. Fans paid fifteen dollars and received a copy of the CD. Then, two days later, Prince arrived in Los Angeles to play the twenty-thousand-seat Staples Center. He reportedly attracted the venue's largest audience ever, selling over nineteen thousand tickets.

By now, VH1's executive vice president for music and talent Rick Krim had received and enjoyed a copy of Prince's video for lead single, "Musicology." "The timing feels right." Krim said. "He was away long enough." VH1 would air it. That same day, Sony released the single to stores while Prince's own music club site offered two new MP3 albums: *The Chocolate Invasion* (tracks offered during the Club's first year) and *The Slaughterhouse* (more songs from the first year). But with the media not interested in joining a club, or paying fees for review copies, reporters focused on his Sony work, *Musicology*.

Monday night, two weeks after the Rock Hall induction, four video monitors in the Staples Center aired Alicia Keys's earnest introduction. The stage was empty save for the old fireman pole and a guardrail on the side with an NPG emblem. Lighting was limited to spotlights. With Keys's final words echoing (". . . the one and only, Prince"), the crowd roared.

Prince walked into view in white clothes, with a red tuxedo coat and hat, and leaped into "Musicology." After some dance moves, he wiped his face with a rag, and brushed off a shoulder. "Los Angeles!" he shouted. On cue, the confetti and purple ribbons fell from the rafters. Then he did the

Purple Rain medley. After tossing his hat into the crowd, he breezed through other works and invited fans onstage. When he saw a female fan trip and fall during "Take Me With U," he quipped, "Too many trips to the bar!"

Backstage, Prince heard the crowd yell for more. He slipped quickly into a sleeveless black turtleneck and matching pants. Back onstage, he saw the chair at center stage. Sitting with an acoustic guitar he offered a gentle "Forever in My Life," written when he thought he and Susannah would be together. Then he did "Little Red Corvette." The eclectic audience of older and younger fans knew every word. Some audience members wept openly. Finally, his own eyes watered while singing "Sometimes It Snows in April's" doleful lyric about hoping to see a dead friend again in Heaven. When it ended, he received a standing ovation. He wept at the adulation and struggled to regain his composure.

Eventually, Prince regrouped. The band came out again. After decades of claiming he resented typecasting, he strapped on his purple electric guitar and admitted, "I love playing this song." He went right into "Purple Rain" and wound up lying on the stage floor, reaching out to touch a few hands in the crowd. "One more!" he yelled. "One more!" But the show was over. As the band kept playing, Prince made his exit down the fireman pole.

Prince continued to make headlines wherever he went. And by March 31, 2004, *The Wall Street Journal* joined in welcoming him back. "Baby, I'm a Star, Again," their headline read. "How a Seeming Has-Been Spent Months Preparing to Reclaim the Center Stage." But with everyone describing *Musicology* as a comeback, Prince asked, "Comeback? I never went anywhere!"

To his dismay, writers kept including the term. Prince just shook his head. He had always made music. The media just stopped focusing on him. "Never had a problem filling arenas." And he never alienated fans, either, he suggested (though message boards might have suggested otherwise). Warner's "restrictive, one-sided contract" was to blame for the ♀, he claimed.

"No regrets whatsoever," he said in a virtual chat hosted by the *Boston Herald*. Any artist, he stressed, would do the same for eight times more money and control of their work. "I wasn't getting anywhere by telling Warner Brothers that they were abusing me."

———

By April 20, 2004, Columbia had filled orders for over a million copies worldwide of *Musicology*. "And with the first copy shipped, we started making money," said Don Ienner. The label had "really high expectations for this," Ienner added, and while there were no guarantees, they hoped to stay in business with Prince for a long time. "How often does an artist of his stature become available on any terms?"

As usual, his work divided critics. Most reviewers called *Musicology* his most competent and commercial work in years. The Associated Press felt it was a relief after almost a decade of "convoluted, self-indulgent albums that only Prince fanatics cared about." *Rolling Stone* had mixed feelings, offering praise in a review subtitled, "Prince can still bring the funk, but we've heard it all before." Either way, *Musicology* debuted at No. 3, with first-week sales of over 191,000, doubling those of *Rave Un2 the Joy Fantastic*. The album stayed in the Top 10. In several other nations, it reached the Top 5.

April 28, MTV's special *The Art of Musicology* drew even more people to his album and shows. The half-hour special aired on MTV, MTV2, VH1, VH1 Classic, and BET, and showed him in concert, playing songs alone on an acoustic guitar. After years of struggle, Prince was finally triumphant. "'Prince is crazy,'" he said. "I knew what people were saying." When he used the ♀, writers cracked jokes; but he was the one laughing. "I knew I'd be here today, feeling each new album is my first."

But his groundbreaking package soon inspired a rash of suspicious articles. *Entertainment Weekly* claimed "Prince schemes to top *Billboard* charts." Labels complained of an "unfair precedent in tallying sales." MTV, however, noted "only the four shows that have taken place since the album's April 20 release have been counted." With fifteen thousand people at each show, SoundScan credited *Musicology* for sixty thousand album sales. "But even with that number subtracted from the total, *Musicology* would still be the third best-selling album, since weekly sales of the No. 4 album, *Now That's What I Call Music! 15*, stand at ninety-eight thousand."

At the same time, Prince's idea was fueling the struggling music business. With concert prices rising 13 percent in the past year, fewer people bought tickets, meaning sales had slowed in the $2.5 billion industry. *Pollstar*'s editor-in-chief Gary Bongiovanni said, "This is a very good marketing strategy." And while Prince's average ticket price was slightly higher than the industry average of $58.71, the extra dollar or two he charged got customers the entire album. Even this price was still reportedly less than half what it cost to see other stars.

Most reporters continued to imply Prince was somehow inflating sales figures, but one wrote this was "perhaps kicking off a music industry revolution." Prince remained impervious to criticism. He called "this bundling situation" his "emancipation," and noted it was a way to get around a biased media. "They pick and choose what they want to focus on," he said of reporters. "We're given prepackaged pop stars every day. They control who's on heavy rotation." Now, he turned the tables. Proudly, Prince said, "the album's in the top ten."

He was just as confident about his other business projects. When HBO executives appeared backstage one night, to propose taping and airing the concert, he heard them say the deal meant having to avoid other TV specials for a year. "Excuse me?" Prince asked. "Oh no. End of discussion. You want to talk about something else? I know you flew a long way. We might as well talk philosophy or something."

One answered, "Well, that's just our policy."

"Well, you keep your policy. You want some pizza? Cause you ain't going to get no concert."

Despite a rash of suspicious articles, Prince kept welcoming reporters backstage. While driving many toward his various dressing rooms in a golf cart he cracked jokes. Behind the wheel one day, he told one, "Hang on. I don't have insurance." Another day, a writer noted the purple silk or tie-dyed fabrics, lit candles, couches, guitars, and keyboards in his dressing room. Prince waved a hand toward all of it. "They do this everywhere we go. Makes it feel like home."

He was more open with them, but some things didn't change. "Like no tape recorders," David Segal of *The Washington Post* reported. Now Prince claimed he didn't like the sound of his voice. He also wouldn't discuss his marriage. But when one writer invoked religion, Prince quickly said he was into spirituality and solutions, not odd ceremonies or conjecture. "I'm very practical. You go Trekkie on me, I gotta go."

Despite his sanitized set list, some interviewers kept referring to explicit songs. He felt he put five on twenty-five albums. "It's more like a dozen," a writer felt, "but no use quibbling." In the end, Prince didn't argue, either. "We've all used shock value to sell things," he said, and early on, he did it to get attention. But even these works included messages about education, literacy, and respect for women. "Go and listen to the verses. All people focus on is the hooks."

His set list also alienated some of his older core audience. Where he once let these fans suggest numbers, he now accepted some wanted to keep reliving their glory days with provocative old numbers like "Darling Nikki." "I'm not mad at them," he said. "I feel for them. It takes all kinds." At the same time, they had to accept he wasn't "that old lady in *Sunset Boulevard*," he said. He wouldn't stay in a mansion, coasting on past glories and preparing for a close-up. "I've changed. I'm a different person." From center stage, Prince stared out into the audience and saw grandmothers, mothers, teens, and children enjoying his music. Some shows, he invited them onstage to dance. During "Purple Rain," he urged crowds to go home and open their Bibles. Ben Margolin, who ran fan site Prince.org, was surprised more people weren't complaining. "I think the hard-core fans are placated because he's playing a lot more guitar."

Even relations with *Rolling Stone* improved. He felt slighted by Jann Wenner's magazine for years, but the rock journal put his face on its May 2004 cover for the first time in more than a decade. In the past, it would have been no big deal. "Once you've done anything, to do it again ain't no big deal, you feel me?" He'd been on the cover with Vanity, and again "when I didn't even do an interview, when I wouldn't talk to them." But now, he was excited about the attention. "Having once revolutionized rock 'n' roll," the *San Francisco Chronicle* wrote, "Prince can now say he defied the rock establishment and survived."

45

BABY I'M A STAR

SOLD-OUT ARENA DATES ACCOUNTED FOR ONLY PART OF *MUSI-cology*'s 632,000 sales in five weeks. But the controversy continued in May. MTV was supportive—understanding Prince wanted older fans to hear his new stuff—but noted he might be putting "unwanted multiple copies in the hands of his followers." A married couple would leave a show with two copies. If they went to another show, they'd have even more. Also fans were receiving copies in a cardboard sleeve, instead of a jewel case with the genuine artwork.

By now, *Pollstar* ranked his tour No. 1 in terms of dollars and units, reporting he had earned $45.7 million and sold 737,097 tickets. In every city, each show attracted about 24,800 people and earned $1.5 million. Reporters expected Prince to gross $45.7 million by June 30 and $100 million by the final show.

One week in early June, Prince's four concerts helped *Musicology* rise from No. 8 to No. 4. "The album also experienced a thirty-five percent rise in weekly sales, to more than ninety-five thousand copies, pushing its total to slightly less than eight hundred thousand," MTV noted. At Sound-Scan and *Billboard*, executives suddenly rethought their policy regarding albums and concert tickets.

Billboard chart editor Geoff Mayfield claimed one-fourth of the album's sales—158,000 or so copies—were from concert tickets. And with Prince planning three or four shows a week until early September, *Musicology* wouldn't leave the charts for any of that time. *Billboard*'s June 5 edition announced the magazine's amended policy. "The consumer must be given the option to purchase a CD with a concert ticket for [the sale] to count toward the chart." Customers had to be free to reject a CD, and pay less for a ticket. The CD's cost also had to be close to what stores charged. "We're not going to let them sell the album for two bucks," said Mayfield.

But it wouldn't apply to *Musicology*. *Billboard* and SoundScan had to keep counting those sales. A week later, *Musicology* dropped a spot, to No. 5, but sold over seventy-two thousand more copies. Then, when Prince took a few days off from touring, the album dropped a little on the chart. But once he resumed touring, it returned to the Top 10 again. Attorney McMillan told the *Hollywood Reporter* they would dole out as many as 1.5 million copies during his summer tour. *Entertainment Weekly* predicted he'd stay in the Top 20 for months. "Almost 2 good 2 B true."

During this same period, Prince took time to react to radio deejays playing his album cut "Call My Name" so many times, the ballad—not even on a single—reached No. 75 on the *Billboard* Hot 100 and No. 27 on the R&B Chart. He quickly filmed a video for this clean-cut ode to monogamy and marriage, piling on scenes of a marriage proposal and wedding

Eventually, Prince sold a million concert tickets. And since he launched the Musicology Tour in March, without an end date, he could tour for decades and have *Billboard* keep tallying album sales.

As summer wore on, CNN/Money called him "the only top-draw performer whose tickets are selling well." Soon Prince said, "We have sold more than three million CDs worldwide, and it will continue."

He announced in an online chat, "The music business as we know it is over."

Teenagers were creating entire albums and artwork on laptops, then uploading them to sites that served as "their own distribution service," Prince said. "I mean, what do we really need record companies for?"

Prince's most successful year ever continued. And now everyone saw what he worked so hard to achieve; what all of the unpredictable decisions and carrying on had been about. At Warner, he would have had to sell 666,666 albums to earn $1 million. Now, 142,857 copies of *Musicology* earned the same amount. And while *Purple Rain* reportedly earned him $19.5 million over twenty years, *Musicology*'s sales of 1.4 million had already brought $9.1 million. He continued to take jabs at his old label in interviews—especially while discussing his masters—but it was part of the act. He had actually softened his position on master tapes. He no longer demanded complete ownership. He'd settle for "more control and more generous financial terms," a reporter said. He also kept thinking about his catalog. With Warner issuing old albums on CD, Prince heard one interviewer mention how *Sign O' the Times* had unpredictable volume levels and muddy sound. Leaping to his feet, Prince yelled, "Tell them that! We need to bring it up to the industry standard!"

Prince kept claiming he wanted remastered, even expanded versions with surround sound from his label. But the demands were accompanied by slights. One night onstage, while ad-libbing during a song, he sang, "Warner Brothers used to be a friend of mine. Now they're just a monumental waste of time."

Warner executives ignored the bluster. They told *The Wall Street Journal* if Prince were more cooperative and helped launch a stronger marketing effort, they'd be "pleased to work closely with him." But when the company reached out to him, for help with DVD editions of *Under the Cherry Moon* and *Graffiti Bridge*, Prince refused. Jon Bream understood why. In *Cherry Moon*, Prince was by far "the worst actor" and seemed natural only when singing "Girls and Boys" in a club. *Graffiti Bridge*, released in 1990, was "dreadful then," Bream added. It was even worse today, playing like a bunch of "poorly lit music videos, shot on a low-budget set."

Purple Rain should have been different. With the film's anniversary approaching, Warner Home Video planned a twentieth-anniversary DVD release. The company first released it on DVD in 1997, as one of the earliest products in this format, but fans viewed that version—no extras, and visuals trimmed to standard TV size—as primitive. Warner hoped to change this with a twenty-seven-dollar reissue.

Warner convinced Wendy, Lisa, Jellybean Johnson, director Magnoli, producer Cavallo, and screenwriter William Blinn to grant interviews. They also included a documentary about the club First Avenue, MTV's coverage of the July 1984 premiere, and eight music videos. Now, executives asked Prince to contribute a commentary track. Though most film creators didn't charge for these, Jon Bream wrote in the Minneapolis *Star Tribune* that Prince "reportedly demanded a fee to participate in the project." He did so, Bream added, during his most successful year as a concert performer, and despite Warner planning to pay royalties for the reissue. Further, Prince supposedly encouraged other cast members to seek payment. In the end, Morris Day and Apollonia didn't do commentaries, either. Bream frowned on the decision in print. Prince was wise to avoid the other two DVDs "but his failure to participate in the reissue of his first movie leaves a black cloud over *Purple Rain*."

46

THIS FRIENDSHIP HAD TO END

IN NOVEMBER, PRINCE WAS WORKING ON HIS NEXT ALBUM, *3121*. One day former drummer Michael Bland got a call out of the blue from Prince's guitar technician, who said, "Prince wants to know where you and Sonny Thompson are at."

They were at a sound check for a jazz show that night in St. Paul.

"Can you guys come out to Paisley Park after you're done?"

When Bland and Thompson left the theater at eleven thirty that night and arrived at the studio, Prince already had the equipment set up and ready to go. "Okay," he told them, "there won't be any mistakes. Just pay attention and go for it."

In three and a half hours, they knocked out eleven or twelve tracks.

After the commercial and critical success of *Musicology*'s more traditional songs, Prince filled *3121* with the usual templates: "Black Sweat" had empty "Kiss"-style funk; "Satisfied" was another in a line of "Adore"-like ballads; "The Word" included some "Mountains"-like acoustic sounds; "Fury" had enough guitar for fans of "Let's Go Crazy." But he also tried something new—Santana-like riffs, and tapping the Spanish market, with "Te Amo Corazón."

He soon added another winner to the lineup. He reconnected with a singer named Tamar Davis. The Houston native had left Girl Tyme, a group with preteen Beyoncé Knowles and Kelly Rowland that competed and lost on the TV talent show *Star Search*. Her solo demo had reached Paisley Park in 1997. Prince liked it. "He flew me and my mom into town to Paisley Park and I recorded 'Somewhere Over the Rainbow,'" Tamar told EURweb. Prince didn't meet the thirteen-year-old but still offered her a production contract.

In the years since, Tamar had moved on, studying music at USC, and joining all-female jazz/funk band Angaza for their album *Light*. Now, Prince had Tamar's friend, choreographer Fatima Robinson, who was helping with one of his videos, invite Tamar to the set. Between takes, Tamar approached to say, "Hey, you did a song (on me) at thirteen."

He remembered, and had her sing something then and there. She did and he thought she could make *3121* even hotter than it was. "So we went in the studio and started singing and ended up writing 'Beautiful, Loved, and Blessed,'" she explained. Its sound so pleased him, Prince helped the young singer create her debut *Milk & Honey* at Paisley Park.

He was about to shop another album around, during a period in which media reports continued to emphasize his recent successes. His Musicology Tour's ninety-six dates attracted almost 1.5 million people. Its reported earnings of $90.2 million inspired *Pollstar* to crown him 2004's top concert draw. *Rolling Stone* had him at twenty-eight on their list of 100 Greatest Artists of All Time. Then, in December 2004, *Rolling Stone* readers named him Best Male Performer and Most Welcome Comeback and—in the same issue—listed him at number five on a list of Top Pop Artists of the Past 25 Years. Since he wasn't reclusive anymore, or suspicious, or lecturing reporters, or denouncing Warner, or going by the unspeakable ♣, a writer noted, "Suddenly, liking Prince didn't feel like such a chore. In fact, it was fun."

At the 2005 Grammy Awards, his *Musicology* ballad "Call My Name" won Best Male R&B Vocal Performance. His title track won another Grammy, for Best Traditional R&B Vocal Performance. They also nominated him for Best R&B Song, Best R&B Album, and Best Male Pop Vocal Performance (for his polemical "Cinnamon Girl"). His success continued in February when the Academy Awards invited him to present an Oscar at that year's ceremony. Then in March, he took a Los Angeles stage to accept a NAACP Image Vanguard Award (during a ceremony televised on Fox). For each appearance, he looked stylish, youthful, and warm, but still—despite a mountain of press written about him in the preceding two decades—somewhat unknowable. Nonetheless, his image as a troublesome rabble-rouser had receded. And major labels were suddenly very open to working with him.

At Universal, Prince hammered out terms for a one-album deal without using an attorney. He didn't need one. Being independent so long—earning good money with things like *Crystal Ball*—he wouldn't sign any deal that didn't benefit him. As always, he brought marketing ideas along, too: renting a house in Los Angeles, renovating it to resemble the sort of party setting he sang about on his title track, including tickets—purple, of course—in select copies of the album, allowing customers that found them to attend a special, intimate show, inviting reporters to this event. Universal liked the sound of his ideas, not to mention his Spanish track "Te Amo Corazón," and the ballad with Tamar. The world's largest major label agreed to release 3121 in early 2006 and expressed interest in Tamar's own album *Milk & Honey*. One thing at a time. "It wasn't a contract," Prince noted. "I don't believe in contracts." It was a handshake deal "but we do sign some agreements to ensure business gets accomplished."

He was thrilled with the arrangement but soon faced Barney Hoskyns, an interviewer for *The Observer* that felt he'd gone from rebuking labels to leaping "aboard the biggest slavery ship of them all." Prince corrected him. "I got a chance to structure the agreement the way I saw fit as opposed to it being the other way around."

In October 2005, Prince focused on promoting the next album, signing an eight-month lease for a ten-bedroom, eleven-bath home on Sierra Alta Way, in West Hollywood. The lease called for a seventy-thousand-dollar monthly rent, thesmokinggun.com reported, and included a nondisclosure agreement barring tenant and landlord from discussing the deal. Then he arranged for laborers to prepare it for the private show by slapping some purple striping on the exterior, painting his ♀ and the number 3121, installing a purple monogrammed carpet in the master bedroom, and adding plumbing and piping to a downstairs bedroom so his beauty salon chairs could have water.

He also threw himself into his video for "Te Amo Corazón," hiring renowned actress Salma Hayek (of *Frida*) to direct, then traveling to a huge Spanish-style house in Marrakesh, Morocco. There, Hayek filmed him standing by a big sun-filled window; walking through a big Spanish-style home; playing his purple guitar while lying in a bed covered with silky sheets and rose petals. She added footage of *Motorcycle Diaries* actress Mia Maestro playing his love interest as she walked around the house, and called it a day.

His next promotional move was a December 13 press conference in Los Angeles, where he showed reporters his new video, sang Hayek's praise, but noted the dainty ballad didn't reflect 3121's sound. Then various Universal Music Group chiefs joined in promoting the clip, with a statement announcing a historic premiere on VH1, broadband channels, and a new mobile telephone service by Verizon.

As December continued, Prince saw new protégé Tamar sign her deal with Universal Republic. The label wanted *Milk & Honey* to include "Beautiful, Loved, and Blessed," which she co-wrote and helped sing. They also wanted it as her lead single. To everyone's surprise, Prince offered no objection and even planned to tour with her, as a guitar-wielding sideman, until the label released her work on August 29.

It was clear that his recent successes had brought about a change of heart—or at least a change of methods—in the once-combative Prince.

As part of The Tamar Presentation Tour, he stood to the side of the stage, letting her croon her title track, his new twin dancers shimmy and shake, and a disc jockey scratch vinyl records on turntables. He also stood near her while she sang "Every Little Step." Soon, they sang together the amorous duets "Red Headed Stepchild," and "Beautiful, Loved, and Blessed." Suddenly they were all over the media—at February's BRIT Awards, on *Saturday Night Live,* during his first appearance on the show in twenty-five years. The tour raised both of their profiles and paved the way for their upcoming works.

Finally, it was time to promote 3121. Three days after *Saturday Night Live,* Prince greeted reporters at the big house in Beverly Hills and played the new album.

Barney Hoskyns, who once joined Prince on the bygone 1999 Tour, attended. But he viewed "Alphabet St." off of 1988's *Lovesexy* as "his last truly great pop song." Instead of great pop music, Hoskyns saw Prince seemingly pour his energy into a protracted campaign against Warner, when he took to writing "Slave" on his face. "I thought the whole thing was pretty grotesque," said Hoskyns, "though we're all now aware of just how exploitative the record industry has been."

In his rented mansion, Prince didn't address Hoskyns, who took his spot in the crowd. As the new album played, Hoskyns didn't think much of 3121 (or much of his output since the 1980s, "though there were some good things on *Emancipation*"). If anything, Hoskyns wondered where Prince had gone wrong, and kept returning to two possible answers. Either "He ran out of creative juice, like most people do," or "He alienated just about anyone who was good for him." Either way, Hoskyns felt Prince was now coasting on past achievements. This new 3121, he decided, seemed "pitched at the mainstream." Some songs sounded like "Prince on autopilot," but a few moments proved "there's still fire in the guy's belly."

When it finished, Prince mounted an improvised stage with his band.

Once more, he stood to one side while Tamar and the Twinz performed. When he stepped forward, it was to say that their music contained no samples. He advanced once more when a song required the kind of feral guitar solo at which Prince excelled. When the show ended at 3:00 A.M., the crowd reacted with "mild bemusement since Prince did very little apart from play guitar in the background," Hoskyns noted. Hoskyns himself was surprised. Twenty years ago, Prince would have played until dawn. Now, he thanked everyone for coming, left the ballroom, and hit the sack.

Warner Bros. Records meanwhile chose this moment to exercise its right to release one last Prince album. Part of the April 1996 agreement that freed him from his obligation to Warner allowed the label to put out two compilations of material he recorded as their artist. Five years ago, Warner had released the first, their single-disc *The Very Best of Prince*, which Nielsen SoundScan had down as selling 1.2 million copies in the United States. Now, Warner believed—after *Musicology* renewed interest in his activities—something called *Ultimate Prince* could do just as well and end the deal.

This time around, though, rather than put a staff producer on the collection, Warner recruited hard-core fans Geoffrey Dicker and Mathieu Bitton as creative consultants. Both wanted the best collection for hard-core fans and casual listeners alike. A Prince fan since hearing "Controversy" at age four, Geoffrey Dicker created a list of forty songs, a mix of original album versions, and remixes for singles that never appeared on CD. Warner and Rhino executives were enthusiastic, so Dicker considered how the songs would appear. After "Purple Medley," listeners would hear three album cuts, three twelve-inch mixes (including "Erotic City"), three more album cuts, then three remixes. Disc 2 would be similar, he figured, starting with a longer "Kiss." They could end the two-hour, twenty-two-track retrospective with "My Name Is Prince," his voice shouting the title.

Mathieu Bitton meanwhile worked for design firm Candy Tangerine. At age ten, Bitton started collecting Prince albums. He was thirteen when he paid fifteen hundred dollars for a copy of the original pressing of *The Black Album*. Ten years later, Bitton had gotten rid of many items but still had a staggering and costly collection of Prince memorabilia. His design for Warner's *Up from the Catacombs: The Best of Jane's Addiction* inspired the invitation onto this project. "I was as shocked as could be," Bitton said of Warner's call. "I didn't know there was a Prince project in the works." Nevertheless, Bitton quickly accepted, and searched Warner's photo archives for shots to include in liner notes. Bitton also carried a mere tenth of his Prince records to a meeting with Warner and Rhino, where stunned executives decided to include a photo of the collection in liner notes. After the photo shoot, Bitton worked for a month on the album's design, toying with a white background and the classic pointy-edged letters from the *Purple Rain* logo.

Then Warner invited Prince to provide input. Despite public jibes against the label, complaints about master tapes, and much talk of how life and earnings improved after leaving Warner, Prince agreed to be involved. (Even more surprising to his longtime followers: He didn't back out.)

Prince decided "Erotic City" and "Sexy MF" shouldn't appear. He also wanted original-album cuts on one disc, and remixes on another. "I don't know why Prince wanted them split out, but he did, and Warner Brothers and Rhino appeased him with that," said Dicker.

February 2, *Billboard* reported, "A week before Prince's new NPG Music Club/Universal album, *3121*, hits stores on March 21, Rhino will unveil a two-disc collection of remastered hits and remixes."

When fans learned of the new Warner album, some accused Warner on online message boards of trying to cash in by releasing its compilation just a week before the new album. Regardless, the label began the sort of aggressive push Prince always said he wanted. Ads for the Best Buy chain mentioned it. Record stores nationwide also publicized it. There were television commercials. Some fans ordered copies from Amazon or in stores like Barnes & Noble. Bitton was thrilled. "This was like, no pun intended, the ultimate project for me," he told PopMatters.com. Dicker told the site he was just as elated. "It's like being a die-hard fan for all these years has paid off."

March 1, Tamar's tour reached Philadelphia's Electric Factory. But Prince kept thinking about Warner's *Ultimate Prince* arriving a week before his own new *3121*. It was only days before the release now: Warner had already shipped promotional copies—which supposedly included his anti-rap "Dead On It"—to a few stores. Customers there had already snatched up some of these.

Nevertheless, Prince asked Warner, at the last moment, to delay the album.

In a remarkable act of conciliation, Warner agreed, Bitton told Pop-Matters.com, "to honor Prince's wishes." Warner could have stood its ground, "could have said, 'Hey, we're putting it out. We don't care,'" Bitton continued. "But they really have respect for Prince, and I hope he sees that." Warner asked retailers to return their copies.

The cancellation devastated its creators, PopMatters.com quoted Dicker as saying. "We had the release date for *Ultimate* long before Prince had the date for *3121*," said Dicker. "And then it kind of came out looking like Warner was riding on the coattails of that, and in reality it was just a really bad coincidence."

In March, some fans searched in vain for *Ultimate Prince*. Coincidentally or not, Prince had his site offer a deluge of material. Then, March 21, Universal had *3121* in stores. Most critics called it his best album since the eighties. The *LA Times* wrote, "Uneven? No question." But it was entertaining. *The New York Times* called it "a friendly, happy, concise album." *Billboard* heard "a testament to the singer's versatility and musicianship." *Blender* said, "The minimalist tracks rate among his best." Other reviewers were more critical. *Entertainment Weekly* heard "his umpteenth disappointment" and "a messier, more self-indulgent affair than its predecessor." The public however loved it. Within a week, they bought 183,000 copies, making *3121* his very first work to debut at No. 1, and his first chart-topper since 1989's *Batman*.

At Rhino, executives scrapped another release date (May 22) for *Ultimate,* leaving many fans wondering if it'd ever see the light of day. Prince meanwhile faced another personal setback. May 24, the Minneapolis *Star Tribune* reported, Manuela, his wife of five years, filed for divorce in Hennepin County. Reporter Cheryl Johnson called her publicist for an interview. In response, she heard, "She's leaving for vacation for the next month. A nice long vacation out of the country, actually." And the divorce file, Johnson learned, was sealed.

Manuela and Prince never publicly revealed why they divorced. But *People* later quoted Prince's personal lawyer as saying it wasn't something Prince wanted. It was Manuela's choice. Prince was as tightlipped as usual about this personal development, and his reaction to it seemed to be none at all. He let his attorney know he wouldn't contest it; worked to keep details out of the media; ignored rumors that claimed he and Tamar were romantically involved; and slowly distanced himself from attempts to land Tamar a new record deal (since Universal dropped her after he left the label, following the release of *3121*). With Manuela moving forward with the divorce, Prince had to find another place to live. He also wanted to keep working, maintaining the momentum caused by two well-received comeback albums. He turned his eye toward Las Vegas—a solution, he felt, to both dilemmas.

Prince's singles and videos continued to do good business with specific audiences: the Latin-tinged ballad "Te Amo Corazón," his soul anthem "Black Sweat" and, in the UK, the rock-styled "Fury." Radio deejays also received a promo copy of "Beautiful, Loved, and Blessed" credited to Tamar.

Prince himself kept promoting the new album, appearing on the season finale of the high-rated TV talent show *American Idol*, playing the Empire Ballroom in Las Vegas with Tamar, performing with her on ABC's *Good Morning America*, in June, and having her join him again at the sixth annual BET Awards in Los Angeles. His online fan club thrilled at every exploit until—he offered another disruption.

July 4, at midnight, Prince unexpectedly ended his five-year-old NPG Music Club site, explaining it couldn't progress further in its current form. It happened the same day British company HM Publishing (owners of Nature Publishing Group, also known as NPG) filed an opposition to the NPG trademark. His lawyer said the events were unrelated.

By now, large segments of Prince's hard-core following viewed Warner Bros. Records as the villain in the Prince story. It came as a surprise to them when, that same July, Warner and Prince actually worked together again. The company's film studio was finishing *Happy Feet*, a four-year-in-the-making computer-animated film about a dancing penguin. Alan Horn, president and chief operating officer of Warner Brothers, got the ball rolling by telling director George Miller, "Look, let's get great music." After sifting through countless songs, they chose "Kiss," for voice-over stars Nicole Kidman and Hugh Jackman to perform as a duet. But they didn't want Kidman singing, "You don't have to be rich to be my girl." They wanted to change it to "pearl." When they asked permission, however, Prince said, "No, you're not gonna change my lyrics," Miller recalled. Warner executives Gary LeMel and Gary Hinkman urged him to see the film. He'd see it fit. "Well, show me the movie," Prince replied. The executives and Miller brought it to Minneapolis. Prince watched a rough cut, Miller recalled, probably the first person to see the whole thing. Near the finale, Prince mounted the viewing room stage, lifted a guitar he had nearby, and strummed, seeking a chord. "Give me two weeks," he said.

Miller asked, "What?"

"I'm going to write a song for it. I don't want any money." They could also change the lyrics. Miller was stunned and touched. The soundtrack and film included "Kiss" as part of a medley, near Elvis Presley's "Heartbreak Hotel," and his new "The Song of the Heart." On August 1, Miller was heard bragging to a reporter about Prince's involvement.

At last, his long relationship with Warner Bros. Records came to a quiet end. August 22, 2006, five months after *3121*'s release, and its own original release date, Warner released *Ultimate Prince* on its Rhino subsidiary. But instead of a glorious end to their historic teaming, the twenty-eight-cut set sat on shelves, barely mentioned by the media. After their aborted attempt at promoting the daylights out of it in March, Warner had seemingly washed its hands of what one reporter called an "end-of-summer dump of the hits package." It came and went so quickly, casual fans barely knew it existed.

47

LIFE CAN BE SO NICE

FEBRUARY 1, 2007, AT LEAST FIVE HUNDRED REPORTERS PACKED
the conference room at the Miami Beach Convention center, for the "Pepsi
Super Bowl Halftime Show Press Conference." As a vindication of his
comeback, Prince found himself invited to headline the event.

Prince was determined to give fans something they had never seen
before.

At the press conference, in a bright orange, Jimi Hendrix–like suit
with flared pants, Prince mounted the stage, and grabbed the microphone. "Contrary to rumor, I'd like to take a few questions now." Someone started asking one. Prince half-turned, cutting him off with a loud
guitar riff. Facing the crowd again, he smiled as if in disbelief at the fact he
got away with that. He started playing "Johnny B. Goode" with two sexy
women in men's dress shirts, The Twinz, on either side of him. Then he
leaped into "Anotherloverholenyohead"—with its fiery solos—before
ending with his lesser-known "Get on the Boat." Before anyone could ask
a question, Prince said, "Thank you. See you at the Super Bowl. Peace."
He left.

"I think he's brilliant," fellow Super Bowl performer Billy Joel told a
reporter. "He's one of the most talented people in the industry today."

February 4, the day of the big game, it rained. But it let up by the time
Prince walked toward the awesome ♀-shaped stage in Miami's Pro Player
Stadium. In his orange and turquoise suit, he held his guitar and prepared
to play for 74,512 people in the stands and the biggest audience of his
life—140 million TV viewers worldwide. Later, the media would report it
was also the third most-watched program in American history (93 million
households watching).

On the field, the well-rehearsed Florida A&M University Marching
Band wore luminous purple on their uniforms. Prince took the stage for
eleven or twelve memorable minutes. He surprised audiences with "All

Along the Watchtower," sections from Ike and Tina Turner's "Proud Mary," and the Foo Fighters' "The Best of You." He also played *Purple Rain* classics "Let's Go Crazy," and "Baby I'm a Star." Instead of mugging for the camera, Prince interacted with the crowd and included many heavy guitar riffs. Tossing his black head rag aside, Prince asked, "Don't it feel good?" The rain started again but he kept playing. Even the most skeptical could be nothing but amazed by what Prince delivered. He closed with "Purple Rain," violet lights outlining his body and ♀-shaped guitar.

In the stands, the audience held flashlights they had received beforehand, aiming them at the stage. Many sang along, the crowd riveted by every note. Critics shared the sentiment. One called it "arguably the best halftime show in Super Bowl history." Another said it was "one of the best ever."

The show more than doubled Prince's album sales, *Billboard* reported. At Amazon.com, people bought more copies of *The Hits/B-Sides*, *The Hits 2*, *Ultimate Prince*, and *3121*. But Warner's *The Very Best of Prince* experienced the biggest leap in sales, going from No. 999 to 38 on Amazon's "Top Sellers" list.

Alan Leeds, who had been by Prince's side for decades, was no less impressed. Already he thought Prince's marketing of *Musicology* and the tour were brilliant. Now he called Prince's decision to play Super Bowl XLI "equally stellar. He took what had been a disaster for Janet Jackson and a dismal nonevent for the Rolling Stones and turned in a landmark appearance that will be remembered for years to come." Prince hadn't had a certifiable hit album in years, but still had the world viewing him as a star and a force.

"If that isn't successful strategy," Leeds added, "I don't know what is."

EPILOGUE: BETTER WITH TIME

AFTER DOZENS OF ALBUMS, PRINCE HAS REMAINED AS PASSION-
ate as ever about innovating musically and professionally. Shortly after his
Super Bowl triumph, Prince began work on a new album, *Planet Earth*.
Planet Earth moved him past the *Musicology* and *3121* pop sound. It offered
heavy guitar, stronger rock, some polished R&B, and even revived disco.
Lyrical themes were more substantial. "Planet Earth" discussed discrimi-
nation on a global scale and called for an end to war; "Chelsea Rodgers"
held a message about the legend of Jimi Hendrix; "Lion of Judah" seemed
to say faith in God would keep him strong during a breakup.

He planned a marathon twenty-one shows at the new twenty-
thousand-seat O2 arena in London. Outside Organization, which helped
promote the shows, publicly claimed they would find him performing his
greatest hits "for the very last time" but during a May 8, 2007, press conference in London, Prince told reporters he would draw from a list of 150
songs and create a different set list each night.

Prince proposed offering what people now called Covermounts (free
CDs with magazines). In the years since he first considered them in the
mid-1990s, many newspapers and magazines had begun including CDs to
lure readers. Before Sony—the label distributing *Planet Earth*—knew it,
Prince had agreed to let British newspaper *The Mail on Sunday* distribute
Planet Earth with their Sunday, July 15, edition. Readers could receive the
entire album for a three-dollar cover price. Prince, meanwhile, was to
receive a reported $500,000 in the deal, and royalties for each copy. This
deal, one writer speculated, may have brought him "more than eight times"
what he earned from *3121* (which sold eighty thousand copies in the UK).

The deal marked the first time a top-selling artist let fans have a full-
length new album in this manner. Various overseas retailers expressed
shock, dismay, and anger but Prince called it "direct marketing," and a
way out of "the speculation business of the record industry."

Before long, the paper's managing director Stephen Miron announced, "The first time anyone will be able to hear *Planet Earth* will be exclusively through *The Mail on Sunday*."

At Sony BMG, executives were stunned. A spokesperson said, "*The Mail on Sunday* deal was not something that we were aware of. That came to light a few days ago." With almost 3 million people about to receive copies with the paper, Sony canceled the United Kingdom release. Yet, a spokesperson noted, "It doesn't change the fact that we're delighted to be working with him." Their global deal was unaffected. "This is a UK-only exemption."

When July 15 arrived, *The Mail on Sunday* headline read: "Free Inside. Prince's New Album. All 10 Tracks . . ." The paper sold the usual 2.3 million copies and the extra 600,000 copies they printed. Retailers continued to fume but *The New York Times* felt this deal showed "he thinks differently about the business."

Prince moved on to his next feat, the twenty-one shows that August and September at London's grand twenty-thousand-seat 02 Arena (each of which had already sold out). Meanwhile, back in America, Sony released *Planet Earth*—nine days after the giveaway—to some of Prince's best reviews in years. *Spin* crowned *Planet Earth* "the year's best pop album." *Vibe* called it "his strangest yet most alluring rock project since 1988's astonishing *Lovesexy*." That first week, *Planet Earth* sold 95,500 copies and debuted at No. 3 on the August 1 Billboard chart. By October, sales climbed to about 298,000, with almost no promotion.

Prince returned to his new home—a thirty-thousand-square-foot estate in a gated community in LA's Beverly Park section. As always, his home reflected his personality: bright purple carpet on the front steps; Mediterranean style furniture; a big gold-colored ♀ over a Lucite grand piano; purple paisley pillows on a couch; purple thrones flanking a fireplace; photos of himself in a Moroccan home in a nearby hallway; and a see-through curtain over the door leading into his bedroom. When he wasn't touring, he welcomed industry executives to the home and discussed new ideas for releasing music. He attended meetings at a local Kingdom Hall, and went out to perform field service. He threw himself into promoting a fifty-dollar coffee table book called *21 Nights* (photos of him playing that London tour at the 02 alongside poems and a CD). "I'm really proud of this," he said of the well-received work.

Eventually, he got back to his next plan.

He was going to create three new albums. The first, *LotusFlow3r*, had roots in sessions for *3121*. He had toured as a backup player for Tamar in 2006 and remembered how much he loved playing guitar. And so he kept writing and recording rock-heavy tracks, until eventually he had too many for one album. Instead of releasing it all, he chose only the best tracks for a single disc. It was a surprising exploration of the dark side of sixties rock. He included his usual R&B tracks and love songs, but his solos were among his most furious to date.

His second album, *MPLSound*, was the product of numerous 2008 sessions back at Paisley Park in Minneapolis. He fused his early drum-machine sound to more mature themes. He soon had an odd but refreshing collection that fit in with current trends but included lyrics that offered a respite from the club-focused monotony of radio. "Better with Time" described aging gracefully; "No More Candy 4 You" expressed disdain for talentless, media-created stars.

The final album of the trio would be *Elixir*, by his newest protégé Bria Valente, a tall white brunette who grew up in Minneapolis and, as a teen, attended a few parties at Paisley Park. Prince's keyboardist Morris Hayes introduced them. Prince liked her voice, songwriting, and interest in Scripture. Bria had become a Jehovah's Witness as well, and now they were working together on her debut. He urged her to fit into an existing niche, "but do something with it that you don't hear." On *Elixir* Valente sounded clean-cut one moment, then smooth as Sade, and even ventured into Doris Day territory. Prince, Hayes, and Valente created the music for the pleasant, string-filled "Everytime," her title track (as moody and intimate as anything on Prince's debut *For You*); and the house-music-styled "2 Nite."

Designer Scott Addison Clay, whose work included high-profile Web sites for the films *The Dark Knight* and *Twilight*, began work on a site called LotusFlow3r, initially created as a means to distribute the three-CD set. Prince had intended for people to join his new fan club for an annual seventy-seven-dollar fee and receive the set as a gift. But by now, The Eagles and AC/DC had released their newest original works exclusively through Walmart, the world's biggest music retailer. Walmart had promoted each with huge in-store displays and choice product placement, and with 1.92 million sales AC/DC's *Black Ice* was 2008's fifth biggest-selling album. It inspired Prince to change his plan for the new set. He wanted to try this, too. But his way.

Prince decided to work with Target. The discount-store chain had worked wonders with Christina Aguilera's greatest hits package in 2008. And while Target had about 1,677 stores—over 800 less than Walmart—the chain had a more upscale image. And Target was open to placing huge displays in prime locations, including right near checkout lines. Exact figures for these deals were unknown but *Time* noted chains usually gave artists in the mid–six figures for their albums and assistance in promoting them.

Either way, Target agreed to start selling a three-disc set—his rock album *LotusFlow3r*, his retro *MPLSound*, and Valente's debut *Elixer*—for an affordable $11.99 starting on March 29, 2009.

Prince started promoting the set and his new site by inviting reporters to his Beverly Park estate. He created another amazing publicity campaign: his site's launch on March 24, a consecutive three-night stand as musical guest on *The Tonight Show With Jay Leno*, then three concerts at Los Angeles's Nokia Theater on March 28 (shows that sold out in a mere 7.7 seconds). Then, the next morning, Target stores nationwide would start selling *Lotusflow3r* for a price lower than what most labels charged for a single disc.

Critics offered mixed reviews. *Entertainment Weekly* called it "Prince's most disappointing set in years." *The Boston Globe* felt it "should have been boiled down to a single disc." But *Rolling Stone* felt it was "intermittently brilliant and a real bargain." *Vibe* called it "a solid offering of tightly conceptualized tunes."

Despite mixed reviews and releasing it directly to only one retail chain, Prince's *LotusFlow3r* still sold 168,000 copies opening week, debuting at an impressive No. 2. ("Other charts say that it was number one," he said.) Either way, with thirty million or so shoppers visiting Target stores each week, *Lotusflow3r* will continue to sell.

Since the start of his career, Prince's influence has been evident. He wasn't the first black artist to include heavy rock on his albums—but he nevertheless moved a new generation to do so. His sexual themes were so inspiring that—while planning his all-genre work *Thriller*—Michael Jackson reportedly asked an associate if he shouldn't include something like Prince's *Controversy* number "Jack U Off." Many people immediately remembered Prince's Vanity 6 when they got a look at Madonna prancing around onstage and in videos in revealing outfits. And the throbbing bass and sexual theme on her classic "Like a Virgin" reminded many of both on Prince's own "Dirty Mind." As the eighties continued, more rock bands began using his fusion of keyboard and rock guitar—and his former protégés carried innovations on to productions like those of Janet Jackson.

Paisley Park Studios put his hometown of Minneapolis on the musical map, and inspired many other musicians to create similar setups. And while the Warner-backed Paisley Park imprint wasn't the resounding success Prince or the label hoped for, it operated for years, introduced new sounds, and revived the careers of aging vets.

It hasn't been a career without missteps. Prince's decision to play black music forms like rap in the nineties cost him large segments of his audience. His open campaign against Warner alienated some listeners. But in taking such chances, Prince showed a nervous artist community that someone could defy a major label and survive. His insistence on operating without the usual agents, concert bookers, distributors, and other intermediaries soon inspired artists to rethink their own professional affairs. This alone would have been enough to get him in the history books. He went on to show artists they could serve as their own digital label, retain ownership of master tapes, and earn more money in the process. Recent years have seen Madonna—Warner's reliable hitmaker—leave the label for a reported $120 million three-album deal with concert promoter Live Nation. U2 also reportedly decided that—while future albums would be for Universal—Live Nation could handle their merchandising and digital rights.

As far as his music is concerned, Prince continues to write memorable works. And traces of his earlier styles are heard on works by artists as diverse as Terence Trent Darby, Seal, Lenny Kravitz, D'Angelo, Pharrell Williams of The Neptunes, Andre 3000 of Outkast, Justin Timberlake, Usher, Britney Spears, Madonna, Ciara, and Beck.

Prince reportedly counseled Michael Jackson on how best to stage a comeback. Jackson wound up making headlines in 2009 by announcing his own residency at London's 02 Arena (fifty shows that immediately sold out), following in Prince's lead. Crossover rap act The Black Eyed Peas, meanwhile, announced their own exclusivity deal with Target for their album The E.N.D. (or The Energy Never Dies).

Back in his California estate, Prince has finally found peace. He is a fastidious middle-aged bachelor that has seen two marriages fail. He has also seen negative reviews of his most recent work. But he remains more open with reporters and fans than perhaps ever. He continues to be a God-fearing, clean-living man. He is happy to be alive and grateful for his friends; and thrilled to be able to choose when he wants to record an album or play a show. He's looking forward to signing deals for his bandmates and protégés. He has found in Target, for now at least, a way of releasing music that allows him the freedom he's spent a career seeking.

He is, he said recently, in "celebration mode."

Acknowledgments

During the decade in which I researched and created this book, many people provided invaluable assistance. For their help, I'd like to thank agent Jacqueline Hackett; editor David Moldawer; and especially editor Yaniv Soha (for his patience, a standard of excellence and curiosity that matched my own, for understanding and helping me refine my vision for this book, and for helping me to get certain parts absolutely right). I'd also like to thank authors Per Nilsen and Alex Hahn. Our musical tastes and view of certain events differ, but their respective works *DanceMusicSexRomance: Prince—The First Decade* and *Possessed: The Rise and Fall of Prince* come highly recommended. I'd also like to thank the many reporters who described Prince's evolution from awkward loner to controversial industry opponent to rock legend with a thirty-album discography and four entertaining films to his credit. These hard-working talents worked at national magazines (*Entertainment Weekly, Rolling Stone, Billboard, Vibe*, and more), local newspapers (including the Minneapolis *Star Tribune*, *The New York Times*, and the *Los Angeles Times*, among many others), and television networks (MTV, BET, PBS, etc.). Then there were people like Alan Leeds, Jill Jones, Neal Karlen, Dez Dickerson, Matt Fink, Bobby Z, Owen Husney, David Rivkin, Tom Garneau, Jill Willis, Sheila E., Anna Garcia, Rosie Gaines, T. C. Ellis, Gayle Chapman, Jellybean Johnson, Touré, Robyne Robinson, Alan Light, Bob Merlis, Paul Peterson, Mayte Garcia, Jesse Johnson, David Z. Rivkin, BrownMark, Paul Peterson, Bob Merlis, Liz Rosenberg, Russ Thyret, and everyone else who either answered questions, confirmed or corrected passages, or reached out. It was an honor hearing from all of you. Further thanks goes to the Prince-related fan sites Prince.org and Housequake.com for insight into what some hard-core fans expect; my readers; Warner Bros. Records; Carmen Ruiz, Matthew Olson, and Mark "Skillz" McCord for ongoing friendship, belief, and support; everyone involved with the classic film *Purple Rain*; and finally, Prince Rogers Nelson himself for so many enjoyable, groundbreaking works.

Index

CPSIA information can be obtained at www.ICGtesting.com
Printed in the USA
LVOW11*2339070716

495493LV00003B/10/P

9 780312 383008